Inspired

Teacher's Book 2

MACMILLAN

Judy Garton-Sprenger • Philip Prowse

with Rachel Bladon and Catherine Smith

Macmillan Education
Between Towns Road, Oxford OX4 3PP
A division of Macmillan Publishers Limited
Companies and representatives throughout the world

ISBN 978-0-230-41514-0

This edition published 2012
First edition published 2008

Original design by Giles Davies Design Ltd and eMC Design Ltd
Page make-up by Expo Holdings, D&J Hunter Design
Illustrated by Kathy Baxendale (pp168, 179), Mark Davis (pp163, 170), Gillian Martin (pp152, 162, 165, 174), Julian Mosedale (pp166, 168, 168, 177, 178, 181) and Simon Smith (pp169, 171).
Cover design based on an original design by Studio Montage

The authors and publishers would like to thank the following for permission to reproduce the following copyright material:
Page 186: ***Dancing In The Street***—Words and Music by Marvin Gaye, William Stevenson, and Ivy Hunter copyright © Jobete Music Inc, USA, Jobete Music (UK) Ltd, London, WC2H 0QY 1960, reprinted by permission of International Music Publications Ltd. All Rights Reserved;
Page 187: ***Footprints In The Frost***—Words and Music by Chris Difford and Glenn Tilbrook, copyright © Virgin Music Publishing Ltd, EMI Virgin Music Ltd, London, WC2H 0QY 1987, reprinted by permission of International Music Publications Ltd and EMI Virgin Music Ltd, London, WC2H 0QY. All Rights Reserved;
Page 188: ***Father and Son***—Words and Music by Cat Stevens copyright © Cat Music Limited/ Sony Music Publishing UK 1970, reprinted by permission of the publisher. All Rights Reserved. International Copyright Secured.
Page 189: ***The Miracle***—Words and Music by Brian May, Freddie Mercury, John Deacon, Roger Taylor copyright © 1989, Reproduced by Permission of Queen Music Ltd/ EMI Music Publishing Ltd, London W8 5SW;

For full photographic acknowledgements please refer to the Student's Book.

Printed and bound in Thailand

2017 2016 2015 2014 2013
10 9 8 7 6 5 4 3

Contents

Inspired

Inspired is a four-level course designed to take teenagers from beginner to intermediate level (CEFR A1–B1+). The course aims to appeal to the modern teenager through imaginative and exciting topics, introduces up-to-date language and expressions, increases confidence through learner independence activities, provides regular opportunities for consolidation and self assessment, and caters to different learning styles. For the teacher it offers everything needed for successful lessons with full support at every stage.

The course offers a dual-entry possibility, and those learners who have already made some progress in English can start with *Inspired 2*.

KEY IDEAS

A fundamental concept in the organization of *Inspired* is that of *difference*.

Different ages

Teenagers are passing through a challenging period of their lives with great physical, social, and psychological changes. A 13-year-old lives in a different world than a 16-year-old. In designing *Inspired*, our aim has been to create a course which grows with its students.

Different abilities

Every class is a mixed-ability class. We see mixed ability not as a problem, but as a fact of life to which we need to respond in our teaching. Our response in creating *Inspired* has been to develop *flexible* materials which offer a variety of learning paths to success.

Different interests

One of the most striking findings of the research phase in preparing this course was the wide variety of different interests among students. We have therefore provided a broad range of materials to engage students in challenging but achievable tasks. The topic syllabus gives the opportunity for cross-curricular and cross-cultural work so that students learn about life and the world at the same time as learning English. Language learning also needs to be fun to be effective, so we have included lots of games, poems, and puzzles, as well as a story in the Workbook and songs in the Teacher's Book.

Different backgrounds

Teenagers come to the language classroom with a wide range of backgrounds—not only in social and educational terms, but also because of different learning histories. Students in the same class may have had positive, negative, or no language-learning experiences at elementary school level; they may have started learning another language, or had private lessons or extra classes in English. Students who started learning English in elementary school may have been exposed to predominantly oral activities, games, and songs, and be surprised by the different demands of the class they are now in.

Inspired aims to provide a safe transition to the new level, and to consolidate and recycle language in fresh contexts.

Different learning styles

We believe that it is important for students to "learn how to learn." We have provided opportunities for students to experiment with different learning styles and develop language learning strategies which suit them. We have tried to make students aware that, while they may have a preferred learning style, they could benefit from experimenting with others.

Different aspirations

Within each teenager there is a young adult in the making, and all have differing goals and aspirations for the future. We have aimed to provide students with practical language skills and a positive attitude toward learning. This will lead them to success in examinations and prepare them for using English in the real world.

Different class sizes and weekly hours

The Teacher's Book provides lesson plans full of extra optional activities which can be given to less confident learners or to fast-finishers, and the Workbook exercises can all be used for self-study. Teachers with more hours at their disposal will find that they have material for considerably more than the 90–120 hours of the core course if they use the optional activities.

KEY FEATURES OF *INSPIRED*

Multi-syllabus

The course has a topic-led syllabus which integrates separate communicative, lexical, grammatical, pronunciation, skills, and learner independence syllabi. This provides a principled approach to vocabulary acquisition and to the development of the four skills. The Contents pages of the Student's Book list the topics, lesson titles, communicative aims, language areas, pronunciation points, skills, and learner independence training.

Reading

At Levels 1 and 2, students encounter new language in the first three lessons of each unit through dialogues and prose texts. The dialogues feature an international group of teenage characters with whom the students can identify, while the prose texts focus on topics of interest and relevance to the students' lives and studies. Dialogues and texts are preceded by pre-reading/listening tasks to develop predictive skills.

Vocabulary and grammar

The topic-led syllabus provides a firm basis for systematic coverage and development of vocabulary. Lessons contain Word Banks and activities to consolidate and extend lexical fields, and students are encouraged to maintain their own vocabulary notebooks. At the back of the Student's Book there is a unit-by-unit Word List with phonemic transcriptions.

There is a clearly structured approach to grammar, leading to fluency activities where students apply the target language in communicative situations. Language Workout boxes at the end of each lesson are cross-referenced with a comprehensive Language File at the back of the Student's Book, which provides full paradigms and explanations of grammatical points with controlled practice exercises.

Pronunciation

The first three lessons of each unit provide explicit work on pronunciation, stress, and intonation arising from the lesson language. Phonemic symbols are given as support where relevant; these are intended for recognition only. There is a Pronunciation Guide at the back of the Student's Book.

Skills development

Careful attention is paid to the development of the four language skills in each unit, both in the first three lessons and in the fourth Integrated Skills lesson. Guided writing, a carefully staged program of tasks, helps the growth of students' writing skills. There is further work on reading and writing skills in the Workbook, together with suggestions for extensive reading.

Learner independence

The Integrated Skills lessons in each unit offer work on the development of learner independence, and this is supported by parallel sections in the Workbook and advice in the Teacher's Book lesson notes.

Cognitive development, language awareness, and enjoyment

Inspired contains a range of activities, such as quizzes and questionnaires, which encourage students to think in English. "Your response" activities after a text or dialogue also encourage the development of critical thinking and personal responses to reading.

Inspired *Extra!* sections at the end of each Student's Book unit contain either a full project, or a Language Links activity focusing on plurilingualism, and a skit for students to act out. There are also word games, puzzles, and limericks. Games can also be found in the Student's Book lessons, and the Workbook contains more puzzles, crosswords, and brainteasers.

Mixed ability

The first three lessons of each unit contain Extension activities for fast-finishers. Inspired *Extra!* also includes both a Consolidation and Extension section which caters to two different ability levels—consolidating and extending language from the preceding four lessons—and a Your Choice! section where students can choose between activities reflecting different learning styles. There are further Consolidation and Extension sections in the Workbook.

Recycling and reviewing

The syllabus regularly recycles new language. In addition to the Consolidation and Extension sections, there are four Review sections in each level, providing further consolidation and learner independence self assessment sections. There are additional Review sections in the Workbook.

Culture and CLIL

Each level also features four Culture sections which build cross-cultural awareness, encourage discussion, develop vocabulary, and lead up to Mini-projects. The Workbook contains further Culture sections with reading, writing, and vocabulary exercises. There is a wealth of CLIL material appropriate to the students' age and level throughout the course, including a dedicated section in each Workbook.

COURSE COMPONENTS

Student's Book

The Student's Book provides 90–120 hours of teaching material within eight units. Each unit has four lessons—each on two pages for ease of use—and an Inspired *Extra!* section. The first three lessons in each unit present and practice new language, and the fourth is an Integrated Skills lesson. Each pair of units is preceded by a Preview, which gives the learner a taste of what is to come, followed by a Review. At the back of the book there is a Language File, a Word List, a Pronunciation Guide, and a list of Irregular Verbs.

Workbook

The Workbook offers exercises which can be done in class or as self-study. It mirrors the Student's Book in its organization, providing a wealth of extra language practice material, integrated skills, and learner independence work, mixed-ability Consolidation and Extension exercises, Culture pages, and Review sections. It includes pronunciation exercises, brainteasers, crosswords, and suggestions for follow-up work. The Workbook also contains CLIL materials linked to other subjects studied in this level, and a unit-by-unit story for extensive reading with language practice activities.

Teacher's Book

The Teacher's Book features a practical approach to methodology with step-by-step lesson notes. There are stimulating ideas for warm-up activities to start each lesson, as well as optional activities throughout the lesson notes. There are follow-up activities at the end of each lesson and suggestions for homework. Useful cultural information is provided to help answer student queries, and downloadable songs with activities are also included. Full audioscripts are integrated within the notes, as are answers to all the Student's Book exercises. There is also a complete Workbook Answer Key.

Tests CD

The editable Tests are designed to cater to mixed-ability classes by providing Standard and Higher Tests for each Student's Book unit. Teachers can use the test that best suits their students and adapt it as necessary. There is also a diagnostic test, three end-of-term tests, and an end-of-course test. Tests include grammar, vocabulary, reading, listening, and writing.

Class Audio CD

All the Student's Book dialogues, texts, and pronunciation exercises are recorded. Recorded items are indicated by the symbol 1.04 in the Student's Book and Teacher's Book.

Inspired Digital

Inspired embraces the digital generation, offering multi-media and interactive solutions for use in class and at home. *Inspired Interactive Classroom* for use with an Interactive Whiteboard or digital projector includes the Student's Book in digital format with integrated audio and answer key, interactive activities, and cultural video clips. *Inspired Practice Online* (www.macmillanpracticeonline.com/inspired) provides self-marking interactive practice activities, videos, and fun language games. The *Inspired Resource Site* (www.macmillanenglish.com/inspired) provides the teacher with extra language practice materials, cross-curricular, and culture lessons, webquests, and a social networking section.

Inspired and the Common European Framework of Reference for Languages

The Common European Framework of Reference for languages (CEFR) is a widely-used standard created by the Council of Europe. In the classroom, familiarity with the CEFR can be of great help to any teacher in identifying students' actual progress and helping them set their learning priorities.

Inspired offers a wide range of teaching materials in various components which give teachers the opportunity to develop all aspects of their students' language ability. The CEFR can be used to follow their progress.

Below are the A2–B1 descriptors (description of competencies) covered in *Inspired* 2 which students are aiming to reach. A1–A2 descriptors are available in the *Inspired 1* Teacher's Book and also on the *Inspired* teacher's websites. A basic level of confidence with the A1–A2 descriptors is expected as students start using *Inspired* 2, and by the end of the course, students should be able to accomplish more of the B1 level. Many of the B1 descriptors talk of greater confidence with the same kinds of ability already described in A2: others only emerge for the first time in B1.

On the teacher's website you will also find a list of unit-by-unit descriptors with suggested targets which you print out and copy for your students to assess themselves. Students can use these at any point to get a detailed picture of their own individual progress.

What is a CEFR Portfolio?

If you are using portfolios as a way of evaluating your students' coursework over the year, you will find a wide variety of opportunities within each *Inspired* unit to provide material for the portfolio.

A portfolio is a way to document a person's achievements. Artists, architects, or designers collect samples of their work in portfolios. The basic idea is that students collect samples of their work in their portfolio. Most of the time, these samples will be texts created by the students, but they could also include photos of classroom scenes, wall displays, audio recordings, and DVDs. All these documents provide evidence of a student's performance, e.g. during a discussion, an oral presentation, or a role-play.

The portfolio consists of three parts: the Language Passport with information about a student's proficiency in one or more languages, i.e. qualifications, the Language Biography where students reflect on their learning process and progress and say what they can do in their foreign language(s), and the Dossier, a collection of materials and data put together by students to document and illustrate their learning experiences.

Although it may be a demanding task to set up in the beginning, the overall aim is for students to be involved in planning, collecting, and evaluating their own work—taking responsibility for their own learning. This may lead to increased participation and autonomy on the learners' part.

	Inspired 2 TB descriptors	Unit 1	Unit 2	Unit 3	Unit 4	Unit 5	Unit 6	Unit 7	Unit 8
Listening A2	I can understand what is said clearly, slowly, and directly to me in simple everyday conversation; it is possible to make me understand, if the speaker can take the trouble.	10	24, 27						
	I can generally identify the topic of discussion around me when people speak slowly and clearly.	10	29	42	53	64		96	104
	I can understand phrases, words, and expressions related to areas of most immediate priority (e.g. basic personal and family information, shopping, local area, employment).			38, 43, 49	55	67		95	
	I can catch the main point in short, clear, simple messages and announcements.			41, 42		67			
	I can understand the essential information in short recorded passages dealing with predictable everyday matters which are spoken slowly and clearly.	7, 16, 17, 18		35, 37, 38, 39, 41	48, 55	61, 62	74, 79, 81, 84	86, 95	103, 107

	I can identify the main points of TV news items reporting events, accidents, etc. when the visual supports the commentary.						78, 81		107
Listening B1	I can follow clearly articulated speech directed at me in everyday conversation, though I sometimes have to ask for repetition of particular words and phrases delivered relatively slowly and clearly.				53	68	84		104
	I can generally follow the main points of extended discussion around me, provided speech is clearly articulated in standard dialect.		29	39	49, 52, 53	61, 62, 64, 70	73, 74, 77, 81	90, 95, 96	103, 104, 107
	I can listen to a short narrative and form hypotheses about what will happen next.				51, 53				
	I can understand the main points of radio news bulletins and simpler recorded material on topics of personal interest		29	37, 41, 43	48, 51, 55	62, 68	77, 79	95	101, 107
	I can catch the main points in TV shows on familiar topics when the delivery is relatively slow and clear.						79		
	I can understand simple technical information, such as operating instructions for everyday equipment.								
Reading A2	I can identify important information in news summaries or simple newspaper articles in which numbers and names play an important role and which are clearly structured and illustrated.	10, 14, 16	26, 28, 30	42, 46, 47	48, 50, 51, 58	64	76	92, 96	100, 102
	I can understand a simple personal letter in which the writer tells or asks me about aspects of everyday life.			47		63			
	I can understand simple written messages from friends or co-workers, e.g. saying when we should meet to play soccer or asking me to be at work early.					63, 67			
	I can find the most important information on leisure time activities, exhibits, etc. in information leaflets.	20	23	38		68	80	94	102, 110
	I can skim small advertisements in newspapers, locate the heading or column I want, and identify the most important pieces of information (price and size of apartments, cars, computers).	20		43	54			92	
	I can understand simple user's instructions for equipment, e.g. a public telephone.								110
	I can understand feedback messages or simple help indications in computer programs.								
	I can understand short narratives about everyday things dealing with topics which are familiar to me if the text is written in simple language.	6, 7, 10, 12, 13, 14, 16, 17, 21	22, 24	36, 47	52, 54	68	76, 78, 80	88, 90, 98	102

Reading B1	I can understand the main points in short newspaper articles about current and familiar topics.		22, 28, 32	44	48, 50, 51, 54, 58		84	92, 96, 98	100, 106
	I can read columns or interviews in newspapers and magazines in which someone takes a stand on a current topic or event and understand the overall meaning of the text.		26	40, 42	58		80, 84	88	
	I can guess the meaning of single unknown words from the context, thus deducing the meaning of expressions if the topic is familiar.		28, 29	44	58		76	94	100
	I can skim short texts (e.g. news summaries) and find relevant facts and information (e.g. who has done what and where).	16	24	38, 44	54	66	74, 84	96, 98	100, 101, 102, 103, 106, 110
	I can understand the most important information in short, simple, everyday information brochures.		28, 30, 32	38		68, 72, 73	82	94, 98	102, 106, 110
	I can understand simple messages and standard letters (e.g. from businesses, clubs, or authorities).								
	In private letters I can understand those parts dealing with events, feelings, and wishes well enough to correspond regularly with a pen friend.					63		93	
	I can understand the plot of a clearly structured story and recognize what the most important episodes and events are and what is significant about them.					66		88	100, 108
Spoken Interaction A2	I can make simple transactions in stores, post offices, or banks.								
	I can use public transportation: buses, trains, and taxis, ask for basic information and buy tickets.								
	I can get simple information about travel.								
	I can order something to eat or drink.					64, 65			
	I can make simple purchases by stating what I want and asking the price.					65			
	I can ask for and give directions referring to a map or plan.					67			
	I can ask how people are and react to news.								
	I can make and respond to invitations.					65			
	I can make and accept apologies.								
	I can say what I like and dislike.	10	26	36	52, 55	73	81	87	
	I can discuss with other people what to do, where to go, and make arrangements to meet.					71		93	
	I can ask people questions about what they do at work and in free time, and answer such questions addressed to me.	9, 10, 17	31	35, 39	49		77	87	

Spoken Interaction B1	I can start, maintain, and close simple face-to-face conversations on topics that are familiar or of personal interest.	15	23, 31	39	51, 55	61, 63, 71	75, 83	89, 93	101, 104, 107
	I can maintain a conversation or discussion, but may sometimes be difficult to follow when trying to say exactly what I would like to.		23, 25, 28	28	55, 56	66, 69	81	95, 96	104, 105, 108
	I can deal with most situations likely to arise when making travel arrangements through an agent or when actually traveling.					69		93	
	I can ask for and follow detailed directions.		25			67			
	I can express and respond to feelings such as surprise, happiness, sadness, interest, and indifference.				52			94, 95, 97	108
	I can give or seek personal views and opinions in an informal discussion with friends.		24, 29, 31	40, 45	50, 55, 56	61, 66	77, 81	89, 90, 96, 99	101, 103
	I can agree and disagree politely.				51			95, 96, 99	
Spoken Production A2	I can describe myself, my family, and other people.	7, 19	29					90	108
	I can describe where I live.	16	23						
	I can give short, basic descriptions of events.		23	45	56, 58			92	107, 108
	I can describe my educational background, my present, or most recent job.								
	I can describe my hobbies and interests in a simple way.	10	26				81		
	I can describe past activities and personal experiences (e.g. last weekend, my last vacation).			37, 45			75, 85	108	
Spoken Production B1	I can narrate a story.				55		75		
	I can give detailed accounts of experiences, describing feelings and reactions.		24		52	61, 72	81	98, 99	108
	I can describe dreams, hopes, and ambitions.								
	I can explain and give reasons for my plans, intentions, and actions.		26	36, 38	50	62, 69, 71	81	88, 92, 96	101
	I can relate the plot of a book or movie, and describe my reactions.			40	56				
	I can paraphrase short written passages orally in a simple fashion, using the original text wording and ordering.			37, 42, 45			75, 81	89	107
Strategies A2	I can ask for attention.	17							
	I can indicate when I am following.	16, 17	29						
	I can very simply ask somebody to repeat what they said.								

Strategies B1	I can repeat back part of what someone has said to confirm that we understand each other.							95	
	I can ask someone to clarify or elaborate what they have just said.	17							
	When I can't think of the word I want, I can use a simple word meaning something similar and invite "correction".								
Language Quality A2	I can make myself understood using memorized phrases and single expressions.	17	25	43	55	65, 69	81	91, 95	107
	I can link groups of words with simple connectors like "and", "but", and "because".		22, 27	41	51, 58				
	I can use some simple structures correctly.	11, 13, 15	23, 25, 27	37, 39, 41, 45	49, 51, 53, 55, 57, 59	63, 65, 67, 71	75, 77, 79, 81, 82	89, 91, 93	101, 103, 105, 110
	I have a sufficient vocabulary for coping with simple everyday situations.	7, 8, 9, 12, 14, 15, 18, 21	22, 23, 24, 25, 26, 33	34, 35, 37, 39, 40, 41, 43, 47	49, 52, 53, 55, 57, 58, 59	60, 63, 64, 65, 67, 71, 73	75, 77	86, 89, 91, 92, 99	101, 103, 105, 107, 110, 111
Language Quality B1	I can keep a conversation going comprehensibly, but have to pause to plan and correct what I am saying—especially when I talk freely for longer periods.						83	99	107, 109
	I can convey simple information of immediate relevance, getting across which point I feel is most important.		25		51, 52		76	89, 91	103, 107
	I have a sufficient vocabulary to express myself with some circumlocutions on most topics pertinent to my everyday life such as family, hobbies and interests, work, travel, and current events.		26, 32, 33	43, 47	51, 53, 54, 55, 57	64, 67, 71	77, 78	89, 91, 99	101, 110
	I can express myself reasonably accurately in familiar, predictable situations.			40, 43	57	71	76	89, 91, 93	107, 109
Writing A2	I can write short, simple notes and messages.	11					82, 83	97	101, 108
	I can describe an event in simple sentences and report what happened when and where (e.g. a party or an accident).	15, 17, 19	30			63	79	95	108, 109
	I can write about aspects of my everyday life in simple phrases and sentences (people, places, job, school, family, hobbies).	13, 15, 19	23	39, 47	57		77, 81, 83	91, 97	101, 109
	I can fill in a questionnaire giving an account of my educational background, my job, my interests, and my specific skills.								
	I can briefly introduce myself in a letter with simple phrases and sentences (family, school, job, hobbies).	19							

	I can write a short letter using simple expressions for greeting, addressing, asking, or thanking somebody.							93	
	I can write simple sentences, connecting them with words such as "and", "but", "because".	15, 17	27, 30	41, 43	58		75, 79		
	I can use the most important connecting words to indicate the chronological order of events (first, then, after, later).					63, 67			107
Writing B1	I can write simple connected texts on a range of topics within my field of interest and can express personal views and opinions.	17, 21	25, 27, 33	39, 43, 45, 47	51, 56, 57	73	77, 79, 81, 82	89	101, 103, 109
	I can write simple texts about experiences or events, e.g. about a trip, for a school newspaper, or a club newsletter.		29	37, 39, 45	49	63, 73	75, 83	91, 95, 99	105, 108
	I can write personal letters to friends or acquaintances asking for or giving them news and narrating events.			41	55		77	95	109
	I can describe in a personal letter the plot of a movie or a book or give an account of a concert.				55, 56, 57				
	In a letter I can express feelings such as grief, happiness, interest, regret, and sympathy.							97	
	I can reply in written form to advertisements and ask for more complete or more specific information about products (e.g. a car or an academic course).								
	I can convey—via fax, e-mail, or a circular letter—short simple factual information to friends or co-workers or ask for information in such a way.								
	I can write my résumé in summary form.								

Using *Inspired*

There are four **Preview** sections in each level of *Inspired*, giving students a brief introduction to the communicative aims and topic/vocabulary areas they will cover in the following two units.

Communicative Aims

Students match pictures with contextualizing sentences or questions to the correct communicative aim from the box. This activity helps prepare students for the context in which they will learn each communicative aim.

Topics and Vocabulary

Categorization activities introduce students to some of the key vocabulary from the following two units, and they are also encouraged through brainstorming to identify other words that they already know for some of the topics.

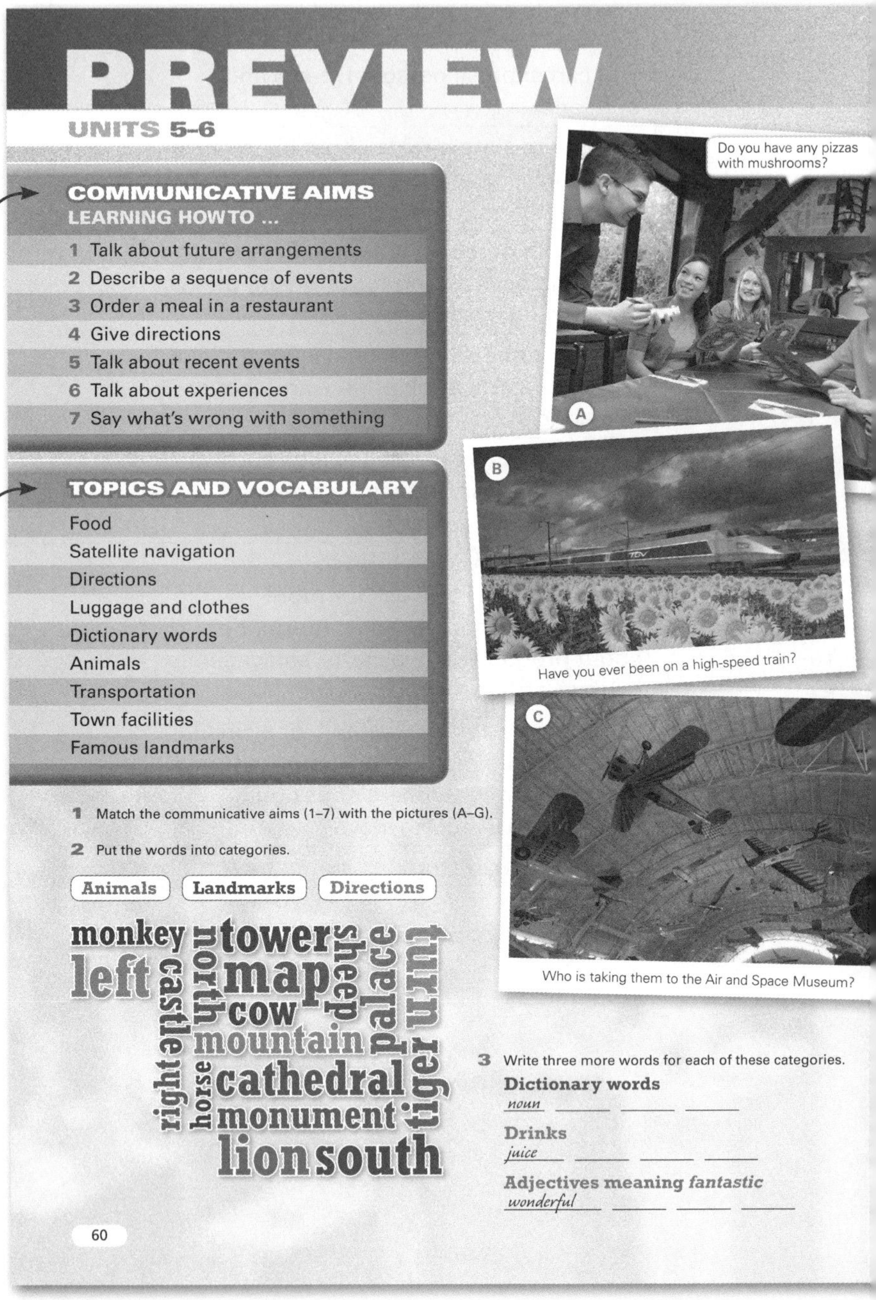

PREVIEW

UNITS 5–6

COMMUNICATIVE AIMS
LEARNING HOW TO ...

1 Talk about future arrangements
2 Describe a sequence of events
3 Order a meal in a restaurant
4 Give directions
5 Talk about recent events
6 Talk about experiences
7 Say what's wrong with something

TOPICS AND VOCABULARY

Food
Satellite navigation
Directions
Luggage and clothes
Dictionary words
Animals
Transportation
Town facilities
Famous landmarks

A — Do you have any pizzas with mushrooms?

B — Have you ever been on a high-speed train?

C — Who is taking them to the Air and Space Museum?

1 Match the communicative aims (1–7) with the pictures (A–G).

2 Put the words into categories.

Animals | Landmarks | Directions

monkey tower left map castle north sheep palace turn cow mountain right horse cathedral monument tiger lion south

3 Write three more words for each of these categories.

Dictionary words
noun ___ ___ ___

Drinks
juice ___ ___ ___

Adjectives meaning *fantastic*
wonderful ___ ___ ___

60

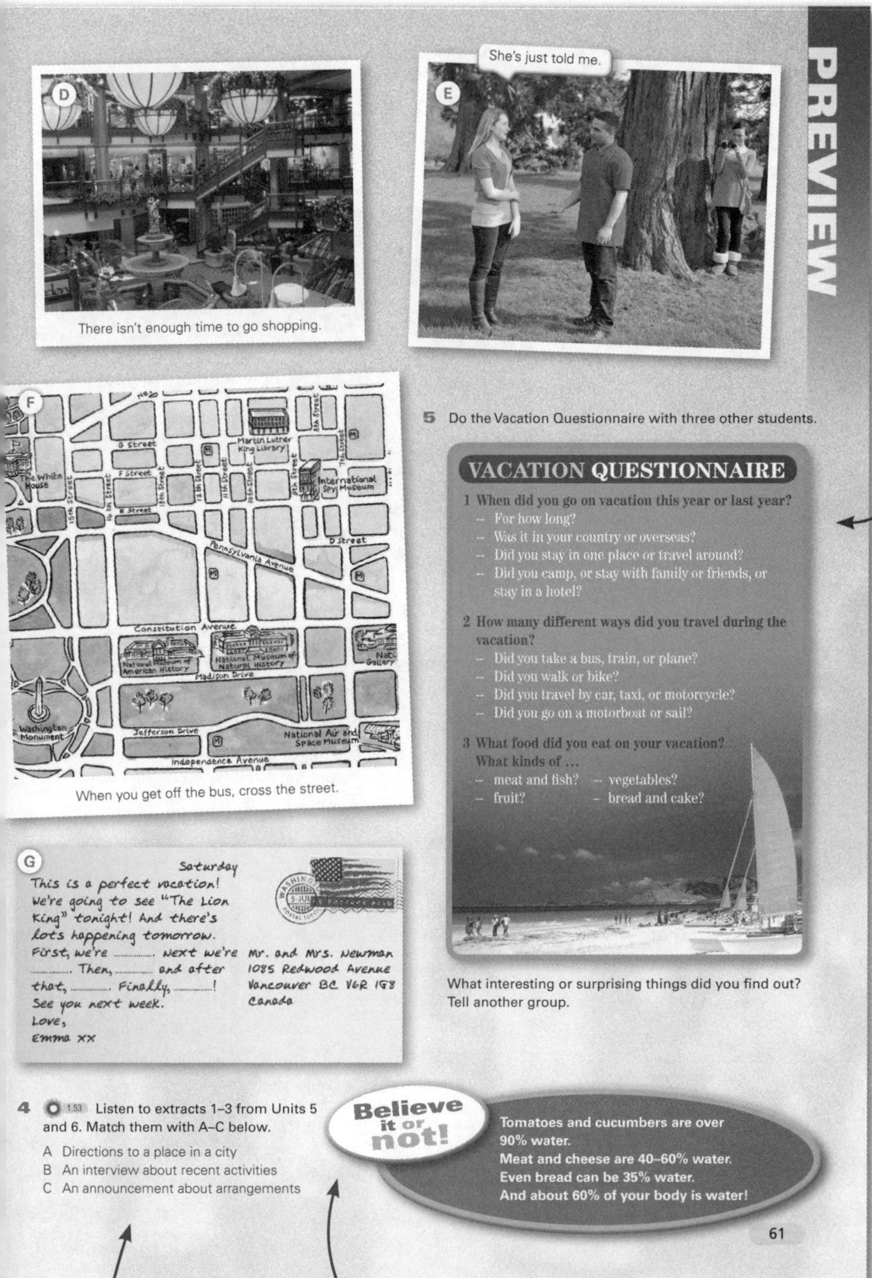
PREVIEW

There isn't enough time to go shopping.

When you get off the bus, cross the street.

4 1.53 Listen to extracts 1–3 from Units 5 and 6. Match them with A–C below.

A Directions to a place in a city
B An interview about recent activities
C An announcement about arrangements

5 Do the Vacation Questionnaire with three other students.

VACATION QUESTIONNAIRE

1 When did you go on vacation this year or last year?
- For how long?
- Was it in your country or overseas?
- Did you stay in one place or travel around?
- Did you camp, or stay with family or friends, or stay in a hotel?

2 How many different ways did you travel during the vacation?
- Did you take a bus, train, or plane?
- Did you walk or bike?
- Did you travel by car, taxi, or motorcycle?
- Did you go on a motorboat or sail?

3 What food did you eat on your vacation? What kinds of ...
- meat and fish?
- vegetables?
- fruit?
- bread and cake?

What interesting or surprising things did you find out? Tell another group.

Believe it or not!

Tomatoes and cucumbers are over 90% water.
Meat and cheese are 40–60% water.
Even bread can be 35% water.
And about 60% of your body is water!

61

Questionnaire
Students complete a questionnaire related to one of the topics from the following two units, to encourage them to personalize their knowledge of the topic. The Teacher's Book provides suggestions for students to use the results of the questionnaire to complete a project.

Believe it or not!
Interesting facts related to one of the topics from the following units.

Listening Preview
Students listen to short extracts from the following units and identify what kind of passage the extracts are taken from or what topic they discuss.

The first three lessons in each unit present **new language**. While these lessons follow a similar pattern up to the After Reading exercise, the subsequent practice activities vary from lesson to lesson, but always include pronunciation and end with writing and Language Workout. Lessons may also include Word Banks and vocabulary exercises, games, and role-plays as appropriate for the lesson aims. There are usually one or two Extension activities for fast-finishers. In every case there is a progression from controlled presentation and practice of new language to freer, more communicative activities.

Lesson heading

The heading shows the unit topic—in this case How do they do it?—and the communicative aim(s) and target language of the lesson.

WARM-UP

The Teacher's Book suggests at least two warm-up activities for each lesson. These may consolidate previously learned language or prepare students for the lesson topic.

1 Opener

The aim of the Opener is to set the scene for the reading text or listening passage, to pre-teach vocabulary, or both.

2 Reading/Listening

The new language is presented in a text or listening passage which is preceded by pre-reading/listening tasks or prediction activities. Students then read the text or listen to the passage. Teachers may then wish to play the recording, pausing to answer queries about language or content, or to ask students to close their books and listen without reading.

3 After Reading/Listening

These exercises use a variety of different formats including true/false, open questions, matching questions and answers, and completion. The aim is intensive reading/listening. After Reading/Listening ends with Your response: an activity which invites the student to personally respond to the text or dialogue.

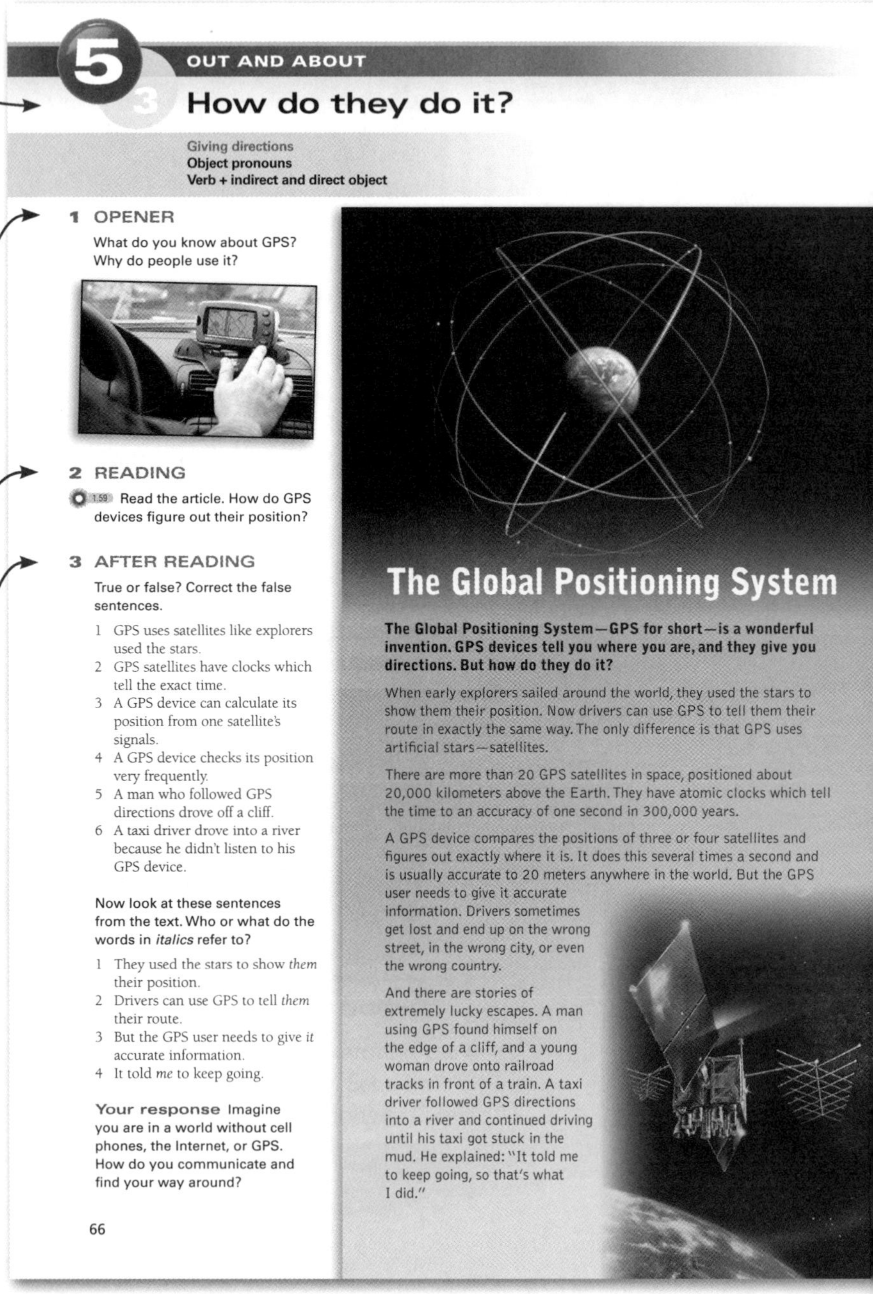

5 OUT AND ABOUT

3 How do they do it?

Giving directions
Object pronouns
Verb + indirect and direct object

1 OPENER

What do you know about GPS?
Why do people use it?

2 READING

1.59 Read the article. How do GPS devices figure out their position?

3 AFTER READING

True or false? Correct the false sentences.

1 GPS uses satellites like explorers used the stars.
2 GPS satellites have clocks which tell the exact time.
3 A GPS device can calculate its position from one satellite's signals.
4 A GPS device checks its position very frequently.
5 A man who followed GPS directions drove off a cliff.
6 A taxi driver drove into a river because he didn't listen to his GPS device.

Now look at these sentences from the text. Who or what do the words in *italics* refer to?

1 They used the stars to show *them* their position.
2 Drivers can use GPS to tell *them* their route.
3 But the GPS user needs to give *it* accurate information.
4 It told *me* to keep going.

Your response Imagine you are in a world without cell phones, the Internet, or GPS. How do you communicate and find your way around?

66

The Global Positioning System

The Global Positioning System—GPS for short—is a wonderful invention. GPS devices tell you where you are, and they give you directions. But how do they do it?

When early explorers sailed around the world, they used the stars to show them their position. Now drivers can use GPS to tell them their route in exactly the same way. The only difference is that GPS uses artificial stars—satellites.

There are more than 20 GPS satellites in space, positioned about 20,000 kilometers above the Earth. They have atomic clocks which tell the time to an accuracy of one second in 300,000 years.

A GPS device compares the positions of three or four satellites and figures out exactly where it is. It does this several times a second and is usually accurate to 20 meters anywhere in the world. But the GPS user needs to give it accurate information. Drivers sometimes get lost and end up on the wrong street, in the wrong city, or even the wrong country.

And there are stories of extremely lucky escapes. A man using GPS found himself on the edge of a cliff, and a young woman drove onto railroad tracks in front of a train. A taxi driver followed GPS directions into a river and continued driving until his taxi got stuck in the mud. He explained: "It told me to keep going, so that's what I did."

Follow-up activities and homework

The Teacher's Book offers optional follow-up activities, usually including a game, to help with mixed-ability teaching and to cope with variable aptitudes and how much time is available. Homework suggestions (usually writing) are also provided for each lesson.

UNIT 5

4 LISTENING

2.02 Look at the map of Washington, D.C. and find the hotel. Then listen to the directions and follow the route on the map. Where do you get to?

5 VOCABULARY

2.02 Listen again and complete the directions with prepositions from the Word Bank.

When you come __1__ the hotel, turn right __2__ 9th Street. Walk straight __3__ 9th Street __4__ the library. Go __5__ Pennsylvania Avenue and walk down __6__ Constitution Avenue. Then turn right and it's the big building on the left. You can't miss it!

Word Bank Prepositions of direction

across along up down past
around through to onto out of

▶ Language File page 119

6 SPEAKING

2.03 Look at the map. You are at the Washington Monument. Ask and answer the question, putting sentences A–D in the correct order. Then listen and check.

Excuse me, can you help me—how do I get to the Spy Museum?

A Then walk six blocks and it's on the right. It isn't far.
B Go across Constitution Avenue and walk up to F Street.
C Walk through the park and turn left onto 15th Street.
D When you get to F Street, turn right.

Now point to places on the map to show where you are, decide where you want to go, and ask each other for directions. Use the Word Bank to help you.

Excuse me, can you tell me the way to the White House?

Extension Use the map to give each other directions to mystery destinations.

7 PRONUNCIATION

Write these words under *walk*, *stop*, or *go*.

block call clock cross hot lost lot most phone post show talk told top wrong

/ɔ/ walk	/ɑ/ stop	/oʊ/ go

2.04 Now listen and check. Repeat the words.

8 WRITING

Write directions from your school to your home.

Turn left outside the school and walk to the bus stop. Catch a bus to ... When you get off the bus, cross the street. I live on the fourth street on the right.

Now read your directions aloud. Don't say the name of your street. Can other students guess where you live?

LANGUAGE WORKOUT

Complete.

Object pronouns

Singular	**Plural**
me	us
____	you
him, her, it	____

Verb + indirect and direct object
Can you tell **me the way**?
... they give **you directions**.
... show **them their position**.

▶**Answers and Practice**
Language File page 118

67

6 Speaking

In the Speaking activity, students use the target language to communicate, in this case asking for and giving directions. This activity often also personalizes the target language and students use it to talk about their own lives and opinions.

Extension

Lessons have one or more Extension activities offering more challenging practice for fast-finishers.

7 Pronunciation

Each of the first three lessons in every unit contains a pronunciation exercise focusing on particular sounds or stress and intonation. The Teacher's Book provides more information about the phonological area being treated and suggests further activities.

8 Writing

Each of the first three lessons in each unit ends with a writing activity. These typically have the dual function of developing writing skills and reinforcing the target language. In this lesson, students write directions from their school to their home.

5 Vocabulary

Lessons may also offer explicit lexical development through Word Banks of lexical sets and vocabulary exercises.

Language Workout

The Language Workout boxes highlight the target language with sentences from the reading text or paradigms for the students to complete. The bottom of the box refers students to the Language File at the back of the book where they can check their answers, find a fuller treatment of the grammatical point, and do a practice exercise focusing on the form of the target language. The Teacher's Book provides suggestions for further practice activities and additional information about the target language.
Teachers may decide when to draw students' attention to the Language Workout, and the Teacher's Book gives suggestions for when it can be used. For example, it may be appropriate to refer to it before learners are expected to produce the target language, and/or for consolidation at the end of the lesson.

The fourth lesson in each unit is an **Integrated Skills** lesson. In these lessons, the four skills support each other, usually moving from a reading text to a listening activity, then a speaking activity based on the listening or reading, and concluding with a writing activity for which the reading, listening, and speaking have prepared the students. The lesson ends with a Learner Independence section.

Lesson heading
The lesson heading identifies the text type, in this lesson, Suggestions and advice.

1 Opener
The aim of the Opener is to introduce the topic or to consolidate and pre-teach vocabulary, or both.

WARM-UP
The Teacher's Book suggests two or three warm-up activities. These may consolidate vocabulary or prepare students for the lesson topic.

2 Reading
There are usually one or two reading activities encouraging detailed reading. Detailed comprehension questions have the dual function of encouraging intensive reading and highlighting the structure of the text in preparation for the subsequent skills activities.

4 Listening
These activities develop intensive listening skills. Here, students listen for the order in which a character plans to visit certain countries, and for the items he is taking with him on his travels.

5 OUT AND ABOUT

4 Integrated Skills

Suggestions and advice

1 OPENER

What do you pack when you go on vacation? Make a list and compare with another student.

READING

2 Read *Welcome to TopTeenTravel!* and match five of these topics with paragraphs 1–5.

Travel light   Keep in touch
Make a list   Think small
Enjoy long journeys   Buy new clothes
Don't take too much

3 Find the highlighted words in the text which mean:

1 books
2 suggestions
3 cloth made from artificial material
4 less heavy than other similar things
5 does not let water through
6 extremely large
7 small backpack for use in the day
8 (group of) things

LISTENING

4 2.05 Steve is telling Lara and Ramón about his planned trip around the world. Listen to the first part of their conversation and number these countries in the order Steve is visiting them.

Australia   Brazil   Chile
New Zealand   Peru   Singapore

68

Get Mail   Write   Contacts   Reply   Forward   Delete   Print

Welcome to TopTeenTravel!

Thank you for choosing TopTeenTravel for your African adventure vacation—we know you're going to have a great time with us! Here are our favorite travel tips to help you get ready for the trip.

1 You know that the tour bus will be crowded, so there won't be room for a big suitcase or backpack. Also remember that you're flying to Africa, so a **huge** backpack isn't a good idea.

2 How much should you take with you? Put everything you want to take on your bed—remember you'll be gone for six weeks. Then look at your things and choose only a third of them! Check that all your **stuff** fits in your bag.

3 And it's not just a question of how many things you take. Choose clothes which are light, and easy to wash and dry. So go for a **polyester** T-shirt, not a cotton one, **lightweight** pants instead of jeans, and a fleece jacket, not a wool sweater. Forget your raincoat and pack a **waterproof** jacket—it's much lighter.

4 You'll often travel for 10 to 12 hours a day. It's a good idea to have some things in your **daypack** to help you pass the time—your MP3 player, **paperbacks**, or some playing cards.

5 And last but not least, don't forget your cell phone—you'll want to tell your family and friends how the trip is going.

See you soon on our adventure vacation! And happy backpacking!

The TopTeenTravel Team

6 Speaking
Students now use their answers from the Listening activity to role-play a conversation between two characters in which one of them makes suggestions and gives advice. The Teacher's Book offers further optional activities.

UNIT 5

LEARNER INDEPENDENCE

5 2.06 Listen to the second part of the conversation and check your answers. Then check (✓) the things Steve is taking with him.

backpack cotton T-shirts jeans raincoat shirts
suit swim trunks tie umbrella wool sweater

6 SPEAKING

Read *Welcome to TopTeenTravel!* again and look at the things that Steve is taking with him. Then role-play a conversation between Steve and either Lara or Ramón. You can use the phrases in the box.

Lara/Ramón	Steve
Ask Steve what he is taking on his trip.	
	Reply.
Make a suggestion.	
	Ask why.
Explain. Ask what else he is taking.	
	Reply.
Make a suggestion and explain.	
	Agree.

Making suggestions and giving advice
Do you think that's a good idea?
Can I make a suggestion?
Maybe you should …
Why don't you …?
What about …?
It's a good idea to …

7 WRITING

Write the dialogue between Lara or Ramón and Steve which you practiced in the role-play.

OR Write an e-mail giving advice to a friend who is going backpacking.

8 What does "knowing" a word mean? Which of these answers do you agree with? Compare with another student.

- Being able to understand it.
- Remembering it when I need it.
- Being able to pronounce it correctly.
- Being able to spell it properly.
- Knowing how to use it grammatically.
- Knowing which other words I can use it with.

9 Dictionaries use abbreviations to give you information about words. Match these abbreviations with their meanings below.

abbrev adj adv aux
C pl sb sing sth U

Word Bank
Dictionary words
countable singular abbreviation
adverb plural something
auxiliary verb (like *be*) adjective
uncountable somebody

Compare these abbreviations with your own dictionary.

10 2.07 **Phrasebook:** Find these useful expressions in Unit 5. Then listen and repeat.

I'm starving!
Are you ready to order?
I'll have that.
What would you like to drink?
Sure—coming right up.
You're impossible!
You can't miss it!
Excuse me, can you help me?
It isn't far.
Last but not least …

Now match these replies with the three questions in the box.

a Yes, can I have a pizza?
b Yes, of course. What's the problem?
c A glass of milk, please.

69

Learner Independence

Learner Independence sections typically include three activities, focusing on learning to learn, vocabulary development, and idiomatic expressions.

8

In this lesson, students look at different interpretations of knowing a word. Discussion may take place in English or their mother tongue, as appropriate to the learner's level. The emphasis here is on learning *how* to learn. The Teacher's Book offers optional activities to further explore this area.

9

The aim here is to learn the meanings of dictionary words and their abbreviations.

10 Phrasebook

This section appears in every unit and helps students learn idiomatic expressions in context. Students find the expressions from within the unit, practice pronunciation, and then complete a small follow-up activity, in this case matching replies with the idiomatic questions they have learned.

Follow-up activities and homework

The Teacher's Book offers optional follow-up activities, usually including a game, to help with mixed-ability teaching and to cope with variable aptitudes and how much time is available. Homework suggestions (usually writing) are also provided for each lesson.

7 Writing

Here, students can choose between writing the dialogue from the Speaking activity or writing an e-mail giving advice. The Teacher's Book suggests that students check each other's work for grammar, spelling, and punctuation, and also provides further optional activities.

Inspired ***Extra!*** follows the Integrated Skills lesson in each unit and always includes, on the left-hand page, a Game/Puzzle, plus either a Project, or Language Links, a Skit, and sometimes a Limerick. On the right-hand page, there are mixed-ability activities giving opportunities for both consolidation and extension, and Your Choice! which allows students to choose from two different activities.

Language Links

The aim of the Language Links section is to raise plurilingual awareness. Here, students are encouraged to see how knowing one or two languages can often help them identify words in other languages.

Game/Puzzle

Here, students solve a riddle and then make up their own riddle. There is often a game on this page, and there are also games throughout the book in the lessons and in the Teacher's Book optional activities.

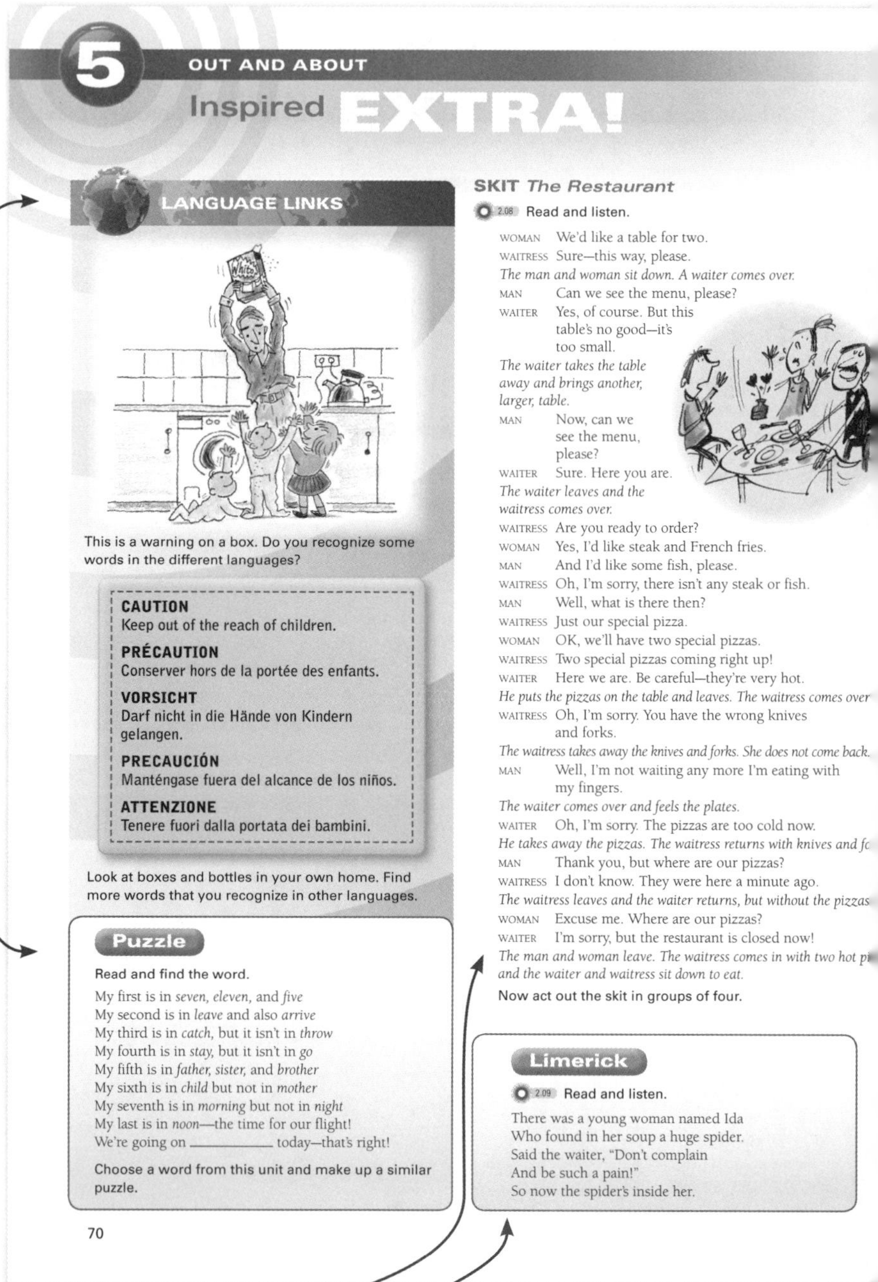

5 OUT AND ABOUT

Inspired EXTRA!

LANGUAGE LINKS

This is a warning on a box. Do you recognize some words in the different languages?

CAUTION
Keep out of the reach of children.

PRÉCAUTION
Conserver hors de la portée des enfants.

VORSICHT
Darf nicht in die Hände von Kindern gelangen.

PRECAUCIÓN
Manténgase fuera del alcance de los niños.

ATTENZIONE
Tenere fuori dalla portata dei bambini.

Look at boxes and bottles in your own home. Find more words that you recognize in other languages.

Puzzle

Read and find the word.

My first is in *seven, eleven,* and *five*
My second is in *leave* and also *arrive*
My third is in *catch*, but it isn't in *throw*
My fourth is in *stay*, but it isn't in *go*
My fifth is in *father, sister,* and *brother*
My sixth is in *child* but not in *mother*
My seventh is in *morning* but not in *night*
My last is in *noon*—the time for our flight!
We're going on __________ today—that's right!

Choose a word from this unit and make up a similar puzzle.

SKIT ***The Restaurant***

2.08 Read and listen.

WOMAN We'd like a table for two.
WAITRESS Sure—this way, please.
The man and woman sit down. A waiter comes over.
MAN Can we see the menu, please?
WAITER Yes, of course. But this table's no good—it's too small.
The waiter takes the table away and brings another, larger, table.
MAN Now, can we see the menu, please?
WAITER Sure. Here you are.
The waiter leaves and the waitress comes over.
WAITRESS Are you ready to order?
WOMAN Yes, I'd like steak and French fries.
MAN And I'd like some fish, please.
WAITRESS Oh, I'm sorry, there isn't any steak or fish.
MAN Well, what is there then?
WAITRESS Just our special pizza.
WOMAN OK, we'll have two special pizzas.
WAITRESS Two special pizzas coming right up!
WAITER Here we are. Be careful—they're very hot.
He puts the pizzas on the table and leaves. The waitress comes over
WAITRESS Oh, I'm sorry. You have the wrong knives and forks.
The waitress takes away the knives and forks. She does not come back.
MAN Well, I'm not waiting any more I'm eating with my fingers.
The waiter comes over and feels the plates.
WAITER Oh, I'm sorry. The pizzas are too cold now.
He takes away the pizzas. The waitress returns with knives and fc
MAN Thank you, but where are our pizzas?
WAITRESS I don't know. They were here a minute ago.
The waitress leaves and the waiter returns, but without the pizzas
WOMAN Excuse me. Where are our pizzas?
WAITER I'm sorry, but the restaurant is closed now!
The man and woman leave. The waitress comes in with two hot pi and the waiter and waitress sit down to eat.

Now act out the skit in groups of four.

Limerick

2.09 Read and listen.

There was a young woman named Ida
Who found in her soup a huge spider.
Said the waiter, "Don't complain
And be such a pain!"
So now the spider's inside her.

70

Skit

The aim of the skits is for students to enjoy using English, while also getting valuable stress and intonation practice. The Teacher's Book has suggestions for using the recording and for acting out the skits.

Limerick

The limerick (here and in Unit 7) also gives useful stress and intonation practice, as well as increasing students' awareness of rhyme. The Teacher's Book encourages students to write their own limericks.

Consolidation

The Consolidation exercises provide further writing practice for less confident students in mixed-ability classes. In this unit, students write sentences about a group's plans for a particular day, a conversation in a restaurant, a set of directions, and vocabulary lists. They are always given sections of the unit to refer back to.

Extension

The Extension exercises provide challenging writing activities for more confident students in mixed-ability classes. In this unit, students brainstorm vocabulary under different categories, extend a word map, write directions from their school to various places, and write an e-mail about a trip.

The Consolidation and Extension exercises are a flexible resource and may be done at the end of the unit or after the relevant lesson. Alternatively, the students can do them as homework. The Teacher's Book provides possible answers.

UNIT 5

CONSOLIDATION

LESSON 1 Look at the schedule on page 62 and write sentences about what the group is doing on Saturday:

in the morning　at lunchtime
in the afternoon　in the evening

In the morning, they're taking a sightseeing tour of Washington, D.C.

LESSON 2 Look at the conversation on page 64 and at the Pizza Paradise menu. Write a similar conversation between the waiter and Ramón and Alex. Ramón likes spinach, and Alex doesn't want any tomatoes or peppers on his pizza.

Waiter: Are you ready to order?
Ramón: Yes, could I have a ...?

LESSON 3 Look at exercise 5 on page 67, and write directions for someone who wants to go from the National Museum of Natural History back to the hotel.

Turn right outside the museum and walk along to 9th Street.

LESSON 4 Look again at pages 68–69 and make lists of items under these headings:

Luggage　*backpack*
Clothes　*T-shirt*

EXTENSION

LESSON 1 Make lists of words for places in a town under these headings.

Places to visit	Performance	Shopping	Food and drink
museum	*theater*	*market*	*restaurant*

LESSON 2 Look at the word map you made in exercise 4 on page 64, and add at least ten more words to the map. You can also add more categories, such as FISH AND SEAFOOD. Use a dictionary to help you.

LESSON 3 You are outside your school. Write short conversations where you give directions to a tourist who is looking for:

- a place for lunch.
- the nearest hotel.

Tourist: Excuse me, can you help me? I'm looking for a place for lunch.

LESSON 4 Imagine you are going on a trip around the world. Write an e-mail to a friend explaining where you are going and what you are taking. Begin like this:

Great news! I'm going on a trip around the world. I'm leaving on ...

YOUR CHOICE!

SUGGESTIONS

- Work in a small group.
- Think of a problem situation, for example:

You're lost in a big city.　You're stuck in an elevator.
You're afraid of heights.　You're always late.

- Take turns telling the rest of the group about the problem and giving each other advice.

Maybe you should ...　Why don't you ...?
What about ...?

I NEVER TRAVEL WITHOUT IT

- Work in a small group.
- Think of an item which you always take with you when you travel. Don't say what it is!
- In turn, mime using or wearing the item to the rest of the group. They ask *Yes/No* questions to find out what your essential item is.
- Finally, explain why you think your item is essential.

71

Project

Projects provide a valuable resource for student creativity, self-expression, and language consolidation. They also allow students of varying abilities to all contribute. Students are encouraged to save their projects to add to their portfolios. While intended for use with the whole class, the projects could also be used for homework or as supplementary material with more confident students in mixed-ability classes. The group size for projects will vary from class to class, but teachers may prefer to have groups of three to six members.

1 Projects require students to go back through the part of the unit which models the writing they will do. Then, students brainstorm ideas, choosing a few to write about.
2 There is then a research phase using reference books, libraries, or the Internet to gather information for the project. This could involve interviewing people, for example, family members.
3 Finally, the group works together to produce their project, reading each other's work, editing, and illustrating it. The Teacher's Book offers suggestions for organization.

Your Choice!

The aim here is for students to choose and do the activity they like best. The activities reflect different learning styles and the aim is to encourage awareness of learning styles and to foster learner independence. Your Choice! activities may involve individual, pair, or group work.

Culture

There are four Culture sections in each level of *Inspired*, providing both factual information and the opportunity for cross-cultural comparisons. The section illustrated here deals with the topic of teenage life.

1 Opener

The aim of the Opener is to introduce the topic and stimulate discussion, often through a quiz. For this lesson, the Teacher's Book provides useful information about teenagers' activities and attitudes. There are further Useful information sections throughout the Teacher's Book.

2 Reading

Here, students read a text in which four girls talk about being teenagers, and identify the character that holds each of the listed views.

5 Culture

1 OPENER

How much do you know about teenagers in the U.S.? Try our Teenage Life Quiz!

2 READING

Read *Girls* and find the answers to these questions.

Who …

1 can't stand being 15?
2 has a boyfriend?
3 plays two instruments?
4 knows people who are worried about how they look?
5 thinks designer clothes are too expensive?
6 wants more independence?
7 enjoys dancing?
8 likes movies?

Teenage Life Quiz

	A	B	C
1 How many American teenagers expect to be famous?	A 10%	B 20%	C 30%
2 What percentage of teenagers say they are usually happy?	A 50%	B 65%	C 80%
3 What do teenagers spend most of their money on?	A Clothes	B Music	C Video games
4 What percentage of teenagers eat a healthy diet?	A 30%	B 50%	C 70%
5 How many hours a month do teenagers watch TV?	A 50	B 75	C 100
6 What percentage of the total U.S. population are teenagers?	A 10%	B 20%	C 30%

What do you think the answers to the quiz are for teenagers in your country

72

Culture

Girls

Isabelle

Some girls want to look like models, so they go on diets when they don't need to and get really thin. And I have friends who spend a lot of money on designer clothes, even boys. They buy expensive jeans and sneakers and stuff. It's a waste of money, really. And others get upset because they can't afford the latest fashions. I just make my own clothes—I'd like to be a fashion designer.

Naomi

I like being 15. I love shopping and going to the movies. And I often watch DVDs with friends, because there isn't much to do in this town for people of our age. Computers? I mainly use my computer for homework and studying for exams, and chatting on the Internet. But I know a guy—he's my boyfriend, actually—and he spends hours playing computer games. They're really addictive.

Anna

I hate being 15, I really do. I get along OK with my parents, but they still treat me like a kid and try to organize my life. It's not that they don't trust me, but they definitely worry too much. I can go to gigs or parties on weekends, but they always want me home early—my friends can stay out much later than me. I can't wait to have more freedom and responsibility.

Jodi

I listen to music in my spare time—I really love it—and I play the violin and the guitar. I actually like classical music best. Some people think it's awful, but I think it's really cool. Of course, when you go to dances it's all hip-hop, rap, and R&B, and that's fine, too. Anyway, you can't dance to classical music, and I love dancing.

3 VOCABULARY

Match the words with their definitions.

1 guy
2 addictive
3 upset
4 kid
5 awful
6 cool

a difficult to stop
b great
c man or boy
d terrible
e child
f worried and unhappy

4 MINI-PROJECT
Teenage life

Are the things that Naomi, Isabelle, Jodi, and Anna say also true about life for teenage girls in your country? Discuss the similarities and differences with another student.

> Naomi says there isn't much to do in her town. But in our town …

Now work together to write about teenage life for girls and/or boys in your country. Read your work carefully and correct any mistakes. Then compare your *Teenage life* report with other students.

73

3 Vocabulary
The Culture section texts provide a rich source of useful new vocabulary, and there is a variety of activity types here to give practice.

4 Mini-Project
The Mini-Projects in the Culture sections typically use the text as a model and invite the students to work in pairs and write about aspects of their own culture.

There are four **Reviews** in each level of *Inspired*. Each Review covers the new language of the preceding two units. The Teacher's Book contains the answers to all the exercises.

Review exercises are contextualized, often using information from the relevant lesson, so that students are creating meaningful sentences.

Reviewed language points include not only main verb tenses but also problem areas such as *some/any* and *much/many/enough*.

The Workbook offers a parallel Review with text and multiple-choice questions, examination-type exercises, and a self assessment Progress Check including "My Learning Diary".

Exercise 1

Each review begins with a text covering the new language from both units.

REVIEW

UNITS 5–6

1 Read and complete. For each number 1–10, choose word or phrase A, B, or C.

No singer has had a career like Kylie Minogue, and no one ___1___ to more people at the same time. ___2___ the Sydney Olympic® Games in 2000, she sang *Dancing Queen* to a worldwide TV audience of 4 *billion* people. Today she is one of the most successful singers the world has ___3___ seen, but she started performing as a child actor in soaps on Australian TV.

Kylie Ann Minogue was born in Melbourne, Australia, on May 28, 1968. Her first TV role came when she ___4___ only 12 years old, and six years later she left school and joined *Neighbours.*

A year later, her first single, *Locomotion*, was a number-one hit in Australia. But it was the next song, *I Should Be So Lucky*, released in January 1988, which made ___5___ a world star. It was the biggest selling hit in the U.K. that year and a big hit in the U.S. "A new star ___6___ arrived," the newspapers said. Now Kylie ___7___ over 50 hit singles around the world.

Kylie discovered she had cancer in 2006, but she was performing again by the end of 2007. Over her long career she ___8___ hundreds of awards, and she is a household name everywhere. But Kylie herself ___9___ changed. Ask her how many records she has sold or how ___10___ money she has, and she smiles her famous smile. She simply enjoys making people happy, and they love her for being herself.

	A	B	C
1	A sang	B sung	C has sung
2	A At	B In	C On
3	A always	B ever	C never
4	A has been	B is	C was
5	A her	B hers	C she
6	A have	B has	C had
7	A is having	B has had	C have had
8	A has won	B wins	C won
9	A hasn't	B doesn't	C wasn't
10	A any	B many	C much

2 2.23 Ask Carrie questions about future arrangements. Listen and write the dates.

Silvana/return to Argentina

When is she returning to Argentina?

On August 31.

1 Silvana/return to Argentina *August 31*
2 Lara/fly home
3 Ramón and Jay/visit Florida
4 Alex/go on vacation
5 Emma/go back to school
6 you/get married

Now write sentences.

1 Silvana is returning to Argentina on August 31.

3 Choose *some* or *any*.

1 I want to buy some/any gifts for my family.
2 Could you lend me some/any money for ice cream?
3 There aren't some/any empty tables in the coffee shop.
4 Would you like some/any water with your meal?
5 I don't have some/any expensive jewelry.
6 Do you sell some/any Spanish newspapers?

4 Complete with *How much/many*, and write the answers.

1 water do you drink every day?
2 meals do you have every day?
3 money do you spend every week?
4 books do you read every month?
5 English words do you learn every week?
6 time do you spend at school every week?
7 sleep do you have every night?
8 times do you wash your hair every week?

5 Emma is talking to Lara about Saturday evening. Complete with object pronouns.

"This evening, some friends called me from Florida. I was talking to ___1___ on the phone and Jay was waiting for ___2___. So Carrie gave Jay a map of Washington, D.C. and told ___3___ the way to the theater. But I don't think Jay listened to ___4___! We looked for the theater, but we couldn't find ___5___, so we asked a police officer to help ___6___. When we ran into the theater, you were all waiting for ___7___. It was great to see ___8___! And we were just in time for the show—I'm glad I didn't miss ___9___."

6 Complete with these prepositions.

across along around at into on past to unde

You can take a three-hour Circle Line cruise all the way ___1___ New York City's Manhattan Island. The cruise starts ___2___ Pier 83 ___3___ the Hudson River. The boat sails south down the Hudson to the Harlem River and then north up the East River back ___4___ the Hudson. There are many famous buildings and attractions ___5___ each river. The boat sails ___6___ the United Nations, and you can see the Statue of Liberty. But don't fall ___7___ the water!

The Circle Line sails ___8___ seven bridges. Once Carrie and her boyfriend walked ___9___ the George Washington Bridge to New Jersey. It was a long walk!

7 Write sentences about what's happened this week.

Alex/play soccer ✓/tennis ✗

Alex has played soccer, but he hasn't played tennis.

1 Jay/speak to his father ✓/mother ✗
2 Silvana and Lara/have a letter ✗/an e-mail ✓
3 Alex/buy a CD ✗/a book ✓
4 Emma/write a postcard ✓/a letter ✗
5 Carrie/make a podcast ✓/a movie ✗
6 we/go to the movies ✗/theater ✓

84

REVIEW

8 Rewrite the sentences using the present perfect with *just*.

Steve had lunch half an hour ago.
Steve has just had lunch.

1 Lara took a shower ten minutes ago.
2 Ramón bought some new sneakers yesterday.
3 Silvana went to bed five minutes ago.
4 Emma sent a text message a few seconds ago.
5 Lara and Alex showed their video an hour ago.
6 Carrie interviewed the President this morning.

9 Ask and answer.

Emma/see the Statue of Liberty ✗
A Has Emma ever seen the Statue of Liberty?
B No, she hasn't.

1 Silvana/made a video before ✗
2 Carrie/visit New York ✓
3 Jay and Emma/be on TV ✓
4 Lara/meet Eminem ✗
5 Ramón/win a contest ✓
6 Alex/lose his camera ✗
7 the contest winners/see the President ✗
8 Steve/go to Italy ✓

Now write sentences.

Emma has never seen the Statue of Liberty.

10 Complete with *much*, *many*, or *enough* and write the answers.

1 Are there too ____ tourists in your city?
2 Is there too ____ traffic on the roads?
3 Have you spent too ____ money this week?
4 Have you watched too ____ TV shows this week?
5 Do you have too ____ TV channels?
6 Do you have too ____ homework?
7 Do you always have ____ sleep?
8 Do you go to bed early ____?

VOCABULARY

11 Complete with nine of these words.

customer fountain magnet menu park position route satellite stadium tie track waiter

1 A ____ is someone who works in a restaurant.
2 A ____ is an artificial object in space which goes around the Earth.
3 A ____ is someone who buys things in a store or a meal in a restaurant.
4 A ____ is a list of the food you can order in a restaurant.
5 A ____ is a green open space in a town or city.
6 A ____ is something that a man wears around his neck over a shirt.
7 A ____ is a piece of metal which attracts objects that contain iron.
8 A ____ is a place where they play soccer, baseball, or football.
9 A ____ is a way to get from one place to another.

12 Match these words with their definitions.

ancient dairy produce engine line market paradise railroad starving statue vegetarian

1 perfect place
2 machine that makes a train, car, or plane move
3 very, very hungry
4 someone who doesn't eat meat
5 butter and cheese, for example
6 place (often outside) with stands where you can buy food, clothes, etc.
7 track that trains travel along
8 opposite of *modern*
9 large stone or metal model of a person or animal
10 people waiting for something one behind the other

13 Match the verbs in list A with the words and phrases in list B.

A	B
1 cross	a contest
2 give	a meal
3 go	a noise
4 make	directions
5 order	shopping
6 play	someone the way
7 tell	an instrument
8 visit	the street
9 win	the zoo

LEARNER INDEPENDENCE SELF ASSESSMENT

Look back at Lessons 1–3 in Units 5 and 6.

How good are you at ...?	✓ Fine	? Not sure
1 Talking about future arrangements Workbook pp52–53 exercises 1–4	☐	☐
2 Describing a sequence of events Workbook p53 exercise 5	☐	☐
3 Ordering a meal in a restaurant Workbook p54 exercise 1	☐	☐
4 Giving directions Workbook p57 exercises 5–7	☐	☐
5 Talking about recent events Workbook pp64–65 exercises 1–4	☐	☐
6 Talking about experiences Workbook pp66–67 exercises 1–3	☐	☐
7 Saying what's wrong with something Workbook p69 exercises 3 and 4	☐	☐

Not sure? Take a look at Language File pages 117–120 and do the Workbook exercise(s) again.

Now write an example for 1–7.

1 We're meeting tomorrow at 11:30.

85

Collocation

All the Review sections include an exercise to raise awareness of the importance of collocation.

Learner Independence: Self Assessment

This Self Assessment section for every two units lists the communicative aims and invites students to rate their confidence in each one. Students who are not sure about their ability in a particular area are referred to the Language File and the relevant Workbook exercises. The Teacher's Book offers guidance on handling this.

Follow-up activities and homework

The Teacher's Book offers optional follow-up activities, usually games. Homework suggestions (usually writing) are also provided.

Vocabulary

Vocabulary exercises include completion, matching words with their definitions, and collocation (in this case matching nouns and phrases).

Welcome!

Language	Communicative Aims	Vocabulary	Optional aids	
Simple present: *be*	Introducing yourself and others Talking about nationality	Countries Nationalities	Warm-up 1: a soft ball (or a ball of paper) Exercise 2 Optional activity: a map of the world	Follow-up activities: small cards; small cards with names of famous people and their countries written on them

WARM-UP 1

Introduce yourself to the class. Say *Hello, I'm … My name is … I'm from …* Walk around the room introducing yourself to individual students and telling them where you are from. Use a soft ball to encourage students to introduce themselves. Throw the ball to a student who then introduces him/herself and says where he/she is from. He/She then throws the ball to another student who does the same. Continue until all the students have introduced themselves.

WARM-UP 2

Ask *What are the main news websites in your country?* Translate *websites*. Explain that in this book there is a news website called World2day. World2day is an imaginary website. It has regular contests that you can complete online to win a prize.

1 Opener

- The aim is to introduce the students to the photo story that runs through the book.
- Ask students to look at the photo on pages 6–7. Ask *Where is this?* Explain that it is San Francisco, a city which many tourists visit every year.
- In pairs, students read the contest questions and see if they know or can guess the answers.
- Play the recording for students to check their answers.

1.02 Recording

The United States of America is one of the largest countries in the world. It has 50 states, and its total population is 300 million. The capital of the United States is Washington, D.C., and the U.S. President lives in Washington, D.C. at the White House. The longest river in the U.S. is the Missouri—it's 3,767 kilometers long!

Competition answers

1 50 2 300 million 3 Washington, D.C.
4 the White House 5 the Missouri

Optional activity

Students change the words and facts in the contest questions to make it into a contest about their country.

2 Reading

- The aim is to introduce the coursebook characters and review introductory personal statements.
- Students read the speech bubbles and find out how many contest winners there are.

Answer

Six

Optional activities

- 1.03 Play the recording of the speech bubbles for students to read and listen. Stop at any words you predict may cause pronunciation problems, e.g. *vacation, sights*, and ask students to repeat.
- Students find the countries and cities mentioned in the speech bubbles on a map of the world.

3 After Reading

- Ask students to read the speech bubbles again and to work in pairs to answer questions 1–10.
- Check the answers by asking different students to ask and answer the questions.

Answers

1	*She's a journalist.*	6	*Silvana*
2	*Emma*	7	*In Recife*
3	*Lara*	8	*Guadalajara*
4	*Ramón*	9	*Silvana*
5	*Alex*	10	*Emma*

Your Response

- Ask any students who have visited the U.S. to tell the class some of the things they liked/didn't like.
- Ask students to work in small groups discussing whether they would like to visit the U.S., and giving reasons for their answers.

4 Speaking

- Ask students to look at the photo again. Hold up your book and point to Silvana. Ask *What's her name?* and elicit *Her name is Silvana.* Ask *Where's she from?* and elicit *She's from Argentina.* Now point at Jay, ask *What's his name?* and elicit *His name is Jay.* Ask *Where's he from?* and elicit *He's from the U.S.A.* Highlight the link between *her/she* and *his/he*. Explain to students that U.S.A. stands for the United States of America and we sometimes call it the U.S.
- Point to another character in the photo and elicit the same questions and answers from the students.
- Students continue the exercise in pairs.

Optional activity

In pairs, one student closes his/her book and the other asks questions about the characters. The student with the closed book answers from memory. They then change roles.

Extension Students write a sentence about each of the contest winners, to say where they are from. Point out to students that some of the winners only say which country they are from, not the city.

Possible answers

Jay is from the U.S.A.
Lara is from Recife in Brazil.
Ramón is from Guadalajara in Mexico.
Emma is from Vancouver in Canada.
Silvana is from Argentina.
Alex is from Australia.

5 Vocabulary

- Ask students to close their books. Write the following countries on the board and elicit the nationalities by saying the name of the country: the U.S.A.—American, Argentina—Argentine, Australia—Australian, Brazil—Brazilian, Britain—British, Canada—Canadian, France—French, Italy—Italian, Mexico—Mexican, Spain—Spanish.
- Drill the country and nationality words in chorus for pronunciation and stress, marking the stress on words with two or more syllables. Point out that nationalities start with a capital letter in English.
- Point to the different characters in the Student's Book and elicit statements from the students about their nationalities like the one in the example, e.g. *Lara is Brazilian.*
- Point to a character and ask *Is he/she Mexican/American/ Brazilian?* and elicit *Yes, he/she is* or *No, he/she isn't.*

Optional activities

- ♦ Clean the board. Call out the names of the characters' countries. Students respond with the appropriate nationalities. Then call out the nationalities and students say the countries.
- ♦ With a confident class, elicit other nationalities by saying the name of the country, e.g. *Japan—Japanese, Peru – Peruvian, India—Indian.*

Follow-up activities

- ♦ Use small cards to start a Vocabulary box. They can write new words on one side of the card and an explanation, illustration, or translation on the other side.
- ♦ **Game** *Celebrity party* Give each student a card (see Optional aids). Set a time limit of three minutes. Students get up and move around introducing themselves and finding out who other students are and where they are from. They then have one minute to write down the name and country or nationality of the people they have met. The student with the most names and nationalities wins.

Homework

Ask students to write a question and answer dialogue of at least four lines about a famous person, using this model:
Who's he/she? His/Her name is …
Where's he/she from? He/she's from …

NOTEBOOK SECTION

Complete the sentences using one of these words: *am, is,* or *are.*

1 I ____ Mexican.
2 Jack ____ from Canada.
3 Carla and Javier ____ Mexican.
4 She ____ from Bogotá in Colombia.
5 They ____ from Chicago.

Answers *1 am 2 is 3 are 4 is 5 are*

Workbook Welcome! pp2–3

PREVIEW

Units 1–2

Activities		**Project**	**Vocabulary**	**Optional aids**
Identifying the function of communicative language	Categorizing vocabulary Contextualizing listening extracts	Birthdays	Music Town facilities Colors Clothes	Follow-up activity: slips of paper for students to write single words on

WARM-UP 1

If students did the homework in the last lesson, ask one student to read out the questions about a famous person and another to give his/her answers. In pairs, students take turns asking and answering the two questions.

WARM-UP 2

Draw three female faces and three male faces on the board. Explain to students that they are the contest winners from *Welcome!* Point to each face in turn, asking *What's his/her name?* and *Where's he/she from?* and eliciting the names and countries of each character.

WARM-UP 3

Ask students to look at the photos and captions/speech bubbles on pages 8–9 and to answer the questions *What do the photos show? Who can you see in the photos?*

1
- The aim is to introduce students to the main areas of communicative language they will cover in the first two units, and to encourage them to think about the function of the language.
- Explain to students that the two boxes at the top of the page show the communicative language and topics/vocabulary they will use in the first two units. Students look at the first box and match the communicative aims 1–8 with the pictures A–H on pages 8–9.

Answers

1 E 2 H 3 C 4 D 5 G 6 A 7 F 8 B

Optional activity

Students write another example sentence or question for each of the communicative aims 1–8. Monitor and help where necessary.

2
- Elicit the meaning of the word *facilities*. Explain to students that words from each of the three vocabulary categories (music, town facilities, and colors) are arranged in the word square. Give students two minutes to write the words in the correct category.
- Students check their answers in pairs and then as a whole class. Point out that *church* could potentially be a kind of music and also a town facility. Also point out that while *blues* is a kind of music, *blue* is only a color.

Answers

Music: jazz, salsa, hip-hop, world, soul, reggae
Town facilities: church, coffee shop, hotel, store, museum, restaurant
Colors: green, red, yellow, brown, purple, blue

Optional activities

- ♦ Students rewrite the lists for music and colors in their notebooks in order, putting the ones they like most first and the ones they like least last.
- ♦ In small groups, students think of as many different words as possible to add to the three categories. Give them a time limit.

3
- Students write the name of each type of clothing under the correct picture.

Answers

1 cap 2 sweater 3 shirt 4 sneakers 5 jacket 6 pants

Optional activity

Game *Word tennis* Students close their books and, in pairs, play Word tennis. One student "serves" the name of a type of clothing, then their partner "returns" a different item and so on. If possible, encourage students to include other names of clothes they know that were not included in the exercise.

4
- The aim of the activity is for students to contextualize a short listening extract by figuring out what kind of passage it is extracted from. Explain to students that they should listen for the main gist of the passage and that it does not matter if they do not understand every word.
- Play the recording. Students match each extract 1–3 with the correct kind of passage A–C.

1.04 Recording

1

People all over the United States celebrate New Year. People often have parties on New Year's Eve. They may stay at home with their family or go out with friends. Many people who live in New York go to Times Square and wait for midnight. At midnight, the people in the square watch a big glass ball drop to the bottom of a tower. People all over the United States watch the "ball dropping" on TV. After midnight, people hold hands and sing a special song. People open bottles of champagne and say "Happy New Year" to each other.

2

In Brazil, people celebrate Carnival in February or March. Every region has its own festival, but Carnival in Rio is the most famous. It lasts four days and millions of people go to it, including 300,000 foreign visitors. It's one of the biggest Brazilian carnivals—and it's the best, say the Cariocas (the people of Rio).

3

CARRIE *Hello and welcome to our World2day podcast and "Five Minutes with ... Jay." Jay is one of the winners of our vacation contest. What's he like? Let's find out. Jay, welcome, where are you from?*

JAY *From the U.S., from Chicago.*

CARRIE *Tell us about you and your family.*

JAY *Well, I'm sixteen and I live at home with my parents and my sister, Zoey.*

CARRIE *And how old is Zoey?*

JAY *She's only three, and she's fantastic.*

Answers

1 C 2 B 3 A

Optional activity

1.04 Play the recording again and ask students a comprehension question about each extract. 1 *The woman is describing New Year celebrations in which country? (the U.S.)* 2 *What famous carnival is the speaker talking about? (the carnival in Rio de Janeiro in Brazil)* 3 *Who is being interviewed? (Jay)*

5
- Give students a few minutes to look through the Birthday Questionnaire. Elicit the meaning of difficult words like *celebrate, ordinary, ideal*.
- Students do the questionnaire in groups of four, making notes about their group's answers, especially any that are interesting or surprising.
- One person from each group moves to another group and gives a brief report about their group's answers, telling them anything interesting or surprising that they found out, e.g. *Most people in our group go out for their birthday, but Kurt always goes on vacation!*
- Point out the "Believe it or not!" fact at the bottom of the page. Go around the class asking students to say when their birthdays are. If anyone has their birthday on the same day as someone else they should call out *Me too!*

Birthday project

Ask students to work in pairs to decide on three or four of the most interesting questions from the Birthday Questionnaire. They prepare a survey sheet, e.g. a tally chart like the one in the example below, and use their sheet to interview all the students in the class.

Birthday project	
celebrate your birthday with your friends	~~IIII~~ I
celebrate your birthday with your family	II
have a birthday party	IIII
don't have a birthday party	IIII
have a birthday cake	~~IIII~~ III
don't have a birthday cake	III

Students write a short report about the results of their survey, illustrating it with drawings or photos from magazines or the Internet (or from home). Encourage students to include a short introduction in their report, then to give the results, and then to try and draw some simple conclusions.
Display the projects in class so that students can look at each other's work.

Follow-up activities

- In groups of four, students brainstorm vocabulary for three other categories from the box on page 8: *jobs and occupations, adjectives*, and *carnivals and festivals*. Give students an example from each category before they start, and tell them they have two minutes for each category to write as many words as they can think of on slips of paper. After the time is up for each of the three categories, students shuffle their slips of paper so they are jumbled out of order. They then swap their slips with another group, and the students then have another two minutes to sort another group's slips into the correct categories.
- Students write four important dates in their notebooks. (These could be birthdays of family or friends, anniversaries, or dates when important things happened to them.) They then show the dates to a partner and talk about them, e.g. *February 4th is my mom's birthday.*

Homework

Ask students to interview someone who is older or younger than them for the Birthday Questionnaire and to write the person's answers down.

1 Do you really speak Chinese?

Communicative Aims	Language	Pronunciation	Vocabulary	Optional aids
Talking about regular activities	Simple present	/s/ chat*s* /z/ doe*s* /ɪz/ watch*es*	Likes and dislikes Regular activities	Follow-up activity: small blank cards

Useful information

San Francisco's Pier 39 at Fisherman's Wharf is home to a colony of California sea lions. These animals have always lived in San Francisco Bay, but they moved to the Pier around 25 years ago. In 2009, many of the sea lions abandoned their famous home, swimming north, some experts think, to the Oregon coast. However, many have now returned, and are a popular—if noisy and smelly—tourist attraction!

WARM-UP 1

Game *Word tennis* Divide the class into two teams. Students "serve" the name of a country to the other team, who must return the nationality, e.g. *Brazil—Brazilian, Italy—Italian, Mexico—Mexican*. Teams change roles after three countries have been "served."

WARM-UP 2

Ask students what they can remember about the characters who won the contest. Ask *Where is Lara from? Who is from the U.S.?* etc. You can divide the class into teams and give a point for each correct answer.

1 Opener

- The aim is to introduce the context for the presentation dialogue in exercise 2.
- Write the words *cats, dogs, computer games, movies* on the board, and ask a student which of the things they like or don't like. (You may need to explain *computer games*.)
- Ask students to write a list of five things they like and five things they don't like. They can use some of the words from the board, but must also think of their own ideas.
- Students work in pairs telling each other about the things they like and don't like, and take notes about their partner.
- Ask some of the pairs to tell the rest of the class about the things their partner likes/doesn't like.

2 Reading

- Students read the dialogue and decide which of the topics the group is talking about.
- Give students three minutes to read the dialogue. Then check answers.
- Encourage students to guess unfamiliar vocabulary from context. Be prepared to translate *surf the Web, chat with people online, do yoga*.
- Review classroom language as it comes up during the lesson. Encourage students to ask *What does … mean?*

Answers

animals languages movies

Optional activity

1.05 Play the recording of the dialogue for students to read and listen. Stop at any words that you predict may cause pronunciation problems, e.g. *home, languages*, and ask students to repeat.

3 After Reading

- Students read the dialogue again and decide if sentences 1–8 are true or false. Ask them to underline the words in the dialogue that help them decide on their answers.
- Check the answers before students write corrections for the false sentences. Monitor and help where necessary.
- Ask students to read their answers to the class.

Answers

1 False. Emma doesn't like sea lions at all.
2 True.
3 False. Jay watches DVDs, but he doesn't go to the movies often.
4 False. Silvana goes to the movies every Saturday.
5 True.
6 True.
7 False. Emma doesn't speak Chinese.
8 True.

Optional activities

- 1.05 Play the recording of the dialogue sentence by sentence for students to repeat for pronunciation and intonation practice. Students act out the dialogue in groups of three. They then change roles. Monitor, listening for problems with intonation and pronunciation. Give feedback to students after the activity.
- Students note down new vocabulary in their notebooks.

Your Response

Ask students to work in pairs discussing the questions. Have some students tell the class about their partner.

4 Listening

- Tell students they are going to listen to some facts about four of the characters.
- Ask students to look at the photographs and tell you who the characters are and where they are from.
- Students listen and complete the sentences. Play the recording twice.

1.06 Recording

Hi, I'm Carrie. Welcome to World2day, and here are some facts about our contest winners. Ramón really likes music and he loves hip-hop and rap. Silvana chats with her friends online every evening in English and Spanish. Lara does gymnastics every Friday afternoon and then she goes swimming in the evening. Alex plays basketball and does karate on the weekend.

Answers

Lara does gymnastics and goes swimming every Friday.
Alex plays basketball and does karate.
Ramón loves hip-hop and rap.
Silvana chats online in English and Spanish.

- Ask different students to read their answers to the class. Elicit extra information, *e.g. Does Lara do gymnastics in the evening? When does Alex do karate? When does Silvana chat with her friends online?*

5 Pronunciation

- Ask students to look at the words in the chart.
- Play the first part of the recording, pausing after each word for students to repeat. Remind students that /s/ is like the noise of a snake, and /z/ like a bee. The difference between /s/ and /z/ is that /s/ is unvoiced, i.e. the sound is produced without using the voice-box in the throat. Get students to say /z/ and feel their throat vibrate. When they say /s/ the throat doesn't vibrate.

1.07 Recording

/s/ *chats drinks eats*
/z/ *does knows loves*
/ɪz/ *watches chooses finishes*

- Ask students to copy the chart into their notebooks.
- Play the second part of the recording. Students write the words from the box in the correct column. Pause after each word to give students time to write.

1.07 Recording

dances goes likes plays speaks teaches

Answers

/s/ *chats*	/z/ *does*	/ɪz/ *watches*
likes	*goes*	*dances*
speaks	*plays*	*teaches*

6 Game

- The aim is to encourage learners to take responsibility for their learning by testing each other.
- Ask three or four students to spell words from the lesson. Use *How do you spell . . .?*
- Divide the class into pairs or teams and ask them to take turns testing each other on ten words from the lesson. Give them time to choose their ten words. The winner is the person or team who gets ten words right.

LANGUAGE WORKOUT OPTION

If you want to pre-teach the language students will be using in the following activities, you may like to go to the Language Workout box now.

7 Speaking

- Read the question in the example aloud: *Do you play soccer every week?* Point out the first line of the chart: *doesn't play soccer every week.* Elicit the questions for the other activities orally around the class. Students then write them in their notebooks.
- Explain that students must move around the classroom asking different students about each activity. When they find someone who does/doesn't do the listed activity, they write his/her name in their chart. The aim is to complete the chart with eight different names.
- Demonstrate the procedure first with two or three confident students. Set a time limit of five minutes.

Optional activity

In groups of four or five, students find one activity that two/three/four/five of them do and one activity that none of them does. They then report back to the class, e.g. *Two of us go swimming. None of us plays tennis.*

Extension Ask a pair of students to read out the first question and answer in the example: *Does Mariela do yoga? / No, she doesn't.* Ask a confident student *Does (name) play soccer every week?* and encourage them to answer *Yes, he/she does.* or *No, he/she doesn't.* Start a question-and-answer chain around the class, with each student answering a question and then asking another student a new question.

8 Writing

- Students write complete sentences in their notebooks to summarize the results in their charts from exercise 7. Go through the examples with the class first. Monitor and help where necessary.
- Describe your daily routines and habits during the week as a model for the second part of the exercise.
- Students think about their habits and routines and write five sentences about themselves. Monitor and help where necessary.

Optional activity

Students exchange their sentences and correct each other's work for spelling, grammar, and punctuation.

Extension Tell students to write five sentences about another student: three true and two false. In pairs they take turns to read their sentences aloud. Each student's partner tries to guess which statements are false. Encourage partners to correct the false sentences, e.g. *False! He/she doesn't speak three languages.*

LANGUAGE WORKOUT

- Ask students to look at the Language Workout box and to complete the sentences. Confident students can complete first and then check, while others can look back at exercises 2 and 3 and then complete.
- Students turn to page 112 of the Language File to check their answers.

  Answers
  go speaks do speak don't doesn't
- Highlight that:
  - we use the simple present to talk about things we do every day, week, month, and to talk about how often we do things.
  - we add *s* for *he/she/it* in the affirmative form.
  - we form questions with *do/does* + verb.
  - we form the negative with *don't/doesn't* + verb.
- Drill the examples in chorus for pronunciation and stress.

Practice

- Students do Practice exercise 1 on page 112 of the Language File. They complete the sentences with the correct form of the verb. Remind students not to forget the third person *s*. Write a large *S* on the board and refer to it during the exercise.
- Check the answers by asking different students to say the completed sentences.

Answers
1 loves 2 goes 3 doesn't like 4 chats 5 doesn't play 6 do 7 Do … see 8 Does … speak 9 do … fly 10 Do … know

Optional activity

Game *Question-and-answer chain* Student 1 asks a question using one of the verbs from the dialogue on page 10, e.g. *Do you chat online?* Student 2 answers *Yes, I do.* or *No, I don't.* Student 2 then asks Student 3 another question. Students who repeat a question are out. This can be played with the whole class or in big groups.

Follow-up activities

- ♦ **Game** *Vocabulary game* Students write new vocabulary from the lesson associated with routines and activities on cards. Collect the cards and divide the class into teams of three or four. One student from each team comes to the front of the class. Choose a card for each student. Show student 1 a card. He/She mimes the meaning of the word to his/her team, which wins a point for a correct guess. Students 2 and 3 then take turns to mime their words to their teams. Continue with different team members and words.
- ♦ Students think of a famous person. They write five sentences to describe what the person does every day. Students work in pairs and try to guess who their partner has described.
- ♦ Add words to the Vocabulary box. Students can write new words from the lesson on one side of a card and an explanation, illustration, or translation on the other side of the card.

Homework

Students write the names of three important people in their lives in their notebooks, for example a friend, a family member, or a celebrity. At home they write sentences to describe these three people's hobbies, routines, and language abilities.

NOTEBOOK SECTION

Complete the sentences using a form of the word in parentheses.

1 John ____ tacos. (love)
2 My friends ____ ____ rap music. (not like)
3 ____ he ____ coffee? (drink)
4 ____ you ____ English? (speak)
5 She ____ ____ to the movies often. (not go)

Answers *1 loves 2 don't like 3 Does, drink 4 Do, speak 5 doesn't, go*

Consolidation and Extension p19

Language File p112

Workbook Unit 1 Lesson 1 pp4–5

Photocopiable notes p153, worksheet p162

2 You're standing on my foot!

Communicative Aims	Language	Pronunciation	Vocabulary	Optional aid
Describing what's happening now	Present progressive Relative pronouns: *who/that*	Syllable stress	Clothes Colors Actions	Follow-up activity: large pieces of paper or card

Useful information

The San Francisco carousel is located on Pier 39 in the Fisherman's Wharf district of the city. Pier 39 is a popular tourist attraction, built on a pier next to the ocean. There are many stores, restaurants, and street performers, as well as an aquarium. It's also home to the famous sea lions. From the pier, you can see the Golden Gate Bridge, the Bay Bridge, and Alcatraz. The two-story carousel is one of Pier 39's most popular attractions. It was made in Italy, and depicts famous San Francisco landmarks, including Lombard Street, Chinatown, and the sea lions.

WARM-UP 1

Game *Memory chain* Student 1 says, e.g. *On Monday I go to school.* Student 2 says *On Monday I go to school. On Tuesday I go to the gym.* Continue around the class adding a new day each time. The eighth student goes back to Monday. Students who cannot remember the chain stop playing and are out.

WARM-UP 2

Game *Alphabet game* The game can be played in groups or as a whole class. Students try to think of a country beginning with each letter of the alphabet, omitting the letters Q and X. Students win one point for each correct country. An extra point could be added for saying in which continent the country is located.

1 Opener

- The aim is to prepare the vocabulary for the following exercises. Ask students to look at the photo on pages 12–13 and to see which items in the box they can find. They check their answers in pairs.

Answers

bag (the girl in the orange top) camera (Alex and Silvana)
hat and sunglasses (the juggler) juggler (on the far right)
map (Steve and Lara) shirt (Ramón)
signs (behind them) umbrella (Jay)
We cannot see a guitar.

2 Reading

- Ask students to read the dialogue and to identify the characters in the photo on pages 12–13. Point to each one and ask *Who's this? Where are they? What are they doing? What are they saying?* Invite as many class suggestions as possible.
- Encourage students to guess unfamiliar vocabulary from context and to ask *What does … mean?*

Optional activity

1.08 Play the recording of the dialogue for students to read and listen. Stop at any words that you predict may cause pronunciation problems, e.g. *famous, juggler*, and ask students to repeat.

3 After Reading

- Students read the dialogue again, and match the questions and answers. Make sure students understand that one of the answers is wrong.
- Check the answers. Ask students to give you extra information where appropriate, e.g. *Is Ramón wearing a jacket? No, he isn't. He's wearing a shirt.*

Answers

1 e 2 g 3 f 4 b 5 i 6 h 7 a 8 d
Wrong answer: c

Optional activities

- ♦ Students act out the dialogue in pairs. Monitor, listening for problems with intonation and pronunciation. Give feedback to the class.
- ♦ Students write true/false statements about the dialogue. Monitor and help where necessary. Divide students into groups to test each other on the dialogue using their true/false statements.

Your Response

- Ask students to work in pairs discussing the questions. After a few minutes, ask each pair to get together with another pair and compare their answers.
- Then ask one student from each group to answer the questions. The emphasis here is on fluency rather than accuracy. Try to avoid interrupting/correcting unless students make mistakes with the target structure.
- Play the recording. Students listen and then describe what actually happened. Compare their original predictions with the recording.

1.09 Recording

RAMÓN *He's running this way! Got you!*
ACTOR *Hey! What are you doing?*
RAMÓN *You're a thief! Look—see what you're holding in your hand. It's that girl's wallet.*
ACTOR *Yes, that's right. It's her wallet. Now can you see that man over there?*
RAMÓN *You mean the man with a video camera?*
ACTOR *Yes. We're making a movie here. I'm not a thief, I'm an actor!*
RAMÓN *Oh no! I'm really sorry!*

Optional activity

Students suggest what happens next. Discuss as a whole class.

4 Pronunciation

- Remind students about syllable stress. Explain that in individual words, one syllable is usually pronounced more strongly, as in the example in their books.
- Play the recording, pausing for students to count the syllables and mark the stress.

1.10 Recording and answers

behind (2) *camera* (2)
happening (3) *jacket* (2) *orange* (2) *umbrella* (3)
video (3) *wallet* (2)

- Check the answers. Ask individual students to say each word aloud, exaggerating the stressed syllable. Ask individual students to tell you where the stress falls.
- Play the recording again for students to repeat the words.

LANGUAGE WORKOUT OPTION

If you want to pre-teach the language students will be using in the following activities, you may like to go to the Language Workout box now.

5 Vocabulary

- Check students understand the words in the Clothes Word Bank.
- Ask a pair of students to read out the first question and answer in the example: *Who's Emma? / She's the one who's wearing a green top and black pants.*
- Ask *Who's Alex?* and invite a confident student to complete the answer in the example: *He's the boy that's standing next to Silvana.*
- Ask the class to continue the questions and answers in pairs, using words from the Clothes Word Bank.

Suggested questions and answers

Who's Ramón? He's the one who's wearing a shirt (and jeans). He's the boy that's standing next to Emma.
Who's Emma? She's the one who's wearing a green top (and black pants/boots). She's the girl that's standing next to Ramón.
Who's Jay? He's the one who's wearing a blue T-shirt (and jeans). He's the boy who has an umbrella.
Who's Steve? He's the one who's wearing a black jacket (and jeans). He's the man who's looking at the map.
Who's Lara? She's the one who's wearing a pink top (and jeans/boots). She's the girl who's looking at the map.
Who's Alex? He's the one who's wearing a red shirt (and blue pants). He's the boy who has a camera.
Who's Silvana? She's the one who's wearing a blue top.
Who's the actor? He's the one who's wearing black clothes.
(NB Students can swap "the one" with "the girl/boy/man" and "who's" with "that's.")

- Ask a few students what questions they asked. Encourage the class to answer.

6 Speaking

- Read out the question and answer in the example.
- In pairs, students ask and answer questions about what people in the photo are doing.
- Ask each pair to read out a question and answer to the class.

Suggested questions and answers

What's Ramón doing? He's talking/standing next to Emma.
What's Emma doing? She's talking/standing next to Ramón.
What's Jay doing? He's listening to Steve.
What's Steve doing? He's talking about San Francisco.
What's Lara doing? She's looking at the map.
What's Alex doing? He's looking at his camera.
What's Silvana doing? She's helping Alex with his camera.
What's the thin man doing? He's taking the girl's wallet.
What's the girl in the orange top doing? She's watching the juggler.
What's the juggler doing? He's juggling!

Optional activities

- ♦ Give students one minute to look at the photo in detail. Students then close their books. Ask quick-fire questions to test their memory (use the suggested questions above). This can be a quiz or a team game. Give one point for a correct answer and an extra point for the correct use of the present progressive.
- ♦ In pairs, one student closes his/her book and the other asks questions.

7 Writing

- Students look at the photo on pages 12–13 and write sentences describing the people without using their names. Encourage them to include information about where they are, what they are wearing, and what they are doing. Go through the example with the class first.
- Students exchange sentences and try to guess the names of the people described.

Extension Ask students to read the example in their book, and then ask one student to go and look out of the classroom window and say one thing that is or isn't happening outside, e.g. *A car is driving along the street.* Tell students to look out the window (you could ask them to do this a few students at a time) and to write down four or five things that are or aren't happening outside. Remind students to listen out for noises as well as looking for things that are happening. Check students' answers and ask a few students to read their sentences aloud.

LANGUAGE WORKOUT

- Ask students to look at the top half of the Language Workout box and explain that we use the present progressive to talk about things that are happening *now*.
- Ask students to complete the sentences in the box. Confident students can complete first and then check, while others can look back at exercise 2 and then complete.
  Ask students to look at the bottom half of the Language Workout box and complete the sentence.
- Students turn to page 113 of the Language File to check their answers.

Answers
wearing are Is is are
that

- Drill the examples in chorus for pronunciation and stress.

Practice

- Students do Practice exercise 2 on page 113 of the Language File. Ask students to write sentences using the present progressive.

Answers
1 *Steve is talking about San Francisco.*
2 *Lara is visiting San Francisco for the first time.*
3 *Are Jay and Lara looking at the map?*
4 *Alex and Silvana aren't holding hands!*
5 *Is the thin man stealing the girl's wallet?*
6 *Jay is holding an umbrella.*
7 *Silvana is watching the juggler.*
8 *Ramón isn't listening to Steve.*
9 *Why are Emma and Ramón running?*
10 *I'm not taking pictures right now.*

Optional activity

Individually, students write three new sentences about the photo using the present progressive. They then jumble up the word order and give the sentences to a partner, who must re-order them. Write an example on the board, e.g. *his hand in man the her putting is bag.*

Follow-up activities

- Draw a word map on the board. Write *CLOTHES* in the center. Elicit different categories from the class and write them on the word map, e.g. different occasions, different seasons, men and women.
- Divide students into small groups to draw their own word map on a large piece of paper or card. Encourage them to think of their own categories, and add as many words as they can. Set a time limit and give out bi-lingual dictionaries if available. The word maps can be displayed in the classroom.
- Students choose to be A or B. Student A looks out the window and answers questions about what is happening outside. Student B asks as many questions as possible and *draws* what is going on. Which pair has the best pictorial representation?

Homework

Students cut out pictures of people from magazines and write sentences to describe what the people are doing and what they are wearing. Ask students to bring their pictures and sentences to the next lesson.

NOTEBOOK SECTION

Complete the sentences using the present progressive.
1 She ____ to music. (listen)
2 They ____ basketball. (not play)
3 What ____ your brother ____? (watch)
4 Are they the ones who ____ pink? (wear)
5 I like the girl that ____. (sing)

Answers
1 *'s (is) listening*
2 *aren't playing*
3 *'s (is), watching*
4 *are wearing*
5 *'s (is) singing*

Consolidation and Extension p19

Language File pp112–113

Workbook Unit 1 Lesson 2 pp6–7

Photocopiable notes p153, worksheet p163

3 It's my sister's birthday

Communicative Aims	Language	Pronunciation	Vocabulary	Optional aids
Talking about possessions	Possessive adjectives and pronouns Possessive 's and s'	/i/ eat /eɪ/ break	Communication technology Personal possessions Jobs and occupations	Exercise 4 Optional activity: a bag

WARM-UP 1

If you set the homework suggested in the previous lesson, stick the students' pictures on the board and write a number next to each one. Students take turns reading out one of their sentences. The other students listen and guess which picture is being described. This could be played as a team game.

WARM-UP 2

Students stand back-to-back and describe what their partner is wearing. Alternatively, students take turns to describe someone in the room and the others guess.

1 Opener

- The aim is to pre-teach the vocabulary for the following exercises and set the scene for the reading text. Find out how many students use Twitter, and ask which other social networking sites they use.
- Students read the words in the box and decide which are most likely to be in the text. Elicit the meaning of *account, password,* and *username*.
- Students do the task individually and then compare their answers in pairs.
- Encourage them to discuss why they expect to find the words they have chosen.

2 Reading

- Ask students to read the text about Twitter to confirm their guesses.

Answers

account cell phone e-mail address Internet password text message username

Optional activity

1.11 Play the recording of the text for students to read and listen. Stop at any words that you predict may cause pronunciation problems, e.g. *messages, tweets*, and ask students to repeat.

- The aim is to read for main ideas and to identify characters. Explain to students that they do not need to understand every word of the text at this stage.
- Give students two minutes to read the text and match the tweets with the characters. Students compare their answers in pairs before checking as a class.
- Elicit the key words in the tweets that helped students make their decisions.

Answers

A Rosie's—interview
B Anna's—writing a song
C Luke's—trying to learn
D Teresa's—pictures
E Scott's—dog, work with animals
F Bill's—I'm having fun in the office

3 After Reading

- The aim is to read for specific information and detail. Set a short time limit. Students could work in pairs to find the answers and write full sentences in their notebooks.
- Check the answers by asking one student to ask a question and choosing another student to answer it.

Answers

1 Linkin Park
2 It's about people's problems and what they can do about them.
3 Luke
4 Teresa's sister's
5 She's in a meeting.
6 Scott's

Your Response

Give students some time to write their own tweet.

LANGUAGE WORKOUT OPTION

If you want to pre-teach the language students will be using in the following activities, you may like to go to the Language Workout box now.

4 Speaking

- Ask students to look at the photos on pages 14–15 and find the objects in the box. Help students with any words they don't know.
- Ask *Whose is the book? Whose are the glasses?* Let students answer both questions and then drill the questions in chorus and individually. Encourage students to

link together *whose≈is* and *whose≈are*. Check that they understand the difference between *who's* (= *who is*) and *whose* (= *who is the owner of*).

- Students ask and answer the questions about the remaining objects in the box. This can be done as a whole class or in pairs.

Answers

1 *Whose is the book? It's Luke's.*
2 *Whose is the camera? It's Teresa's.*
3 *Whose are the cell phones? They're Bill's.*
4 *Whose is the dog? It's Scott's.*
5 *Whose are the glasses? They're Bill's.*
6 *Whose is the guitar? It's Anna's.*
7 *Whose is the laptop? It's Bill's.*
8 *Whose is the microphone? It's Rosie's.*
9 *Whose is the pen? It's Bill's.*
10 *Whose is the pink shirt? It's Anna's.*
11 *Whose is the stethoscope? It's Scott's.*

- Introduce the second part of this exercise by picking up students' objects and asking the wrong owner *Is this yours?* Elicit *No, it isn't mine. It's hers/his/Maria's*, etc.
- Point out the guitar on page 14, and ask *Is it Bill's guitar?* Elicit *No, it isn't his. It's Anna's*. Drill the example exchange chorally and individually.
- Students ask and answer questions about the photos in pairs. Check answers with the class.

Answers

1 *Is it Luke's microphone?*	*No, it isn't his. It's Rosie's.*
2 *Are they Teresa's glasses?*	*No, they aren't hers. They're Bill's.*
3 *Is it Rosie's camera?*	*No, it isn't hers. It's Teresa's.*
4 *Is it Bill's pink shirt?*	*No, it isn't his. It's Anna's.*
5 *Are they Scott's cell phones?*	*No, they aren't his. They're Bill's.*
6 *Is it Anna's dog?*	*No, it isn't hers. It's Scott's.*

Optional activity

Game *Whose is this?* Ask each student to secretly give you an object. Place the objects in a bag. Take one object out at a time. In pairs, students note the name of the object and who the owner is. Then pick up each object in the same order and ask *Whose is this?* Elicit guesses from students, e.g. *It's Angel's* before checking, e.g. *Angel, is this pen yours?*

5 Pronunciation

- Ask students to look through the words in the box.
- Play the first part of the recording, pausing after each word for students to repeat.

1.12 Recording

break eat great meal mean
meet plane play speak take

- Ask students to copy the chart into their notebooks and write the words in the correct column.
- Play the second half of the recording for students to check their answers.

1.12 Recording and answers

/i/ *eat, meal, mean, meet, speak*
/eɪ/ *break, great, plane, play, take*

6 Vocabulary

- Students match the definitions with jobs from the Word Bank. Explain to students that there are six extra jobs in the Word Bank.
- Students check answers in pairs and then with the whole class. Encourage students to say whole sentences when giving their answers, e.g. *A photographer is someone who takes pictures.*

Answers

a *photographer*	d *reporter*
b *actor*	e *vet*
c *musician*	f *PA (personal assistant)*

Extension Students choose two other jobs from the Word Bank and write definitions for them. In pairs, they read out their definitions and see if their partner can guess the job. Invite some students to read out their definitions for the rest of the class to guess.

Suggested answers

firefighter—someone who helps put out fires
nurse—someone who cares for sick people
pilot—someone who flies planes
receptionist—someone who helps people when they arrive at a hotel or office
teacher—someone who gives lessons
waiter—someone who brings food or drinks to the table in a coffee shop or restaurant

Optional activity

Put students in groups, and give each student a job from the Word Bank. They write the name of the job on one piece of paper and the definition on another. Students mix their papers up and then, in their groups, match the definitions with the jobs.

7 Speaking

- The aim is to contrast the simple present and present progressive. Refer students to the Language File on pages 112–113, which explains the use of these two tenses.
- In pairs or as a class, students follow the first example. They then look back at the photos and tweets on pages 14–15, and the jobs in the Word Bank on page 15, and make notes about what job each person does and what they are doing at the moment.
- Students then take turns to ask and answer questions about the people, saying what they do and what they are doing now.

Suggested answers

What does Rosie do? She's a reporter.
What's she doing? She's waiting to interview Linkin Park.
What does Anna do? She's a musician.
What's she doing? She's writing a song.
What does Luke do? He's an actor.
What's he doing? He's trying to learn his lines for a play.
What does Teresa do? She's a photographer.
What's she doing? She's having a meal in a restaurant for her sister's birthday.
What does Scott do? He's a vet.
What's he doing? He's giving his dog Goldie a health check.
What does Bill do? He's a PA.
What's he doing? He's having fun in the office.

8 Writing

- Ask students to read the example.
- Students work individually, writing sentences describing what each of the characters in the photos does and is doing right now.
- In pairs students compare their sentences.

Suggested answers

Anna is a musician and she's writing a song about people's problems and what they can do about them. It's called You Can Get it Right *and she hopes we like it.*
Luke is an actor and he's trying to learn his lines for a play, which starts tomorrow. Everyone else knows their lines.
Teresa is a photographer and she's having a meal in a great restaurant for her sister's birthday. She's taking lots of pictures.
Scott is a vet, and he's giving his dog Goldie a health check. He works with hundreds of animals, but he only has one of his own.
Bill is a PA, and he's going on Twitter. His boss says he can't go on Twitter at work. But she's in a meeting, and it's his lunch break, so he's not working! He's having fun.

Extension Write the name of a famous celebrity on the board, and ask students *What does he/she do?* Then ask *What do you think he/she is doing right now?* Elicit suggestions from students, reminding them to use the present progressive. Ask students to think of three celebrities and to write sentences about them like the one in exercise 8, to say what they do and what students think they are doing right now.

LANGUAGE WORKOUT

- Ask students to look at the top half of the Language Workout box and to complete the chart. Confident students can complete first and then check, while others can look back at exercise 2 and then complete.
- Students turn to page 113 of the Language File to check their answers.

Answers

our mine your their

- Highlight the difference between possessive adjectives and possessive pronouns (*pronouns are not used with nouns*). Point out that we don't use *the* with possessive adjectives or possessive pronouns, i.e. *It's ~~the~~ mine.*
- Drill the examples in chorus for pronunciation.
- Ask students to look at the bottom half of the Language Workout box. Highlight that we can use the possessive *'s* form with or without a noun, e.g. *It's Emma's bag./It's Emma's.*

Practice

- Students do Practice exercise 3 on page 113 of the Language File. They complete the sentences with the possessive pronouns and check their answers in pairs.

Answers

1 yours, mine 2 ours, theirs 3 hers, his 4 yours, ours

- Students do Practice exercise 4 on page 113 of the Language file. They write phrases using 's or s' and then check their answers in pairs.

Answers

1 my parents' car
2 the teacher's glasses
3 the children's school
4 your doctor's name
5 his sisters' books
6 the people's clothes
7 students' work
8 Alex's watch

Homework

Students write a short paragraph about a family member's job. They define the job, and say what the person usually does and what he/she is doing right now.

NOTEBOOK SECTION

Circle the correct option in each sentence.

1 *Who/Whose* cell phone is ringing?
2 Do you have *my/mine* CDs?
3 That isn't my dog. It's *Juan's/Juans'*.
4 Those are *her/hers* earrings.
5 Excuse me, that's *our/ours*.

Answers

1 Whose 2 my 3 Juan's 4 her 5 ours

Consolidation and Extension p19
Language File p113

Workbook Unit 1 Lesson 3 pp8–9
Photocopiable notes p153, worksheet p164

4 *Integrated Skills* Personal profiles

Skills

Reading Connecting ideas: magazine interview
Listening Checking details of personal information
Speaking Interviewing
Writing Personal profile

Learner Independence

Finding the meaning
Personal phrasebook

Vocabulary

Personal information
Useful expressions

WARM-UP 1

Check students' memories of the job vocabulary from Lesson 3, exercise 6. Give the job definitions and ask students to write the jobs down in their notebooks without looking in the Student's Book. Check their answers and their spelling.

WARM-UP 2

Give students a short test on vocabulary from previous lessons. If you have started a Vocabulary box, choose words from the box. Give students definitions and ask them to write down the word. Check their answers and their spelling.

1 Opener

- The aim is to encourage students to predict before reading. Ask students where Lara is from. Tell students to close their books and ask them the two questions. Students discuss their guesses in pairs.

2 Reading

- The aim is to read and connect ideas by matching questions and answers, and to review personal information. Explain to students that extracts like this one from the World2day website appear throughout the book.
- Students read through the interview once before completing it with the correct sentences. With a less confident class, start the exercise with the whole class.
- Play the recording for students to listen and check their answers.

1.13 Recording

CARRIE *Lara is one of the winners of the World2day vacation contest. What's she like? Find out here!*
Hi, Lara. Where do you live?
LARA *In Recife in Brazil, but right now I'm staying at the Bridge Hotel in San Francisco.*
CARRIE *What are your favorite clothes?*
LARA *It depends. I often wear jeans and a sweatshirt, but I like dresses in the summer.*
CARRIE *And your favorite colors?*
LARA *That's easy. Pink and black!*
CARRIE *What is your favorite English word?*
LARA *"Cool." Americans say "cool" all the time!*
CARRIE *What makes you angry?*
LARA *People who don't listen.*
CARRIE *What makes you happy?*
LARA *Sunshine and blue skies!*
CARRIE *How do you relax?*
LARA *I listen to music.*
CARRIE *What languages do you speak?*
LARA *Portuguese, of course, and Spanish. And I'm learning English.*
CARRIE *Is there someone very important to you?*
LARA *What do you mean? Do I have a boyfriend? I'm not telling you! But my mother is very important to me.*
CARRIE *Is there something special you do every day?*
LARA *That's difficult. Let me think. I know. I try to help someone every day.*
CARRIE *What are you reading right now?*
LARA *An English book called* L.A. Winners. *It's great!*
CARRIE *Thank you, Lara!*

Answers

1 c 2 d 3 a 4 b 5 e

Optional activity

Students read and act out the interview in pairs.

3

- Students read Ramón's answers to some of the questions in the profile and decide which questions they match.

Answers

1 *What makes you happy?*
2 *What makes you angry?*
3 *How do you relax?*
4 *Is there someone very important to you?*
5 *Is there something special you do every day?*

Optional activities

♦ Students interview you, asking similar questions.
♦ In small groups, students make up answers to five of the questions in the interview to give to another group. Groups exchange answers and guess the questions.

4 Listening

- The aim is to listen for specific details. Students read the profile. Confirm that students know what to do. Ask them to predict what the incorrect information is. Tell them not to worry about correcting the mistakes on the first listening.
- Play the recording. Students listen to check details and note the mistakes. They compare their answers in pairs before you play the recording again.

1.14 Recording

CARRIE *Hello and welcome to our World2day podcast and "Five Minutes with ... Jay." Jay is one of the winners of our vacation contest. What's he like? Let's find out. Jay, welcome, where are you from?*
JAY *From the U.S., from Chicago.*
CARRIE *Tell us about you and your family.*
JAY *Well, I'm sixteen and I live at home with my parents and my sister, Zoey.*
CARRIE *And how old is Zoey?*
JAY *She's only three and she's fantastic.*
CARRIE *Ah, that's nice ... And tell me, what are your favorite clothes?*
JAY *That's easy—shorts and T-shirts.*
CARRIE *And your favorite colors?*
JAY *Hmm. Red, white, and blue.*
CARRIE *And what's your favorite word?*
JAY *I don't have a favorite word.*
CARRIE *OK ... and what makes you angry?*
JAY *Nothing!*
CARRIE *Wow! That's great! Right, Jay, now tell me: what makes you happy?*
JAY *My friends—it's great to be with good friends.*
CARRIE *How do you relax?*
JAY *I play with DJ in the park—she's my dog.*
CARRIE *DJ ... nice name ... right. And what languages do you speak?*
JAY *I speak English and I'm learning Spanish.*
CARRIE *Spanish? Great! And is there someone very important to you?*
JAY *Not one person, but my friends are very important to me. I'm missing them now that I'm in San Francisco.*
CARRIE *And is there something special you do every day?*
JAY *I read for half an hour every night. I love it!*
CARRIE *Thank you, Jay. That's great.*
JAY *Thank you.*

- Play the recording again for students to correct the mistakes. They check their answers in pairs. Play the recording again if necessary.

Answers

1 ~~*New York*~~ *Chicago*
2 ~~*17*~~ *16*
3 ~~*green*~~ *blue*
4 ~~*His favorite word is "Yes"*~~*. He doesn't have a favorite word.*
5 ~~*French*~~ *Spanish*
6 ~~*watches TV*~~ *reads*

Optional activities

♦ In pairs, Student A covers the text and tells Student B everything he/she remembers about Jay. Student B listens and checks in the book.
♦ Students close their books and remember as many questions from the article on page 16 as they can.
♦ Students write the correct information about Jay in full sentences in their notebooks. Monitor and help where necessary.

5 Speaking

- In pairs, students act out an interview using the questions in the profile of Lara on page 16. Students sit across from each other. Student A writes in his/her notebook while Student B answers. Then they change roles.

Optional activity

Students go around the class choosing different people to interview. Set a time limit and tell students to ask as many questions as they can.

6 Writing

- The aim is to write a personal profile using a model for guidance. Students read Jay's profile again and match each paragraph with the questions. Check the answers with the class.

Answers
Paragraph 1
Where do you live?
What are your favorite clothes?
Paragraph 2
And your favorite colors?
What is your favorite English word?
What makes you angry?
What makes you happy?
Paragraph 3
How do you relax?
What languages do you speak?
Is there someone very important to you?
Is there something special you do every day?

- Students write a similar three-paragraph profile based on the answers from their interview in exercise 5. Remind students not to forget the third person *s*. Write a large *S* on the board and refer students to this as you monitor. Give students a few minutes to check their paragraphs for grammar, spelling, and capital letters. They then give it to another student to check.

Optional activity

Ask students to tell you something interesting about the student they interviewed.

7 Learner Independence

- The aim is to identify students' preferred way of finding the meaning of new words and to encourage them to experiment with other ways. Write three or four words or phrases from the previous lessons on the board, e.g. *account, password, receptionist, chat with people online*. Do students remember the meanings of these words? Ask *How can you find out the meaning of these words?* Find out who has a dictionary and if it is monolingual or bilingual. Discuss the advantages and disadvantages of these two types of dictionaries.
- Students look at the list in exercise 7 and mark from 1 to 6 (1 = best) their favorite way of finding a word. They compare their order with another student's.
- Elicit feedback from the class and compare the advantages and disadvantages of each method. Encourage students to try and find the meaning of the word themselves before asking for help. Equally, it is better to guess from the context before consulting a dictionary or asking for help.
- Suggest that students try out a new way of finding out the meanings of words for a week and then report back to the class.

8

- The aim is to encourage students to develop their own store of words and expressions in English. Ask students to look back through the unit and tell you expressions they like and want to learn. Write five or more of their chosen expressions on the board. Ask students to help you find the best translation by guessing or using a dictionary.
- Ask students to copy the expressions and translations into their notebook under the heading of Personal Phrasebook: Unit 1.
- Then ask students to find five more expressions to translate and write into their notebooks. Circulate and help students to find correct translations of the expressions.
- Emphasize the importance of reviewing the expressions in their Personal Phrasebooks at home.

9 Phrasebook

- Ask students to look through the unit and find the expressions, and to notice how they are used.
- Then play the recording for students to listen to and repeat the idiomatic expressions.

1.15 Recording and answers
Of course not. (Emma, Lesson 1, ex 2)
It's a joke! (Emma, Lesson 1, ex 2)
What's happening? (Ramón, Lesson 2, ex 2)
Let me see! (Ramón, Lesson 2, ex 2)
Ow! (Emma, Lesson 2, ex 2)
Hey! (Ramón, Lesson 2, ex 2)
I hope you like it. (Tweet B, Lesson 2, ex 3, not recorded)
It depends. (Lara, Lesson 4, ex 2)
What do you mean? (Lara, Lesson 2, ex 3)

- Students can add expressions that they like to their Personal Phrasebooks. Help with translation.
- Ask students to work in pairs to make up the four-line dialogues. Ask some confident pairs to act out their dialogues in front of the class.

Follow-up activities

♦ Write jumbled sentences from previous lessons on the board for students to re-order.
♦ Quick dictation: dictate five sentences from the recording in exercise 4. Students exchange their sentences and correct each other's work.

Homework

Students try out the methods from the Learner Independence section to learn new vocabulary.

NOTEBOOK SECTION

Complete the sentences using one of these words: *Where's, Who's, Whose, What's, What.*
1 ____ your favorite animal?
2 ____ Puerto Rico?
3 ____ your favorite singer?
4 ____ boyfriend is he?
5 ____ are your favorite colors?

Answers
1 What's 2 Where's 3 Who's 4 Whose 5 What

Consolidation and Extension p19

Workbook Unit 1 Lesson 4 pp10–11

Inspired EXTRA!

LANGUAGE LINKS

- Check that students understand the meaning of *Congratulations* and ask them to work in pairs to think of situations when you might say the word, e.g. when someone passes a school exam, gets engaged/married, etc.
- Ask students to share their ideas with the class.
- Give students two minutes to work in pairs matching the words for *Congratulations* with the correct language.

Answers

Congratulazioni!—Italian
Gefeliciteerd!—Dutch, Félicitations!—French
¡Felicitaciones!—Spanish, Glückwünsche!—German,
Parabéns!—Portuguese, Pozdravlyayu!—Russian

- Ask students if anyone can say any of the words, and encourage them to demonstrate, letting the class repeat.
- Ask students if they know how to say *please* and *thank you* in other languages.

Game Spelling Chain

- Review the pronunciation of the letters of the alphabet.
- Read the instructions in the Student's Book with the class. Demonstrate the example with three confident students. Point out that A can't say anything at the end because he/she doesn't know any words starting with X.
- Divide the class into two teams and play the game.

Skit The Train Conductor

- The aim is for students to enjoy using their English while also getting valuable stress and intonation practice. Ask students to look at the cartoon and elicit train vocabulary: *ticket, station, train conductor*. Ask *What does a train conductor do?*
- With a more confident class, play the recording with books closed. Then play it again with books open. With a less confident class, play the recording while students follow in their books, and then again with books closed.

1.16 **Recording**

See text on page 18 of the Student's Book.

- Divide the class into two groups and play the recording again, with one group repeating in chorus as the Waiter/ Conductor and the other as the Passenger. Encourage students to exaggerate stress and intonation.
- Ask students to close their books and play the recording again. Then ask students to work in groups of three and read the skit aloud. Choose several groups to act out the skit in front of the class.

Language File pp112–113

Consolidation

Lesson 1

Suggested answers

Silvana loves sea lions. She goes to the movies on Saturdays. She goes to yoga on Saturdays.
Emma doesn't like sea lions at all. She thinks dogs are OK. Cats are her favorite pets. She has two cats at home. She does yoga every Tuesday. Her mom teaches yoga. She doesn't speak Chinese.
Jay loves dogs. He never plays computer games. He surfs the Web and chats with people online. He watches DVDs. He doesn't go to the movies often.

Lesson 2
For possible answers, read the dialogue and look at the answers to exercises 5, 6, and 7.

Lesson 3
Refer students to their *Clothes* word map (Lesson 2) for ideas.

Lesson 4
If necessary, point out that the three paragraphs in Jay's profile follow the order of the questions in Lara's interview.

Extension

Lesson 1
Students' own answers.

Lesson 2
Students' own answers.

Lesson 3

Suggested answers

Whose is the purple dress? It's Rosie's.
Whose is the black jacket? It's Bill's.
Whose is the grey shirt? It's Bill's.
Whose is the blue top? It's Scott's.
Whose is the colorful T-shirt? It's Luke's.

Lesson 4
Remind students to write three paragraphs.

YOUR CHOICE!

The aim is to give students more learner independence and help them identify their preferred ways of learning. Encourage students to choose an activity that they feel less comfortable with if they want a challenge or are aware that they need practice in a particular area.
Who Am I? gives students the opportunity to practice free writing.
Whose is This? gives students the opportunity to practice speaking.

Workbook Unit 1 Inspired EXTRA! pp12–13

1 CULTURE

Welcome to the U.S.

Useful information

Golden Gate Bridge
The Golden Gate Bridge was built at a cost of $33 million and ten workers' lives. Its International Orange color was selected because it provided visibility in the fog for passing ships. Movies that feature the Golden Gate Bridge include: *Interview with a Vampire* (1994), *Star Trek VI: The Undiscovered Country* (1991), *A View to a Kill* (1985), and *Vertigo* (1958).

Walt Disney World® Resort
Four theme parks are the heart of Walt Disney World® Resort: Magic Kingdom, Epcot, the Disney–MGM Studios, and Animal Kingdom.

Universal's Islands of Adventure®
The park is based on the idea of a journey, where visitors leave a port to visit six islands, each of which has a theme. The Wizarding World of Harry Potter is the new island. The park is the ninth most popular theme park in the U.S.

Kennedy Space Center
The Kennedy Space Center is located on Merritt Island, between Miami and Jacksonville on Florida's Atlantic coast. The Center is the base for the space shuttles, and is the launch site for every U.S. human space flight since 1968. As well as being home to the Center, Merrit Island is also an important wildlife sanctuary, with eagles, alligators, panthers, and snakes.

Hollywood
The word "Hollywood" is synonymous with the U.S. movie industry, even though today many studios have moved into the surrounding area. For many years, the area was in decline, with many landmarks threatened with demolition. However, Hollywood is currently undergoing a revival, with many new developments, and the opening of fashionable bars, clubs, hotels, and restaurants.

Niagara Falls
Niagara Falls were formed when glaciers receded at the end of the last ice age, and water from the newly-formed Great Lakes carved a path through the Niagara Escarpment en route to the Atlantic Ocean. They are renowned both for their beauty, and as a valuable source of hydroelectric power.

Times Square
Times Square is named after the Times Building (now One Times Square), the former offices of the New York Times newspaper. It has become an iconic world landmark, and a symbol of its home city.

The Grand Canyon
The Grand Canyon was created by the Colorado River over six million years, exposing nearly two billion years of the Earth's history.

Georgia Aquarium
Highlights include a living reef, whale sharks, animals from the polar regions of the world, and an overhead river.

1 Opener

- The aim is to arouse the students' interest in the topic of the U.S.A.
- Ask students to look at the photos of famous places in the States. Ask if anybody knows any of them and what they are called.
- Students look at the headings of the U.S. sightseeing guide A–I and try to match the places with the photos.

2 Reading

- Students read the guide and check their answers.

Answers
A 4 B 8 C 1 D 9 E 3 F 6 G 7 H 5 I 2

- Check that students understand all the questions.
- Students find the answers in the sightseeing guide.
- Check the answers orally with the whole class.

Answers
1 The Hollywood Wax Museum
2 The Georgia Aquarium
3 Times Square
4 Niagara Falls
5 Walt Disney World® Resort
6 Kennedy Space Center

Optional activity

♦ Ask students to close their books. Give a quick quiz: say a fact about one of the places and students have to name the place.

3 Vocabulary

- Students work individually to match the words with the definitions, and then compare their answers in pairs.

Answers
1 e 2 c 3 a 4 g 5 f 6 d 7 b

4 Mini-project Sightseeing guide

- Ask students to work in pairs or small groups and choose three well-known places in their town or country. Then students take turns to describe one place and the others have to name the place.
- In pairs, students choose one place and write a short description of it using the questions and the U.S. sightseeing guide to help them.
- Students could also do extra research to find information about the place they have chosen.
- Encourage them to illustrate their work with photos or extra information from magazines, newspapers, or the Internet, or with drawings.
- When students have written their descriptions, ask them to check their work and then join with other pairs and put their descriptions together to make a sightseeing guide.

NOTEBOOK SECTION

Draw lines to match a place on the left with a location on the right.

1 Hollywood	Washington, D.C.
2 Niagara Falls	New York
3 U.S. Capitol	Los Angeles
4 Times Square	San Francisco
5 Golden Gate Bridge	U.S. and Canada

Answers

1 Los Angeles
2 U.S. and Canada
3 Washington, D.C.
4 New York
5 San Francisco

Workbook Culture pp14–15

1 It's the best street party

Communicative Aims	Language	Pronunciation	Vocabulary
Comparing things	Comparative and superlative adjectives	/ə/ festiv*a*l	Carnivals and festivals Adjectives

WARM-UP 1

Game *Teacher* Write _ _ _ _ _ _ _ _ _ _ on the board. Divide the class into two teams who take turns to guess a letter. If they call out a correct letter, e.g. *P*, you write it in the correct place(s), e.g. P _ _ _ P _ _ _ _ _. If they call out a letter that is not in the word, e.g. *S*, write that letter on the board and write the first letter of *teacher* on one side of the board. The aim is for students to guess the word, e.g. *pickpocket*, before you complete the word *teacher*. The team that guesses the most words wins.

WARM-UP 2

Elicit the names of the characters in Unit 1. Ask *Where's he/she from?* Divide the students into groups and give them two minutes to write as many sentences as they can about the characters. If necessary, give prompts, e.g. *What does Jay like? What are Lara's favorite colors?* The group with the most correct sentences wins.

1 Opener

- The aim is to introduce the topic of carnivals and festivals. Elicit the meaning of the words in the Word Bank, and be prepared to help students with *carnival*, *costume*, *parade*, *stage*, and *stall*.
- Brainstorm the names of festivals in their country. Make a list on the board, putting the most important one first. Ask students *What time of year is the festival? Do you usually go? What happens at the festival?*
- In pairs, students talk about these festivals, using the words in the Word Bank to help them.

Useful information

The word *carnival* comes from a Latin phrase meaning *goodbye meat*. Carnivals were traditionally religious festivals celebrated between Epiphany on January 6 and Shrove Tuesday, the last day before Lent (40 days before Easter).

2 Reading

- Explain that the Rio de Janeiro carnival is the most famous carnival in Brazil, and the New Orleans carnival is in Louisiana in the U.S.
- Ask students to guess which of the carnivals is bigger, and which lasts longer.
- Students read the *Carnivals* text and check their answers.

Answers

The Rio de Janeiro carnival is bigger.
The New Orleans carnival lasts longer.

- Elicit the meaning of unfamiliar vocabulary, e.g. *ball* (= *dance*), *spectacular, cosmopolitan, exotic*.

Optional activity

1.17 Play the recording of the text for students to check their answers.

3 After Reading

- Students read the text again and decide if the sentences are true or false.
- Check the answers before students write corrections for the false sentences. Ask students to read their answers to the class.

Answers

1 *False. Each parade lasts ten to twelve hours.*
2 *True.*
3 *False.*
4 *False. It starts in January.*
5 *True.*
6 *False. It's the biggest in North America. The Rio carnival is the biggest in the world.*

- Students read *Carnivals* again and complete the chart for Rio and New Orleans.
- Ask some students to read their answers to the class.

Answers

	Rio	*New Orleans*
When?	*February or March*	*January and February*
How long?	*four days*	*from January to "Fat Tuesday"*
How many people?	*millions*	*up to a million*
What kind of music?	*samba*	*jazz and other kinds of music*
How expensive?	*very expensive*	*less expensive than Rio*
What's special about it?	*It's the biggest and most spectacular carnival in the world.*	*It's the best street party and largest carnival in the U.S.*

Optional activities

- 1.17 Play the recording of the text for students to read and listen. Stop at any words that you predict may cause pronunciation problems, e.g. *carnival, festival, parade*, and ask students to repeat.
- Ask more comprehension questions about the Rio and New Orleans carnivals, e.g. *How many foreign visitors go to the Rio carnival?*
- Students find five adjectives to describe a carnival and four words related to music in the texts and copy them into their notebooks. Decide as a class which words to put on cards for the Vocabulary box.

Your Response

- Ask students to choose one of the festivals they talked about in exercise 1, or another festival they know well.
- Students complete the chart with the necessary information for this festival. Point out that they don't all have to describe the same festival.

Optional activity

In pairs, students interview each other about the festival they have written about, using the question prompts from the chart, e.g. *When is your festival?*

LANGUAGE WORKOUT OPTION

If you want to pre-teach the language students will be using in the following activities, you may like to go to the Language Workout box now.

4 Speaking

- Ask *Which carnival lasts longer, Rio or New Orleans?* Elicit a full answer and write it on the board.
- Ask *Is your festival bigger than Rio? Is it an important festival?* Write the full answers on the board. Elicit an appropriate connecting word to make one complete comparative sentence, e.g. *My festival is smaller than Rio, but it is one of the most important festivals in my country.*
- Ask students to make other comparative sentences. If necessary, give adjective prompts, e.g. *big, colorful, famous, exciting*. The students could first write the sentences and then read them to a partner.

Optional activity

Students say a mixture of true and false comparative sentences about the carnivals in the text or their own festival. The class or their partner has to say whether each sentence is true or false.

5 Pronunciation

- Say the /ə/ sound. Tell the students that this is the most common sound in English. Many different spelling combinations can produce the /ə/ sound.
- Play the recording. Students listen and repeat.
- Students copy the words into their notebooks and circle the /ə/ sound. Play the recording again if necessary.
- Ask individual students to tell the class their answers.

1.18 Recording and answers

/ə/ *festiv(a)l*

carniv(a)l *fam(ou)s* *gi(a)nt* *milli(o)n* *p(a)rade*
reg(io)n *samb(a)* *spec(ia)l* *stadi(u)m* *thous(a)nd*

Optional activity

Write the words *breakfast, computer, language, country, guitar, actor, jacket* on the board. Students identify the three words which do not contain the /ə/ sound. This could be played as a team game.
(Answers: country, language, guitar)

6 Speaking

- Choose three cities from different regions of the students' country. Explain that the students have to compare the three cities using the ideas in the box and adjectives from the Word Bank. Check comprehension of the words in the box and in the Word Bank (students may need help with *attractions, atmosphere, popular*).
- Go through the example with the class. Elicit sentences for age and size with the whole class.
- Students make more sentences as a whole class or in pairs.

Extension The aim is to encourage learners to take responsibility for their learning by testing each other. In pairs, one student closes the book and the other tests him/her on eight of the comparative and superlative forms from the Language File on page 114. The other student reads out an adjective, and their partner has to give the correct comparative and superlative forms. Then they change roles. Each student keeps a record of their partner's score, giving them two points for each correct answer. Ask how many students got 16 points. Confident students can test each other on other adjectives they know.

Optional activity

Ask students for the comparative and superlative forms of the adjectives in the Word Bank.

7 Writing

- Students write at least six sentences comparing the three cities from exercise 6. Set a time limit of ten minutes.
- Students exchange sentences and check each other's work for spelling and grammar.

Optional activity

Students look at the *Carnivals* text again and find all the comparative and superlative adjectives in the text in preparation for the Language Workout.

Extension Students choose their favorite city, and write a paragraph about it for a tourist brochure. Encourage students to use lots of superlative adjectives to encourage people to visit their city. Ask a few confident students to read their paragraphs to the rest of the class.

Optional activity

In groups, students read their tourist brochures to each other and vote on the city they would most like to visit.

LANGUAGE WORKOUT

- Ask students to look at the Language Workout box and complete the chart. Point out that they can find all the comparative and superlative forms in the *Carnivals* text.
- Students turn to page 114 of the Language File to check their answers.

  Answers

  smaller the largest the biggest
  noisier the most famous more exciting
  the most exciting the best less three
- Highlight that:
  - one-syllable adjectives ending in one vowel + one consonant double the final consonant in the comparative and the superlative forms, as in *big, bigger, the biggest.* (But we do not double *-w, -x, -y* at the end of words.)
  - adjectives ending in *-y* change the *y* to *i* and add *-er/-est,* as in *noisy, noisier, the noisiest.*
  - some two-syllable adjectives and all adjectives of three or more syllables form the comparative with *more* and the superlative with *most.*
- Drill the examples in chorus for pronunciation and stress.

Practice

- Students do Practice exercise 5 on page 114 of the Language File. They complete the sentences with the correct form of the adjectives in brackets. Students check each other's work.

Answers

1 larger 2 biggest 3 best 4 most exciting
5 less expensive 6 better 7 worst 8 longer
9 noisiest 10 least expensive

Optional activity

Students make other sentences using the adjectives in the Word Bank on page 23, e.g. *Rafael Nadal is the best tennis player in the world.* Students could then give each other prompts like *Nadal, good* to elicit sentences from their partner.

Follow-up activity

Game *Comparisons* Ask students to name two animals. Put them into pairs and ask them to write a sentence comparing the two animals. The first pair with a correct sentence wins a point. Continue the game using actors, singers, and countries. Tell students they are not allowed to repeat adjectives.

Homework

Students imagine they are at a carnival and write a description of what they can see and hear, and what they are doing.

NOTEBOOK SECTION

There is an error in each sentence. Rewrite the sentences correctly.

1 NewYork is colder Los Angeles.
2 Shakira is the most good singer.
3 Rio is the excitingest city in the world.
4 That cell phone is expensiver than this one.
5 Books are most interesting than movies.

Answers

*1 NewYork is **colder than** Los Angeles.*
*2 Shakira is **the best** singer.*
*3 Rio is **the most exciting** city in the world.*
*4 That cell phone is **more expensive than** this one.*
*5 Books are **more interesting** than movies.*

Consolidation and Extension p31

Language File p114

Workbook Unit 2 Lesson 1 pp16–17

Photocopiable notes p154, worksheet p165

2 We should stay together

Communicative Aims	Language	Pronunciation	Vocabulary	Optional aids
Giving advice Saying where things are	*should* and *shouldn't*	/s/ sixty /ʃ/ shirts	Social customs Prepositions of place Town facilities	Language Workout Practice exercise 6 Optional activity: cards with places and events on them, e.g. *a party, the movies*

WARM-UP 1

Brainstorm adjectives and write them on the board. Student 1 chooses an adjective, Student 2 says the comparative, and Student 3 says the superlative and then chooses another adjective for the next student. Continue around the class.

WARM-UP 2

Put anagrams for words related to festivals and music, e.g. *NABD* (band), *LATLS* (stall), *SCUMOTE* (costume) on the board for students to solve.

WARM-UP 3

Ask students what they remember about the New Orleans Carnival from Lesson 1. Ask *When does it take place?*, etc.

1 Opener

- The aim is to introduce the context for the Reading dialogue in exercise 2. Students think about the question in pairs or small groups, using the words in the box to help them.

Optional activity

Ask students to write six sentences about problems at festivals or carnivals, using a word from the box in each one, e.g. *It is easy to get lost from friends or family if there are big crowds.*

2 Reading

- Ask students to identify the contest winners in the photo. Ask *What is Steve's job? (He's the tour guide.).*
- Ask students to read the dialogue and answer the question.

Answer

Steve gets angry because some of the group won't stay together.

Optional activity

1.19 Play the recording of the dialogue for students to read and listen. Stop at any words that you predict may cause pronunciation problems, e.g. *stall, vacation,* and ask students to repeat.

3 After Reading

- Ask the students to find the expressions *get lost, stay together, go away, taking care of, go by yourself* in the dialogue. Students use the context to try to translate these. Test comprehension by giving the translation and asking individual students to say the English equivalent.
- Students read the dialogue again and answer the questions with short answers.
- They check their answers in pairs. Ask students to read their answers to the class.

Answers

1 *Emma and Alex.*
2 *Because Steve is taking care of them.*
3 *No, she doesn't.*
4 *Because he doesn't think it is safe for her to go by herself.*
5 *In half an hour.*
6 *The International Coffee Shop.*

Optional activity

Students write true/false statements about the dialogue and test each other in small groups.

Your Response

Ask students to discuss the question in groups, giving reasons for their answers. Brainstorm other things young people disagree with adults about. Discuss why they think there is a difference of opinion.

LANGUAGE WORKOUT OPTION

If you want to pre-teach the language students will be using in the following activities, you may like to go to the Language Workout box now.

4 Speaking

- The aim is to practice *should/shouldn't* in the context of the students' own country. Ask students to read the first question on the questionnaire and elicit feedback. Encourage students to use *You should/shouldn't …* Monitor the pronunciation of *should/shouldn't*.
- Ask the students to read the rest of the questions. Be prepared to translate or demonstrate *take your own food, cheek, shake hands, immediately, guest*.
- Students work on their own and decide on the appropriate answers. They compare their choices in pairs, saying the full sentence.
- Elicit feedback on any differences of opinion.

Answers

Some answers are subjective and there may be differences of opinion. Students could justify different choices.

5 Pronunciation

- Demonstrate the two sounds: /s/ sounds like a snake and /ʃ/ is the sound English speakers make when they want people to be quiet.
- Play the recording and ask students to repeat the tongue-twister. Then students practice the tongue-twister in pairs, and say it as fast as possible!

1.20 **Recording**

/s/ /ʃ/ *She has sixty shirts and sixty-six skirts—she should stop shopping!*

Optional activity

Students make up and practice more tongue-twisters using the sounds /s/ and /ʃ/.

6 Vocabulary

- Elicit the prepositions: stand next to the desk and ask *Where am I?* Put your book under the table and ask *Where is it?*, etc. Initially, you could provide the answer yourself and drill it in chorus. Then choose a confident student and tell him/her to stand between two things or people. Continue with other students and different instructions.
- Ask students to look at the illustrations of prepositions of place in the Word Bank.
- Highlight the difference between *across from*, meaning *facing each other*, and *in front of*. Refer students to page 114 of the Language File.
- Ask questions about the photo on page 24, e.g. *Where is Steve?*
- Students complete the sentences. Ask different students to read their answers to the class.

Answers

1 next to 2 in front of 3 between 4 across from 5 behind 6 near

Optional activity

Students give each other instructions using the prepositions, e.g. *Stand in front of the table.*

Extension Demonstrate this game with the whole class. Describe where an object is in the classroom (see the example) and encourage them to guess what the object is. Once students have understood, they can play in pairs, taking turns to describe where three objects are to their partner.

7 Vocabulary

- Students work in pairs with their books closed. Give them two minutes to write down as many places as possible which you can find in a town. Ask the pairs with the most to read them to the class and then ask other pairs to add to the list. Check comprehension by asking *What can you buy there? What do you do there?*
- Ask if there are any additional places in the Word Bank on page 25. Check comprehension by asking the questions again about each place in the Word Bank.
- Demonstrate the example with a confident student.
- Students continue either as a question-and-answer chain around the class or in pairs.

Optional activity

Ask a student to draw the center of their town on the board with one or two places marked in. Write the rest of the town facilities on the board. Then ask the students where these other places are.

8 Role-play

- Ask students to read the phrases in the boxes.
- Use the town map in exercise 7 and elicit an example of a complete conversation, beginning with the questions and answers in the book. Write it on the board and drill it in chorus for pronunciation and intonation. Leave the conversation on the board.
- Demonstrate the exercise a couple of times with confident students playing the part of the local. Vary the places you want to get to. Students then act out dialogues in pairs.

Extension Ask students to write down the facilities from the Word Bank that can be found in their town, or in a town they know well. In pairs, students act out more dialogues like those from exercise 8, but this time asking and answering questions about their own town, or a town they know well.

9 Writing

- Explain that an English-speaking friend is coming to visit. Ask the students to use the ideas in the questionnaire to write some advice for them. Read the example with the class. Set a time limit of ten minutes. Tell students that they can also think of other situations where it is important to do the right thing, and write more sentences about these.

Useful information

Students may be interested to know what, under normal circumstances, is "right" in the U.S.:

1 You should take flowers and arrive on time.
2 You should shake hands firmly.
3 You should say thank you and open the gift immediately.
4 You should say hello and/or your name/phone number.
5 You should wait until others are eating and eat everything on your plate.

Optional activity

Ask students to write two more questions for the questionnaire on page 24 about other situations where it is important to do the right thing.

LANGUAGE WORKOUT

- Ask students to look at the Language Workout box and complete the sentences. Point out that they can find all the answers in the dialogue and After Reading questions.
- Students turn to page 114 of the Language File to check their answers.

Answers

should shouldn't should

- Highlight that:
  - *should* and *shouldn't* are used to show that you think something is a good/bad idea and to give advice/warnings.
  - *should/shouldn't* always has the same form: it doesn't add *-s* in the third person singular.
  - *should/shouldn't* is followed by the infinitive without *to*.
- Drill the examples in chorus.

Practice

- Students do Practice exercise 6 on page 114 of the Language File. Ask students to close their books. Explain that the text in the exercise lists three *don'ts* and two *dos* for the carnival. Ask the students to try to guess what they are. Write all their ideas on the board.
- Students open their books and check their ideas.
- Students read the *Dos and Don'ts* again and complete the sentences. This could be done in pairs or as a short test. Ask different students to read their answers to the class.

Answers

1 shouldn't 2 should 3 shouldn't; should 4 shouldn't 5 should

Optional activity

Game *What should you do?* Students work in pairs. Each pair takes one event or place card (see Optional aids). The students write sentences about what you should and shouldn't do in that place. Then they read their sentences in groups and the other students guess the event/place.

Follow-up activity

Draw a blank diagram from the answers below on the board. Don't include the words except for "bank." Ask students to copy it. Then dictate the following sentences for students to complete the diagram:
The drugstore is between the bank and the hairdresser's.
The post office is across from the hairdresser's.
The flower shop is next to the post office, on the right.
The newsstand is across from the flower shop.
The travel agency is across from the drugstore.
Where is the coffee shop?

Answers

bank	*drugstore*	*hairdresser's*	*newsstand*
coffee shop	*travel agency*	*post office*	*flower shop*

Homework

Students prepare similar puzzles to the one above.

Students update their vocabulary notebooks with the places in the Town facilities Word Bank and with pictures to illustrate all the prepositions of place.

NOTEBOOK SECTION

There is an error in each sentence. Rewrite the sentences correctly.

1 You should to drink lots of water.
2 He shoulds relax.
3 Do I should go to the hospital?
4 She should eats healthy food.
5 They don't should stay out late.

Answers

1 You should drink lots of water.
2 He should relax.
3 Should I go to the hospital?
4 She should eat healthy food.
5 They shouldn't stay out late.

Consolidation and Extension p31
Language File p114
Workbook Unit 2 Lesson 2 pp18–19
Photocopiable notes p154, worksheet p166

3 I love going to festivals

Communicative Aims	Language	Pronunciation	Vocabulary	Optional aids
Talking about likes and dislikes Saying what people can do	Verb/Preposition + gerund	Syllable stress	Music	Exercise 1 Optional activity: samples of different kinds of music

WARM-UP 1

Ask the students to remember what you should and shouldn't do at a carnival.

WARM-UP 2

If you set the homework suggested in the previous lesson, students work out each other's puzzles.

1 Opener

- The aim is to present and review music vocabulary. Ask the students to look at the pictures on pages 26–27. Elicit what the pictures show (a music festival) and ask students to guess where they were taken (in Britain). Ask students *Do you go to music festivals or watch them on TV?* Write a list on the board of music festivals students have been to or watched.
- Ask students to look at the Music Word Bank and ask *What kind of music do you like listening to?* Ask students to suggest musicians and bands who play the different kinds of music. Find out which kind of music is most popular in the class.

Optional activity

Play samples of different kinds of music (see Optional aids). Students listen and identify the kind of music.

2 Reading

- Ask students to look at the list of topics in the box. They then read the article and say which topics the article talks about. Encourage them to guess unfamiliar vocabulary from context.

Answers

mud money music trash weather

Optional activity

1.21 Play the recording of the text for students to read and listen. Stop at any words that you predict may cause pronunciation problems, e.g. *friendly, atmosphere*, and ask students to repeat.

3 After Reading

- Students read the text again and complete the sentences. Ask different students to read out their answers.

Answers

1 like 2 mind 3 stand 4 hate 5 bad 6 interested 7 good

Optional activities

- ♦ Students personalize the sentences, e.g. *I love waiting in line in the rain. I can't stand getting muddy.* and tell a partner.
- ♦ Students write sentences containing each of the answers to exercise 2, e.g. *There is lots of mud at Glastonbury*.

Your Response

- Give students two minutes to make notes in their notebooks about all the things they would and wouldn't like about going to a festival like Glastonbury.
- In pairs, students discuss the question, using their notes to give reasons.

Optional activity

Have a class vote to see how many students would/ wouldn't like to go to a festival like Glastonbury. Ask students to suggest the things they would/wouldn't like about it, and make two lists on the board.

Useful information

Glastonbury Festival is the biggest open-air music and performing arts festival in the world, and it takes place every year over a weekend at Worthy Farm in the south-west of England. The first festival was held in 1970 and 1,500 people came. Tickets cost £1 (less than $2), and included free milk from the farm. Now, more than 130,000 people come for the weekend, paying nearly £200 (around $325) for a ticket. As well as music, Glastonbury features dance, comedy, theater, and circus shows.

4 Pronunciation

- Play the recording. Students listen and repeat.
- Ask students to copy the words into their notebooks and mark the stress. Play the recording again for them to check.

1.22 Recording and answers

atmosphere dangerous enjoy fantastic
festival friendly interested security

Optional activity

Students work in pairs or small groups and look through the book for other words with the same stress pattern as *atmosphere*, *enjoy*, and *friendly*. This could be done as a contest and when one pair/group thinks they have six words, they write them on the board.

LANGUAGE WORKOUT OPTION

If you want to pre-teach the language students will be using in the following activities, you may like to go to the Language Workout box now.

5 Speaking

- Elicit from students the difference between *Do you like …?* and *Do you mind …?* (If you like doing something, you actively enjoy it, but if you don't mind doing something, it is usually an unpleasant or boring thing that you are happy to do anyway.)
- Ask students which of the things in the box normally go with the question *Do you like …?* and which with *Do you mind …?* Explain that some of the things go with both questions.
- Model the example questions and point out that the gerund (verb + *-ing*) is used after both questions. Give students five minutes to write questions beginning *Do you like …?* and *Do you mind …?* They can use the phrases in the box and add their own ideas.
- Students interview each other in pairs, asking the questions they have written, and then swap partners with another pair so they each interview two students. Tell students to note down their partners' answers.

Suggested answers

Do you mind/like sleeping in a tent?
Do you mind standing up all day?
Do you like listening to live music?
Do you like/mind being in a large crowd?
Do you mind paying a lot for a ticket?
Do you like hearing new bands?
Do you mind being a long way from the stage?
Do you mind waiting in line for the bathroom?
Do you like/mind getting covered in mud?

Extension Point out the example sentence to students. They write sentences about the students they interviewed. Encourage them to link their sentences (as in the example), but remind them that they will need to use *but* if they are including positive and negative statements in their sentences, e.g. *Mercedes likes listening to live music but she doesn't like standing up all day.* Point out to students that if their partner answers *Yes* to the question *Do you mind …?* we usually say *I do mind …* or *I don't like …* rather than *I mind …*

6 Listening

- Tell students that they are going to listen to Sara from Festival Radio interviewing Holly and Matt. Ask them to read the chart and the possible answers in the box. Students work in pairs to predict the answers.
- Play the recording. Students listen and check their predictions.

1.23 Recording

SARA *Hi, Holly, and welcome to Festival Radio—I'm Sara. How are you doing?*
HOLLY *I'm good—I'm having a fantastic time here.*
SARA *That's great, Holly. And tell me, what do you like doing at Glasto?*
HOLLY *I love meeting old friends—it's great!*
SARA *And what do you hate doing?*
HOLLY *Uh … I can't stand getting wet! And it never stops raining!*
SARA *I know what you mean—the weather's terrible. Now, what are you good at?*
HOLLY *That's easy—dancing, especially to hip-hop. But …*
SARA *But what?*
HOLLY *I'm really not good at getting up early. This morning I missed my favorite hip-hop band.*
SARA *Oh, no—that's too bad! Actually, I'm pretty bad at getting up early too. Well, thank you Holly, and enjoy the rest of the festival!*
HOLLY *Thanks, Sara—bye!*
SARA *And now here's Matt—hello!*
MATT *Hi!*
SARA *Now Matt, tell us something you love about festivals.*
MATT *Oh, let me think, there's so much—well, I love staying up late. I really love nighttime.*
SARA *Uh-huh. Something you hate?*
MATT *I can't stand getting lost. And last night, I couldn't find my way back to my tent!*
SARA *Oh, no! You don't want to end up in the wrong tent! But tell me, Matt, what are you good at?*
MATT *I think I'm good at making new friends … but I'm really bad at talking to girls.*
SARA *I don't believe you! I enjoy talking to you a lot! Thank you, Matt.*

Answers

	Holly	Matt
Loves	*meeting old friends*	*staying up late*
Hates	*getting wet*	*getting lost*
Good at	*dancing*	*making new friends*
Bad at	*getting up early*	*talking to girls*

- Model the four questions in the examples, stressing love, hate, good, bad. Students repeat in chorus.
- Give students time to ask for relevant vocabulary.
- Copy the chart onto the board and demonstrate.
- Students ask and answer questions in pairs to complete the chart.

Optional activity

With a confident class, encourage students to ask follow-up questions, e.g. *What kind of movies do you like?*

7 Writing

- Ask students to close their books. Prompt students to "dictate" sentences to you about what Holly likes and doesn't like, and write them on the board. Ask students to spell some words. Highlight any omissions/ problems.
- Students copy the sentences from the board and use them as a model to write about Matt and the person they interviewed.

Extension Change *Holly* in the text on the board to *I* and elicit the necessary grammar changes, i.e. remove third person *s* and change *is* to *am*. Students write about themselves.

LANGUAGE WORKOUT

- Ask students to complete the Language Workout box. Point out that they can find all the answers in the text from exercise 2.
- Students turn to page 115 of the Language File to check their answers.

  Answers

  playing waiting getting being getting in
- Highlight that:
  - the gerund (verb + *-ing*) is used like a noun.
  - the gerund is used after some verbs and all prepositions.
- For the spelling of verb + *-ing*, see Language File page 113 under Present Progressive.

Optional activity

Students look through the text in exercise 2 and find examples of the gerund.

Practice

- Students do Practice exercise 7 on page 115 of the Language File. Students read and complete the sentences. This could be done in pairs or as a short test.
- Ask different students to read and spell their answers.

Answers

1 being 2 dancing 3 doing 4 waiting 5 camping 6 listening 7 talking 8 speaking

Optional activity

Give students a quick spelling test of words which are often incorrectly spelled in the gerund: *studying, going, being, swimming, playing, doing, celebrating, making.*

Follow-up activity

Game *Find someone who …*

Write the following on the board:
Find someone who …
loves _____ hates _____ is good at _____
is bad at _____

Students copy and complete the sentences with appropriate vocabulary of their choice. They pass their completed sentences to a different student, who has to ask questions to find someone for each category. When a student has four names they win.

Homework

Students write about a member of their family or a famous person/character, explaining what they love, don't mind, don't like, can't stand, are good/bad at.

NOTEBOOK SECTION

Draw lines to make complete sentences.

1 She's good	in animals.
2 You shouldn't be rude	for my mother.
3 He's interested	with his girlfriend.
4 I'm waiting	to people.
5 He's chatting	at using computers.

Answers

1 She's good at using computers.
2 You shouldn't be rude to people.
3 He's interested in animals.
4 I'm waiting for my mother.
5 He's chatting with his girlfriend

Consolidation and Extension p31

Language File p115

Workbook Unit 2 Lesson 3 pp20–21

Photocopiable notes p154, worksheet p167

4 *Integrated Skills* Celebrations

Skills
Reading Topics and details: The New Year Around the World article
Listening Choosing the best answers: New Year's Eve in the U.S.
Speaking Interviewing
Writing Description of a celebration

Learner Independence
Learning words
Self assessment

Vocabulary
New Year's Eve
Useful expressions

Optional aids
Opener: a map of the world

WARM-UP 1

If you set the homework suggested in the previous lesson, ask a student to read their text aloud without saying who it is about. The other students listen and guess the age of the person.

WARM-UP 2

Ask *When is New Year's Eve? And New Year's Day?* Review how to say dates. Tell them they are going to read about how the new year is celebrated around the world. Brainstorm anything they know about how other countries celebrate.

1 Opener

- The aim is to encourage students to predict before reading. Ask students to look at the photos on pages 28–29 and take turns describing what they can see to a partner. Have them see if their partner can guess which photo they are describing. Help with necessary vocabulary, e.g. *fireworks, suitcase, dragon*. Then ask them to guess which countries' festivals the photos illustrate. It may help them to look at a map of the world.

2 Reading

- The aim of the matching activity is to identify topics and to confirm guesses in exercise 1. Students read the text and match the paragraphs with the photos. To check, say the letter of a photo and ask *Which country is this?*

Answers
Photo A—Brazil *Photo B—Italy* *Photo C—Japan*
Photo D—Venezuela *Photo E—China*
Photo F—Thailand

- Have students read the text again and answer the questions 1–8. Have them check their answers with a partner.

Answers
1 *In Japan.*
2 *In Venezuela.*
3 *They wear white clothes.*
4 *They go to the beach and jump over the waves seven times. Then they throw flowers into the ocean and make wishes for the new year. Some people light candles.*
5 *In Italy.*
6 *On April 13.*
7 *15 days.*
8 *In Italy.*

- Read the example questions out loud. Students repeat in chorus. With a confident class, students ask and answer similar questions about the text in pairs.
- With a less confident class, write *When do people celebrate the new year in …? Where do people eat/drink/throw water/…? What do people in … do/eat/drink/…?* on the board.
- Ask the whole class some of these questions. After three or four, encourage the student who answers to make a question for another student. Continue as a question-and-answer chain around the class or in pairs.

Optional activity

Students write questions and answers, then jumble them. They ask another student to match each question and answer.

3 Listening

- Ask students if they know anything about the new year in the U.S.
- Read the questions aloud and ask students to suggest possible answers to check comprehension.
- Play the recording. Students listen for specific information and note the answers. Play the recording again, pausing to check the answers to each question.

1.24 Recording

People all over the United States celebrate New Year. People often have parties on New Year's Eve. They may stay at home with their family or go out with friends. Many people who live in New York go to Times Square and wait for midnight. At midnight, the people in the square watch a big glass ball drop to the bottom of a tower. People all over the United States watch the "ball dropping" on TV. After midnight, people hold hands and sing a special song. People open bottles of champagne and say "Happy New Year" to each other.

Answers

1 A 2 B 3 B 4 A 5 B

4 Speaking

- Students interview each other, taking turns to ask and answer questions.

5 Writing

- The aim is to give students guidelines for writing a description of an event. Read the notes on the typical structure of a description with the class.
- Students write their paragraphs following the structure.
- For a less confident class, write the following prompts on the board:
  In … we celebrate New Year's Eve on …
  People eat … and they drink … They often …
  At midnight they …
  After midnight they …
- Students correct each other's work.

6 Learner Independence

- The aim is to identify students' preferred way of learning new words and to discuss the advantages and disadvantages of each method.
- Students look at the list and mark from 1–7 (1 Best) their favorite ways of learning new words.
- Elicit feedback on the most popular methods. Suggest students try a new way of learning words for a week and then report back to the class.

7

- The aim is to encourage students to assess their language skills and to think about ways of developing skills. Ask students to assess themselves for each skill on a scale of 1–4. Encourage them to be as honest as possible. Point out that successful learners identify their weaknesses and work on areas where they have difficulty.
- Students work in pairs and compare their self assessments. Do they agree with each other's assessment? Go around the class and check that your assessment tallies with theirs. If students have underestimated themselves, you can raise their self-esteem. You may like to repeat this activity every month—if students keep a record of their assessments, they can compare them and measure their own progress.
- Brainstorm ways of improving each skill and write suggestions on the board, for example: Listening—listen to English language radio shows; Speaking—listen to a recording of a text or dialogue and read it aloud at the same time; Reading—try to read an English book (a graded reader) every week; Writing—write letters to a penpal.

8 Phrasebook

- Ask students to find the idiomatic expressions in Unit 2.
- Play the recording for students to listen and repeat.

1.25 Recording and answers

Dialogue, page 24
I don't know. (Jay, Lesson 2, ex2)
Come here! (Steve, Lesson 2, ex2)
Why not? (Emma, Lesson 2, ex2)
Bye! (Emma, Lesson 2, ex2)
It isn't safe. (Jay, Lesson 2, ex2)
I'm coming with you. (Jay, Lesson 2, ex2)
Now listen up! (Steve, Lesson 2, ex2)
OK? (Steve, Lesson 2, ex2)
Come back! (Steve, Lesson 2, ex2)

Text, page 26
The only problem is … (man, Lesson 3, ex2)

- Read the example dialogue with a confident student. Ask students to work in pairs and write another four-line dialogue using at least two of the expressions.
- Ask confident pairs to act out their dialogues for the rest of the class. Students can add expressions that they like to their Personal Phrasebooks.

Follow-up activity

Students write about what they enjoy/don't like/are good/bad at doing in English, e.g. *I enjoy speaking English, I'm good at learning vocabulary,* etc.

Homework

Students write a paragraph about a memorable New Year's Eve. They describe what they did and who they were with.

NOTEBOOK SECTION

Complete the sentences using a form of the word in parentheses.

1 I love ____ late. (sleep)
2 I can't stand ____ in line! (stand)
3 He hates ____ late. (be)
4 José ____ talking to people. (love)
5 Cathy enjoys ____ in the ocean. (swim)

Answers

1 sleeping 2 standing 3 being 4 loves 5 swimming

Consolidation and Extension p31

Workbook Unit 2 Lesson 4 pp22–23

Inspired EXTRA!

Optional aids
Project: photos and pictures from newspapers or magazines of festivals or public celebrations, e.g. Independence Day
Game: sheets of paper

Project
Festivals and celebrations

1
- Explain to students that the aim of this project is to write about a festival or public celebration. If you have brought photos or pictures into class, show them to the students. Remind them about the articles in Unit 2, Lessons 1 and 3, and look at the photos (the top one is a rehearsal for Independence Day celebrations in India and the bottom one is a concert at a folk festival in Russia) and the example project.
- Divide students into groups and appoint an "editor" for each group.
- Give students two minutes to make a list of festivals or public celebrations they know or have information about. Then each group chooses one to write about.

2
- Hold a class brainstorming session to generate ideas they can use to write about their chosen festivals.
- Students look at the prompts and make notes about their festival or celebration. They may need to use the Internet or find information at home.

3
- Each person in the group writes a short text to contribute to their project.
- Students put their work together and read through the texts carefully to correct any mistakes. They copy their texts out neatly. The editor selects the order of the texts while others work on illustrating their project with photos from magazines or the Internet, or drawings.
- Students show their work to other groups. Display the projects in the classroom if possible.

Game Write a poem!

- Read the poems aloud to the class. Draw students' attention to the poem "patterns" beneath each one.
- Students write their own poems, saying what they love/hate and are good/bad at, and thinking of prepositions and nouns for a *Preposition* poem. Point out that the lines don't need to rhyme. Encourage students to be as creative and amusing as possible.
- Collect the poems and shuffle them. Then read some of them out to the class and ask students to try to identify the writer of each poem.

Consolidation

Lesson 1
Students' own answers.

Lesson 2
If necessary, give students prompts, e.g. *noticeboard, poster.*

Lesson 3

Answers
Lara loves swimming. She hates losing things. She's good at writing poems, but she's bad at getting up early.
Alex loves taking pictures. He hates flying. He's good at playing the guitar, but he's bad at dancing.

Lesson 4
Students' own answers.

Extension

Lesson 1
Start with a brainstorming session to generate ideas for people/bands and appropriate adjectives, e.g. *popular.*

Lesson 2
Students' own answers.

Lesson 3
Students' own answers.

Lesson 4
Refer students to the questions in Project exercise 2.

YOUR CHOICE!

The aim is to give students more learner independence and help them to identify their preferred ways of learning. Encourage students to choose an activity that they feel less comfortable with if they want a challenge or are aware that they need practice in a particular area.
Musical Festival Advice gives students the opportunity to reinforce the language they have learned by writing.
Superlative You! gives students the opportunity to practice speaking with a partner.

You may now like students to do the song *Dancin' In The Street.* See p161 for the notes and p186 for the worksheet.

Language File pp114–115

Song—photocopiable notes p161, worksheet p186

Workbook Unit 2 Inspired EXTRA! pp24–25

Units 1–2

Optional aids

Follow-up activities: slips of paper, each one with a target vocabulary item from Units 1 and 2 written on it

1 Give the students two minutes to read the text and say how many different events are mentioned. (*seven—Independence Day, Chinese New Year, Cherry Blossom Festival, Cinco de Mayo, Carnival San Francisco, Halloween, Christmas*). Students read the text again and choose the appropriate word for each space. Do the first one together as an example. This can be done in pairs or individually as a short test.

Answers
1 A 2 C 3 B 4 C 5 A 6 B 7 C 8 C 9 A 10 C 11 A 12 B

Optional activity

Confident students can first attempt the task without looking at the word options.

2 Students complete the sentences with the correct simple present form. Less confident students could first decide which verb goes in each sentence.

Answers
1 chats 2 am not 3 watches 4 Does … speak 5 calls 6 doesn't like 7 go 8 Does … drink 9 doesn't do 10 eats 11 doesn't play 12 get

3 Students complete the sentences with the correct present progressive form.

Answers
1 is telling 2 Are … holding 3 is helping 4 Is … standing 5 are making 6 Are … listening

4 Students write questions using the words given and then answer them. Do the first one together. Note: warn students to be careful about items 5 and 6 (plural possessive ending in s'). Check the answers by asking one student to read the question and then choose another student to answer. Students then ask and answer the questions in pairs.

Answers
1 *Whose watch is this? It's Ramón's. It's his.*
2 *Whose bag is this? It's Carrie's. It's hers.*
3 *Whose book is this? It's Lara's. It's hers.*
4 *Whose jacket is this? It's Steve's. It's his.*
5 *Whose DVDs are these? They're my parents'. They're theirs.*
6 *Whose sandwiches are these? They're the dancers'. They're theirs.*

5 Students complete the sentences with the appropriate form of the adjectives in parentheses. With a less confident class, the students could first decide which form, comparative or superlative, is required for each example, before completing the sentences.

Answers
1 the largest 2 the most exciting 3 better 4 worse 5 the most popular 6 the biggest 7 more expensive 8 less well known

6 Ask students to read the advice. Note: *strangers* = people you don't know (not foreigners). Students rewrite the advice using *should/shouldn't*.

Answers
You shouldn't ride with strangers, or get into a stranger's car.
You shouldn't stay out very late and you shouldn't walk home by yourself.
You should remember to carry a cell phone.
You should make sure you have enough money for a taxi home if necessary.
You should check the times of the last trains and buses.

7 Point to the people in the photo on pages 12–13 and check that students know their names. Students complete the sentences with the appropriate prepositions. Do the first one together as an example.

Answers
1 between 2 next to 3 behind 4 in front of 5 near

Optional activity

Students write a similar exercise for each other, based on people and things in the classroom.

8 Tell students that they need to choose the correct verb and form the gerund. Do the first one together as an example.

Answers
1 being 2 dancing 3 waiting 4 waiting 5 learning 6 being 7 going 8 giving 9 getting

Vocabulary

9 Confident students can first cover the list of words and try to work out what the definitions refer to. Students match the nouns with their definitions. Point out that there are three nouns that don't have definitions.

Answers
1 pickpocket 2 candle 3 parade 4 joke 5 drugstore 6 newsstand 7 outside 8 costume 9 guide 10 remember

Optional activities

- Students write definitions for the three extra nouns (*crowd, medicine, pilot*).
- Students write definitions of other words from Units 1 and 2. They exchange definitions with another student and guess each other's words.

10 Remind students that it is very helpful to learn common idiomatic verb + noun phrases of this kind.

Answers

1 *change some money*	6 *make a wish*
2 *chat online*	7 *play games*
3 *do yoga*	8 *speak a language*
4 *get up early*	9 *stay at a hotel*
5 *hold hands*	10 *wear glasses*

11 Students choose the word in each group that is different from the others in some way. Point out that they should be able to explain their choices. Do the first one together as an example.

Answers

1 *cost (all the others are directly related to festivals)*
2 *costume (all the others are adjectives)*
3 *street (all the others are prepositions of place)*
4 *hotel (all the others are similar in meaning)*
5 *bank (all the others are stores)*
6 *suitcase (all the others are words related to computers)*

Optional activity

Fast finishers make other odd word groups to test each other.

Learner Independence Self Assessment

- Explain to students that the aim of the self assessment is to encourage them to check their own progress and take any necessary action to improve. Point out that the list 1–8 covers areas of functional language from Units 1 and 2. Students check the "Fine" box for functional language that they feel confident using, but put a question mark in the "Not sure" box for functional language that they have difficulty with or still cannot use confidently.
- Encourage students to look at the Language File and re-do exercises from the Workbook in areas where they have problems. They may also like to re-do exercises from the lessons and from the Consolidation and Extension sections in Units 1 and 2.
- Students write an example sentence for each language area in the list. You may like to elicit the grammar students need for each example before students write sentences, e.g. *Talking about regular activities: simple present.* Students can refer back to the lessons and the Language File.
- Ask students to compare their sentences with a partner's, and to discuss and correct any mistakes.
- Check their sentences and note down language areas for future practice.

Follow-up activities

- **Game** *Tic-Tac-Toe* Draw this grid on the board:

comparative and superlative adjectives	clothes	possessive adjectives and pronouns
preposition/ verb + gerund	town facilities	should/ shouldn't
/i/ and /eɪ/	prepositions of place	/ə/

  Divide the class into two teams. Team A are the Os and Team B are the Xs. Team A chooses a square first. On a grammar square they must make a correct sentence, on a vocabulary square you give a definition and they must say the word, and on a pronunciation square they must say words which contain the sounds. If they answer correctly, write O in the appropriate square. If they answer incorrectly, Team B can answer and win the square. The first team to get a line of three Os or Xs in any direction wins the game.
- **Game** *Don't say the word* To test students on vocabulary from previous lessons, put them into groups. Select one student from each group and give them some of the slips of paper (see Optional aids). That student has one minute to explain to his/her group as many of those words as possible without using the words themselves. For every word that the group guesses, they get one point.

Homework

Students update their vocabulary notebooks.
Students write a paragraph about typical teenage birthday celebrations (people, food and drink, etc.).

NOTEBOOK SECTION

Complete the sentences using a form of the word in parentheses.
1 ____ he ____ her often? (call)
2 He should ____ more. (practice)
3 Who ____ you ____ for? (wait)
4 She ____ ____ in this photo. (smile)
5 James Bond never ____. (die)

Answers

1 Does, call 2 practice 3 are, waiting
4 's (is) smiling 5 dies

Language File pp112–115

Workbook Review Units 1–2 pp26–27

Units 3–4

Activities		Project	Vocabulary	Optional aids
Identifying the function of communicative language	Categorizing vocabulary Contextualizing listening extracts	First time/Last time questionnaire	Transportation Jobs and occupations Feelings Buildings Performance TV shows	Follow-up activity: small slips of paper

WARM-UP 1

Game *Teacher* Play with words from Units 1–2. See Unit 2, Lesson 1, Warm-up 1 for more details.

WARM-UP 2

Divide the class into two teams and ask students questions about the first two units to see how much they can remember. Encourage students to look back through Units 1 and 2 to find the answers if necessary. You may like to use the questions below or add your own:
What are the names of the contest winners? (Silvana, Emma, Jay, Ramón, Alex, and Lara) What was their prize? (A vacation in San Francisco) Who is the group's tour guide? (Steve) Which two famous carnivals did you learn about in Unit 2? (Rio and New Orleans) Why did Steve get angry with some of the group at the carnival? (Because he wanted them to stay together) What is Britain's biggest open-air music festival? (Glastonbury) In which country do people throw flowers into the sea on New Year's Eve? (Brazil) Where is the cherry blossom festival? (Japan)
Check answers and see which team got the most questions right.

WARM-UP 3

Ask students to look at the pictures and captions/speech bubbles on pages 34–35 and to answer the questions: *What do the pictures show? Who can you see in the pictures?*

1 • The aim is to introduce students to the main areas of communicative language they will cover in Units 3 and 4, and to encourage them to think about the function of the language. Explain to students that the two boxes at the top of the page show the communicative language and vocabulary/topics they will use in the next two units of *Inspired*. Students look at the first box and match the communicative aims 1–6 with the pictures A–F on pages 34–35.

Answers
1 C 2 E 3 A 4 F 5 D 6 B

Optional activity

Students write another example sentence or question for each of the communicative aims 1–6. Monitor and help where necessary.

2 • Explain to students that words from each of the three vocabulary categories (transportation, jobs and occupations, and feelings) are arranged in the word square. Give students two minutes to write the words in the correct category.

• Students check their answers in pairs and then as a whole class.

Answers
Transportation: car, plane, bicycle, train, bus, boat
Jobs: actor, pilot, musician, teacher, doctor, scientist
Feelings: worried, happy, angry, tired, sad, scared,

Optional activities

♦ In groups, students think about a time this week when they had any of the feelings in the list. They explain to the rest of the group why they felt a particular way.
♦ In small groups, students think of as many different words as possible to add to the three categories. Give them a time limit.

3 • Elicit the meaning of the three word-family names. Ask students to work in pairs to think of three more words for each family.

Suggested answers
Buildings: museum, church, temple, school, bank, house, store, station, office block, apartment building
Performance: band, dancer, actor, movie star, rock singer, ballerina, orchestra
TV shows: cartoon, talk show, drama, documentary, game show, music program, news program, reality show, science fiction, soap (opera), sports program, talent show, thriller

Optional activity

Confident students may like to write three words for each of the remaining word families in the box (inventions, time reference words, British English, recorded music, adverbs, and grammar words). Explain to students that time reference words are words that are used with times and dates, e.g. *on, at*.

4 • The aim of the activity is for students to contextualize a short listening extract by working out what kind of passage it is extracted from. Explain to students that they should listen for the main gist of the passage and that it does not matter if they do not understand every word.

• Play the recording. Students match each extract 1–3 with the correct passage A–C.

1.26 Recording

1

The people of San Francisco were asleep when the earthquake happened at 5:12 a.m. on Wednesday, April 18, 1906. The earthquake wasn't long, only a minute, but it was extremely strong. A fire started after the earthquake and spread quickly. Everything was very dry, and the city fire department didn't have any water. People think that the fire caused 90% of the damage to the city.

2

EMMA *You know, my brother Ryan fell overboard last year.*

JAY *Really? What happened? What was he doing?*

EMMA *He was sailing with a friend off the coast of Africa. At first, it was a beautiful day and the sun was shining. But then the weather suddenly got worse and there was a terrible storm. They were sailing in a small boat and they knew it was very dangerous.*

JAY *Yeah, sure.*

3

Medical drama series are always popular and one of the best is Scrubs, *which takes place in a hospital and a medical school. The lives and loves of doctors, nurses, and their patients are what a hospital series is all about. There's both comedy and tragedy in this fast-moving show, which is action-packed with accidents, serious illnesses, and emergencies, as well as romance.*

Answers

1 B 2 C 3 A

Optional activity

1.26 Play the recording again and ask students a simple comprehension question about each extract. *1 Which historical event is the speaker talking about? (The San Francisco earthquake) 2 What accident are Emma and Jay talking about? (Emma's brother falling overboard) 3 Which TV show is the speaker talking about?* (Scrubs)

5 • Give students a few minutes to look through the First Time Last Time questionnaire. Point out the speech bubbles around the questionnaire and explain that there are many different ways of saying when things happened.

• Students do the questionnaire in groups of four, making notes about their group's answers, especially any that are interesting or surprising.

• One person from each group moves to another group and gives a brief report about their group's answers, telling them anything interesting or surprising that they found out, e.g. *Most people in our group went to the movies for the first time when they were very young, but Anna went to the movies for the first time last year!*

• Point out the "Believe it or not!" fact at the bottom of the page. Ask students to guess what the fourth most common noun is. (way)

First Time Last Time project

Students first write down their own answers to the questionnaire.
They then interview a partner and write down their answers.
Students then write a First Time Last Time report comparing their partner's answers with their own.
Encourage students to swap with their partner and correct each other's work.
Display the projects in class.

Follow-up activities

♦ Students think of three other questions to add to each section of the First Time Last Time questionnaire. They ask and answer the new questions with their partner.

♦ In groups of four, students brainstorm vocabulary for three of the categories from the box on page 34: *transportation, TV shows,* and *feelings*. Hand out slips of paper to each student. Give students an example from each category before they start, and tell them they have two minutes for each category to write as many words as they can think of on slips of paper. After the time is up for each of the three categories, students shuffle their slips of paper so they are jumbled out of order. They then swap their slips with another group, and the students then have another two minutes to sort another group's slips into the correct categories.

Homework

Ask students to interview someone in their family with the First Time Last Time questionnaire, and to write a paragraph about their answers.

1 A fire started after the earthquake

Communicative Aims	Language	Pronunciation	Vocabulary	Optional aids
Talking about past events (1)	Simple past: affirmative and negative	/d/ design<u>ed</u> /t/ laugh<u>ed</u> /ɪd/ invent<u>ed</u>	Buildings and places Inventions	Exercise 4 Optional activity: a box or hat and cut-up cards for Bingo

WARM-UP 1

Write today's date on the board. Say it twice and ask students how we say it (*June 20th*). Now write the year 1666. Ask students how we say it (*as two separate numbers—16, 66*). Now write the year 2011 and ask students how we say it (*twenty eleven or two thousand and eleven*).

WARM-UP 2

Write some examples of dates on the board. As a class or in large groups, students find out as many students' birthdays as they can and write them in their notebooks. Students then write three dates that are important to them in their notebooks. In pairs, students take turns to find out why each date is significant.

1 Opener

- The aim is to pre-teach vocabulary for the following exercises and set the scene for the presentation text. Ask students to look at the picture on page 36. Ask *What famous event does the picture show?* and establish that it shows the fire which followed the San Francisco earthquake in 1906.
- Use the picture to explain the meaning of new vocabulary in the box, e.g. *buildings, flames, smoke.*
- Students work in pairs and write sentences describing the picture using the words in the box. Ask them to try to use all the words.
- Invite pairs to read out their sentences. Build up a description of the picture on the board.

Suggested answer

The picture shows a city street on a hill. There are people sitting on chairs and standing in groups on the street. A lot of buildings are burning, and there are flames and clouds of smoke.

2 Reading

- Encourage students to predict information in the text by asking *When did the earthquake happen? What happened after the earthquake? How many buildings did it destroy? How many people died?* Students write down their guesses and then read to check.
- Ask students what they read in the text that most surprised them.

Suggested answers

The fire after the earthquake caused more damage than the earthquake.
Some people weren't afraid of the fire. They sat in the street and watched it.

Optional activity

1.27 Play the recording of the text for students to read and listen. Stop at any words that you predict will cause pronunciation problems, e.g. *population, damaged,* and ask students to repeat.

3 After Reading

- Students read and listen to the text again and decide if sentences 1–10 are true or false.
- Check the answers before students write corrections for the false sentences.
- Ask students to read their answers to the class.

Answers

1 *False. The earthquake was in 1906.*
2 *False. The fire started after the earthquake.*
3 *True.*
4 *False. He borrowed a new camera.*
5 *False. He took pictures of the fire.*
6 *True.*
7 *False. The fire burned for four days.*
8 *False. The fire destroyed 500 blocks.*
9 *True.*
10 *False. People think at least 3,000 people died.*

Your Response

- Tell students to work in pairs discussing which of their possessions they would most like to save from a fire. Students take notes about their partners' answers, and then report back to the rest of the class.

LANGUAGE WORKOUT OPTION

If you want to pre-teach the language students will be using in the following activities, you may like to go to the Language Workout box now.

4 Vocabulary

- Make this a competitive exercise. Students race to find the past tense of these verbs from the text in exercise 2.

Answers

(Irregular verbs are in bold)
*become—**became*** *borrow—borrowed*
*build—**built*** *caused—caused* *come—**came***
destroy—destroyed *die—died* *discover—discovered*
*go—**went*** *lose—**lost*** *report—reported* *sit—**sat***
*spread—**spread*** *stand—**stood*** *start—started*
*take—**took*** *walk—walked*

- Refer students to the list of Irregular Verbs on page 127. Tell students that there are more regular than irregular verbs in the English language, but there are about 100 frequently used irregular verbs and it's a good idea to learn them by heart.

Optional activities

♦ **Game** *Bingo* Students make their own bingo cards in their notebooks (a grid with three columns and three rows). Write 20 infinitives with an irregular past on the board and on small cards (see Optional aids). Students choose nine and write them in the boxes in their grid. Jumble the cards up in a hat or a box. Go around the class asking students to pick one out without looking and say the past tense aloud to the class. Students who have the infinitive cross it out on their bingo card. The first student to cross out all nine boxes shouts *Bingo!* and wins the game. You can repeat the game writing the past tense on the board and cards to check that students know the infinitive form.

♦ **Game** *Word tennis* See Unit 1, Lesson 1, Warm-up for details, but use the simple present and simple past of verbs.

5 Speaking

- Introduce this quiz by pointing to the pictures and eliciting the name of each item.
- Go around the class asking individual students to make simple past sentences using the verbs in parentheses.
- Read the speech bubbles to the class. Ask students to work in pairs and match the sentences with the pictures.
- Play the recording for students to listen and check.

1.28 Recording and answers

1 *In 1885, Karl Benz built the first car.*
2 *In 1860, Antonio Meucci made the first phone call.*
3 *In 1961, Yuri Gagarin was the first person to travel in space.*
4 *In 1928, Walt Disney made the first cartoon movie with sound.*
5 *In 1939, Igor Sikorsky designed the first helicopter.*
6 *In 1895, the Lumière brothers showed the first movies.*
7 *In 1938, László Biró invented the first ballpoint pen.*
8 *In 1826, Joseph Niepce took the first photograph.*
9 *In 1475, William Caxton printed the first book in English.*

- Ask students to write sentences like the example. Play the recording again for them to check.
- Check the answers by asking students to read out their sentences.

Optional activity

Give students two minutes to look at the dates and inventors. They then close their books. Ask quick-fire questions to test their memories, e.g. *Who built the first car?* This can be an individual or team game.

Useful information

Antonio Meucci developed the telephone and gave a public demonstration of his "teletrofono" in 1860. But he did not have enough money to patent it properly. In 1876, the Scot, Alexander Graham Bell, who shared a laboratory with Meucci, patented the telephone. Meucci took Bell to court, but died in 1899. 113 years later, in June 2002, the U.S. Congress recognized Meucci as the inventor of the telephone.

6 Listening

- Ask *What do you know about Walt Disney?* Students read the text and find out more about Disney.
- Ask them to predict what the incorrect information is. Suggest that they underline the mistakes as they listen. Tell them not to worry about correcting the mistakes on the first listening.
- Play the recording. Students listen to check details and underline the mistakes. They compare their answers in pairs before you play the recording again.

1.29 Recording and answers

*Walt Disney was born in **Chicago** in 1901 and he went to art school there. He started Walt Disney Studios with his **brother** on October 16, 1923. He married Lillian Bounds in **1925**, and it was she who thought of the name Mickey Mouse. Disneyland, one of the world's first theme parks, opened in California on July **17**, 1955. Disney planned another park in Florida, but he died on **December** 15, 1966 before it opened.*

- Play the recording again for students to correct the mistakes.
- Read the example with a confident student. Check the answers by asking a student to read a sentence containing a mistake to another student in the class. The second student responds with the correct answer.

Extension In pairs, students look back at the *San Francisco Earthquake* in exercise 2. One student makes a false statement about the events, for example *The earthquake happened during the day.* Their partner listens and responds with the correct answer: *No, it didn't! It happened at 5:00 a.m. in the morning.* In their pairs, students take turns making false statements and correcting them.

7 Pronunciation

- Focus on the three pronunciations of the *-ed* ending. Explain that *-ed* is pronounced /t/ after unvoiced sounds, e.g. *walked*, /d/ after voiced sounds, e.g. *designed*, and /ɪd/ for some consonant sounds, e.g. *invented*.
- Emphasize that the difference between /d/ and /t/ sounds is minimal and that students can hear it better if they link the verb to a word that begins with a vowel sound, e.g. *walked≈around*, *designed≈an*.
- Play the first part of the recording, pausing for students to write the verbs in the correct column.

1.30 Recording

designed destroyed invented laughed reported
showed started walked watched

- Play the second part of the recording for students to check their answers.
- Drill the words chorally and individually.

1.30 Recording and answers

/d/ *designed destroyed showed*
/t/ *laughed walked watched*
/ɪd/ *invented reported started*

Optional activity

Read out the verbs from exercise 7. Students raise their left hand if it is a verb with a /t/ ending, their right hand if it is a verb with a /d/ ending, and put a hand on their head if it has an /ɪd/ ending. Count to three before students raise their hands to stop them from copying each other.

8 Writing

- Students imagine they were in San Francisco at the time of the earthquake. Help them visualize this by pointing at the picture on page 36 and asking: *Where are you? Who are you with? What can you see/smell/hear?*
- Students refer to the questions in their books and the text in exercise 2 to help them write a diary entry.
- Students exchange texts and check each other's work for grammar, spelling, and punctuation.

Extension Students think about last weekend, and write some true and false answers to the questions in exercise 8. Students then read out their sentences to another student. Their partner has to guess which sentences are true and which are false.

LANGUAGE WORKOUT

- Ask students to look at the Language Workout box. Explain that the simple past refers to completed actions in the past. Ask students to complete the sentences.
- Students turn to page 115 of the Language File to check their answers.

Answers

were wasn't weren't
started damaged carried
didn't

- Highlight that:
  - *for I, he, she, it* we use *was*; for *we, you* (singular and plural), *they* we use *were*. Point out that the verb *to be* is easier in the past than in the present as there are only two forms, not three!
  - regular simple past verbs end in *-ed* and forms are the same for all persons. Refer students to the Language File for spelling rules, i.e. most verbs add *-ed*, but verbs that end in *-e* add *-d*, and verbs that end in *-y* drop the *-y* and add *-ied*.
  - the change from present to past in the negative form is simple: students change one word (*don't/doesn't* to *didn't*).
- Drill the examples in chorus for pronunciation and stress.

Follow-up activity

Students read *The San Francisco Earthquake* again and find words for different buildings and places. They design a word map, writing *Buildings and Places* in the center of the map, and decide on different categories, e.g. *public places, stores*, etc. They add as many extra words as they can to the existing categories.

Homework

Students write a short biography of a famous dead person. They can find out information from an encyclopedia or the Internet.

Students write a newspaper article describing the San Francisco earthquake. They think of a name for their newspaper and a headline for their article.

NOTEBOOK SECTION

Complete the sentences using the simple past form of the word in parentheses.

1 He ____ his girlfriend from school. (marry)
2 Most people ____ asleep. (be)
3 I ____ what happened. (not know)
4 She ____ very angry. (become)
5 They ____ up and ____ away. (stand, walk)

Answers

1 married 2 were 3 didn't know 4 became 5 stood, walked

Consolidation and Extension p45
Language File p115

Workbook Unit 3 Lesson 1 pp28–29
Photocopiable notes p155, worksheet p168

2 Did you have fun?

Communicative Aims	**Language**	**Pronunciation**	**Vocabulary**	**Optional aids**
Talking about past events (2)	Simple past: questions and short answers Adverbial phrases of time	Syllable stress	Famous landmarks Daily activities Adjectives	Warm-up 1: 10–15 small objects and a small cloth

WARM-UP 1

Game *Kim's game* Place 10–15 small objects on your table, e.g. a wallet, a book. Hold up the objects one by one and ask students to tell you the names, e.g. *There is a pen.* Give students one minute to memorize all the objects. Ask students to close their eyes. Remove some of the objects or cover them with a cloth. In pairs, students have two minutes to write down all the missing or hidden objects using *There was/There were*. Ask students to tell you what is missing or covered.

WARM-UP 2

Students think of as many everyday activities as they can, e.g. *go shopping, go to the gym*. Write them on the board and ask students to change the present to past tense, e.g. *go—went*. Use one of the activities to drill the question *When was the last time you (went shopping)?*, etc. In pairs, students ask and answer the question. They change partners and tell their new partner what their first partner did and when.

1 Opener

- The aim is to arouse students' interest in San Francisco.
- Students look at the photos on pages 38–39. Ask *Who can you see? Where are they in San Francisco? What do you know about these places in the city?*
- Students read *San Francisco Facts* and match the attractions with the photos.

Answers

cable car—B
Grace Cathedral—C
Chinatown—D
California Academy of Sciences—A

- Check comprehension of new vocabulary, e.g. *spectacular, steep, communities, exhibits, multimedia*. Ask general questions to check overall comprehension of the text, e.g. *How many cable car lines are there? When did work start on the cathedral?*

Optional activity

In pairs, students read out the text, changing the dates and numbers, e.g. *The cathedral was completed in 1910 (not 1964).* Their partner listens and reads, calling out *Stop!* and giving the correct answer every time they hear a wrong number or date.

2 Reading

- Explain that the group is talking about where they went in San Francisco that morning.
- Ask students to read the conversation and to complete it by writing the correct place for each number.
- Play the recording so students can check their answers. Then check the answers with the whole class. Explain that *Hi, guys* is an informal greeting to a group of people.

1.31 Recording and answers

ALEX *Hi, guys. Did you have fun this morning?*
SILVANA *Yes, we did. It was awesome! First we went to the California Academy of Sciences.*
JAY *And we saw a great exhibit about the earthquake.*
SILVANA *Then we took a bus downtown and went up Nob Hill to Grace Cathedral. We spent an hour there.*
ALEX *Did you climb up Nob Hill?*
SILVANA *No, we didn't. We took a cable car. And then we went to Chinatown and visited a spectacular temple.*
JAY *Emma didn't. She was really lazy!*
EMMA *I wasn't lazy—I was thirsty! I sat outside and had a long cold drink! And the others were exhausted when they came out.*
SILVANA *Well, we walked a lot! My feet hurt!*
EMMA *And what happened to you, Alex? Were you asleep all morning?*
ALEX *No, I wasn't!*

Optional activity

1.31 Play the recording again, pausing after each line for students to repeat. Monitor pronunciation.

3 After Reading and Listening

- Students read the dialogue again. They answer the questions in their notebooks, giving more information in their answers if necessary.
- Ask individual students to read their answers to the class.

Answers

1 *They went to the California Academy of Sciences.*
2 *No, they didn't. They saw an exhibit.*
3 *They took a bus.*
4 *They spent an hour on Nob Hill.*
5 *No, she didn't.*
6 *No, she wasn't. She was thirsty.*
7 *Yes, they were (exhausted).*
8 *No, he wasn't.*

Optional activity

Ask early finishers to find eight adjectives and eight irregular past verbs in the dialogue.

Your Response

Tell students to work in groups discussing which of the places from page 38 they would most like to visit and why, and which they think is the least interesting and why. Ask a confident student from each group to take notes, and then report back to the rest of the class.

4 Pronunciation

- Check students know the meaning of the words in the box. Ask them to give definitions, in English if possible.
- In pairs, students read the words to each other and count the number of syllables in each word.
- Play the recording once, pausing after each word for students to repeat. Ask individual students to tell you the number of syllables in each word. Before listening again, ask students to work in pairs and mark the stress.
- Play the recording again. Check the answers.
- Drill the words chorally and individually for pronunciation and stress.

1.32 Recording and answers

academy 4   cathedral 3   community 4
earthquake 2   exhausted 3   exhibit 3
restaurant 3   spectacular 4   temple 2   theater 3

LANGUAGE WORKOUT OPTION

If you want to pre-teach the language students will be using in the following activities, you may like to go to the Language Workout box now.

5 Listening

- Books closed. Explain to students that they are going to hear Alex talking about what he did this morning. Ask students to note down all the different activities they hear. Play the recording. Students check their answers by looking at the actions in exercise 5.

1.33 Recording

SILVANA *And what about you, Alex? What did you do this morning?*
ALEX *OK, first I surfed the Net—that was from nine to ten o'clock. They have really good computers in the hotel. Then at ten I went to a music store for an hour.*
SILVANA *Did you buy anything?*
ALEX *No, everything I liked was too expensive. Then I was really hot and tired, so at about eleven o'clock I had ice cream in a coffee shop.*
SILVANA *And then?*
ALEX *And then I came to the park and sat in the sunshine and waited for you!*
EMMA *Now that's what I call really lazy!*

- Play the recording again for students to listen and match the actions with the times.
- Check the answers, making sure that students know the past tense of all the verbs and pronounce the times correctly.

Answers

9:00—10:00 He surfed the Internet.
10:00—11:00 He went to a music store.
11:00—12:00 He had ice cream in a coffee shop.
12:00—1:15 He sat in the park.

- Ask two students to read the example question and answer aloud, making sure they complete the answer. Students then continue asking and answering in pairs.

Optional activity

Game *Ten guesses* Tell students you went somewhere yesterday. They try and discover where you went by asking a maximum of 10 questions. Students call out their guess *Did you go to the bank yesterday?* Wait for a full question before answering *Yes, I did.* or *No, I didn't.*

Extension The aim is to encourage learners to take responsibility for their learning by testing each other. Divide the class into pairs or teams and ask them to take turns to test each other on ten simple past forms. Give them time to first choose ten verbs each. One student in each pair or team reads out the verbs, pausing after each one to give their partner or team time to say the correct simple past form. After they have read out their ten verbs, their partner or another student has a turn. If necessary, demonstrate the game with a confident student. The winner is the person or team who gets ten words right in the fastest time.

6 Speaking

- Ask students to think about their last weekend. Give them three minutes to write six weekend activities using the past tense.
- In pairs, students exchange lists. Ask them to look at the example dialogue and at the adverbial phrases of time in the Language Workout box at the bottom of page 39.
- Choose a pair to read out the examples.
- Pairs ask each other up to 20 questions about last weekend to find out exactly *when* their partner did the things in the list. They write down their partner's answers in their notebooks.
- Elicit feedback. Ask *Did any of you do the same things at the same time?*
- Students write a summary of their partner's last weekend. They exchange texts and check for spelling, grammar, and punctuation.

7 Writing

- Ask students to write their diaries for last Saturday and Sunday. Tell them to pay particular attention to simple past forms and adverbial phrases of time. Encourage them to continue writing diary entries in English.

Extension Students read the text on page 38 (*San Francisco Facts*) again. They think of three or four places in their own town, and find out information about them. They then write one or two sentences about each place.

LANGUAGE WORKOUT

- Ask students to look at the first half of the Language Workout box. Remind them of the word order in questions and the use of the auxiliary in short answers.
- Ask students to complete the sentences in the box. Confident students can complete first and then check, while others can look back at exercises 2 and 3 and then complete.
- Students turn to page 115 of the Language File to check their answers.

  Answers
  did Did didn't Was were irregular
- Drill the examples chorally and individually for pronunciation and stress.
- Look at the second half of the Language Workout box to see some time phrases.

Practice

- Students do Practice exercise 8 on page 115 of the Language File. Students complete the questions on their own. Check the answers by asking individual students to read out their questions.
- Students read *San Francisco Facts* and the dialogue again to find the answers.
- As a class or in pairs, students take turns to ask and answer the questions.

Answers

1	*did … go*	*They went to the California Academy of Sciences.*
2	*did … see*	*They saw an exhibit.*
3	*was*	*In 1964.*
4	*did … start*	*In 1910.*
5	*Did … spend*	*Yes, they did.*
6	*Did … climb*	*No, they didn't. They took a cable car.*
7	*Was*	*Yes, she was.*
8	*Did … have*	*No, she didn't. She had a cold drink.*
9	*Were*	*Yes, they were.*
10	*Did … visit*	*No, he didn't.*

Follow-up activities

- ♦ Students update their *Building and Places* word map (see Unit 3, Lesson 1) with all the new places from this lesson.
- ♦ Students see how many words they can make from SPECTACULAR. Students may only use the letters "a" and "c" twice. The student with the most words wins.

Homework

Students write their schedule for today.

Ask students to learn irregular verbs from the list on page 127 at the back of their books. You may like to give students short, regular tests on these irregular verbs.

NOTEBOOK SECTION

There is an error in each sentence. Rewrite the sentences correctly.

1 When they went to the beach?
2 They left on the morning.
3 Jack go home?
4 Was they tired after the game?
5 Did you saw her?

Answers

1 When did they go to the beach? 2 They left in the morning. 3 Did Jack go home? 4 Were they tired after the game? 5 Did you see her?

Consolidation and Extension p45

Language File pp115–116

Workbook Unit 3 Lesson 2 pp30–31

Photocopiable notes p155, worksheet p169

3 It was coming straight toward him

Communicative Aims	Language	Pronunciation	Vocabulary	Optional aids
Describing what was happening Asking for and giving reasons	Past progressive *Why? because …* (reason)	/w/ why	Meteorites Transportation	Follow-up activity: long slips of paper

WARM-UP 1

Review irregular verbs. Say the infinitive of the verb, and students write the past form. Check and ask students for an example sentence.

WARM-UP 2

Students brainstorm as many places and past time expressions as they can. Write these in two columns on the board. Students then use the places and expressions to ask each other questions, e.g. *Were you in the park yesterday?*

Useful information

Meteorites are objects from outer space that land on Earth. Most meteorites break up when they enter the Earth's atmosphere, but about 500 reach the Earth's surface every year, some as small as a marble and others as large, or bigger than, a basketball. As they fall, meteorites often make loud noises and give out strange lights.

1 Opener

- The aim is to encourage students to predict before reading a text.
- Set the scene for the reading by asking students to look at the headline and photos at the top of page 40.
- Ask students *What is a meteorite?* Explain that it is a piece of rock that falls from space and lands on the ground. Check comprehension of the words in the box. Ask students to write down the words they expect to find in the newspaper article.
- Then let them compare their answers in pairs, explaining to their partner why they think they will find each word in the article.

2 Reading

- Ask students to read the article and check their answers to exercise 1. Then check the answers with the class.

Answers

atmosphere ball crash escape ground hit hole magnetic rock roof water

Optional activities

- ♦ 1.34 Play the recording of the article for students to read and listen. Stop at any words that you predict will cause pronunciation problems, e.g. *meteorite, thunder,* and ask students to repeat.
- ♦ Ask students to write a sentence for each of the words that they found in the newspaper article, e.g. *The girl threw the* ***ball****.*

3 After Reading

- Students read the questions and find the answers in the article.
- Ask students if they can explain the term "the chance is about 1 in 100 million." Explain that if the chance of a meteorite hitting someone is 1 in 100 million, it means that for every 100 million meteorites, only one usually hits someone.
- Ask individual students to read out their answers.

Answers

1 *Gerrit/He was walking to the school bus.*
2 *Gerrit/He saw a ball of light.*
3 *Gerrit/He felt a pain in his hand, and heard an enormous bang.*
4 *No, it was small. We can see it in the photo, and the article talks about the "tiny" piece of rock.*
5 *The meteorite/It was traveling at about 500 kilometers per hour when it hit Gerrit.*
6 *No, it is extremely rare for meteorites to hit people.*
7 *No, it didn't.*
8 *No, she was asleep.*

Your Response

- In pairs, ask students to discuss whether they believe Gerrit's story, and to give their reasons. Ask them to feed back their partners' answers to the rest of the class.
- Hold a class vote to see whether most students in the class believe Gerrit's story or not.

LANGUAGE WORKOUT OPTION

If you want to pre-teach the language students will be using in the following activities, you may like to go to the Language Workout box now.

4 Speaking

- Ask students to work in pairs, taking turns to ask questions 1–5 and to give the correct answer from a–e.
- Then check by asking pairs of students to read out the questions and answers.

Answers

1 e   2 d   3 a   4 b   5 c

- Go through the example sentence with the class and complete it. If necessary, do number 2 together with the class as a second example.
- Students write the sentences in their notebooks.

Answers

1 *Gerrit's ears were ringing for hours because there was an enormous bang when the meteorite hit the ground.*
2 *The meteorite made a hole in the ground because it was falling so fast.*
3 *Most meteorites are magnetic because they contain iron.*
4 *Most meteorites don't reach the Earth because they burn up in the atmosphere.*
5 *Most meteorites land in water because water covers more than two-thirds of the Earth.*

5 Listening

- The aim is to understand a short anecdote and to listen for detail. Tell the students they are going to hear Emma talking about an accident that happened to her brother. Before they listen, ask them to read sentences 1–9. Elicit the meaning of new vocabulary, e.g. *overboard, sail, coast, storm, emergency.* Point out that the past progressive is often used when telling a story.
- Play the recording. Students listen and decide if sentences 1–9 are true or false. Ask them to note down the false information as they listen.

1.35 Recording

EMMA *You know, my brother Ryan fell overboard last year.*
JAY *Really? What happened? What was he doing?*
EMMA *He was sailing with a friend off the coast of Africa. At first, it was a beautiful day and the sun was shining. But then the weather suddenly got worse and there was a terrible storm. They were sailing in a small boat and they knew it was very dangerous.*
JAY *Yeah, sure.*
EMMA *So, Ryan called the emergency number on his cell phone. They were sailing back when the boat hit a rock and they both fell into the ocean!*
JAY *Oh, no!*
EMMA *And then the boat started to sink!*
JAY *What happened?*
EMMA *A helicopter rescued them.*
JAY *Were they both OK?*
EMMA *Yes, they were. It was a lucky escape. But my brother wasn't happy because he lost his cell phone!*

- Check true or false answers. Students listen again and write corrections for the false sentences.
- Students check their answers in pairs. If necessary, play the recording again for students to check.

Answers

1 *False. He fell overboard last year.*
2 *True.*
3 *True.*
4 *False. The weather got worse.*
5 *False. They were sailing in a small boat.*
6 *True.*
7 *False. They were sailing back when the boat hit a rock.*
8 *False. A helicopter rescued them.*
9 *False. He lost his cell phone.*

- Students write a paragraph about Ryan's lucky escape based on the three true and six corrected sentences.

Optional activity

Confident students can write the story with their books closed. Remind them to use both the simple past and the past progressive.

6 Pronunciation

- Demonstrate the /w/ sound and point out that both *w* and *wh* are pronounced /w/ in English.
- Play the recording and ask students to repeat the tongue-twister. Then students practice the tongue-twister in pairs, and say it as fast as they can.

1.36 Recording

/w/ Why was the white whale whistling when it was swimming in the wonderful warm water?

Optional activity

Students make up and practice more tongue-twisters using the /w/ sound.

7 Vocabulary

- The aim is to help students organize vocabulary. Ask students to look at the Word Bank and at the word map. Check they know the meaning of the words.
- Students categorize the words according to *air/water/land transportation*. They copy the word map into their notebooks and add words from the Word Bank. Point out that students can add their own words too.

Answers

Air: *helicopter, plane, rocket, spaceship*
Water: *boat, ship, speedboat*
Land: *bicycle, bus, car, taxi, train*

Extension The aim is to encourage learners to take responsibility for their learning by testing each other. Ask students to read the example speech bubbles first. Point out that they are a chain of word associations and each new word relates to the previous word. Let students read out the example chain in pairs, taking turns. Suggest another word to start a chain, *e.g. train*. Students work in pairs to continue the chain.

8 Writing

- Read out the instructions and the example. Give students time to think about their own lucky escape. Point out that it can be real or imagined.
- Highlight that the four questions in the instructions provide a structure for students to use in their writing. Students write a short paragraph using the simple past and the past progressive.
- Students exchange texts and check for spelling, grammar, and punctuation before you collect their work.

Extension Ask students to remember a time when they heard some dramatic news, e.g. about something that happened in the world, or in their family. Ask them to think about what they were doing and how they felt. Tell students to write another short paragraph, again using the simple past and past progressive. Students read their texts to each other in pairs, and answer their partner's questions about what happened.

LANGUAGE WORKOUT

- Ask students to look at the top half of the Language Workout box. Explain that we use the past progressive to describe what was happening at a particular time in the past. Draw a time line on the board.

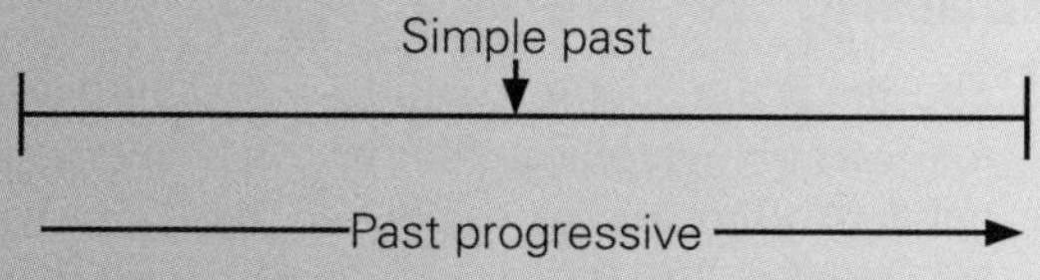

- Ask students to complete the sentences in the box.
- Students turn to page 116 of the Language File to check their answers.

Answers
was were wasn't was Was

- Tell students that *was* and *were* are usually stressed at the start of a question (*Was* /wɒz/ *he feeling all right?*) but not elsewhere in a question (*What were* /wɜr/ *you doing?*) or in statements (*She was* /wəz/ *taking pictures.*).
- Drill the examples chorally and individually.
- Look at the bottom half of the Language Workout box to see how *why* and *because* are often used together.

Practice

- Students do Practice exercise 9 on page 116 of the Language File. They look at the photos on pages 38–39 again and in pairs describe what was happening. Students complete the sentences on their own.
- Ask individual students to read out their sentences. Check students use the weak and strong forms of *was/were* correctly.

Answers
*1 wasn't riding 2 were smiling 3 weren't looking
4 Was … standing, was 5 Was … eating, wasn't
6 Was … having, were 7 Was … taking, wasn't
8 Was … raining, was shining*

Follow-up activity

Game *What were you doing?* Divide the class into four groups. Give each student two slips of paper. On one they write the first half of a sentence using the past progressive, e.g. *I was sleeping*, and on the other they write the second half of a sentence using *when* + simple past, e.g. *when the phone rang*. Students fold the slips in half and make two piles (beginnings and endings). Students shuffle each pile once. Each student in the group takes one slip from both piles and reads them to the group in the correct order. If the sentence makes sense, they keep the slips.

Homework

Students research information about a famous person who is no longer alive from their country, e.g. a writer, a musician, or an artist, for the next lesson.

NOTEBOOK SECTION

Complete the sentences using the past progressive form of the words in parentheses.

1 It ____ when I arrived. (rain)
2 He fell because he ____. (not look)
3 What ____ you ____ when he saw you? (do)
4 People ____ during the movie. (talk)
5 Why ____ they ____ at him? (laugh)

Answers *1 was raining 2 wasn't looking 3 were, doing 4 were talking 5 were, laughing*

Consolidation and Extension p45

Language File p116

Workbook Unit 3 Lesson 3 pp32–33

Photocopiable notes p156, worksheet p170

4 *Integrated Skills* Biography

Skills

Reading Topics and time reference: *William Shakespeare* biography
Listening Dates and numbers: biography of Charles Dickens
Speaking Exchanging information
Writing Short biography

Learner Independence

Word association
Word maps

Vocabulary

Time reference words
Theater
Jobs and occupations
Useful expressions

Optional aids

Warm-up 2: cards with names of famous people
Exercise 4 Optional activity: small cards for the Vocabulary box
Exercise 9 Optional activities: small pieces of paper with jobs written on them

WARM-UP 1

Review transportation vocabulary from the previous lesson. Give definitions of different types of transportation for students to guess. They write the words down in their notebooks. Check their answers and their spelling.

WARM-UP 2

Game *Twenty questions* Write names of famous people on cards. Choose one of the cards. Students have twenty guesses to find out who you are by asking different questions, e.g. *Are you dead or alive? Are/Were you a man or a woman? Are/Were you married?* This game can be played in groups or in pairs.

WARM-UP 3

Play *Teacher* (see Unit 2, Lesson 1, Warm-up 1 on page 43) with a word from the Vocabulary box.

Useful information

Romeo and Juliet—a summary
Romeo Montague and Juliet Capulet lived in Verona in Italy, and when they met, it was love at first sight. But their families hated each other, so Romeo and Juliet got married in secret. Soon after, a close friend of Romeo's, Mercutio, had a fight in the street with Juliet's cousin Tybalt, and Tybalt killed Mercutio. Romeo was so upset that he killed Tybalt. Now Romeo's life was in danger, so he said goodbye to Juliet and left Verona. Meanwhile, Juliet's parents decided she should marry a man named Paris. Juliet went to ask a friar for help, and he suggested a plan. He gave her a drug to make her sleep for 42 hours so that people thought she was dead. When she woke up, she could join Romeo. Unfortunately, Romeo returned to Verona, found Juliet's body, and killed himself. When Juliet woke up and saw Romeo lying dead next to her, she killed herself with his knife.

1 Opener

- The aim is to pre-teach the vocabulary for the following exercises and to introduce the topic of William Shakespeare.
- Ask students *What do you know about William Shakespeare? Do you know the movie* Romeo and Juliet *with Leonardo DiCaprio and Claire Danes?* In pairs, students have a minute to write down as much information as they know about Shakespeare's life and work. Elicit feedback—which pair has the most information?
- Students read the words in the box, and decide which are most likely to be in the text. Elicit the meaning of *playwright* (point out the spelling—*wright* is from an Old English word meaning *work*, so a playwright is someone who writes or "makes" plays) and *tragedies* (a *tragedy* is a play which usually involves a death and is the opposite of *comedy*).
- Ask students to scan the text about Shakespeare to confirm their guesses.

Answers
actor performance play playwright tragedies

2 Reading

- The aim is to read for main ideas to identify topics and to present biographical information. Check students understand the topic titles before they start the exercise. Explain that they do not need to understand every word of the text at this stage.
- Give students two minutes to read the text and match four of the topics with the paragraphs. Students compare their answers in pairs before checking as a class.
- Elicit the key words in the paragraphs and titles that helped students make their decisions.

Answers
1 The first years 2 Early career 3 Fame and fortune 4 Later life

3

- The aim is to review time reference words and to develop awareness of text cohesion. Check students know how to use the words in the box by asking for example sentences.
- Students read the text in more detail and complete it with the words in the box. Students compare their answers in pairs.
- Play the recording for students to listen and check their answers. Ask students which of the words have capital letters because they start a new sentence. (*By, Between, Finally, After*).

1.37 Recording and answers
William Shakespeare
William Shakespeare was born (1) ***in*** *April, 1564 in Stratford-upon-Avon, in the middle of England. He went to school in Stratford, and he probably became a teacher. In 1582,* (2) ***when*** *he was 18, he married Anne Hathaway, and they soon had three children.*
In the late 1580s, he decided to leave Stratford and try to find work in London. (3) ***By*** *this time, there were several theaters in the city—the first public theater opened in London in 1567. Shakespeare joined an acting company, and soon he was also writing plays. He quickly became a well-known actor and playwright.*
(4) ***Between*** *1589 and 1600, Shakespeare wrote about 20 plays, including* A Midsummer Night's Dream *and* Romeo and Juliet. *His plays were extremely popular and there were even special performances for Queen Elizabeth I! Shakespeare* (5) ***soon*** *became the most important playwright in the country. He was now a rich man, and was a part-owner of the Globe Theater, which opened in 1599. He lived and worked in London* (6) ***for*** *many years, but he often went home to see his wife and children in Stratford.*
Shakespeare's success continued into the (7) ***next*** *century, when he wrote some of his most famous tragedies, including* Hamlet *and* Othello. *In all, he wrote 37 plays, and he also wrote many beautiful poems.* (8) ***Finally,*** *he returned to Stratford in 1611, and he lived there* (9) ***until*** *he died, aged exactly 52,* (10) ***on*** *April 23, 1616. In his will, he left his wife his second-best bed!* (11)***After*** *his death, two actor friends collected all his plays and published them in 1623. Today, 400 years* (12) ***later****, he is one of the most famous writers in the world, and there are many movies of his plays.*

4

- The aim is to read for specific information and detail and to review biographical information. Set a short time limit. Students could work in pairs to find the answers and write full sentences in their notebooks.
- Check the answers by asking one student to ask a question and choose another student to answer it.

Answers
1 *He was born in April, 1564 in Stratford-upon-Avon, England.*
2 *He got married in 1582 to Anne Hathaway.*
3 *They had three children.*
4 *He started writing plays some time in the late 1580s.*
5 *He wrote 37 plays.*
6 *He also wrote beautiful poems.*
7 *He died on April 23, 1616.*
8 *He is important today because he is one of the world's most famous writers.*

Optional activities
- ♦ Students make a list of sequencing words and prepositions of time in their notebooks. They illustrate the meaning of each word with an example sentence.
- ♦ Students choose five words from the text to add to the class Vocabulary box.

5 Listening

- Students close their books. Ask them to name famous writers from their country. Ask *What do you know about …? What did he/she write? When was he/she born?*, etc. Tell them they are going to listen to a text about a famous British author. Play the recording for students to listen and then tell you who the author is.

1.38 Recording
Charles Dickens
Charles Dickens was born on February 7, 1812 in Portsmouth, on the south coast of England. In 1823, the Dickens family moved to London, but his father lost his job and the family had no money. Charles left school in 1824, and when he was only twelve years old, he started working in a factory!
But things became easier. In 1833, Dickens started writing stories for newspapers, and in 1836 he wrote his first novel, The Pickwick Papers. *In the same year, he married Catherine Hogarth and they later had ten children.*
In 1842, Dickens visited the United States for the first time, and wrote a book about his visit called American Notes. *In the book, he criticized slavery in the U.S.*
Between 1836 and 1865, Dickens wrote fourteen major novels, including Oliver Twist *and* David Copperfield. *His novels were extremely successful and he became the most popular writer in the country. He also wrote lots of stories, including the ghost story* A Christmas Carol.
Dickens worked extremely hard at everything he did. He died suddenly on June 9, 1870 at the age of fifty-eight, after a tour of the U.S. He was the most popular English writer of the nineteenth century. Today, over a hundred forty years later, his books are still bestsellers and there are many movies of his novels.

- Give students time to familiarize themselves with the chart. Make sure they understand that they are listening for dates and numbers.
- Play the recording again. Students listen and note the answers. They check their answers in pairs.
- Play the recording again, pausing to check the answers to each question.

Answers

February 7, ***1812***	*Born in Portsmouth …*
1823	*Family moved to London.*
1824	*Left school, started working …*
1836	*First novel:* The Pickwick Papers.
1836	*Married Catherine Hogarth, had* ***10*** *children.*
1842	*Visited the U.S. …*
1836–65	*Wrote* ***14*** *major novels …*
June 9, ***1870***	*Died … Most popular English writer of* ***19****th century.*
Over ***140*** *years later*	*His books …*

Optional activities

♦ In pairs, one student covers the chart and the other asks him/her questions about Charles Dickens, focusing on the dates and numbers, e.g. *When was he born?*

♦ With a confident class, ask further comprehension questions about the listening text, e.g. *At what age did he start working in a factory? How did he die?* Lead a class discussion about the differences between life in those times and now.

6 Speaking

- The aim is to exchange information about biographical details using the simple past. Ask students to look at the questions in exercise 4 and make any necessary changes to make them relevant to Dickens, e.g. change *plays* to *novels*.
- Read the example question and answer with a confident student. Students continue asking and answering questions in pairs.

Answers

1 When and where was he born?
He was born on February 7, 1812 in Portsmouth, England.
2 When did he get married? Who did he marry?
He got married in 1836 to Catherine Hogarth.
3 How many children did they have?
They had ten children.
4 When did he start writing novels?
He started writing novels in 1836.
5 How many novels did he write? He wrote 14 novels.
6 When did he die? He died on June 9, 1870.
7 Why is he important today?
He is important today because his books are still bestsellers and many movies have been made of them.

Optional activity

With less confident students, divide the class into Student As and Bs. They prepare questions for each other from the chart. Student As prepare questions from 1812–33 and Student Bs from 1836–now.

7 Writing

- The aim is to write a short biography using a model for guidance. In pairs, students choose a famous person and note down as much information as they can. If you set the homework suggested in the last lesson, students use their research information for their notes. They could also find information in an encyclopedia or from the Internet.
- Students write four paragraphs based on their notes, using the topics from exercise 2 and time reference words from exercise 3. Tell them to refer back to the biography on page 42 for help with text structure.
- Students exchange texts and check grammar, spelling, and capital letters.
- Students read their corrected texts to the class without saying the famous person's name. Other students listen and try to guess who he/she is.

Optional activity

With a less confident class, brainstorm the names of three or four famous people that students know something about and write them on the board. Individually, they choose one famous person and make notes. Set a short time limit. Elicit as much information as possible from students about each famous person and write it on the board before asking students to write four paragraphs.

8 Learner Independence

- The aim is to review different ways of learning new words. Write three or four words from the lesson on the board, e.g. *theater, novel, bestseller*. Do students remember the meanings of these words? Ask *How do you remember a word?*
- Go through the different techniques of word association listed and discuss how different techniques may be more appropriate for different words.
- Students choose some words they wish to learn from Unit 3 and write them in their notebooks with an associated word/sound/color/picture.
- Check by eliciting examples from students.

Optional activity

Write twenty words on the board. Give students 30 seconds to memorize the words. Give them a minute to write down as many as they can. Which words did students remember and why? Did they use any of the techniques discussed to help them?

9

- The aim is to show that grouping words according to topic in word maps can aid memory. Students copy the word map, and then work in pairs to add as many jobs and occupations as they can. Set a short time limit.
- Elicit different words from their word maps and write them on the board.

Optional activities

- ♦ Students number the jobs on their maps from *best* to *worst paid* and *most boring* to *most interesting*. Elicit their suggestions and try to develop a class discussion.
- ♦ **Game** *Twenty questions* Give out small pieces of card with different jobs written on them (see Optional aids). In small groups, students try to guess each other's job by asking no more than 20 questions. See Warm-up 2 from this lesson for more details.

10 Phrasebook

- Ask students to find the expressions in Unit 3.
- Play the recording. Pause after each expression for students to listen and repeat.

1.39 Recording and answers

Did you have fun? (Alex, lesson 2, ex2)
It was awesome! (Silvana, lesson 2, ex2)
What happened to you? (Emma, lesson 2, ex2)
There was an enormous bang! (article, lesson 3, ex2)
It's extremely rare. (article, lesson 3, ex2)
As far as we know, … (article, lesson 3, ex2)
She wasn't feeling well. (article, lesson 3, ex2)

- Ask individual students to identify and read out the two exclamations. Write them on the board. Students work in pairs and think of new situations where they could use them. Go through the example first.
- Ask pairs to share their ideas with the class and write all appropriate ideas under the exclamations on the board.

Suggested answers

It was awesome! *Talking about a movie/book/play/concert.*
There was an enormous bang! *Talking about a fireworks display/an accident.*

Follow-up activities

- ♦ Students draw two columns titled *Shakespeare* and *Dickens* in their notebooks. Dictate some of the facts, numbers, and dates from the text on page 42 and the chart on page 43 for students to write in the columns. Divide students into small groups and give them three minutes to look back through the lesson and find what each fact, date, or number refers to. Check the answers by asking each group in turn to give their answers. They get one point for a correctly pronounced answer and another point for a correct fact.
- ♦ Write some life events on the board in a random order, e.g. *be born, go to college, get married, die, go to school, have children, start work*. Elicit other typical life events. In pairs, students number the events in the order they think they should happen. Elicit feedback, recording variations on the board. Discuss the differences, encouraging students to use sequencing words where possible.

Homework

Students use the methods suggested in the Learner Independence exercises to learn new vocabulary from the previous lessons.

Students interview a family member and make notes about significant events in his/her life. They then write a short biography, describing events in as much detail as they can.

NOTEBOOK SECTION

Complete the questions using *was* or *did*. Complete the answers using *in*, *on*, or *at*.

1 When ____ Shakespeare born? ____ 1564.
2 When ____ your birthday? ____ Friday.
3 When ____ school start? ____ September.
4 When ____ he call? Late ____ night.
5 What time ____ the sun rise? ____ 6:00 a.m.

Answers

1 was, In
2 was, On
3 did, In
4 did, at
5 did, At

Consolidation and Extension p45

Workbook Unit 3 Lesson 4 pp34–35

Inspired EXTRA!

Optional aids

Game: two different-colored board pens or pieces of chalk

LANGUAGE LINKS

- Ask students to read out the dates and numbers and check that they are saying them correctly.
- Give students two minutes to read the two articles and make notes about what the dates and numbers refer to.
- Check answers with the whole class.

Answers

1604—When the first dictionary appeared
250 million—The number of English-speakers in the U.S. today
1620s—When people emigrated to North America
1475—When William Caxton printed the first book in English
6 million—The number of people who spoke English in Shakespeare's time

- Ask students to discuss the question in pairs and then take a class vote to see which answer everyone thinks is correct. It is C—there are at least one million words in English. No one knows exactly how many words there are because the number keeps increasing.

Game Link-up

- The aim of the game is to recycle vocabulary from Unit 3. Draw the grid in the Student's Book on the board.
- Go through the instructions with the class. Show how teams could link, e.g. C to A, B, or H and point out that they can zigzag. Emphasize that teams should try to block each other.
- Divide the class into two teams and play the game. Each time a team wins a square, circle the letter (in a different color for each team) on the grid. You can use these questions:
  What A is a person who designs buildings? (architect)
  What B is a method of transportation with two wheels? (bicycle)
  What C is a large and important church? (cathedral)
  What D is a book where you write what happens to you every day? (diary)
  What E is a dangerous situation, like a fire or an accident? (emergency)
  What F is what you see when there is a fire? (flames)
  What H is a flying machine? (helicopter)
  What K is a measurement of distance? (kilometer)
  What M is a rock from space? (meteorite)
  What N is loud? (noisy)
  What P is a person who writes plays? (playwright)
  What Q is sometimes a king's wife? (queen)
  What R covers a building? (roof)
  What S travels very fast in water? (speedboat)
  What T is a play with an unhappy ending? (tragedy)
  What W do you find in rivers, lakes, and oceans? (water)

Skit Shakespeare

- The aim is for students to enjoy using their English while also getting valuable stress and intonation practice.
- Explain that the skit is about two tourists visiting the exhibit at the Globe Theater. Ask students to read the first line of the skit and elicit that the exhibit is about the theater in Shakespeare's time.
- With a confident class, play the recording with books closed. Then again with books open. With a less confident class, play the recording once while the students follow in their books, and then again with books closed.

1.40 Recording

See text on page 44 of the Student's Book.

- Divide the class into two equal groups and play the recording again, with one group repeating in chorus as the Woman and the other group as the Man. Encourage students to exaggerate stress and intonation.
- Ask students to close their books and play the recording again. Then ask students to work in pairs and read the skit aloud. Choose several pairs to act out the skit in front of the class.

Optional activity

Make an audio or video recording of students performing the skit.

Consolidation

Lesson 1

Less confident students can find sentences from the lesson, but encourage them to create their own new sentences if possible.

Lesson 2

Suggested questions and answers

What did Silvana, Jay, and Emma do in the morning? They went to the California Academy of Sciences.
When did Silvana, Jay, and Emma go to the California Academy of Sciences? In the morning.
What exhibit did they see? An exhibit about the earthquake.
How did they get downtown? They took the bus.
What did they do on Nob Hill? They visited the cathedral.
How did they get up Nob Hill? They took a cable car.
What did they do after that? They visited a temple.
Who stayed outside? Emma.
What did she do? She had a drink of water.

Lesson 3
Students' own answers.

Lesson 4

Suggested answer

ME *When and where were you born?*
GHOST *I was born in April, 1564 in Stratford-upon-Avon.*
ME *When did you get married?*
GHOST *I got married in 1582.*
ME *Who did you marry?*
GHOST *Anne Hathaway.*
ME *How many children did you have?*
GHOST *We had three children.*
ME *When did you start writing plays?*
GHOST *In 1589.*
ME *How many plays did you write?*
GHOST *I wrote 37 plays.*
ME *What else did you write?*
GHOST *I also wrote lots of poems.*
ME *When did you die?*
GHOST *On Apri 23, 1616.*
ME *Why are you important today?*
GHOST *Because I'm one of the most famous writers in the world!*

Extension

Lesson 1
Students' own answers.

Lesson 2

Suggested answer

ME *Hi, Alex! Did you have fun this morning?*
ALEX *Yes, I did. It was awesome! First I surfed the Internet from nine to ten o'clock. Then I went to a music store. I spent an hour there.*
ME *Did you buy anything at the store?*
ALEX *No, I didn't. But at about eleven o'clock, I was really hot and tired, so I went to a coffee shop and I bought an ice cream.*
ME *And then what did you do?*
ALEX *I came to the park and sat and waited for you!*
ME *You were really lazy!*
ALEX *No, I wasn't!*

Language File pp115–116

Lesson 3

Suggested answers

Steve was telling everyone about San Francisco. He was wearing a raincoat and blue jeans. He was standing next to Lara.
Lara was listening to Steve and looking at a map. She was wearing a red top and blue jeans. She was standing next to Alex.
Alex was looking at his camera. He was wearing a red shirt and blue pants. He was standing next to Silvana.
Silvana was helping Alex with his camera. She was wearing a blue top and blue jeans. She was standing next to a girl in an orange top.
The girl in the orange top was watching the juggler. She was wearing an orange top and black pants.
The thin man was taking the girl's wallet. He was wearing a black shirt and black pants.
Ramón was talking to Emma. He was wearing a checked shirt and blue jeans. He was standing next to Emma.
Emma was talking to Ramón. She was wearing a green top and black pants. She was standing next to Jay.

Lesson 4
Students' own answers.

YOUR CHOICE!

The aim is to give students more learner independence and help them to identify their preferred ways of learning. Encourage students to choose an activity that they feel less comfortable with if they want a challenge or are aware that they need practice in a particular area.
Simply the Best! gives students the opportunity to practice speaking about a personal topic.
Survey: Transportation gives students the opportunity to practice speaking by interviewing other people.

Workbook Unit 3 Inspired EXTRA! pp36–37

3 CULTURE

Hello New York!

Optional aids

Mini-project: information and pictures of students' home town

1 Opener

- Ask students some general questions about New York City, e.g. *Is it in the east or west of the U.S.? (East) Is it by the ocean? (Yes) Is it the U.S. capital? (No, Washington, D.C. is.)*
- Ask students to take the quiz in pairs.

2 Reading

- Have students read the text to check their answers. Check the answers with the whole class. Are they surprised by any of the answers?

Answers
1 B 2 C 3 C 4 B

- Ask students to look at the photo on page 46, and explain that it is a view of New York looking west over the Hudson River to New Jersey. Ask *What's the name of the island in the center of New York?* (Manhattan) *What's the name of the tall skyscraper on the left?* (the Empire State Building)
- Students read and listen to the text *The First New Yorkers*. Ask quick comprehension questions: *What happened in …? (1524, 1609, 1624, 1626, 1664) What do these words mean? (cookie, nitwit, poppycock)*. With a confident class you may wish to do this with the books closed, or in pairs with one student asking the questions (written on the board) and the other answering.
- Ask students to read the first paragraph of the text again and number the events. Students compare their answers in pairs. Check as a whole class.

Answers
1 C 2 A 3 D 4 E 5 B

Useful information

New York City was the U.S. capital from 1785 to 1790.

Optional activity

Students make up true/false statements about the text. Put them into pairs to take turns deciding whether their partner's statements are true or false.

3 Vocabulary

- Students work on their own and match the words with the definitions. They compare their answers in pairs.

Answers
1 c 2 f 3 a 4 e 5 d 6 b

4

- Ask *What British music do you listen to? What British English words do you know?*
- Students work in pairs to match the lists of American and British words. Check the answers by asking one student to say the American English word and then choose another student to say the British English equivalent.

Answers

apartment—flat
parking lot—car park
railroad—railway
sneakers—trainers
store—shop
cell phone—mobile phone
drugstore—chemist's
French fries—chips
garbage, trash—rubbish
movie—film

5 Mini-project

- As a whole class, brainstorm information about the students' town's history, using the questions as prompts. Write their ideas on the board. It would be useful for you to be able to contribute some facts if necessary. Alternatively, students could find information in tourist guide books or on the Internet.
- Students work in pairs to write a short history of their town, using the first paragraph of *The First New Yorkers* and the questions to help them.
- Encourage students to illustrate their work with photos or other information from local newspapers, tourist information booklets, the Internet, or with drawings.
- Ask students to correct their work carefully and then to swap with other pairs.

NOTEBOOK SECTION

Circle the correct option in each sentence
1 The police *stopped/stoped* the traffic.
2 I was *takeing/taking* a photo.
3 I hope it's *sunnyer/sunnier* tomorrow.
4 She wasn't *listening/listenning*.
5 He *carried/carryed* my bags for me.

Answers *1 stopped 2 taking 3 sunnier 4 listening 5 carried*

Workbook Culture pp38–39

1 If we mix red and green ...

Communicative aims	**Language**	**Pronunciation**	**Vocabulary**	**Optional aids**
Talking about cause and effect	Open conditional with *if/when*	/əl/ animal	Feelings Digital cameras	Warm-up 2: a digital camera

WARM-UP 1

Game *Taboo* Divide the class into two groups. One student from each group comes to the front of the class and sits down with their back to the board. Write a place on the board, e.g. *Grace Cathedral*, and three "taboo" words, e.g. *church, San Francisco, building*. Groups define and describe the place to their team member at the front, but they cannot use the "taboo" words in their definitions. The first student to guess the place wins a point for their group.

WARM-UP 2

Use a digital camera to take pictures of the class. Pass the camera around so that students can see the pictures. Have a contest to choose the best caption for each picture. You could print some of the pictures to display with their captions.

1 Opener

- The aim is to introduce the context for the Reading dialogue. Give students two minutes to think about pictures they have taken recently. In small groups, students tell each other about the pictures. Anyone in the class who does not have a camera can write down the last time someone took a picture of them.

2 Reading

- Students read the text and write down one fact they learned from it. Make a list of the new facts students learned on the board.
- Elicit the meaning of unfamiliar vocabulary, e.g. *instant, computer chip, pixel, images, filter, process*.

Optional activity

1.41 Play the recording of the text for students to read and listen. Stop at any words you predict may cause pronunciation problems, e.g. *digital cameras, traditional, pixels, calculations,* and ask students to repeat.

LANGUAGE WORKOUT OPTION

If you want to pre-teach the language students will be using in the following activities, you may like to go to the Language Workout box now.

3 After Reading

- Ask students to look at the beginnings and endings. Then they work individually, re-reading the text and matching.
- Students check the answers in pairs. Then check the answers with the whole class.

Answers

1 d 2 f 3 b 4 c 5 a 6 e

Optional activity

Early finishers look back through the text for examples of the open conditional.

4 Vocabulary

- Ask students to find the words listed in the text. They then work on their own to match the words and definitions.
- Students check the answers in pairs.
- Check the answers with the whole class by asking one student to say a word and choose another student to give the matching definition.

Answers

1 instant 2 pixel 3 digital 4 primary colors
5 compare 6 make calculations

5 Pronunciation

- Play the recording once for students to listen. Then play it again for them to listen and repeat.
- Ask *Which word does not end in the sound* /əl/*?*

1.42 **Recording**

animal capital digital example hotel
impossible middle model noodle pixel
simple special travel whistle

Answer

Hotel /el/

6 Listening

- Students listen to the recording and decide if sentences 1–7 are true or false.
- Check the answers before students write corrections for the false sentences.
- Ask students to read their answers to the class.

1.43 Recording

CARRIE *Could I talk to you for a minute, Emma?*
EMMA *Sure, Carrie.*
CARRIE *Let's sit over there—it's a bit quieter. I'm worried about you, Emma—you don't look very happy. Tell me—is something the matter?*
EMMA *This sounds silly, I know, but it's about Jay and Ramón. I really like both of them. And they both want to see me again after the vacation. But I don't know what to say.*
CARRIE *I see. You mean that it's hard for you to show your feelings.*
EMMA *Yes, that's it. I don't always say what I feel. To tell the truth, I was rude to both of them. I didn't mean to be, but …*
CARRIE *If you like a boy, you're rude because you want to hide your feelings. Maybe you're nervous.*
EMMA *I'm not usually nervous when I meet people. Actually, I really like meeting new people. But I don't like it if people tell me what to do.*
CARRIE *So why don't you see both boys after the vacation?*
EMMA *Because they want me to choose one of them!*

Answers

1 True. 2 False. It's hard for Emma to show her feelings. 3 False. She's not usually nervous when she meets people. 4 True. 5 True. 6 True.

Extension In pairs, students discuss Emma and her problem. Encourage them to write a sentence summarizing their ideas that they can read to the rest of the class, e.g. *We think Emma is not being fair to Jay and Ramón, and we think she should decide which of them she wants to see.*

7 Writing

- Ask students to read the statements and answer any vocabulary queries.
- This activity works well when students are paired with someone they do not know too well.
- Students compare their completed statements. Then ask the class for examples of accurate statements—there is often a high percentage of inaccurate completions and lots of laughter.
- Students correct the statements that are wrong.

Extension Students work on their own and complete the statements for themselves. Make sure they understand that they should add five more of their own. With a less confident class, brainstorm a list of possible further statements and put them on the board. Collect the statements and read some out for the class to guess who wrote them.

Consolidation and Extension p57
Language File p116

LANGUAGE WORKOUT

- Ask students to complete the Language Workout box. Confident students can complete first and then check, while others can look back at exercise 2 then complete.
- Students turn to page 116 of the Language File to check their answers.

Answers
see happens take like
simple present

- Highlight that:
  - we use the open conditional to talk about cause and effect.
  - we can use both *if* and *when* in open conditional sentences.
  - the *if/when* clause can follow the main clause.
- Drill the examples chorally and individually for pronunciation and stress.

Practice

- Students do Practice exercise 10 on page 116 of the Language File. They match the sentence beginnings with the endings.
- Check the answers by asking individual students to read a sentence beginning and another to supply the correct ending.

Answers
1 c 2 e 3 b 4 d 5 a

Follow-up activity

Allow students a limited time to see how many words they can make from CAMERA. Students may only use the letter "a" twice. The group with the greatest number of words wins.

Homework

Students make a new word map for Cameras. Students complete the statements in exercise 7 about a family member.

NOTEBOOK SECTION

Complete the sentences with a form of the word in parentheses.

1 She forgets things when she ____ nervious. (get)
2 When you ____ ready, call me. (be)
3 What happens if he ____? (not remember)
4 When I ____ this button, nothing happens. (press)
5 Click here if you ____ "Spanish". (want)

Answers *1 gets 2 're (are) 3 doesn't remember 4 press 5 want*

Workbook Unit 4 Lesson 1 pp40–41
Photocopiable notes p156, worksheet p171

4 PERFORMANCE

2 Which will we choose?

Communicative Aims	Language	Pronunciation	Vocabulary
Making predictions	Simple future: *will/won't*	/ɪ/ will /i/ we'll	Recorded music

WARM-UP 1

Students write three sentences about themselves using open conditionals, and include one false piece of information. In pairs, they read their sentences to each other and try to identify the false information.

WARM-UP 2

Write jumbled sentences with open conditionals from the previous lesson on the board. Students re-order the sentences.

1 Opener

- The aim is to introduce the context for the rest of the lesson. Students discuss the questions in pairs or in small groups.
- Invite individual students to report back to the rest of the class about when, where, and how their partner listens to music.

2 Reading

- Point at the five photos on pages 50–51, and elicit the different ways of listening to music that are shown. Ask students if they have ever listened to music on a phonograph, a record player (LPs), or a cassette player.

Answers

1 phonographs 2 LPs 3 cassettes 4 CDs 5 MP3 players

- Elicit suggestions for other ways of listening to music.
- Students read through the article once, and then complete it with the correct words from the Word Bank. With a less confident class, start the exercise with the whole class. Explain to students that they will need to read the whole sentence, and in one case the following sentence too, before filling in the blanks.
- Play the recording for students to listen and check their answers.

1.44 Recording and answers

Eighteen seventy-seven
Thomas Edison invented the phonograph, which recorded sound on cylinders. Four years later, Charles Tainter invented the first flat disc record. Which were the most popular: cylinders or records? Surprisingly, (1) ***records*** *weren't popular for another fifty years. Until the nineteen twenties, most people listened to music on cylinders on a phonograph.*

Nineteen twenty-eight and nineteen forty-eight
In nineteen twenty-eight, Dr. Fritz Pfleumer invented tape recording in Germany, but tape recorders weren't available in the U.S. until twenty years later. Also, in nineteen forty-eight, the invention of the LP (long-playing record) meant that people could hear more music on each record—around twenty-three minutes a side. Which did people choose: tapes or LPs? Most people chose (2) ***LPs****, but after Sony introduced the Walkman in nineteen seventy-nine, more and more people listened to* (3) ***cassette tapes****.*

Nineteen eighty-two
Compact discs appeared in nineteen eighty-two. At first they were very expensive, but by the nineteen nineties they were more popular than both LPs and cassettes. But how much longer will CDs be popular? Apple introduced the first iPod® in two thousand and one, and more and more people bought Internet-based MP3 players.

The future
MP3 or CD: which will we choose? Most people think that (4) ***MP3 players*** *will soon replace* (5) ***CDs****. The big question is: what will replace MP3 players? We won't know the answer to that question for a few years.*

3 After Reading

- Students read and listen to the whole article again and decide if sentences 1–6 are true or false.
- Check the answers before students write corrections for the false sentences. Monitor and help where necessary.
- Students check each other's work.

Answers

1 True.
2 False. Thomas Edison invented the phonograph.
3 True.
4 True.
5 True.
6 False. Most people think that MP3 players will replace CDs.

Optional activity

Early finishers look back through the article and find sentences with *will/won't*.

LANGUAGE WORKOUT OPTION

If you want to pre-teach the language students will be using in the following activities, you may like to go to the Language Workout box now.

Your Response

- In small groups, students talk about what they think will replace MP3 players, and how they think we will listen to music in ten or twenty years' time. Ask them to make some definite predictions.
- One student from each group talks for one minute to the rest of the class about how his/her group believes we will listen to music in the future.

4 Pronunciation

- Say the two sounds and words at the top of the chart. Ask *What's the difference?* (/i/ is a longer sound, e.g. *tree*).
- Play the first part of the recording pausing after each word for students to repeat.

1.45 Recording

/ɪ/ *will live fit it sit tin fill*
/i/ *we'll leave feet eat seat teen feel*

- Play the second part of the recording. Students write the words they hear and compare their answers in pairs.
- Check by asking individual students to say and spell the words.

1.45 Recording and answers

will leave fit it seat tin feel

Optional activities

- ♦ Students close their books. Write two examples of /ɪ/ and /i/ words on the board. Students copy the words into their notebooks. Dictate the other words from exercise 4 in a random order. Students write the words in the appropriate column.
- ♦ In pairs, students dictate words from the two columns for their partner to write.
- ♦ In pairs, students test each other's spelling of the words in exercise 4.
- ♦ Elicit other words with the same sounds.

5 Speaking

- Explain to the class that they are going to read about five different situations and decide what will happen next, choosing from three options A, B, and C.
- Give students two minutes to work individually choosing one option for each situation.
- Read the example exchange with a confident student.
- Students work in pairs and use the options they have chosen to talk about what they think will happen. Encourage them to follow the model examples. Monitor and make sure students are using *will/won't* correctly.
- Students listen to the recording and compare their predictions with what actually happens. Check students' comprehension by asking which prompts were correct. Play the recording again if necessary.

1.46 Recording

1
LARA *Emma, do you want to go shopping with me and Silvana?*
EMMA *What a great idea! I want to buy some gifts.*
2
STEVE *This is my dog—she's called Daisy.*
JAY *Can I take her for a walk in the park?*
3
SILVANA *Happy Birthday, Lara—here's a small gift for you.*
LARA *Thank you so much! It's my favorite color!*
4
ALEX *Hey, Ramón, let me take some pictures of you!*

Answers

1 C 2 C 3 B 4 C

Extension Review expressions for agreeing and disagreeing with an opinion, e.g. *I agree* and *I don't agree*. Ask students to look at the photo on page 64, and the lesson title (*Could I borrow some money?*) and to read the prediction in the example: *I think they'll go to a pizza restaurant.* In pairs, students look at other lesson titles and pictures in Units 5–8 to make predictions. Ask a student to read out his/her prediction. Ask students if they disagree. Ask one who disagrees to make another prediction.

Optional activity

Students make up their own predictions about the characters and the events to come.

6 Writing

- Write *Travel, Work, Home,* and *Relationships* on the board. Point out the example in the book, and ask a confident student to make a prediction about one of these areas of his/her life.
- Students now write a paragraph making predictions about what they think/hope will happen in their lives. Monitor and provide help where necessary.
- Students exchange texts and check each other's writing for grammar, spelling, and punctuation.
- Ask students to read out their predictions to each other in small groups. Encourage students to say whether they agree or disagree with each person's predictions.

Optional activity

While students are reading out their predictions to each other, ask them to take notes. They then write a paragraph about the most interesting predictions in their group.

LANGUAGE WORKOUT

- Ask students to complete the sentences in the Language Workout box. Confident students can complete first and then check, while less confident ones can look back at exercise 2 and then complete.
- Students turn to page 116 of the Language File to check their answers.

  Answers
  will won't will will
- Highlight that:
  - we can use *will/won't* to talk about hopes and predictions in the future.
  - *will/won't* always has the same form: it doesn't add *-s* in the third person singular.
  - *will/won't* is followed by the infinitive without *to*.
  - we use contractions in spoken English, e.g. *I'll*.
- Drill the examples chorally and individually for pronunciation and stress.

Practice

- Students do Practice exercise 11 on page 116 of the Language File. They complete the sentences using the correct form of *will/won't*. Students check each other's work.

  Answers
  1 will 2 will 3 won't 4 will 5 won't 6 won't

Optional activity

Ask students to make a prediction about their favorite sports team using *will/won't*. Make sure they understand *prediction* (= something you think will happen in the future).

Follow-up activities

♦ Students make a word map for *Music*. They look back over the lesson and add as many words as they can to their map. If possible, give students dictionaries so they can add more words.

♦ **Game** *I hope you'll agree* Students make predictions in note form about these five topics, *Movies, Fashion, Weather, Music, Sports*. Set a short time limit and tell students to stand up and mingle. The first student to find someone who agrees with all of his/her predictions wins the game.

Homework

Students write predictions about their friends and family.

NOTEBOOK SECTION

Complete the sentences using *will* or *won't*.

1 I think she ____ say yes. ✓
2 ____ you see her again? ✓
3 He ____ get here on time. ✗
4 They ____ start if we're not there. ✗
5 When you go, I ____ miss you! ✓

Answers
1 'll (will)
2 Will
3 won't
4 won't
5 'll (will)

Consolidation and Extension p57

Language File p116

Workbook Unit 4 Lesson 2 pp42–43

Photocopiable notes p156, worksheet p172

3 You spoke too fast

Communicative Aims	Language	Pronunciation	Vocabulary	Optional aids
Talking about the way people do things	Adverbs of manner	Syllable stress	Feelings Performance	Exercise 6 Optional activity: cards for the Vocabulary box

WARM-UP 1

Write the following questions on the board:

Do you think you'll ever …
- *get married to a foreigner?*
- *visit Brazil?*
- *live in another country?*
- *be famous?*

In pairs, students ask their partner about the future using *Do you think you'll ever …?* and the experiences on the board. They then report the most interesting predictions back to the class.

WARM-UP 2

Review basic rules for adjectives, i.e. they have the same form in singular and plural; adjectives go before the noun, by writing some sentences with typical student errors in a tic-tac-toe grid on the board, e.g. *I like differents sports. She was a girl very pretty.* In two groups, students take turns to find the mistake in each sentence. If they find it, they place their X or O in the square. The first group with three in a row wins.

1 Opener

- The aim is to introduce the context for the Reading dialogue. Ask students to choose the best adjectives to describe how the whole group feels.

Answer
The group is looking sad.

- With books closed, students predict what Steve is saying to the group.

2 Reading

- Students read the dialogue to check their predictions about what Steve is saying.

Answer
Steve is saying that the director isn't going to use the group's scene in the movie.

Optional activity

1.47 Play the recording of the dialogue, pausing after each line for students to repeat. Focus on pronunciation and intonation. Students act out the dialogue in groups of four.

3 After Reading

- Students read the questions and answers. Then they read the dialogue one more time.
- Students match the questions and answers on their own. Make sure they understand that two answers are not needed. Set a short time limit and check the answers.

Answers
1 h 2 d 3 a 4 g 5 b 6 e
Wrong answers: c and f

Optional activities

- ♦ Students write true/false sentences about the dialogue and test each other in groups.
- ♦ Students find examples of adverbs of manner in the dialogue in preparation for exercise 5.

Your Response

- Ask the class to think of situations when they have to perform in front of people, e.g. acting in a role-play, playing music, doing gymnastics. Write their suggestions on the board.
- In pairs, students discuss how they feel when they are performing, whether they enjoy it and why/why not.
- Invite a few confident students to tell the class how they or their partner feel about performing.

4 Pronunciation

- Ask students to look at the words in the box. Tell them to copy the chart into their notebooks. Play the recording. Students listen and write the words in the correct column.
- Students listen again to check their answers.

1.48 Recording and answers
director everyone exercise extremely happily normally properly rehearsal tomorrow

▪■▪ *director extremely rehearsal tomorrow*
■▪▪ *everyone exercise happily normally properly*

- Play the recording again, pausing after each word for students to repeat.

Optional activity

Students look through the book for other words with the same stress patterns. This could be done as a contest and when one pair/group thinks they have six words for each pattern, they write them on the board.

LANGUAGE WORKOUT OPTION

If you want to pre-teach the language students will be using in the following activities, you may like to go to the Language Workout box now.

5 Listening

- Ask students to look at the photo on page 53. Explain that for the first part of the Listening they have to identify which action each drama exercise involves.
- Play the first part of the recording once. Students check their answers in pairs.
- Check the answers with the whole class.

1.49 Recording

OK. Here are two acting exercises for your bodies and voices. These exercises are quick, easy, and a lot of fun. Are you ready for the first one? It's about how you move. I want you to move around the room in the way that I tell you. For example, when I give you the adverb "quickly," I want you to run around the room. Is that clear? The second exercise uses your voice. I'll give you an adverb, for example, "happily," and I want you to talk in that way. You can say anything you like, it's how you say it that is important.

Answers

1 move   2 talk

- Check students know the meaning of the adverbs in the Word Bank.
- Explain that they are going to hear the characters speaking in some of these ways. Tell them to match each character with an adverb from the Vocabulary box as they hear them speak.
- Play the second part of the recording, pausing after each character has spoken for the students to guess the adverb.

1.49 Recording

STEVE *OK! Moving in the manner of the adverb was fun, wasn't it? Now let's do talking in the manner of the adverb. I've got some cards here with adverbs written on them. When I give you a card, I want you to talk in the manner of the adverb. Then we'll all try and guess what your adverb is. OK? Here are your cards. Now, Alex. You go first.*
ALEX *Excuse me, can I look at your map, please? Thank you!*
ALL *Politely.*
STEVE *Now Emma.*
EMMA *Don't tell me what to do! I'm not a child. I can take care of myself.*
ALL *Angrily!*
STEVE *Jay.*
JAY *It's very noisy in here. All these people are talking. I can't hear anything.*
ALL *Loudly!*
STEVE *Silvana.*
SILVANA *Oh, it's a lovely day and I'm feeling great. Everything is wonderful.*
ALL *Happily!*
STEVE *Lara.*
LARA *I thought the visit to the movie studio was a lot of fun and I really enjoyed myself.*
ALL *Quietly.*
STEVE *And last but not least—Ramón!*
RAMÓN *I'm very glad that we're doing these exercises so we can show the director that we're really good actors.*
ALL *Quickly.*
STEVE *Good job everyone!*

Answers

1 Alex—politely
2 Emma—angrily
3 Jay—loudly
4 Silvana—happily
5 Lara—quietly
6 Ramón—quickly

Extension Ask individual students to come to the front. Quietly ask them to move in the manner of an adverb from the Word Bank in exercise 5 for the others to guess, e.g. *dance slowly.* Then do the speaking exercise from the recording in the same way. These could be played as team games.

Optional activities

- Before students do the drama exercises, play the recording again and ask them to note down what each member of the group says. Less confident students listen to each sentence and first say how many words it has. Check the answers by asking students to say each sentence in the manner in which the sentence was said. Monitor pronunciation and intonation.
- Students choose five adverbs of manner from the box and write sentences in their notebooks to illustrate meaning, e.g. *I sing loudly in the shower.*

6 Vocabulary

- In pairs, students match the definitions with six of the nouns in the Word Bank.
- Students check the answers in pairs and then as a whole class.

Answers

1 studio   2 scene   3 rehearsal   4 character   5 stage   6 director

Extension Give students five minutes to choose five more words from the Word Bank and write definitions.
In pairs, students read out their definitions without saying the words. Their partner has to guess the word.
With the whole class, elicit the best definition for each of the remaining words in the Word Bank, writing them on the board.

Optional activities

- In pairs, students test each other, taking turns to read the definitions from the book or the board for their partner to say the words.
- Students copy the vocabulary onto cards, putting the definition on the back. These can be added to the Vocabulary box.

7 Writing

- Ask students to think of a character in a movie or TV series. Read out the questions. Students work in pairs asking and answering the questions about their characters.
- Students work individually and write short answers to the questions in their notebooks. Then they use their notes to write a short paragraph about their character.

Optional activities

- Students read out their text, without naming the character, to a partner who has to guess who it is.
- With a less confident class, write a paragraph on the board eliciting sentences from students. They use the paragraph as a model to write about their own character.

LANGUAGE WORKOUT

- Ask students to look at the Language Workout box. Ask *How do you form adverbs of manner?* (adjective + *-ly*).
- Ask students to complete the words in the Language Workout box. Confident students complete first and then check, while less confident ones look back at exercise 2 and complete.
- Students turn to page 117 of the Language File to check their answers.

Answers
badly normally properly fast well

- Highlight that:
  - adverbs of manner describe the verb, i.e. *how* we do something.
  - the usual position of adverbs of manner in a sentence is *after* the verb.

Practice

- Students do Practice exercise 12 on page 117 of the Language File. Students use some of the adverbs in the Language Workout box to complete the sentences.
- Ask individual students to read out their answers.

Answers
1 well 2 normally, fast 3 properly 4 badly 5 hard

Optional activity

Game *Word tennis* Divide the class into two teams. Students "serve" an adjective to the other team, who must return the adverb. Teams change roles after three adjectives have been "served."

Follow-up activity

Write jumbled sentences containing adverbs of manner for students to re-order correctly.

Homework

Students invent an imaginary movie or TV character. They write a short paragraph using the questions in exercise 7 to help them.

NOTEBOOK SECTION

Complete the sentences using a form of the word in parentheses.
1 You eat so ____! (slow)
2 She finished her math homework ____. (easy)
3 He walked ____ across the room, and kissed her. (confident)
4 They sang ____ (nice) and danced ____ (good), too.
5 I was carrying it very ____. (careful)

Answers
1 slowly 2 easily 3 confidently 4 nicely, well 5 carefully

Consolidation and Extension p57

Language File p117

Workbook Unit 4 Lesson 3 pp44–45

Photocopiable notes p157, worksheet p173

4 Integrated Skills TV shows

Skills		Learner Independence	Vocabulary	Optional aids
Reading Topics: Classic TV Series guide *Listening* Choosing the best answers: conversation about a TV series	*Speaking* Interviewing *Writing* Description of a TV series	Word combinations Grammar words	TV shows Grammar words Useful expressions	Follow-up activities: cards for Vocabulary box

WARM-UP 1

Write jumbled sentences on the board with adverbs of manner from the previous lesson. Students re-order the sentences.

WARM-UP 2

In pairs, students ask each other what sports, musical instruments, languages, and other activities they play/speak/do well or badly. Elicit feedback, asking students to tell you something interesting about their partner.

1 Opener

- The aim is to introduce the context for the Reading text. Ask students *What are the names of popular TV shows in your country?* and write some of their answers on the board.
- Ask students to say what kind of show each one is, choosing from the words in the Word Bank.
- Read through the words in the Word Bank, eliciting the meaning of each different type of TV show. In pairs, students think of examples for each one.

Optional activity

Students number the different kinds of TV shows in the Word Bank from 1–14 to show which they like best (1 = favorite, 14 = least favorite).

2 Reading

- The aim is to read a text for specific information. Students read and match the paragraphs with the pictures. Set a time limit of two minutes.

Answers
1D 2A 3C 4B

- Ask students to read the paragraph titles. Answer any vocabulary questions. Ask them to choose a title for each paragraph, noting down the words that help them decide.
- Play the recording while students listen and check their answers.

1.50 Recording
See text on page 54 of the Student's Book.

Answers
1 Family Life
2 Life and Death
3 Office Favorite
4 Extraordinary People

- Draw four columns on the board and label them with the paragraph titles. Check the answers and ask students to tell you the key words in each paragraph.

Optional activities

♦ Give students one minute to memorize all they can from paragraph 3. Students close their books. Read out the text including some false information, e.g. *In* Ugly Betty, *smart, friendly Betty Groening works in an office …* Students shout *Stop!* when they hear incorrect information and correct it.
♦ Students make a word map of *TV shows*.

3 Listening

- Ask students to look at the photo on page 55. Ask *Who are the main characters in this series? What do you think it's about?*
- Play the recording. Students listen and note the answers.
- Play the recording again, pausing to check the answers to each question

1.51 Recording

JAY *So what's your favorite TV series, Carrie? Is it* The Simpsons?
CARRIE *No, it isn't, actually. It's* Changing Times.
JAY *What's it about?*
CARRIE *It's about people who live and work in a small town. You know, it's like any soap—there are always problems!*
JAY *And where does it take place?*
CARRIE *In San Lorenzo—it's an imaginary town in the U.S.*
JAY *How often is it on?*
CARRIE *Every weekday—Monday to Friday.*
JAY *Really? What was the most exciting episode?*
CARRIE *Hmm … in one episode, two people escaped from a burning building, but only just in time.*
JAY *Wow! And what's happening now?*
CARRIE *They're looking for a murderer, and I think I know who it is!*
JAY *Hey, life sounds quite exciting in San Lorenzo!*

Answers
1 A 2 B 3 B 4 B 5 A 6 B

4 Speaking

- Give students time to think about their answers to the questions and to ask for necessary vocabulary. Students take turns asking and answering questions about their favorite TV series.

5 Writing

- The aim is for students to write a paragraph using the questions to provide a structure. Ask students to read through *CLASSIC TV SERIES* again. Then, individually or in pairs, they choose a popular TV series to write about. Ask students to look at the questions and make notes to answer them. Students work individually to write a paragraph using their notes to guide them.
- Students exchange paragraphs and read them for interest, and to check spelling and punctuation.

Optional activities

♦ Students include one piece of false information in their paragraph. Students exchange paragraphs and try to identify the false information.
♦ Students do not write the name of the TV series at the top of their paragraphs. Collect their writing and read out the texts. Students try to guess which TV series it is.

Learner Independence

6 • The aim is to encourage students to think about the ways in which words combine. Ask students to look at the verbs and adverbs in the boxes. Ask *Which words go together?* In pairs, students match as many adverbs as possible with the verbs. Make sure they understand that they can use each adverb more than once.
- Ask students to write the most useful word combinations in their vocabulary notebooks.

Answers
eat: carefully, hungrily, quickly, slowly
drink: carefully, quickly, slowly, thirstily
listen: carefully
look: angrily, carefully, happily, quickly, slowly,
speak: angrily, carefully, quickly, slowly
understand: easily, quickly, slowly
walk: angrily, carefully, happily, quickly, slowly
write: carefully, quickly, slowly
(These are the most probable combinations; others, like "listen hungrily" may, of course, be possible in certain contexts.)

Optional activity

Students perform the actions for others to guess the verb and adverb. This can be a team game.

7 • The aim is to help students use dictionaries effectively by ensuring that they understand basic grammatical terms. Ask students to do the exercise and then compare their answers in pairs.

Answers
at: preposition boring: adjective camera: noun
dancing: gerund make: verb slowly: adverb
they: pronoun to see: infinitive

- Ask students to look through the Language File from Units 1–4 to find these grammar words.

8 Phrasebook

- Ask students to look through the unit to find the expressions, and to look at how they are used.
- Play the recording, pausing after each expression for students to repeat.

1.52 Recording and answers
The big question is … (Reading, Lesson 2)
I have some bad news. (Steve, Lesson 3, ex 2)
Oh, thats too bad! (Jay, Lesson 3, ex 2)
I don't understand. (Emma, Lesson 3, ex2)
It doesn't make sense. (Emma, Lesson 3, ex2)
That's crazy! (Emma, Lesson 3, ex2)

- Students can add expressions that they like to their Personal Phrasebooks. Help with translation.
- Ask students to work in pairs to make up the four-line dialogues. Invite some pairs to act out their dialogues in front of the class.

Follow-up activities

♦ **Game** *Word tennis*. One student "serves" the name of a type of TV show, and their partner "returns" the name of a show.
♦ Students choose five words from the lesson to write on vocabulary cards.

Homework

Students make up their own TV series using the ideas from the lesson.

NOTEBOOK SECTION

Complete the sentences using *good* or *well*.
1 She writes very ____. She wrote a ____ story.
2 Their songs are very ____.
3 They get along ____ together.
4 I have some ____ news for you.
5 Did you know her ____?

Answers
1 well, good 2 good 3 well 4 good 5 well

Consolidation and Extension p57

Workbook Unit 4 Lesson 4 pp46–47

4 PERFORMANCE

Inspired EXTRA!

Optional aids

Project: photos and pictures from newspapers, magazines, or the Internet of popular TV shows

Project TV Shows

1

- Explain to students that the aim of this project is to write about their favorite TV shows. If you have brought pictures into class, show them to the students.
- Divide students into groups and appoint an "editor" for each group.
- Give students five minutes to do a survey of the group's favorite TV shows, and to make a list of the ten most popular shows in the group.

2

- Students look back at the work they did in Unit 4, Lesson 4, writing about a TV series.
- The group chooses three shows to write about from their list of favorite TV shows.

3

- Hold a class brainstorming session to generate ideas that students can use to write about their shows.
- Students look at the prompts and make notes about their shows. They may need to use the Internet or find information at home.
- Point out the text about *Dancing with the Stars*, which gives an example of what students can write.

4

- Each person in the group writes a short text about one of the shows.
- Students put their work together and read the texts through carefully to correct any mistakes. They copy their texts out neatly. The editor selects the order of the texts while others work on illustrating them with photos from magazines or drawings.
- Students show their work to other groups.

Game Word Square

- Write the word square on the board. Read the instructions with the class and show on the board how you can make the word PLAY but not PART.
- Students work in pairs. Set a time limit of five minutes (more for a less confident class).

Consolidation

Lesson 1
Students' own answers.

Lesson 2

Suggested answers

2 *Jay won't say he's afraid of dogs, he'll ask if he can take the dog for a walk.*
3 *Lara won't say thank you and then try and exchange it, she'll say she loves black.*
4 *Alex won't start dancing, he'll take some pictures.*

Lesson 3
Students' own answers.

Lesson 4
Students' own answers.

Extension

Lessons 1–4
Students' own answers.

YOUR CHOICE!

The aim is to give students more learner independence and help them to identify their preferred ways of learning. Encourage students to choose an activity that they feel less comfortable with if they want a challenge or are aware that they need practice in a particular area.
Half-minute Talks gives students the opportunity to speak freely about a topic of their choosing.
Saying Words in Two Ways gives students the opportunity to focus on one particular learning area.

You may now like students to do the song *Footprints In The Frost*. See p161 for the notes and p187 for the worksheet.

Language File pp116–117

Song–photocopiable notes p161; worksheet p187

Workbook Unit 4 Inspired EXTRA! pp48–49

Units 3–4

1 Students complete the text choosing the appropriate word or words. Do the first one together as an example. This can be done in pairs or individually.

Answers

1 was getting *2 beautifully* *3 finished* *4 didn't accept* *5 because* *6 well* *7 nervous* *8 hard* *9 want* *10 badly*

2 Students complete the sentences with the correct simple past form. Less confident students could first decide which verb goes in each sentence.

Answers

1 married *2 died, was* *3 lived* *4 worked* *5 wrote* *6 destroyed* *7 took* *8 went*

3 Ask students to look at the example. Read it with a student. Do the first one together if necessary as an extra example.

Answers

1 Did Jay take a cable car? Yes, he did.
Did he walk up the hill? No, he didn't.
2 Did Ramón and Silvana visit a theater? No, they didn't.
Did they see an exhibit? Yes, they did.
3 Did Lara lose her camera? No, she didn't.
Did she take lots of pictures? Yes, she did.
4 Did the group have a picnic? Yes, they did.
Did they go to a restaurant? No, they didn't.
5 Did Emma visit the temple? No, she didn't.
Did she wait outside? Yes, she did.

1 Jay took a cable car. He didn't walk up the hill.
2 Ramón and Silvana didn't visit a theater. They saw an exhibit.
3 Lara didn't lose her camera. She took lots of pictures.
4 The group had a picnic. They didn't go to a restaurant.
5 Emma didn't visit the temple. She waited outside.

4 Students complete the time expressions with the correct prepositions.

Answers

1 in 2 on 3 at 4 in 5 in 6 on 7 at 8 on 9 in

Optional activity

Fast finishers write similar gapped time phrases to test each other, e.g. ____ 2:15, _____ the morning, etc.

5 Students use the prompts and write full sentences.

Answers

1 Alex was taking pictures when he dropped his bag.
2 Lara was doing gymnastics when she hurt her foot.
3 Jay and Emma were dancing when they saw Steve.
4 Carrie was recording an interview when the phone rang.
5 Ramón was listening to music when he fell asleep.

6 Students write sentences with the simple past + *because* and the past progressive.

Answers

1 Steve stayed in the hotel because he was taking care of the group.
2 Emma got lost because she was not thinking.
3 Jay and Lara didn't play tennis because it was raining.
4 Ramón took a hot shower because he was feeling cold.
5 Silvana didn't dance because her feet were hurting.

7 Students match the beginnings with endings to make the full sentences.

Answers

1 C 2 D 3 E 4 B 5 A

8 Refer students back to exercise 1, which introduces Angie. Ask the students to read her conversation with her boyfriend, Nick, all the way through before they complete it with *will* or *won't*.

Answers

1 will 2 will 3 will 4 won't 5 won't 6 will 7 won't 8 will 9 won't 10 Will 11 will 12 will

9 Students complete the sentences with the correct adverbs formed from the adjectives in the box. Less confident students can form the adverbs as a class first before completing the sentences.

Answers

1 quietly 2 early 3 happily 4 well 5 nervously 6 politely 7 late 8 slowly 9 easily

Vocabulary

10 Students complete the sentences with the words in the box.

Answers

1 documentary 2 primary 3 tragedy 4 building 5 career 6 bestseller

11 Confident students can first cover the list of words and try to work out what the definitions refer to.

Answers

1 well-known 2 community 3 rudely 4 exhausted 5 roof 6 rescue 7 boat 8 occupation 9 playwright 10 century

Optional activity

Students write definitions of other words from Units 3 and 4. They exchange definitions with another student and try to guess each other's words.

12 Remind students that it is very helpful to learn common idiomatic expressions of this kind.

Answers

1 fall overboard *2 have fun* *3 make sense*
4 press a button *5 rehearse a play* *6 take place*
7 tell a story *8 work hard*

Learner Independence Self Assessment

- Explain to students that the aim of the self assessment is to encourage them to check their own progress and take any necessary action to improve. Point out that the list 1–6 covers areas of functional language from Units 3 and 4. Students check the "Fine" box for functional language that they feel confident using, but put a question mark in the "Not sure" box for functional language that they have difficulty with or still cannot use confidently.
- Encourage students to look at the Language File and re-do exercises from the Workbook in areas where they have problems. They may also like to re-do exercises from the lessons and from the Consolidation and Extension sections in Units 3 and 4.
- Students write an example sentence for each language area in the list. You may like to elicit the grammar students need for each example before students write sentences, e.g. *Talking about past events: Simple past.* Students can refer back to the lessons and the Language File.
- Ask students to compare their sentences with a partner's, and to discuss and correct any mistakes.
- Check their sentences and note down language areas for future practice.

Follow-up activities

- ♦ Write a sentence on the board, e.g. *I don't like pizza.* In pairs, students say the sentence in the manner of an adverb for their partner to guess.
- ♦ One student says a verb and the other suggests an adverb to use with it, e.g. *walk—quickly*.
- ♦ **Game** *Tic-Tac-Toe* Draw this grid on the board:

feelings	open conditional	Adverbs of manner
Grammar words	*Won't*	Recorded music
Will	Television shows	/ɪ/ or /i/

See Follow-up activities in Review Units 1–2 for complete instructions.

Homework

Students look at the weather forecast in a newspaper. They write a short paragraph using *will* and *won't* to predict next week's weather in three or four places in their country. If the weather is likely to be similar to this week's, they can write about places in different parts of the world.

NOTEBOOK SECTION

There is an error in each sentence. Rewrite the sentences correctly.

1 He looking the other way when he fell.
2 I slept really comfortable.
3 You shouldn't go to bed so lately.
4 When you're tired, you making mistakes.
5 I was running when I was hurting my foot.

Answers

*1 He **was looking** the other way ...*
*2 I slept really **comfortably.***
*3 You shouldn't go to bed so **late.***
*4 When you're tired, you **make** mistakes.*
*5 I was running when I **hurt** my foot.*

Language File pp115–117

Workbook Review Units 3–4 pp50–51

Units 5–6

Activities		Project	Vocabulary	Optional aids
Identifying the function of communicative language	Categorizing vocabulary Contextualizing listening extracts	Vacations	Animals Landmarks Directions	Follow-up activity: slips of paper for students to write single words on

WARM-UP 1

Students look back at Units 3–4 in their books, and talk in pairs about the activities or reading texts that they enjoyed or didn't like. Encourage them to give reasons for their feelings.

WARM-UP 2

Put anagrams for words related to food on the board, e.g. *ZAZIP* (pizza), *CUJIE* (juice), *DERBA* (bread), *ECKA* (cake), *SATAP* (pasta). Students work out the anagrams and then use each word in a sentence.

WARM-UP 3

Ask students to look at the pictures and captions/speech bubbles on pages 60–61 and answer the questions *What do the pictures show? Who can you see in the pictures?*

1 • The aim is to introduce students to the main areas of communicative language they will cover in Units 5–6, and to encourage them to think about the function of the language.

• Explain to students that the two boxes at the top of the page show the communicative language and vocabulary/topics they will use in these two units of *Inspired*. Students look at the first box and match the communicative aims 1–7 with the pictures A–G on pages 60–61.

Answers

1 C 2G 3A 4 F 5 E 6 B 7D

Optional activity

Students write another example sentence or question for each of the communicative aims 1–7.

2 • Elicit the meaning of the word *landmarks*. Explain to students that words from each of the three vocabulary categories (animals, landmarks, and directions) are arranged in the word pool. Give students two minutes to write the words in the correct category.

• Students check their answers in pairs and then as a whole class. Help students with any difficult vocabulary, e.g. *palace, tower, cathedral, monument.*

Answers

Animals: monkey, cow, sheep, horse, lion, tiger,
Famous landmarks: castle, tower, palace, mountain, cathedral, monument
Directions: left, north, map, turn, right, south

Optional activity

In small groups, students think of as many different words as possible to add to the three categories. Give them a time limit.

3 • Explain to students that the words in color are three more vocabulary categories. Elicit the meaning of Dictionary words. Ask students to work in pairs thinking of three more words for each category. Students can look in their dictionaries if they need help thinking of Dictionary words.

Possible answers

Dictionary words: noun, countable, singular, abbreviation, adverb, plural, auxiliary verb, something, adjective, uncountable, somebody
Drinks: juice, tea, coffee, soda, lemonade, beer, wine, milk
Adjectives meaning fantastic: wonderful, great, amazing, awesome, super, terrific

Optional activity

Confident students may like to write three words for each of the remaining categories in the box (food, satellite navigation, luggage and clothes, transportation, and town facilities).

4 • The aim of the activity is for students to contextualize a short listening extract by working out what kind of passage it comes from. Explain to students that they should listen for the main gist of the passage and it does not matter if they do not understand every word.

• Play the recording. Students match each extract 1–3 with the correct kind of passage A–C.

1.53 Recording

1 *OK—can you all be quiet for a minute? I want to tell you about some changes to the arrangements for tomorrow, so listen up. First of all, we're not leaving the hotel tomorrow morning at nine thirty—we're leaving at ten o'clock, so you can stay in bed for an extra thirty minutes! After lunch, we're going to visit the museums.*

2 *When you come out of the hotel, turn right onto 9th Street. Walk straight along 9th Street past the library. Go across Pennsylvania Avenue and walk down to Constitution Avenue. Then turn right and it's the big building on the left. You can't miss it!*

3 CARRIE *Alex—let's hear what you've done this week. Have you taken any pictures?*
ALEX *Oh yes, I've taken lots of pictures!*
CARRIE *Have you bought any gifts?*
ALEX *No, I haven't. But I'm going to buy some tomorrow.*
CARRIE *What about sports—have you played any sports this week?*
ALEX *No, I haven't had time!*

Answers

1 C 2 A 3 B

Optional activity

1.53 Play the recording again and ask students a simple comprehension question about each extract.
1 *What is the change the speaker talks about?* (They aren't leaving the hotel at 9:30, they're leaving at 10 o'clock.)
2 *Which street is the hotel on?* (9th Street)
3 *When is Alex going to buy gifts?* (Tomorrow)

5
- Give students a few minutes to look through the Vacation Questionnaire.
- Students do the questionnaire in groups of four, making notes about their group's answers, especially any that are interesting or surprising.
- One person from each group moves to another group and gives a brief report about their group's answers, telling them anything interesting or surprising that they found out.
- Point out the "Believe it or not!" fact at the bottom of the page.

Vacation project

Ask students to think of other questions they could add to the Vacation Questionnaire, e.g. *What did you do? Did you visit any interesting places? What did you take with you?*
Students make notes about their own vacation this year or last year, using the questionnaire and the other questions they thought of.
Students write a short report about their last vacation, using their notes. They may like to illustrate their report with cuttings from vacation brochures, drawings, or their own pictures.
Display the projects in class so that students can look at each other's work.

Follow-up activities

- ♦ In groups of four, students brainstorm vocabulary for three other categories from the box on page 60: *luggage and clothes, transportation,* and *town facilities*. Give students an example from each category before they start, and tell them they have two minutes to write as many words as they can think of for each category on slips of paper. After the time is up for each of the three categories, students shuffle their slips of paper so they are jumbled out of order. They then swap their slips with another group, and the students then have two minutes to sort another group's slips into the correct categories.
- ♦ Students put away the notes they made when they were interviewing other students in their group for the Vacation Questionnaire. Then they write down everything they can remember about the other students' vacations. Give them two minutes. In their groups, students talk about what they remembered and what they forgot.

Homework

Ask students to write a short paragraph beginning "*On my ideal vacation, I will …*" Students plan their ideal vacation, and say where they will go, where they will stay, and what they will do.

1 What's happening tomorrow?

Communicative Aims	Language	Pronunciation	Vocabulary	Optional aids
Talking about future arrangements Describing a sequence of events	Present progressive: future Sequencing adverbs	/ŋ/ -ing /n/ in	Sightseeing	Exercise 9: entertainment section from local newspaper or leisure guide Homework: pictures of tourist destinations

WARM-UP 1

Ask *Can you remember the places our group visited in Unit 3, Lesson 2? Can you spell them?* (Nob Hill, Grace Cathedral, Chinatown, the California Academy of Sciences)

WARM-UP 2

Write some periods of time on the board in minutes, e.g. *15 minutes, 90 minutes, 130 minutes*. In pairs, students decide how to say them more naturally. Do the first one together, e.g. *a quarter of an hour.* Check students' answers (*an hour and a half, two hours and ten minutes*). They can then write their own time periods and test each other.

Useful information

The Lion King is a musical based on the 1994 Disney movie of the same name, with music by Elton John and lyrics by Tim Rice. The musical was first performed on Broadway in 1997, and is still running today.

1 Opener

- The aim is to arouse interest in what the group are doing on Saturday. Ask students to look at the photos on page 62 and to guess what they show.
- Tell them to look at the schdeule for Saturday and to match the photos with four of the events in the schedule. Check students understand *subway* (the Washington, D.C. underground railroad). Check pronunciation of the times.

Answers

A—Visit the National Museum of Natural History.
B—Take a sightseeing bus tour.
C—Leave for the theater: The Lion King.
D—Visit the National Air and Space Museum.

Optional activity

In pairs, one student reads out a time from the schedule and the other reads out the event.

2 Listening

- Play the recording. Students look at the schdeule and note down changes in the arrangements. They compare their answers in pairs.

1.54 Recording

OK—can you all be quiet for a minute? I want to tell you about some changes to the arrangements for tomorrow, so listen up. First of all, we're not leaving the hotel tomorrow morning at nine thirty—we're leaving at ten o'clock, so you can stay in bed for an extra thirty minutes!

After lunch, we're going to visit the museums. But we aren't taking the subway, we're going by bus. It's easier to take the bus—and it's nicer! I'm taking some people to the National Air and Space Museum, and Carrie is taking a group to the National Museum of Natural History.

And then we're going to The Lion King *in the evening. It starts at seven thirty and we want to be sure that we're at the theater in good time, so we're leaving the hotel fifteen minutes earlier—we're leaving at six thirty. So please be ready to leave by six thirty. All right—is that clear? Any questions?*

- Play the recording again and check the answers.

Answers

They're leaving the hotel at ten o'clock, not nine thirty.
They aren't taking the subway to the museums, they're going by bus.
They're leaving for the theater at six thirty, not six forty-five.

3 After Listening

- Check that students understand all the questions.
- Students find the answers in the schedule. Tell them to write full sentences. Point out that their answers should reflect the three corrections that have been made to the schedule.
- Check the answers by asking one student to read a question and another student to answer it.

Answers
1 *They are leaving the hotel at ten o'clock.*
2 *They are taking a sightseeing bus tour at ten thirty.*
3 *They are having lunch in Pizza Paradise (restaurant).*
4 *Steve is taking them to the Air and Space Museum.*
5 *Lara is going to the National Museum of Natural History.*
6 *No, Alex isn't going to the Air and Space Museum. (He's going to the National Museum of Natural History.)*
7 *They are spending two and a half hours at the museums.*
8 *They are leaving for the theater at six thirty p.m.*

Optional activity

Early finishers look at the questions and find examples of the present progressive with future meaning.

Your Response

- Students use their answers from exercise 1 to make a list of the events from the schdeule.
- In pairs, they discuss which they think is the best event of the day, giving reasons.
- Hold a class vote to see which is the most popular.

LANGUAGE WORKOUT OPTION

If you want to pre-teach the language students will be using in the following activities, you may like to go to the Language Workout box now.

4 Speaking

- Read the example questions and answers with a student. In pairs, students take turns to ask and answer questions about the arrangements.

5 Listening

- Students read through the list of different activities and predict the order before listening.
- Play the recording once. In pairs, students compare answers. Ask students to tell you the order of events.

1.55 Recording

And we have another full day for you on Sunday. First, we're starting with a visit to the National Zoo at ten o'clock, and we're spending two hours there. Next—at twelve thirty—we're having a picnic lunch at Fletcher's Boat House down by the river. Then, after lunch, there's plenty of time for shopping in Georgetown, and you can buy all kinds of souvenirs and gifts there. After that, at four o'clock, we're taking a paddleboat trip on the river for an hour. And finally, at the end of the afternoon, at five o'clock, we're walking along the Reflecting Pool. It's really beautiful, so don't forget your cameras!

Answers
1 B 2 E 3 A 4 D 5 C

- Students complete the schedule. Point out that the order of events in the first part of the exercise will help them.
- Play the recording again and check the answers.

Answers
10 a.m.–noon *Visit the National Zoo.*
12:30 p.m. *Have lunch at Fletcher's Boat House.*
2 p.m. *Go shopping in Georgetown.*
4 p.m. *Take a paddleboat.*
5-5:30 p.m. *Walk along the Reflecting Pool.*

LANGUAGE WORKOUT OPTION

If you want to pre-teach the language students will be using in the following activities, you may like to go to the Language Workout box now.

6 Speaking

- Write *When? At … on … / How long? For …* on the board. Check students understand that *How long …?* is used to talk about length of time.
- Ask two students to read the example questions and answers. Make sure they know how to use the expressions on the board.
- In pairs, students ask and answer questions about what the group is doing on Sunday, using the words on the board and referring to the schedule.
- Explain to students that the present progressive is often used with the sequencing adverbs *first*, *next*, *then*, *after that*, and *finally* for future arrangements, e.g. *First, they're visiting the National Zoo.*
- Ask students to look at the schedule again and work in pairs to tell each other what the group are doing on Sunday using the sequencing adverbs.

Extension Students make notes on what they are planning to do next weekend. In pairs, students talk about their own arrangements for next Saturday and Sunday, using the present progressive with sequencing adverbs. Ask a confident student to tell the rest of the class about their arrangements for the weekend.

7 Writing

- Students copy the postcard into their notebooks and complete it with full sentences. Make sure students understand that they can refer to the answers in exercise 5 to help them.

Answers
First, we're visiting the National Zoo. Next, we're having lunch at Fletcher's Boat House. Then we're going shopping in Georgetown and after that, we're taking a paddleboat trip. Finally, we're walking along the Reflecting Pool!

8 Pronunciation

- Play the first part of the recording, pausing after each word for students to repeat.

1.56 Recording

/ŋ/ *-ing going rang sung thing wing*
/n/ *in go in ran sun thin win*

- Play the second part of the recording. Students write the words they hear and compare their answers in pairs.
- Check by asking individual students to say and spell the words.

1.56 Recording and answers

going ran sung thing win

9 Writing

- Students copy the headings into their notebooks and make short notes. You could bring in the entertainment section from a local newspaper for students to look at.
- Ask students to look at the example sentence. Students write five or more sentences describing this weekend's entertainment using the present progressive.

Extension Brainstorm places and events in the students' town/city that would be interesting for tourists. In pairs, students plan a day out in their town/city for tourists. They then work individually, writing a schedule like the one in exercise 1. Students correct their partner's work. Ask confident students to read out their schedule to the class.

LANGUAGE WORKOUT

- Ask students to complete the sentences in the top half of the Language Workout box. Confident students complete first and then check, while less confident ones look back at exercises 1 and 3 and complete.
- Students turn to page 117 of the Language File to check their answers.

Answers

*We're **returning** to the hotel at 5:30 p.m.*
*They aren't **having** lunch at the hotel.*
*What time **are** they **having** lunch?*
*Who **is taking** them to the Air and Space Museum?*
*How much time **are** they **spending** at the museums?*

- Highlight that "future arrangements" are the kind of things you write in your agenda. We use the present progressive to talk about definite future plans.
- There is little difference between going to and the present progressive, and usually either can be used.
- Students may try to use the simple present and the present progressive to talk about the near future, e.g. *What do you do tonight?*
  Look at the bottom half of the Language Workout box for information on sequencing adverbs.

Practice

- Students do Practice exercise 13 on page 117 of the Language File. They write sentences using the present progressive.

Answers

1 Steve is visiting the Air and Space Museum tomorrow.
2 He's not/He isn't spending all afternoon at the museum.
3 Are they visiting the museums in the morning?
4 We're taking a bus tour before lunch.
5 What time are they returning to the hotel?
6 We aren't/We're not going to the show tonight.
7 Are you coming to my party this evening?
8 I'm meeting my friends in the coffee shop at 6:30.

Follow-up activities

- ♦ Students look back through the lesson and find words to add to their *Buildings and places* word map (see Unit 3, Lesson 1, Follow-up activities).
- ♦ Students write a "busy agenda" for the weekend. They include as many arrangements as possible, e.g. *seeing the doctor,* and leave two times free. In pairs, students find a time when they are both free and arrange to do something together.

Homework

Give each student a different picture (see optional aids). Students write a short "postcard" describing where they are and what their arrangements are over the next two days using sequencing adverbs.

Ask students to think of an event that the tourist office in their town might organize and make a poster for it.

NOTEBOOK SECTION

Complete the sentences using one of these words:
at, for, in, on, by.

1 When are they arriving? ____ the morning.
2 Are they coming ____ plane?
3 How long are they staying? ____ a week.
4 When are they leaving? ____ Saturday.
5 When are we going to see them? ____ lunchtime.

Answers

1 In 2 by (not "in") 3 For 4 On 5 At

Consolidation and Extension p71

Language File p117

Workbook Unit 5 Lesson 1 pp52–53

Photocopiable notes p157, worksheet p174

2 Could I borrow some money?

Communicative Aims	Language	Pronunciation	Vocabulary	Optional aids
Ordering a meal in a restaurant	*some* and *any* *How much/many?* Countable and uncountable nouns *Can/Could* for requests	/ʊ/ good /u/ food	Food	Exercise 4 Optional activities: small cards for the Vocabulary box

Useful information

There are approximately 60,000 pizza resturants in the United States. Each man, woman, and child in the U.S. eats an average of 46 slices of pizza a year. Over 5 billion pizzas are sold worldwide each year. According to a recent survey, children between the ages of 3 and 11 prefer pizza over all other food groups for lunch and dinner.

Pizza-makers have tried virtually every type of food on pizzas, including peanut butter and jelly, and bacon and eggs. 62% of Americans prefer meat toppings on their pizza, while women are twice as likely as men to order vegetable toppings.

WARM-UP 1

If students wrote postcards in the last lesson, collect all the texts and the pictures/postcards. Number the texts and pictures and put them up on the board in random order. Students look at the texts and match them to the postcards/pictures. This can be played as a team game.

WARM-UP 2

Write *What's your favorite food? What's your favorite restaurant?* on the board. Students ask and answer the questions in small groups. Demonstrate by talking about your preferences first.

1 Opener

- The aim is to prepare vocabulary for the lesson. You may wish to share some of the facts in *Useful information* with the class.

2 Reading

- Students look at the pizza menu on page 65. Explain that Emma, Jay, and Silvana are having lunch at this pizza restaurant. Students read the dialogue and write the name of the appropriate pizza in the spaces.
- Elicit answers but don't say if the students are right at this stage. Check students understand the meaning of *starving* and *impossible*. Encourage them to work out the meaning from the context.
- Play the recording. Students check their answers.

1.57 Recording and answers

EMMA *Let's choose something to eat. I'm starving!*
WAITER *Are you ready to order?*
EMMA *Yes, could I have a (1)* ***Mediterranean*** *pizza?*
JAY *What's that?*
EMMA *It's a pizza with cheese, tomatoes, olives, and garlic.*
JAY *Oh, could I have that too? But I don't want any olives.*
SILVANA *Do you have any pizzas with mushrooms?*
WAITER *There's a (2)* ***Four Seasons*** *pizza—with cheese, tomatoes, mushrooms, ham …*
SILVANA *No, I don't want any meat. I'm a vegetarian.*
WAITER *Then why don't you have a (3)* ***Country*** *pizza? It has mushrooms, and there isn't any meat in it.*
SILVANA *OK, I'll have that. And I'd like some garlic bread.*
WAITER *And what would you like to drink?*
SILVANA *A cola, please.*
WAITER *How many colas?*
EMMA *Two.*
JAY *And can I have some water, please?*
WAITER *Sure, coming right up.*
JAY *Emma … how much money do you have?*
EMMA *About $40. Why?*
JAY *Because I don't have any. Could I borrow some?*
EMMA *Jay, you're impossible!*

Optional activities

- 1.57 Play the recording again, pausing after each line for students to repeat. Focus on pronunciation and intonation. Students act out the dialogue in groups of four. You could choose one group to perform it for the rest of the class.
- Students write true/false sentences about the dialogue and test each other in groups.

3 After Reading

- Students work in pairs. Ask them to complete the sentences using information and expressions from the dialogue.
- Ask a student to read out the sentence/question and to choose another student to complete/answer it.

Answers

1 We know that Emma is very hungry because she says ***"I'm starving."***
2 Jay doesn't want any ***olives*** *on his pizza.*

3 *Silvana wants* ***mushrooms*** *on her pizza.*
4 *Silvana doesn't want any meat because she's a* ***vegetarian****.*
5 *Silvana also orders some* ***garlic bread****.*
6 ***Two****.*
7 ***$40****.*
8 *Jay wants to borrow some* ***money****.*

Optional activity

Students work in pairs. One student closes the book. His/Her partner reads out the names of the different pizzas and they try to remember the ingredients. Then pairs exchange roles.

Your Response

In pairs, students talk about which pizza they would like to order from the menu. Encourage students to give their reasons, saying *I like/don't like …, I'm a vegetarian, I want/don't want …*

Optional activity

Brainstorm other pizza toppings, helping with vocabulary, and tell students to design their perfect pizza by listing the toppings it will have and giving it a name.

4 Vocabulary

- The aim is to show that grouping words according to topic in word maps can help memory. Check that students know the meaning of the four main categories (*vegetables, meat, dairy produce, fruit*) by asking for an example of each one.
- Students copy the word map, and then work in pairs to add as many foods as they can. Point out that they can use the foods from this lesson and any other food words they know. Set a short time limit.
- Elicit different words from their word maps, asking students to spell them, and then write them on the board.

Optional activities

- ♦ Students copy the vocabulary onto cards for the Vocabulary Box, putting the definition on the back.
- ♦ **Game** *Teacher* Play with food words. See Unit 2, Lesson 1, Warm-up 1 for more details.
- ♦ **Game** *Memory chain* This is best played in groups of six to ten. Student 1 says *I went shopping this morning and I bought some …* Student 2 repeats this and adds another food item. This continues around the group. A student who repeats or forgets is out.

Extension This game can be played with the whole class, in teams, or in pairs. Less confident students may wish to prepare by making lists of nouns before they start. The first student or team calls out a food word, and the second student or team says whether it is countable or uncountable. They get one point for a correct answer.

5 Pronunciation

- Write *good* and *food* on the board. Elicit their pronunciation and write the phonetic symbols beside each word.
- Students write the words in the correct column.
- Play the recording. Students listen and check their answers.

1.58 Recording and answers

/ʊ/ *good cook could look took would*
/u/ *food choose fruit group juice through*

- Play the recording again, pausing after each word for students to repeat.

Optional activity

Divide the class into small groups or pairs. Groups/Pairs think of six other words for each sound. This could be presented as a contest and when one group/pair thinks they have all twelve words, they say them to the class. Other groups can add words.

LANGUAGE WORKOUT OPTION

If you want to pre-teach the language students will be using in the following activities, you may like to go to the Language Workout box now.

6 Role-Play

- Ask students to read the phrases in the boxes. Ask three confident students to read the example conversation. Point out that students should use the menu on page 65.
- Divide the class into groups of three. One student is the waiter and the others are the customers. If your class doesn't divide into threes, have extra customers. Demonstrate first with yourself as waiter and two confident students as customers.
- Students act out the situation. Waiters write down the orders to make it as realistic as possible. Students change roles and repeat the role-play until they have all been the waiter. Monitor and make a note of any frequent errors in the target language for class correction later.

Optional activities

- ♦ With a less confident class, you may want to elicit the dialogue between waiters and customers on the board. Then remove parts of the dialogue from the board. Students continue practicing the dialogue from memory. Eventually remove all the dialogue.
- ♦ With a more confident class who have completed the role-play, write simple word prompts on the board, e.g. *ready? pizza/like? How much/many want? drink?* Students close their books and repeat the role-play using the prompts on the board.

7 Writing

- Students write out their dialogues from exercise 6, using the dialogue in exercise 2 and the prompts in exercise 6 for guidance.
- Students exchange dialogues and check each others' work for spelling, punctuation, and grammar.

Extension Students work on their own and write their ideal restaurant menu. Encourage them to include appetizers, main courses, desserts, and drinks. Students arrange their chairs as in a restaurant and do the role-play in pairs, one playing the waiter and the other the customer. Then they change roles and do the role-play again.

Optional activity

With a less confident class, students write a short menu following headings you write on the board. Brainstorm a few examples before students begin.
Name of restaurant: …
Appetizers: *mixed salad*
Main courses: *pizza*
Desserts: *ice cream*
Drinks: *orange juice*
Students act out their role-play in front of the class.

LANGUAGE WORKOUT

- Ask students to complete the sentences in the Language Workout box. Confident students can complete first and then check, while less confident ones can look back at exercise 2 and then complete.
- Students turn to pages 117–118 of the Language File to check their answers.

  Answers
  some any some any
  much many much many
- Highlight that:
  - uncountable nouns cannot be used in the plural: you cannot add an *s*. (Students will probably be familiar with the concept of countability, especially in a food context.)
  - *people* has no *s*, but is a plural countable noun and should be learned as an exception.

Optional activity

Game *Left or Right* Write *Countable* on the left-hand side of the board and *Uncountable* on the right-hand side. Tell the students that you're going to call out a noun and they have to point to the correct side of the board. For example, you say pizza and they point to the left, you say cheese and they point to the right. Have all the students stand up to play the game and when they get it wrong they sit down. The last one standing is the winner.

Practice

- Students do Practice exercises 14 on page 117 and 15 on page 118 of the Language File. Students complete the sentences with *some* or *any* and *much* or *many.*

Answers Exercise 14
1 some 2 any 3 any 4 some 5 some 6 any
7 some 8 any 9 any 10 some

Answers Exercise 15
1 many 2 many 3 much 4 much 5 many

Follow-up activities

- ♦ Elicit from students all the food and drink items from the lesson and write them on the board. Students interview each other asking *How much (cheese) do you eat in a week? How much (milk) do you drink in a week?* Ask them to note the quantities and feed back interesting information to the class.
- ♦ **Game** *Alphabet game* The game can be played in groups or as a whole class. Students think of a food or drink beginning with each letter of the alphabet (except Q, U, X, Y, and Z). Students win one point for each correct word. An extra point could be given for saying if the food is healthy or not. The team with the most points wins.

Homework

Students write ten sentences about what they usually eat and say how healthy the choice of food is.

NOTEBOOK SECTION

Complete the sentences using one of these words:
much, many, some, any.
1 How ____ gigabytes does it have?
2 Could I have ____ ice for my drink?
3 She didn't know how ____ it cost.
4 Do you have ____ clothes to give away?
5 They didn't have ____ blue ones.

Answers
1 many 2 some 3 much 4 any (or many) 5 any

Consolidation and Extension p71

Language File pp117–118

Workbook Unit 5 Lesson 2 pp54–55

Photocopiable notes p157, worksheet p175

3 How do they do it?

Communicative Aims	Language	Pronunciation	Vocabulary	Optional aids
Giving directions	Object pronouns Verb + indirect and direct object	/ɔ/ walk /ɑ/ stop /oʊ/ go	Satellite navigation Prepositions of direction	Follow-up activities: local maps from the tourist information office

WARM-UP 1

Vocabulary contest. In pairs, students have two minutes to write down as many places of interest as possible in a typical capital city. Ask the pair with the most to read them to the class and then ask the other pairs to add to the list. For each place ask *What can you do there?*

WARM-UP 2

Ask more confident students in the class *How do you get to school? How long does it take you?* Students continue asking and answering in small groups. Ask *Who takes the longest to get to school?*

1 Opener

- The aim is to introduce the context for the Reading dialogue.
- Students discuss the questions in pairs.

2 Reading

- Students read the article and answer the question.

Answer

They compare the positions of three or four satellites.

Useful information

There are many different kinds of GPS devices, some of which are for use on foot (often for people hiking), and others for use in aircrafts or cars. As well as telling you where to go and giving you your location, GPS devices can show you the best route somewhere and can help you avoid traffic jams and speed cameras. You can even buy a GPS device now that gives you information about historical places you are passing. By 2015, it is expected that there will be more than 400 million GPS users.

Optional activity

1.59 Play the recording of the text for students to read and listen. Stop at any words you predict may cause pronunciation problems, e.g. *artificial, 20,000, accuracy, 300,000* and ask students to repeat.

LANGUAGE WORKOUT OPTION

If you want to pre-teach the language students will be using in the following activities, you may like to go to the Language Workout box now.

3 After Reading

- Students read the article again and decide if sentences 1–6 are true or false.
- Check the answers before students write corrections for the false sentences. Monitor and help where necessary.
- Ask students to read their corrections to the class.

Answers

1 True.
2 True.
3 False. It calculates its position by comparing the position of three or four satellites.
4 True.
5 False. The man found himself on the edge of a cliff.
6 False. The taxi driver drove into a river because he followed GPS directions.

- Students look at the text and find what each word in italics refers to. Do the first sentence together. Ask *Who/What does "them" refer to?* Students find the sentence in the dialogue and look at who/what the pronoun refers to (early explorers).

Answers

1 early explorers 2 drivers 3 the GPS device
4 the taxi driver

Optional activities

- ♦ Ask more comprehension questions about the text, e.g. *What does GPS stand for? What do GPS devices use to show them their position? How many satellites are there in the GPS? What happened to the young woman who was using a GPS device?*
- ♦ Students write four more True/False statements about the text and give them to their partner. They check each other's answers.

Your Response

Students discuss the questions in small groups. Encourage them to think of how people communicated before they had cell phones and the Internet (landlines, fax, telegraph, letter, etc.) and how they found their way around (maps, asking for directions, etc.).

4 Listening

- The aim is to practice following directions. Make sure students know where they are starting from (the hotel). Play the recording, pausing and playing each section again if necessary. Students follow the route and say where they get to.

2.02 Recording

See exercise 5 below.

Answer

National Museum of Natural History

Optional activities

- ♦ 2.02 Play the recording again, pausing after each sentence for students to repeat. Focus on pronunciation and intonation.
- ♦ Read out more directions for students from the hotel (or another starting point) to other places on the map. See if they can follow the directions and tell you where you got to.

5 Vocabulary

- Ask students to look at the prepositions of direction in the Word Bank, and check they understand the meanings clearly.
- Students listen to the recording again and complete the directions using the prepositions from the Word Bank.

2.02 Recording and answers

When you come (1) out of the hotel, turn right (2) onto 9th Street. Walk straight (3) along 9th Street (4) past the library. Go (5) across Pennsylvania Avenue and walk down (6) to Constitution Avenue. Then turn right and it's the big building on the left. You can't miss it!

Optional activities

- ♦ Confident students can try to complete the directions first without listening to the recording, and then listen to check their answers.
- ♦ Give students a minute to study the Prepositions of Direction Word Bank. Students copy the diagrams without the words and then test each other.

6 Speaking

- Make sure students know where they are starting from (the Washington Monument). Read the question. Students then work individually putting sentences A–D in the correct order to give instructions.
- Ask a pair of students to model the dialogue, with one asking the question and the other reading the instructions in the correct order.
- Play the recording so students can check their answers.

2.03 Recording

WOMAN *Excuse me, can you help me—how do I get to the Spy Museum?*

MAN *Walk through the park and turn left onto 15th Street. Go across Constitution Avenue and walk up to F Street. When you get to F Street, turn right. Then walk six blocks and it's on the right. It isn't far.*

WOMAN *Thanks a lot.*

Answers

C, B, D, A

- Focus on the map again. In pairs, students ask each other for directions from one place to another. Point out the example question, and encourage them to use the directions in exercises 5 and 6, and the prepositions of direction in the Word Bank.

Optional activity

In pairs, students write a short dialogue asking for and giving directions from one place to another. They practice the dialogue and then perform it in front of the rest of the class.

Extension Students agree on a starting point on the map and then give each other directions. Their partner has to follow the directions and say where they got to.

7 Pronunciation

- Focus on the three sounds. Read the three words aloud. Students listen and repeat.
- Point out that /oʊ/ is a diphthong—a combination of two sounds.

- Ask students to copy the three pairs of words and sounds into their notebooks and to write the words from the box under the correct one.
- Play the recording for students to check their answers.

2.04 Recording and answers
/ɔ/ *walk call cross lost talk wrong*
/ɑ/ *stop block clock hot lot top*
/oʊ/ *go most phone post show told*

- Play the recording again for students to repeat the words.

Optional activities

- ♦ Students write a sentence which includes as many words as possible from one column.
- ♦ In pairs, students test each other's spelling of the words in the exercise.
- ♦ Elicit other words with the same sounds and write them on the board.

8 Writing

- Give an example by giving directions from your school to a place in town. Then ask students to tell each other the way from the school to three different places.
- Using the model for guidance, students write directions to their home from the school. Monitor and provide help where necessary.
- In small groups or in pairs, students read out their texts without mentioning the name of their street. Their partner/group guesses the name of their street.

LANGUAGE WORKOUT

- Ask students to complete the object pronouns section of the Language Workout box. Confident students can complete first and then check, while less confident ones can look back at exercise 2 and then complete.
- Students turn to page 118 of the Language File to check their answers.

Answers
you them

- Ask students to look at the *Verb + indirect and direct object* section of the Language Workout box. Explain that many verbs can have two objects, and refer students to page 118 of the Language File.

Practice

- Students do Practice exercise 16 on page 118 of the Language File. They complete the sentences with object pronouns. A less confident class could identify who the missing object pronoun refers to before completing the sentences.

Answers
1 them 2 her 3 it 4 me, us 5 him 6 you

- Students do Practice exercise 17 on page 118 of the Language File. They put the words in the right order to make sentences. Remind students to use a capital letter at the beginning of each sentence.

Answers
1 *We asked someone the way.*
2 *Could you send me an e-mail?*
3 *He bought her a gift.*
4 *Will you tell us a joke?*
5 *I wrote them a thank-you note.*
6 *They gave me some flowers.*

Optional activity

Game *Word tennis* Divide the class into two teams. Students "serve" a subject pronoun to the other team, who must "return" the object pronoun. Teams change roles after three subject pronouns have been "served."

Follow-up activities

- ♦ Students use local maps to practice asking for and giving directions. They ask and answer where places are and how to get there.
- ♦ Students think of as many examples as possible for these three categories: *famous singers/groups, food, TV shows*. Write their examples on the board. Drill the question *What do you think of ...?* Students ask each other's opinions of the examples in pairs and practice object pronouns, e.g. *I love them, I don't like it*, etc. Demonstrate with one or two confident students first.

Homework

Students write a dialogue between a tourist who is lost and a police officer using the map in exercise 4 and the dialogue in exercise 6 as a model.

NOTEBOOK SECTION

Circle the correct option in each sentence.
1 Where's my camera? I can't find *them/it*.
2 Would you please give this to *her/she*?
3 Please reserve a room for *us/we*.
4 Here. I'll give *you/yours* my umbrella.
5 There's a message to call he/him.

Answers
1 it 2 her 3 us 4 you 5 him

Consolidation and Extension p71

Language File p118

Workbook Unit 5 Lesson 3 pp56–57

Photocopiable notes p158, worksheet p176

4 Integrated Skills
Suggestions and advice

Skills

Reading Topics: Welcome to TopTeen-Travel travel guide
Listening Checking details: conversations about travel plans
Speaking Role-play: making suggestions and giving advice
Writing Dialogue or e-mail about vacations

Learner Independence

Knowing a word
Dictionary abbreviations

Vocabulary

Luggage and clothes
Dictionary words
Useful expressions

Optional aids

Exercise 10 Follow-up activity: cards for the Vocabulary box

WARM-UP 1

Write jumbled sentences on the board including object pronouns. Set a time limit for students to work in pairs to re-order them.

WARM-UP 2

If you set the homework suggested in the previous lesson, ask students to role-play each other's dialogues in pairs, and ask confident pairs to act out their dialogues in front of the class.

WARM-UP 3

Game *Memory chain* The first student says *I went on vacation and I took (a toothbrush).* The second student repeats the line, adding something new. Continue around the class until the list of things becomes too long to remember.

1 Opener

- The aim is to engage the students' interest in the text and personalize the topic. This can be done as a whole class activity with a less confident class. Supply extra vocabulary where necessary.

2 Reading

- The aim is to increase students' awareness of text structure, in particular, topics and paragraphs. Students read and match the topics with the paragraphs. Point out that they may only need to read the first one or two lines of each paragraph to find the information they need. Remind students that there are two topics they will not need.

Answers
1 Think small 2 Don't take too much 3 Travel light
4 Enjoy long journeys 5 Keep in touch

3

- Students find the highlighted words and match them with the definitions. Then they compare answers in pairs.

Answers
1 paperbacks 2 tips 3 polyester
4 lightweight 5 waterproof 6 huge
7 daypack 8 stuff

Optional activities

- Ask students to create *wh-* comprehension questions about the text, e.g. *What isn't a good idea? Why are lightweight pants better than jeans? Why shouldn't you take a raincoat?*
- Give students five minutes to memorize all they can from the text. Students close their books. Read out the text including some false information, e.g. *There will be room in the tour bus for a big suitcase.* Students shout *Stop!* when they hear incorrect information and correct it.
- Students find words in the text to add to their word map for *Clothes* (see Unit 1, Lesson 2, Follow-up activity).

4 Listening

- Play the recording of the first part of the conversation. Students listen and number the order in which Steve is visiting the countries. Play the recording again if necessary, but do not check the answers yet.

2.05 Recording

LARA	*Steve, what are you doing when we all go home?*
STEVE	*You'll never guess—I'm flying around the world!*
RAMÓN	*Wow! I've always wanted to do that.*
LARA	*Yeah! Where are you going?*
STEVE	*First, I'm flying from San Francisco to Rio de Janeiro in Brazil. I'm staying with a friend there for a week, and then I'm taking a flight across South America to Lima.*
LARA	*That's in Peru, right?*
STEVE	*Right. I want to go to Cuzco in Peru and see the fantistic ruins at Machu Picchu. After that, I'm flying south to Santiago in Chile. There's an amazing desert in Chile called the Atacama Desert. It's three thousand meters high and they say it never rains there.*
RAMÓN	*Never? Really? Are you staying long in Chile?*
STEVE	*For a couple of weeks. The Atacama Desert is one thousand six hundred kilometers north of Santiago. Then I'm taking a very long flight to Auckland in New Zealand, and from there on to Sydney in Australia. I'm spending three weeks backpacking in Australia and finally flying back to San Francisco via Singapore.*
LARA	*What a trip! That's six different countries in six weeks!*

5

- Play the beginning of the second part of the conversation for students to check their answers to exercise 4 (up to where Ramón says *and finally Singapore*).

Answers

1 Brazil 2 Peru 3 Chile 4 New Zealand 5 Australia 6 Singapore

2.06 Recording

LARA	*What a trip! That's six different countries in six weeks!*
RAMÓN	*So, let me see—first, you're going to Brazil, and next …*
LARA	*Next it's Peru, and then Chile. And after that, you're going to New Zealand.*
RAMÓN	*And then Australia, and finally Singapore.*
STEVE	*That's right! I'm really looking forward to it. I've already started packing some things.*
LARA	*What are you taking with you?*
STEVE	*Well, I have an old suitcase, but I'm thinking of getting a big backpack.*
RAMÓN	*Do you think that's a good idea?*
STEVE	*Why not? Then I can take lots of stuff. I have lots of cotton T-shirts, and I'm taking a thick wool sweater because it can get cold in the Atacama Desert. And a raincoat in case it does rain in the desert!*
LARA	*But hold on a minute—maybe you should …*
STEVE	*And of course, I'm taking several pairs of jeans. That's quite a lot already. But I'm not taking a suit or a tie. And I'll buy some shirts in Rio. And swim trunks—Brazilian swim trunks are great!*
LARA	*Steve, can I make a suggestion?*
RAMÓN	*Yes, Steve, there are one or two things I wanted to say, too.*
STEVE	*OK. Go ahead.*
LARA	*Well, why don't you …?*

- Ask students to look at the list of clothes/accessories in the box. Make sure they know what they all are. With a less confident class, you might like to predict what items Steve is taking based on the countries he is planning to visit.
- Play the second part of the conversation all the way through. Students listen and check the items Steve is taking with him. Ask students to compare their answers in pairs.
- Play the recording again for students to check their answers. Explain that *swim trunks* are like shorts and are for boys and men; *swimsuit and bikini* are words for female swimwear.

Answers

backpack cotton T-shirts jeans raincoat wool sweater

6 Speaking

- Read out the role-play instructions and the *Making suggestions and giving advice* box.
- Ask students to read *Welcome to TopTeenTravel!* again and to look at the things they checked in exercise 5.
- Do the role-play with a confident student or elicit suggestions for each stage and build the dialogue on the board.
- Students do the role-play and then exchange roles and repeat it.

Optional activities

- ♦ With a less confident class, you may want to write the dialogue between Steve and Lara/Ramón on the board and then remove parts of the dialogue from the board. Students continue practicing the dialogue from memory. Eventually, remove all the dialogue.
- ♦ Ask different groups to perform their role-plays for the rest of the class

7 Writing

- The aim is for students to write a dialogue or an e-mail using the role-play as a framework. Ask students to look back at the role-play instructions and at the text on page 68 for help. Students choose whether to write the dialogue or the e-mail and then work individually.
- Students exchange texts and read them, first for interest, and then again to check spelling and punctuation.

Optional activities

- ♦ Students work on the dialogue in pairs, each writing the part of one speaker.
- ♦ Students cut up the dialogue into separate lines, which they mix up. Another student or pair has to put the lines back into the correct order.
- ♦ Students writing the e-mail can write a reply, asking why their friend is making suggestions, replying and agreeing.

8 Learner Independence

- The aim is to encourage students to think about what "knowing" a word really means. Ask students to decide which of the statements they agree with, and discuss them with another student. Each statement refers to a different aspect of "knowing": *comprehension, recall, phonology, orthography, syntax,* and *collocation*.

Optional activities

- ♦ Students think of examples of words which they can understand but not pronounce, or pronounce but are not able to spell.
- ♦ Have a class vote on which answers most students agree with. Ask *Why?* about statements where a number of students disagree.

9

- The aim is to help students use dictionaries effectively by ensuring that they understand the abbreviations used. Ask students to match on their own and then compare their answers in pairs.

Answers

abbrev—abbreviation, adj—adjective, adv—adverb, aux—auxiliary verb (like be*), C—countable, pl—plural, sb—somebody, sing—singular, sth—something, U—uncountable*

- Ask students to look at the introduction to their dictionaries to see if the same abbreviations are used. Ask students to find uses of the abbreviations in their dictionaries.

10 Phrasebook

- Ask students to look through the unit and find the idiomatic expressions, and look at how they are used.
- Play the recording for students to listen and repeat.

2.07 Recording and answers

I'm starving! (Emma, Lesson 2, ex 2)
Are you ready to order? (Waiter, Lesson 2, ex 2)
I'll have that. (Silvana, Lesson 2, ex 2)
What would you like to drink? (Waiter, Lesson 2, ex 2)
Sure—coming right up. (Waiter, Lesson 2, ex 2)
You're impossible! (Emma, Lesson 2, ex 2)
You can't miss it! (voice, Lesson 3, ex 5)
Excuse me, can you help me? (voice, Lesson 3, ex 5)
It isn't far. (voice, Lesson 3, ex 5)
Last but not least … (voice, Lesson 4, ex 2)

- Students can add expressions which they like to their Personal Phrasebooks. Help with translation.
- Ask students to match the replies to the four questions. With a confident class, you could do this orally.

Answers

a Are you ready to order?
b Excuse me, can you help me?
c What would you like to drink?

Follow-up activities

- ♦ Students write four-line dialogues using at least two of the expressions from exercise 10.
- ♦ Allow students a limited time to see how many words they can make from BACKPACKERS in small groups. Students may only use letters *a*, *c*, and *k* twice in a word. The group with the greatest number of words wins. Other students can add to the winning list. Possible words include: *as, are, back, pack, sack, sea, car, cap, ask, bar, bear, be, ace, papa, park, bark, peak, spare, spear,* and plurals of all the nouns which don't have *s* in them.
- ♦ Students choose five words from the lesson to write on vocabulary cards. These can be added to the Vocabulary box.

Homework

Students make a list of suggestions for clothes that a visitor to their country should bring at different times of the year.

Using their dictionaries to help them, students find an example of every kind of dictionary word in exercise 9.

NOTEBOOK SECTION

There is a countable/uncountable error in each sentence. Rewrite the sentences correctly.

1 I'd like some spaghettis.
2 How many money do you have?
3 He never has some money.
4 I don't like hamburger.
5 Would you like a cheese?

Answers

*1 I'd like some **spaghetti**. 2 How **much** money do you have? 3 He never has **any** money. 4 I don't like **hamburgers**. 5 Would you like (**some**) cheese?*

Consolidation and Extension p71

Workbook Unit 5 Lesson 4 pp58–59

Inspired EXTRA!

Language links

- Have students look at the cartoon and ask if they find it funny.
- In small groups, students talk about the warning. Ask them to guess what the different languages are (English, French, German, Spanish, Italian). See if they can find any words they recognize, either because they are similar to words in their own language or in another language they know, or because they know the languages the warnings are written in. Ask students to make a list of things that might have this warning on the packet.

Optional activity

Students close their books. Write the French, German, Spanish, and Italian warnings on the board (but not the English one) and see if students can guess what they mean.

Puzzle

- Students work out the puzzle in pairs.

Answer
V-A-C-A-T-I-O-N

- Write the puzzle on the board and then erase the "clue" words to give a structure like this:
  My first is in _____, _____, and _____
  My second is in _____ and also _____
  My third is in _____, but it isn't in _____
  My fourth is in _____, but it's also in _____
  My fifth is in _____, _____, and _____
  My sixth is in _____ but not in _____
  My seventh is in _____ but not in _____
  My last is in _____—the time for our flight!
  We're going on _____ today—that's right!
- As you erase the words at the end of the lines, point out the rhymes. Explain that rhymes are fun but not essential.
- Ask students to write their own puzzle. Make it clear that students don't have to follow this structure and they can choose a longer or shorter final word. Students work in pairs or small groups to write the puzzles. Students can read out their puzzles or write them on the board.

Skit The Restaurant

- The aim is for students to enjoy using their English while also getting valuable stress and intonation practice. Ask students to look at the cartoon and establish that the skit is set in a restaurant.
- With a more confident class, play the recording with books closed. Then play it again with books open. With a less confident class, play the recording once while the students follow in their books, and then once again with books closed.

2.08 Recording
See text on page 70 of the Student's Book.

- Divide the class into four equal groups and play the recording again, with one group repeating in chorus as the Woman, one as the Man, one as the Waitress, and one as the Waiter. Encourage students to laugh and exaggerate stress and intonation.
- Ask students to close their books and play the recording again. Then ask students to work in groups of four and read the skit aloud. Choose several groups to act out the skit in front of the class.

Optional activity

Make an audio or video recording of students performing the skit.

Limerick

- Explain that a limerick is a funny five-line poem in which the first two lines usually rhyme with the fifth line and the third and fourth lines rhyme with each other.
- Play the recording for students to read and listen. Then play the recording again with books closed.

2.09 Recording
See text on page 70 of the Student's Book.

Optional activities

- ♦ Students learn the limerick by heart.
- ♦ Students can try to write their own limericks. Point out that lines 1, 2, and 5 usually have three stresses or beats, while lines 3 and 4 only have two beats.

Consolidation

Lesson 1

Suggested answers

At lunchtime, they're having lunch at Pizza Paradise. In the afternoon, they're visiting the Air and Space Museum or the National Museum of Natural History. In the evening, they're going to the theater/going to see The Lion King.

Lesson 2

Suggested answer

WAITER	*Are you ready to order?*
RAMÓN	*Yes, could I have a Surprise pizza, please?*
ALEX	*What's that?*
RAMÓN	*It's a pizza with cheese, tomatoes, spinach, and a fried egg.*
ALEX	*Oh, I don't want any tomatoes.*
WAITER	*There's a Country pizza—with cheese, onions, peppers, and mushrooms.*
ALEX	*No, I don't want any peppers.*
WAITER	*Then why don't you have a Tropical pizza? There aren't any tomatoes or peppers in that.*
ALEX	*OK, I'll have that.*

Lesson 3

Suggested answers

Luggage *backpack, suitcase, bag*
Clothes *T-shirt, pants, jeans, sweater, raincoat, jacket, swim trunks, shirt, suit, tie*

Extension

Lesson 1

Suggested answers

Places to visit	*museum, art gallery, church, cathedral, park, zoo*
Performance	*theaters, movie theater, concert hall*
Shopping	*market, department store, shopping mall*
Food and drink	*restaurant, coffee shop, snackbar, bar*

Lesson 2
Students' own answers.

Lesson 3
Students' own answers.

Lesson 4
Students' own answers.

YOUR CHOICE!

The aim is to give students more learner independence and help them to identify their preferred ways of learning. Encourage students to choose an activity that they feel less comfortable with if they want a challenge or are aware that they need practice in a particular area.
Suggestions gives students the opportunity to work in a group choosing a problem situation and talking about it using functional language for giving advice.
I Never Travel Without It gives students the opportunity to act out a mime and answer questions individually about an item of their choice.

Language File pp117–118

Workbook Unit 5 Inspired EXTRA! pp60–61

Teenage life

Useful information

A recent survey shows that teenagers in the U.S. spend an average of 25 hours a week watching TV, and only five or six hours doing homework or with the family. 75% of boys aged up to 16 frequently play a team game, compared with 42% of girls. The sport most played by boys is football, while girls prefer more individual activities such as swimming and athletics.

In another survey, almost 85% say that they get along well with their parents. Just one in five teenagers say they argue with their parents. However, while nearly three-fourths of teenagers say that it is important for parents to listen to their children, only 41% of parents share that view.

1 Opener

- The aim is to arouse interest in the reading text.
- Ask students to look at the photo of U.S. teenagers on pages 72–73. Ask *How old are they? What are they wearing? What are they doing? Do they look happy? Do they look like teenagers in your country? Why/Why not?*
- Ask students to take the quiz in pairs and then compare their answers with another pair.
- Check the answers with the whole class. Are they surprised by any of the answers?

Answers
1 C 2 B 3 B 4 A 5 C 6 A

- Ask students to work in pairs and answer the quiz questions for teenagers in their own country.
- In what ways do students think teenagers in their country are the same as teenagers in the U.S.?

2 Reading

- Students read the text about four U.S. teen girls and find the answers to the questions. They compare their answers with a partner.
- Check the answers with the class.

Answers
1 Anna 2 Naomi 3 Jodi 4 Isabelle 5 Isabelle 6 Anna 7 Jodi 8 Naomi

Optional activity

- Ask students *Which of the four girls is most similar to you in attitude? Which is the most different? Which one would you most like to meet?*

3 Vocabulary

- Students close their books and work individually for five minutes, matching the words with the definitions.
- Then tell students to read the texts once more so they can check their answers.
- Check the answers with the class by asking one student to say a word and then to choose another student to say the definition.

Answers
1 c 2 a 3 f 4 e 5 d 6 b

- Note that the meaning of the word *guy* here is exclusively male. However, *guys* can be used to refer to a mixed male/female group. Check comprehension of other words in the texts, e.g. *models, diets, waste, responsibility.*

4 Mini-Project Teenage Life

- Explain that the four girls are typical American teenagers. Write these headings on the board: *Parents, Problems, Future, Leisure activities*, and brainstorm words to write under each heading. Point out that the girls are talking about their attitudes to life as teenagers. Read the example and ask students to work in pairs discussing the similarities and differences between the life the girls describe and life for teenage girls in their country.
- Encourage each pair to make a statement to the class like the one in the example.
- Still in pairs, students write about teenage life for girls and/or boys in their country. They may like to do a class survey to include in their report, or to interview one or two students and include their comments. Encourage them to illustrate their report with drawings and photos.
- Remind students to correct their work carefully.
- Ask each pair to team up with another pair and to show each other their reports and compare their findings.

NOTEBOOK SECTION

Draw lines to match the items in the two columns.

1 can't wait	advice
2 do	a diet
3 give	to see you
4 make	homework
5 go on	a suggestion

Answers
1 can't wait to see you
2 do homework
3 give advice
4 make a suggestion
5 go on a diet

Workbook Culture pp62–63

1 Have you recorded everything?

Communicative Aims	Language	Pronunciation	Vocabulary
Talking about recent events	Present perfect Present perfect with *just*	/f/ enough, photograph	Activities Animals

WARM-UP 1

Game *Word association* Divide students into groups of three or four. Student A thinks of a word from the previous unit, e.g. *suitcase*. Student B has to say a word associated with suitcase, e.g. *travel*. Student C has to say a word associated with travel, e.g. *train*, and so on. Students can challenge each other to explain their word associations.

WARM-UP 2

Ask students to work in pairs or groups, and to list as many animals as possible in three minutes. The pair/group with the longest list wins.

1 Opener

- The aim is to introduce the context for the Reading dialogue. Brainstorm ideas for things you could make a two-minute video about. Discuss the question as a whole class, encouraging individual students to suggest things they would like to make a video about.

2 Reading

- Students cover the dialogue and look at the photo on page 74. Elicit that Emma is filming Silvana and Ramón with a video camera, and ask students to guess who Silvana and Ramón are talking about.
- Students read the dialogue to see if they predicted correctly that Silvana and Ramón are talking about Emma.
- Ask general comprehension questions about the dialogue, e.g. *What does Ramón think about Emma? What does Silvana say about Emma?*

Optional activity

2.10 Play the recording of the dialogue, pausing for students to repeat. Focus on pronunciation and intonation.

3 After Reading

- Students read the dialogue again and decide if sentences 1–6 are true or false.
- Check the answers before students write corrections for the false sentences. Monitor and help where necessary.
- Ask students to read their corrections to the class.

Answers

1 False. Ramón hasn't had an argument with Emma.
2 True.
3 False. Emma has been really mean to Ramón.
4 False. Emma hasn't said a word to Ramón all day.
5 True.
6 False. She has recorded their conversation.

Your Response

- Read out the question and ask the class what they think. Have a class vote to see how many students think Emma has recorded Silvana and Ramón's conversation.
- Play the dialogue. Students listen to see if their ideas were right.

2.11 Recording

EMMA *Let's play back the recording.*
RAMÓN *I have tried to talk to her, but she's been really mean to me.*
EMMA *Oh! Who are you talking about? Me?*
SILVANA *Emma likes you a lot—she just told me.*
EMMA *Silvana, how could you?*
SILVANA *Oh no! You've broken the camera!*
EMMA *No, I haven't! I've only taken out the memory card.*
SILVANA *Oh, Emma, come on! We want to make a video.*
EMMA *I don't want to make a video. I'm going back to the hotel. I've had enough!*

Answer

Emma has recorded Silvana and Ramón's conversation.

- Ask students to talk in pairs about what they think will happen next. Encourage them to tell their ideas to the whole class.

Optional activities

- ♦ 2.11 Play the recording, pausing for students to repeat. Focus on pronunciation and intonation. Students act out the dialogue in groups of three.
- ♦ Students write more true/false sentences based on the second part of the dialogue and test each other in small groups.
- ♦ Early finishers look through the dialogue and note down all the examples of the present perfect in preparation for the next exercise.

LANGUAGE WORKOUT OPTION

If you want to pre-teach the language students will be using in the following activities, you may like to go to the Language Workout box now.

4 Listening

- Explain to students that they are going to hear Carrie's interviews with Lara and Alex for World2day. Check students understand the phrases in the left-hand column of the chart.
- Play the recording. Students complete the chart with checks and crosses as they listen. You may like to pause after Carrie's interview with Lara and check students' answers before playing the rest of the recording.

2.12 Recording

CARRIE *Welcome to World2day! Let's find out what Lara has done this week. Lara, can I ask you a few questions?*
LARA *Sure, go ahead.*
CARRIE *First of all, have you taken any pictures?*
LARA *No, I haven't—I'm not good at taking pictures!*
CARRIE *I don't believe you! What about shopping—have you bought any gifts?*
LARA *Yes, I've bought some gifts for my family.*
CARRIE *That's great. And have you played any sports?*
LARA *Yes, I've played ping-pong twice!*
CARRIE *All right—and have you sent any e-mails this week?*
LARA *No, I haven't, but I've sent some postcards.*
CARRIE *Cool. Now, tell me, have you been to a party?*
LARA *Yes, some Brazilian friends had a party yesterday. It was great.*
CARRIE *OK! Last question—have you had fun this week?*
LARA *Yes, it's been fantastic!*
CARRIE *Good! And thank you, Lara. And now, Alex—let's hear what you've done this week. Have you taken any pictures?*
ALEX *Oh yes, I've taken lots of pictures!*
CARRIE *Have you bought any gifts?*
ALEX *No, I haven't. But I'm going to buy some tomorrow.*
CARRIE *What about sports—have you played any sports this week?*
ALEX *No, I haven't had time!*
CARRIE *And have you sent any e-mails?*
ALEX *Yes, I've sent lots of e-mails to my friends.*
CARRIE *And, um, Alex, have you been to a party this week?*
ALEX *No, I haven't. But I'm looking forward to the farewell party.*
CARRIE *That's wonderful—and please don't be late!*
ALEX *No, I won't!*
CARRIE *And finally, have you had fun this week?*
ALEX *Oh yes, I've had a great time.*

Answers

	Lara	*Alex*
... pictures?	✗	✓
... gifts?	✓	✗
... sports?	✓	✗
... e-mails?	✗	✓
... party?	✓	✗
... fun?	✓	✓

5 Speaking

- Ask two students to read the example questions and answers. Make sure students understand that the information is from the completed chart in exercise 4.
- Students work in pairs, taking turns to ask and answer questions based on their completed charts from exercise 4: Student A asks about Lara and Student B asks about Alex. With a less confident class, check students have completed the chart correctly before they work in pairs.

Answers

A Has Lara taken any pictures?
B No, she hasn't. Has Alex taken any pictures?
A Yes, he has. Has Lara bought any gifts?
B Yes, she has. Has Alex bought any gifts?
A No, he hasn't. Has Lara played any sports?
B Yes, she has. Has Alex played any sports?
A No, he hasn't. Has Lara sent any e-mails?
B No, she hasn't. Has Alex sent any e-mails?
A Yes, he has. Has Lara been to a party?
B Yes, she has. Has Alex been to a party?
A No, he hasn't. Has Lara had fun?
B Yes, she has. Has Alex had fun?
A Yes, he has.

- Ask students to change partners and interview each other to complete the final column of the chart. To demonstrate the activity, invite students to ask you the six questions (*Have you bought any gifts?*, etc.), and answer them. Encourage students to ask follow-up questions.

Optional activities

- ♦ Do the first part of the exercise as an open class activity to check the answers to exercise 4.
- ♦ Ask students to brainstorm other possible recent activities. Write cues on the board, e.g. *play basketball, use a computer, see a movie*. Students interview each other.

6 Speaking

- Ask students to read the phrases in the box. Check they understand *break a plate, make a silly noise, take a shower.*
- Play the recording and pause after the first sound. Read the example sentence aloud. Continue with the recording, pausing after each sound for students to choose the appropriate phrase and say what has just happened.

2.13 Recording
Eight sound effects

Answers
1 Someone has just made a silly noise.
2 Someone has just taken a shower.
3 Someone has just opened a gift.
4 Someone has just told a joke.
5 Someone has just broken a plate.
6 Someone has just kissed someone.
7 Someone has just answered the phone.
8 Someone has just sent an e-mail.

Optional activity

Game *What's just happened?* Divide the class in two groups. One student from each group comes to the front and sits down with their back to the board. Write a sentence on the board, e.g. *He/She has just taken a shower.* The groups tell their team member how they feel now, e.g. *You have wet hair, You feel clean.* The first student to guess the sentence wins a point for their group.

Useful information

Rock Creek Park
Rock Creek Park is a large park which runs down through the middle of urban Washington, D.C. The main section of the park covers 1,754 acres, which is twice the area of Central Park in New York City. The park was established in 1890, and is managed by the National Park Service. Parts of the park are very wild, with a stream, woods, and equestrian trails. Other parts include a tennis stadium, the National Zoo, and a nature center. It is a popular place for jogging, biking, and walking, especially on weekends, when some of the roads that run through the park are closed to cars.

7 Vocabulary

- Ask students to look at the pictures on page 75. Ask *Which animals can you name? Where do you find these animals?* (squirrel, duck, cow, deer)
- Ask students to read the text and find out where they can see these animals in Washington, D.C.

Answers
squirrel—Rock Creek Park
duck—National Zoo
cow—National Zoo
deer—Rock Creek Park

- Ask further comprehension questions about the text, e.g. *Where can you see lions and tigers? What other animals can you see in the National Zoo, Kid's Farm?*

Optional activity

Ask students what they know about parks, zoos, and wildlife in their country. Ask *Who are city farms for?* (*Children, particularly those who don't get out of the city often.*)

Extension Describe an animal to students, e.g. *It has a long tail, it has a hairy body, and it can climb trees.* Elicit the name of the animal (*a monkey*). In pairs, students describe animals to each other without saying their names. Their partners have to guess which animal they are describing.

8 Pronunciation

- Check students know the meaning of the words in the box. Ask them to give definitions, in English if possible.
- Ask students to read the words to each other and mark the ones which they think contain the sound /f/.
- Play the recording once for students to check their answers. Ask students which pairs of letters can make the sound /f/: (*gh, ph*) but *gh* is never pronounced /f/ at the beginning of a word, e.g. *ghost* /goʊst/.
- Play the recording again, pausing after each word for students to repeat in chorus.

2.14 Recording and answers
bought enough laugh lightweight
photograph right thought

Optional activities

- In pairs, students test each other's spelling of the words in the Vocabulary box.
- Ask students to think of other words like *right* where *gh* is silent, e.g. *through, weigh, sightseeing, fight, flight, night, high.*

9 Writing

- Ask students to look at the hand-written example. Point out that *once/twice* are irregular forms; from three onwards we use *times: three times, four times,* etc. These adverbial phrases of frequency usually go at the end of the clause or sentence.
- Students write their sentences on their own. Monitor and provide help where necessary.
- Students exchange texts and check each other's use of the present perfect.
- Elicit feedback about any interesting information.

Extension Have students look at the example sentence. Then students write similar sentences about the student they interviewed in exercise 5.

LANGUAGE WORKOUT

- Ask students to complete the sentences in the Language Workout box. Confident students can complete first and then check, while others can look back at exercise 2 and then complete.
- Students turn to page 119 of the Language File to check their answers.

Answers

been hasn't said Have have Have ... had haven't has 've/have just just

- Highlight that:
  - we can use the present perfect to talk about recent completed actions or events. We don't say the exact time of the action or event, but we can refer to an unfinished period of time, e.g. *all day, today, this week.*
  - we can use the present perfect with *just* to talk about very recent events.
  - we form the present perfect with *have* + past participle. Regular past participles have the same form as the simple past, i.e. *-ed.*
- Refer students to the list of Irregular Verbs on page 127 and explain that irregular past participles fall into three groups:
  Group 1: all three forms are different
  Group 2: two forms are the same
  Group 3: all three forms are the same.
- Drill the examples chorally and individually.

Optional activity

Drill affirmative, negative, and question forms by changing the sentences in the box, e.g. Teacher: *She has been mean to me. Negative.* Students: *She hasn't been mean to me.*

Practice

- Students do Practice exercise 18 on page 119 of the Language File. They complete the exercise individually.
- Ask individual students to read their answers to the class. Ask them for the answers to questions 4 and 5. (*No, he hasn't. No, they haven't.*)

Answers

1 Emma has just filmed Ramón and Silvana.
2 She has recorded everything they said.
3 She hasn't said anything to Ramón today.
4 Has Ramón been rude to Emma?
5 Have they just had an argument?
6 We haven't broken anything.

Follow-up activities

♦ Students make a word map for *Animals*. They make the distinction between wild and domestic animals and add as many animals as they can. If you did Warm-up 2, use the lists the pairs/groups made. The word maps could be displayed in the classroom.

♦ **Game** *Alphabet game* The game can be played in groups or as a whole class. Students think of an animal beginning with each letter of the alphabet, (except Q, U, and X). Students win one point for each correct animal. An extra point could be added for saying whether the animal is wild or domestic.

Homework

Students write about the animals in their local park or zoo.

Write expressions from the lesson on the board, e.g. *I'm not kidding. I've had enough.* Students make up short dialogues to illustrate their meaning. As a warm up in the next lesson, they read out their dialogues, omitting the expressions for other students to guess.

NOTEBOOK SECTION

Complete the sentences using the present perfect form of the verb in parentheses.

1 I ____ anything all day. (not eat)
2 He ____ very hard lately. (try)
3 I'm sorry. I ____ just ____ the bad news. (hear)
4 We ____ much homework this week. (not do)
5 ____ you ____ Jill today? (see) No, I ____.

Answers

1 haven't eaten
2 hasn't tried
3 've (have), heard
4 haven't done
5 Have, seen, haven't

Consolidation and Extension p83

Language File p119

Workbook Unit 6 Lesson 1 pp64–65

Photocopiable notes p158, worksheet p177

2 Have you ever ...?

Communicative Aims	Language	Pronunciation	Vocabulary	Optional aids
Talking about experiences	Present perfect with *ever/never* Indefinite pronouns and adverbs	Word stress in compound nouns	Transportation	Warm-up 2: pictures from magazines Warm-up 3: small cards with infinitives written on them, a hat or box Writing: pieces of paper

WARM-UP 1

If students made up dialogues for their homework in the last lesson, they read them out, omitting the expressions. Other students have to try and guess what the missing expressions are.

WARM-UP 2

Bring in a variety of different pictures (Optional aids) to use as flashcards. Use the pictures to ask questions using the present perfect, e.g. *Have you ever eaten Indian food?* Elicit short answers from students. Give students some of the pictures for them to ask questions in an open class activity.

WARM-UP 3

Game *Bingo* Play *Bingo* (see Unit 3, Lesson 1, page 60) with past participles.

1 Opener

- The aim is to introduce the context for the Reading text. Ask students to look at the photos on page 76. Ask students if they can guess where the trains are (top to bottom: Shanghai, China; France; Japan). Then discuss the questions with the class (the Shanghai train has no wheels, because it moves using magnets).

2 Reading

- Students read the article and discuss the question in pairs. Ask students to tell the class their ideas.
- Elicit the meaning of *links, technology, engine, brakes, magnets, attract, repel, float, cushion, reality, commercial*.

Optional activity

2.15 Play the recording of the article for students to read and listen.

3 After Reading

- Students choose the best words to complete the sentences or answer the questions.
- Check the answers with the whole class.

Answers

1 A 2 C 3 B 4 A 5 C 6 B

Optional activity

Early finishers look back through the text and note examples of the present perfect for exercise 4.

Your Response

- Ask students to discuss the question in groups. Each group should appoint a note-taker, who writes down their arguments.
- After ten minutes, ask each note-taker to write his/her group's arguments on the board, so that the whole class's arguments are presented. Encourage students to comment on other groups' arguments, e.g. if they disagree with anything or notice that several of the groups have had the same idea.

LANGUAGE WORKOUT OPTION

If you want to pre-teach the language students will be using in the following activities, you may like to go to the Language Workout box now.

4 Speaking

- Students use the *Life Questionnaire* to interview each other. Ask a confident student an example question and elicit the answer. Students continue asking and answering questions and note down the answers. Depending on space, students could get up and move around asking as many people as they can in a limited time, or interview each other in small groups.
- Students tell a partner and then the class what they've found out about other students' experiences.

Optional activity

Confident students can ask their partner follow-up questions using the simple past if they receive the answer *yes*, e.g. *When/Where/Who did you …?* Make it clear that *Have you ever …?* asks about a general life experience, but that follow-up questions with *did you* are about specific times and details.

Extension Ask a student to read out the hand-written example. Students then write similar sentences about three students. They exchange texts and check each other's use of the present perfect.
Ask some students to read out their texts, without naming the students, for others to guess who they are talking about.

5 Listening

- Before they listen, students look at the pictures on page 77, read the captions and say what the pictures show (*an old car, a covered wagon, a steam train, a street car*).
- Play the recording once for students to number the pictures from 1 to 4.
- Students compare their answers in pairs. Check the answers with the class.

2.16 Recording

RAMÓN *What a great museum! I've never been anywhere like this. Look at that picture of a covered wagon!*
SILVANA *My guidebook says that they were very slow. It took a whole day to travel 15 kilometers—and some people went all the way from the east coast to the west coast by wagon.*
RAMÓN *So when did the railroad come?*
SILVANA *Around 1830. And look, there's a picture of the first railroad to go from the east coast to California.*
RAMÓN *The one with two engines? What does it say?*
SILVANA *It says "Trains meeting in Utah, 1869." It was America's first transcontinental railroad.*
RAMÓN *Hey. Let's get on this. It's an old streetcar from Washington in 1900. Can you see the conductor?*
SILVANA *Yes, I can see him, but we can't get on the streetcar! It's an exhibit. Now I want to look at some of the old cars in this museum.*
RAMÓN *Come on, then! They're over here.*
SILVANA *Wow! Look at that old red Ford.*
RAMÓN *It's great. I'd love to drive that.*
SILVANA *It says that Elvis Presley drove it.*
RAMÓN *Elvis? I'm sure he had a more modern car than that!*
SILVANA *No, it was in a movie—in 1957.*
RAMÓN *Oh, right. Well, let's start filming our video!*

Answers
1 B 2 C 3 D 4 A

- Play the recording again, pausing and replaying if necessary. Students listen and choose the correct information. Check the answers by asking individual students to read out their completed sentences.

Answers
A drove, 1957 B a day, 15 C railroad, 1869 D can't

Optional activity

Ask further comprehension questions, e.g. *When did the railraod come?* With a confident class, students listen and note down as much information as they can about the exhibits at the museum. They compare in pairs and report to the class.

6 Vocabulary

- Ask students to look at the examples. Explain that they are compound nouns, i.e. a combination of two nouns to make a word.
- Students work in pairs and write compound nouns made from the words in A and B.
- Do not check the answers yet.

7 Pronunciation

- Play the recording once for students to check their answers to exercise 6.

2.17 Recording and answers
bus driver, bus station, bus stop, bus ticket, car driver, bus schedule, car engine, car wash
railroad crossing, railroad engine, railroad station, railroad track
train driver, train station, train ticket, train schedule

- Play the recording again, pausing after each compound noun for students to repeat.
- In pairs, students mark the stress in pencil. Play the recording again for students to check their answers, then drill chorally and individually. The stress is on the first word in these compound nouns.

Optional activity

Game *Teacher* Play with transportation words. See Unit 2, Lesson 1 for more details.

8 Game

- The aim is to encourage learners to take responsibility for their learning by testing each other. Divide the class into pairs/teams and ask students to take turns testing each other on ten past participles. Give students time to choose ten verbs before they start. The winner is the one who gets ten participles right in the fastest time.

9 Writing

- Using the *Life Questionnaire* for prompts and the model sentence for guidance, students write about their own personal experiences on pieces of paper (see Optional aids). Confident students can add details about their experiences using the simple past. Monitor and provide help where necessary.

Extension Tell students something about yourself using *never*, e.g. *I've never been to Washington, D.C.* Encourage students to guess whether the sentence is true or false.
Using the model sentence for guidance, students write five sentences about themselves with *never*, three of which are true and two of which are false. They exchange sentences in pairs and their partner guesses the false information.

LANGUAGE WORKOUT

- Ask students to look at the top half of the Language Workout box. Confident students can complete first and then check, while others can look back at exercise 2 and then complete.
- Students turn to page 119 of the Language File to check their answers.

Answers

Have ... ever you ever never had has never ever

- Highlight that:
  - we can use the present perfect to talk about experiences at an indefinite time in the past.
  - *ever* = at any time. It is often used in questions with the present perfect.
  - *never* = at no time.
  - *ever* and *never* go before the past participle in present perfect sentences.
- Drill the examples chorally and individually for pronunciation and stress.
- Students turn to page 119 of the Language File to check their answers.

Answers

anything everywhere someone

- Highlight that:
  - we use *anyone/thing/where* in negative sentences and questions.
  - indefinite pronouns are singular, so we use singular verbs with *any/every/no/someone.*
  - we can also use *any/every/no/somebody* instead of *any/every/no/someone.*
- Drill the examples chorally and individually for pronunciation and stress.
- Ask students to complete the bottom half of the Language Workout box.

Practice

- Students do Practice exercise 19 on page 119 of the Language File. They complete the sentences with *ever/ never*. Do the first one together as an example.
- Check the answers with the class. Point out the use of *been* in sentences 1, 2, and 6 and explain that *go* has two possible past participles: *gone* (= *gone and not returned*) and *been* (= *gone and returned*).

Answers

1 never 2 ever 3 ever 4 never 5 ever 6 never

- Students do Practice exercise 20 on page 119 of the Language File. They complete the text with indefinite pronouns and adverbs. Do the first one together as an example.
- Check the answers with the class. Point out that *no one* is written as two words, while all the other indefinite pronouns and adverbs are written as one word.

Answers

1 someone/somebody 2 everywhere 3 everything 4 everyone/everybody 5 anyone/anybody 6 anything 7 anywhere 8 anyone/anybody 9 anything 10 No one/Nobody

Follow-up activity

Write some irregular past participles on the board. Students write five *Have you ever ...?* questions using the participles and ask their partner. Students change pairs and interview a new partner.

Homework

Students add words from this lesson to their *Transportation* word map (see Unit 3, Lesson 3).
Students find out more about high-speed trains, and write a paragraph about them. Encourage them to find out what they are called and where they go from/to.

NOTEBOOK SECTION

Circle the correct option in each sentence.

1 Have *ever you/you ever* eaten octopus?
2 I've never *been/went* to his house.
3 We've never *saw/seen* her so happy!
4 Where *you have/have you* been?
5 That was the funniest movie *I've/I* ever seen.

Answers

1 you ever 2 been 3 seen 4 have you 5 I've

Consolidation and Extension p83

Language File pp119–120

Workbook Unit 6 Lesson 2 pp66–67

Photocopiable notes p158, worksheet p178

3 Too many tourists

Communicative Aims	**Language**	**Pronunciation**	**Vocabulary**
Saying what's wrong with something	*too much/too many* *(not) enough*	/ʧ/ much /ʃ/ shop	Town facilities

WARM-UP 1

In pairs, give students two minutes to note down all the famous places they can remember in Washington, D.C. The pair with the most places reads out their list and others add to it. Ask *Have you ever been to Washington, D.C.? Would you like to go there? Which places would you most like to visit?*

WARM-UP 2

Write jumbled sentences on the board including the present perfect + *ever/never*. Set a time limit for students to re-order them in pairs.

1 Opener

- The aim is to pre-teach and recycle vocabulary. Ask students to look at the photos on page 78. Which of the listed items can they see? You may like to tell them that they can find nine of the items in the photos.

Answers

actors (A) football players (C) helmets (C) plants (D) a stadium (C) a spy (B) a stage (A) stairs (D) stores (D)

- We can't see a church or a market.
- Ask *What are these places?* Ask students which place they would most like to visit and why.

2 Reading

- Students read about Lara and Alex introducing their video *City Sights*. Ask *What is the video about?*

Answer

The video is about places in Washington, D.C. that they haven't had enough time to visit.

Optional activities

♦ 2.18 Play the recording of the dialogue for students to read and listen. Stop at any words you predict may cause pronunciation problems, e.g. *city sights, voice,* and ask students to repeat.

♦ Students note examples of *too much, too many,* and *enough* in preparation for the Language Workout.

3 After Reading

- Students read the dialogue again, and match the questions and answers. Make sure students understand that two answers are not needed.
- Check the answers.

Answers

1 c 2 e 3 a 4 g 5 d
Wrong answers: b and f

Your Response

- With the whole class, brainstorm ideas for interesting places in the students' town.
- In small groups, the students choose four places they would like to include in a video about their town, giving reasons.
- Ask one student from each group to read out the places they chose for a video, and make a tally next to each place, so you can see which four places were the most popular choices. Encourage students to explain why they chose each one.

4 Listening

- Explain to students that they are going to hear Steve talking about the places shown in the photos. Play the recording. Students listen to the descriptions and number the photos in the order they hear about them.

2.19 Recording

STEVE *For fantastic shopping, go to Georgetown Park in northwest Washington, D.C. It's a very popular shopping mall, and sometimes there are too many people. But it has over 100 stores, restaurants, and coffee shops, so it's a great place to spend your time. But don't spend too much money!*
Have you done enough shopping? Then why don't you go to a show? There are some famous theaters in downtown Washington, D.C., including Ford's Theater—where President Lincoln was shot dead in 1865—and the Shakespeare Theater. Another great place is the National Theater on Pennsylvania Avenue—it has lots of musicals.
Have you ever wanted to know more about spying? Then visit the International Spy Museum—it's the only one of its kind in the world. The museum is full of exciting exhibits, including pictures of famous spies, movies about spying, and information about secret missions.

Do you like sports? Then why don't you go to a football game? Washington, D.C. has a famous football team, the Washington Redskins, who play in yellow and dark red. The only problem is getting in—too many people want tickets, because the Redskins are very successful! Washington also has a great soccer team, D.C. United, and their uniforms are black and white.

Answers

1 D 2 A 3 B 4 C

- Ask students to read the quiz and to try and remember the information from the recording.
- Students listen again and choose the correct information in the *City Sights Quiz*. Pause and replay sections of the recording if necessary.
- Check the answers, asking students if they remember the exact words from the recording that helped them decide on their answers.

Answers

northwest, 100
downtown, 1865, musicals
world, pictures
yellow, black

Optional activity

Ask further comprehension questions about the listening text, e.g. *Where is the National Theater? What sport do the Redskins Play?*

LANGUAGE WORKOUT OPTION

If you want to pre-teach the language students will be using in the following activities, you may like to go to the Language Workout box now.

5 Writing

- Ask students to read the situations and prepare their answers. Monitor and provide help where necessary.
- Ask a confident student to read out a situation and question, and then choose another student to answer.
- In pairs, students continue, taking turns to ask and answer the questions.

Suggested answers

1 There's too much noise.
2 They don't have enough money.
3 He has bought too many gifts.
4 She makes too many mistakes.
5 There are too many channels.
6 They don't have enough (free) time (to relax).

Optional activity

Students write similar sentences and questions. They read them out for a partner to answer.

6 Pronunciation

- Write *much* and *shop* on the board. Elicit their pronunciation and write the phonetic symbols beside each word.
- Play the first part of the recording, pausing after each word for students to repeat.

2.20 Recording

/tʃ/ *much cheese choose chair watch*
/ʃ/ *shop she's shoes share wash*

- Play the second part of the recording. Students write the words they hear. Pause after each word to give students time to write.

2.20 Recording and answers

she's choose chair wash

Extension Ask students to think of six other words for each sound and write them under the correct heading in their notebooks. Students can use their dictionaries to help them. This could be done as a contest, and when one pair/group thinks they have twelve words in total, they read them to the class. Other pairs/groups can add to the lists.

Optional activities

- Students close their books. Test them on spelling the target words in this lesson.
- **Game** *Longest Sentence* Students make sentences using as many of the words in the chart as possible in each sentence. They test each other's pronunciation. They could dictate their sentences to each other.

7 Speaking

- Ask two confident students to read out the example. Divide the class into small groups. One student describes a place and the others guess what it is. Remind students to use the prompts in the box for ideas, and to follow the style of the example.

Optional activity

With a less confident class, give students two minutes to note down their descriptions. They then describe their places to each other in pairs. Change pairs and ask students to describe the places again without looking at their notes.

Extension Students work in small groups and discuss their town. Find out what they think.

8 Writing

- Students work on their own. Encourage them to include *too much/many* and *enough* as often as possible and to use the model sentences for guidance.

Optional activities

- Students read out their descriptions for others to guess the places.
- Students exchange texts and check each other's work for spelling, punctuation, and grammar.

LANGUAGE WORKOUT

- Ask students to look at the Language Workout box and complete the first three sentences. Confident students can complete first and then check, while others can look back at exercise 2 and then complete.
- Then ask them to try to work out the rule for using *too much/many* and complete the sentences about uncountable and plural countable nouns. Students also complete the sentence in the bottom half of the Language Workout box.
- Students turn to page 120 of the Language File to check their answers.

Answers

too many too many much
many

- Highlight:
  - *too much* + uncountable nouns, *too many* + countable nouns, *too* + adjective.
  - they all mean *more than necessary* and therefore have a negative meaning.
  - *enough* goes before nouns and after adjectives/adverbs; *not … enough* can express the same as *too*, e.g. *not quiet enough* = *too loud/noisy*.
- Drill the example sentences chorally and individually for pronunciation and stress.

Practice

- Students do Practice exercise 21 on page 120 of the Language File. They complete the sentences individually and then check each other's work.

Answers

1 many 2 much 3 many 4 enough 5 much
6 enough 7 many 8 enough

Optional activity

Students draw two columns labeled *too much/too many*. Dictate countable and uncountable nouns. Students write them in the correct column. Check the answers.

Follow-up activities

- Write this sentence from Practice exercise 21 on the board: *I think there's too much trash on TV.* Hold a class discussion. Divide the class into two groups and give students time to note down their arguments before beginning the discussion. The focus here is on fluency, so do not interrupt to correct mistakes. Note them down for later attention.
- Students compare the advantages and disadvantages of city and country life. Elicit sentences with *too much/many* and *not … enough*.
- Students make a page in their notebook to list uncountable nouns, e.g. *noise, money, traffic,* and important exceptions, e.g. *people*. So far, they have seen few uncountable nouns outside the food lexical set.

Homework

Students write a letter of complaint to their town/city mayor. They complain about three different things which are wrong in their town/city and suggest ways to improve them. You could help them by supplying prompts, e.g. *tourists, jobs, traffic, pollution, entertainment, parks.*

Students write a paragraph with the title *There are too many cars on the roads.* They say if they agree or disagree and suggest what could be done to improve traffic and the environment.

NOTEBOOK SECTION

Circle the correct option in each sentence
1 Do you have *enough/much* money to buy that?
2 There's too *many/much* traffic in the city.
3 There are too *many/much* cars on the roads.
4 The store closed. It wasn't busy *enough/much.*
5 They didn't give me *many/much* information.

Answers
1 enough
2 much
3 many
4 enough
5 much

Consolidation and Extension p83

Language File p120

Workbook Unit 6 Lesson 3 pp68–69

Photocopiable notes p158, worksheet p179

4 *Integrated Skills* Favorite places

Skills

Reading Note-taking: favorite places facts
Listening Note-taking: description of a place
Speaking Interviewing
Writing Description of a favorite place

Language

Conjunctions: *and, but, because*

Learner Independence

Working with other students
Peer assessment

Vocabulary

Famous landmarks
Useful expressions

Optional aids

Follow-up activity: cards for vocabulary

WARM-UP 1

Game *Teacher* Play with words for animals. See Unit 2, Lesson 1 for further details.

WARM-UP 2

Game *Taboo* Play *Taboo* (see Unit 4, Lesson 1, page 75) with words related to cameras.

1 Opener

- The aim is to encourage students to predict before reading and to pre-teach vocabulary. Ask students to look at the photos on page 80 and guess the places. Don't confirm or deny their guesses at this stage.
- Ask students to describe what they can see in the photos, and elicit vocabulary: *ruins, pillars, fountains, statue, torch.*

2 Reading

- Students read for main ideas and match the descriptions with four of the photos.

Answers

Jay D Steve A Lara E Ramón C

- Ask students to read the text again for specific information and to make notes to complete the chart for Steve, Lara, and Ramón.
- Draw the chart on the board. Ask different students to read you their answers.

Answers

	Jay	*Lara*	*Steve*	*Ramón*
Place	*Statue of Liberty*	*Cristo Redentor statue*	*Library of Celsus*	*Alhambra*
Country	*U.S.*	*Brazil*	*Turkey*	*Spain*
Date	*1885*	*1931*	*AD 110-135*	*14th century*
Size	*46m high*	*30m high*	*21m wide, over 16m high*	*142,000 sq m in area*
Getting there	*Ferry*	*Car, taxi, or train*	*Tour bus from Selçuk, or a 30-minute walk*	*Walk from downtown Granada*
Problems	*Too many visitors*	*When there are too many passengers, it takes a long time to reach the top*	*Gets extremely hot in the middle of the day in the summer*	*Visitor numbers are limited, so you need to buy your ticket in advance*

- Ask students to look at the questions below the chart. In pairs, students ask and answer questions about the four places using the notes in the completed chart. Confident students could take turns to answer questions with their books closed.

Useful information

The Alhambra was a fortress from the 9th century, but it was rebuilt and developed over the following centuries by the Moors, Berber tribes from modern-day Algeria and Morocco who had arrived in Spain in 711. After many battles, Spanish and European soldiers took most of Spain back from the Moors in the 13th century, but the ruler of the kingdom of Granada negotiated for Granada's independence. It was not until 1479 that Granada fell and Moorish rule came to a complete end in Spain.

Optional activities

- ♦ Ask quick-fire questions about the places such as *Which country gave New York the Statue of Liberty? How many steps are there to the top?* Alternatively, students could write comprehension questions to test each other.
- ♦ Give students one minute to memorize all they can in Jay's description. Students close their books. Read out the text, adding some false information, e.g. *It arrived by ship in 1985.* Students shout *Stop!* when they hear incorrect information and correct it. Students could continue this game in pairs with the different descriptions.
- ♦ Tell students you have a fantastic memory and dramatically close your book. Ask them to ask you questions about the text. Students then continue in pairs.

3

- Ask students to find examples of the conjunctions *and, but, because* in the reading texts on page 80 and to note how they link ideas in and between sentences.
- Ask students *Where is the Eiffel Tower? Has anyone been there?* Ask students to read the text about the Eiffel Tower all the way through, ignoring the gaps. Then students read the text again and complete it.
- Check the answers by asking individual students to read their completed sentences out to the class.

Answers

1 and 2 because 3 and 4 But 5 because 6 and 7 but 8 because 9 because

Optional activity

Students write four or five sentences with *and, but,* and *because*. They could write about a famous monument in their country. Then they copy their sentences, omitting the conjunctions, and give them to a partner to complete.

4 Listening

- Explain to students that they are going to hear Emma talking about her favorite place and establish that it is photo B on page 80. Ask *How tall do you think the statue is? How wide is it? What does it look like?* Teach *angel*.
- Play the recording. Students listen and make notes to complete the chart in exercise 2 for Emma.

2.21 Recording

My sister lives in Newcastle in England, and my favorite place is near there. It's called the Angel of the North and it's a statue, but what a statue! In fact, it's definitely the largest statue in Britain and it's one of the largest in the whole world.

The Angel of the North was put up in February, nineteen ninety-eight. The arms of the statue are fifty-four meters long—as long as the wings of a big plane—and it's twenty meters high. The statue weighs two hundred tons. Getting there is easy—it's very close to the highway and thirty-three million drivers see it every year. But this is sometimes a problem, because too many drivers slow down to look at it.

- Play the recording again, pausing to check the information for each section of the chart.

Answers

Name	*Emma*
Place	*Angel of the North—statue*
Country	*England*
Date	*1998*
Size	*Arms 54m long; 20m high*
Getting there	*By car*
Problems	*Drivers slow down to look at it*

Useful information

The Angel of the North is the creation of Antony Gormley, a leading British sculptor who was born in 1950. He has shown his work in galleries and museums around the world and has had major exhibitions in the U.S.A., China, Japan, Australia, and Norway.

Optional activities

- ♦ Students write a paragraph about the Angel of the North using the information in the chart.
- ♦ In pairs, students ask and answer questions about the Angel of the North using the information in the chart. Confident students could take turns to answer questions with their books closed.

5 Speaking

- Students use the questions in exercise 2 to help them interview each other about their favorite places. They take turns asking and answering questions. Demonstrate the interview, with students asking you questions.
- Monitor and provide help, but do not correct students during this activity.
- Elicit feedback on the most interesting places.

Optional activity

With a less confident class, give students time to think about their answers and ask for vocabulary.

6 Writing

- Individually or in pairs, students decide on a favorite place and note down as much information as possible. They can refer back to the questions in exercise 2. They then write a paragraph based on their notes. They can refer back to exercise 3 and the texts on page 80.

Optional activities

- ♦ Students include one piece of false information in their writing. They exchange texts and check grammar, spelling, and punctuation and try to identify the false information.
- ♦ Students read out their texts but do not say the name of their favorite place. Their partner must listen and guess.

7 Learner Independence

- The aim is to encourage students to learn from each other and experiment with ways of organizing vocabulary. Read out the rules of the game. Demonstrate by asking students to brainstorm all the vocabulary connected with clothes they can remember in one minute. Ask *How many words did you think of?*
- Students continue in pairs.

Optional activity

Students look back in their books and at their word maps and make a list of further topics for word races.

8

- The aim is for students to assess their own and each other's learning skills, and to develop positive strategies to deal with difficulties. Students work in pairs. Ask them to assess themselves and their partner for each skill on a scale of 1–4 (1 = not very good, 4 = very good). Encourage them to be as honest as possible.
- Students compare their scores. Do they agree with each other's assessment? Go around the class and check that your assessment of each student's skills tallies with theirs. Ask students to try at least one new strategy in an area where they feel uncertain.
- If you repeat this activity regularly, students can keep a record of their assessments and measure their progress.

9 Phrasebook

- Ask students to find the expressions in Unit 6.
- Play the recording for students to listen and repeat the expressions.

2.22 Recording and answers

You're kidding, right? (Ramón, Lesson 1, ex 2)
I'm not kidding. (Silvana, Lesson 1, ex 2)
Hey, cheer up! (Silvana, Lesson 1, ex 2)
Here she comes. (Ramón, Lesson 1, ex 2)
Don't make too much noise. (Alex, Lesson 3, ex 2)
It's absolutely stunning. (Steve, Lesson 4, ex 2)
The easiest way to get there is … (Ramón, Lesson 4, ex 2)
But there's one problem … (Ramón, Lesson 4, ex 2)
It's a good idea to … (Ramón, Lesson 4, ex 2)

- Students match the functional descriptions a–d with the expressions.

Answers

a Hey, cheer up! *b You're kidding, right?*
c It's a good idea to … *d It's absolutely stunning.*

- Students can add phrases they like to their Personal Phrasebooks.

Optional activities

- ♦ Students look at the functional descriptions a–d and try to think of functional descriptions for the other expressions in the box.
- ♦ Ask students to work in pairs and write a four-line dialogue using at least two of the expressions in the box. Invite confident pairs to act out their dialogues for the rest of the class.

Follow-up activities

- ♦ **Game** *Just a minute* Students talk for a minute on one of the topics they chose in exercise 7. If they repeat information or hesitate, another student can challenge and take over for the rest of the minute. Students score points for challenging correctly or for finishing in a minute. Award two points for students who talk for a minute with no challenges.
- ♦ Students add to their word map *Buildings and Places* from Unit 3, Lesson 1, Follow-up activities. They look back through the lesson and find as many words as they can to write on their map.
- ♦ Students choose five words from the lesson to write on vocabulary cards.

Homework

Students write an advertisement for a vacation in one of the places described in the lesson.

Students research and write about a famous monument or building in their country or abroad.

Students review vocabulary from this unit.

NOTEBOOK SECTION

Complete the questions with one of these words:
What, Where, When, How, How long.

1 ____ is it? It's in the mountains.
2 ____ do you get there? By bus or car.
3 ____ can you do there? Watch birds and swim.
4 ____ does it take to get there? About five hours.
5 ____ is a good time to go? In July or August.

Answers

1 Where 2 How 3 What 4 How long 5 When

Consolidation and Extension p83

Workbook Unit 6 Lesson 4 pp70–71

Inspired EXTRA!

Optional aids
Game: sheets of paper

Project Wonders of the World

1

- Elicit the meaning of *Wonders of the World*. Explain to students that wonders of the world are old or new buildings or natural sights that people find amazing or extraordinary. The aim of this project is to find out and write about one of the wonders of the world.
- Divide students into groups and appoint an "editor" for each group.
- Point out the examples of wonders of the world on page 82: the Pyramids in Egypt, Sydney Opera House, and the Grand Canyon, and the example project about the Pharos. Give students two minutes in their groups to make a list of wonders of the world. Write all the class' ideas on the board. Then each group chooses a wonder to write about.

2

- Students in each group look at the prompts and decide which areas each person is going to write about. Then they make notes about their wonders. They may need to use the Internet or find information at home.

3

- Each person in the group writes a short text about the wonder to contribute to their project. Remind them to look at the project on page 82 for an example of style.
- Students put their work together and read the texts through carefully to correct any mistakes. They copy their texts out neatly. The editor selects the order of the texts while others work on illustrating the project with photos from magazines or the Internet, or drawings.
- Students show their Wonders of the World projects to other groups. Display them in the classroom if possible.

Game Alphabet Poem

- Read the poem to the class. Point out that each line of the poem starts with a different letter of the alphabet, and usually with a past participle because most of the verbs are present perfect. Hand out a sheet of paper to each student.
- Students write their own poems. Explain that they can reuse verbs from the poem in their books, e.g. *answered, been*, but should try to change the phrases.
- Collect the poems and shuffle them. Read them out and ask students to identify the writer of each poem.

Language File pp119–120

Song—photocopiable notes p161, worksheet p188

Consolidation

Lesson 1

Suggested answers
They've …
visited San Francisco / watched a juggler / seen a musical
been for a ride on a cable car / danced at a street fair /
visited a movie studio
They haven't …
visited New Orleans / seen a soccer game / met the U.S. president

Lesson 2
Students' own answers.

Lesson 3
Students' own answers.

Lesson 4
Students' own answers.
Refer students back to exercise 2 on page 81.

Extension

Lessons 1–4
Students' own answers.

YOUR CHOICE!

The aim is to give students more learner independence and help them to identify their preferred ways of learning. Encourage students to choose an activity that they feel less comfortable with if they want a challenge or are aware that they need practice in a particular area.
What Have I Done? gives students the opportunity to practice prepositions, general vocabulary, and speaking skills by taking part in a group memory game. *
Observation Quiz gives students the opportunity to practice town facilities vocabulary and writing skills with a partner.

*Adapted from Kim's memory game variation 6 p164 *Games for Language Learning* by Andrew Wright, David Betteridge and Michael Buckby (3rd edition, CUP)

You may now like students to do the song *Father And Son*. See p161 for notes and p188 for the worksheet.

Workbook Unit 6 Inspired EXTRA! pp72–73

Units 5–6

1 Ask students what they know about Kylie Minogue. What do they expect to read about? Give students three minutes to read the text and check general comprehension and any vocabulary queries.
Students choose the appropriate word for each space. Do the first one together as an example. This can be done in pairs or individually as a short test.

Answers
1 C 2 A 3 B 4 C 5 A 6 B 7 B 8 A 9 A 10 C

Optional activity

Confident students can first attempt the task without looking at the words.

2 Students listen to the example dialogue and follow in their books. Elicit the remaining questions 2–6. Then play the rest of the recording. Students repeat the questions and write the dates (using abbreviations). Students compare their answers in pairs. Play the recording again. Check the answers. Students write sentences with dates in full.

2.23 **Recording and answers**
Ask Carrie questions about future arrangements, like this:
STEVE *Silvana/return to Argentina*
When is she returning to Argentina?
CARRIE *On* ***August thirty-first****.*
Listen and write the dates. Now you.
1
STEVE *Silvana/return to Argentina*
When is she returning to Argentina?
CARRIE *On* ***August thirty-first****.*
2
STEVE *Lara/fly home*
When is she flying home?
CARRIE *On* ***September fourth****.*
3
STEVE *Ramón and Jay/visit Florida*
When are they visiting Florida?
CARRIE *On* ***September second****.*
4
STEVE *Alex/go on vacation*
When is he going on vacation?
CARRIE *On* ***October fifteenth****.*
5
STEVE *Emma/go back to school*
When is she going back to school?
CARRIE *On* ***September seventh****.*
6
STEVE *you/get married*
When are you getting married?
CARRIE *On* ***November twenty-first****!*

Answers
1 Silvana is returning to Argentina on August 31.
2 Lara is flying home on September 4.
3 Ramón and Jay are visiting Florida on September 2.
4 Alex is going on vacation on October 15.
5 Emma is going back to school on September 7.
6 Carrie is getting married on November 21.

3 When you check the answers, ask students to explain their choice of *some* or *any*.

Answers
1 some 2 some 3 any 4 some 5 any 6 any

4 Check the answers for the first part of the exercise with the whole class. Students then write their answers to the questions and compare their answers in pairs.

Answers
1 How much 2 How many 3 How much
4 How many 5 How many 6 How much
7 How much 8 How many

5 Students read and complete the text with object pronouns. Do the first one together as an example.

Answers
1 them 2 me 3 him 4 her 5 it 6 us 7 us 8 you 9 it

6 Students read and complete the text with prepositions. Do the first one together as an example.

Answers
1 around 2 at 3 on 4 to 5 along 6 past 7 into 8 under 9 across

Optional activity

Allow students a short time to read the text. Students close their books. Then ask the students questions.

7 Students write sentences, following the example. Warn them to be careful with item 6: in this case, the correct past participle of *go* is *been*.

Answers
1 Jay has spoken to his father, but he hasn't spoken to his mother.
2 Silvana and Lara haven't had a letter, but they've had an e-mail.
3 Alex hasn't bought a CD, but he has bought a book.
4 Emma has written a postcard, but she hasn't written a letter.
5 Carrie has made a podcast, but she hasn't made a movie.
6 We haven't been to the movies, but we've been to the theater.

Optional activity

Fast-finishers can write similar sentences about what's happened to them this week.

8 Make sure students realize that the present perfect + *just* replaces simple past + time phrase.

Answers
1 Lara has just taken a shower.
2 Ramón has just bought some new sneakers.
3 Silvana has just gone to bed.
4 Emma has just sent a text message.
5 Lara and Alex have just shown their video.
6 Carrie has just interviewed the President.

9 Remind students of the position of *ever* in questions. In pairs, students take turns to ask and answer. Check the answers by asking pairs to ask and answer to the class before students write full sentences.

Answers
1 Has Silvana ever made a video before? No, she hasn't.
2 Has Carrie ever visited New York? Yes, she has.
3 Have Jay and Emma ever been on TV? Yes, they have.
4 Has Lara ever met Eminem? No, she hasn't.
5 Has Ramón ever won a contest? Yes, he has.
6 Has Alex ever lost his camera? No, he hasn't.
7 Have the contest winners ever seen the President? No, they haven't.
8 Has Steve ever been to Italy? Yes, he has.
1 Silvana has never made a video before.
2 Carrie has visited New York.
3 Jay and Emma have been on TV.
4 Lara has never met Eminem.
5 Ramón has won a contest.
6 Alex has never lost his camera.
7 The contest winners have never seen the President.
8 Steve has been to Italy.

10 Students write *much*, *many*, or *enough* in the gaps. Check the answers and ask students to explain their choices.

Answers
1 many 2 much 3 much 4 many 5 many 6 much 7 enough 8 enough

Vocabulary

11 Students can race to complete the definitions. There are three words in the box that they will not need.

Answers
1 waiter 2 satellite 3 customer 4 menu 5 park 6 tie 7 magnet 8 stadium 9 route

12 Confident students can first cover the list of words and try to work out what the definitions refer to.

Answers
1 paradise 2 engine 3 starving 4 vegetarian 5 dairy produce 6 market 7 railroad 8 ancient 9 statue 10 line

13 Remind students that it is very helpful to learn common idiomatic verb + noun phrases of this kind.

Answers
1 cross the street
2 give directions
3 go shopping
4 make a noise
5 order a meal
6 play an instrument
7 tell someone the way
8 visit the zoo
9 win a contest

Learner Independence Self Assessment

- Explain that the aim of the self assessment is to encourage them to check their own progress and take any necessary action to improve. Point out that the list 1–7 covers areas of functional language from Units 5 and 6. Students check the "Fine" box for functional language that they feel confident using, but put a question mark in the "Not sure" box for functional language that they have difficulty with.
- Encourage students to look at the Language File and re-do exercises from the Workbook in areas where they have problems. They may also like to re-do exercises from the lessons and from the Consolidation and Extension sections in Units 5 and 6.
- Students write an example sentence for each language area in the list. Students can refer back to the lessons and the Language File.

Follow-up activity

Game *Which word am I thinking of?* Divide the class into two groups, A and B. Write *In the town* on the board. Demonstrate by saying *Group A, I'm thinking of a word beginning with the letter P*. Group A call out possible words, e.g. *post office, playground*, until they get your word *park*. Then start the game: a student from one group says the first letter of a word and the students in the other group try to guess it. If a team guesses the word, they get a point.

Homework

Students write a questionnaire to test each other's knowledge of their town/city. They can use the *City Sights Quiz* on page 79 of the Student's Book as a model.

Students bring their vocabulary notebooks up to date.

NOTEBOOK SECTION

Complete the sentences using these words: *have, has, had.*
1 He ____ never ____ a girlfriend.
2 I ____ a girlfriend before I moved here.
3 ____ you ever ____ a black eye?
4 Did she ____ chocolate or vanilla?
5 I ____ n't ____ anything to drink today.

Answers *1 has, had 2 had 3 Have, had 4 have 5 have, had*

Language File p117–120

Workbook Review Units 5–6 pp74–75

PREVIEW

Units 7–8

Activities		Project	Vocabulary	Optional aids
Identifying the function of communicative language Categorizing vocabulary	Contextualizing listening extracts	Questionnaire	Household items The Arctic Body Language Feelings Animated movies Animals	Follow-up activity: slips of paper for students to write single words on

WARM-UP 1

Students look back at Units 5–6 in their books, and talk in pairs about the activities or reading texts that they enjoyed or didn't like. Encourage them to give reasons for their feelings.

WARM-UP 2

Game *Teacher* Play with animal words. See Unit 2, Lesson 1 for further details.

WARM-UP 3

Ask students to look at the pictures and captions/speech bubbles on pages 86–87 and to answer the questions *What do the pictures show? Who can you see in the pictures?*

1 • The aim is to introduce students to the main areas of communicative language they will cover in Units 7–8, and to encourage them to think about the function of the language. Explain to students that the two boxes at the top of the page show the communicative language and vocabulary/topics they will use in these two units of *Inspired*. Students look at the first box and match the communicative aims 1–7 with the pictures A–G on pages 86–87.

Answers

1G 2F 3E 4D 5C 6B 7A

Optional activity

Students write another example sentence or question for each of the communicative aims 1–7. Monitor and help where necessary.

2 • The aim of the activity is for students to contextualize a short listening extract by working out the topic of the passage. Explain to students that they should listen for the main gist of the passage and it does not matter if they do not understand every word.

• Play the recording. Students match each extract 1–3 with one of the topics in the box.

2.24 Recording

1

Here's some exciting news about the next World2day contest. The rules are very simple. The contest is free, so you don't have to pay to enter it. The winners will be on the Web, but you don't have to send a photograph yet—wait until you've won! Remember, you have to send in your answers by September 1. Anyone can enter—you don't have to be an expert—this is a contest for everyone.

2

Dynamic Earth

This is a fascinating exhibit which shows how living things interact with each other. See how human beings adapt to different habitats, from the hot desert to the frozen north, and how we are changing the environment.

3

There are twenty-four pictures for every single second of film, so in one minute each character can move up to one thousand, four hundred forty times! The filmmakers often only manage to shoot a few seconds of film a day, so it can take years to make a whole animated movie.

Answers

1 Rules 2 Exhibits 3 Animated movies

Optional activity

2.24 Play the recording again and ask students a simple comprehension question about each extract. 1 *When do you have to send in your answers?* (By September 1st) 2 *What are we changing?* (the environment) 3 *How many pictures are there for each second of film?* (twenty-four).

3 • Elicit the meaning of the three vocabulary categories (household items, the Arctic, body language). Explain to students that words from each category are arranged in the word pool. Give students two minutes to write the words in the correct category.

• Students check their answers in pairs and then as a whole class. Help students with any difficult vocabulary, e.g. *gesture, igloo*.

Answers

Household items: knife, plate, cup, fork, spoon, glass
The Arctic: snow, winter, polar bear, igloo, ice, cold
Body language: smile, friendly, polite, gesture, shake hands, kiss

Optional activity

In small groups, students think of as many different words as possible to add to the three categories. Give them a time limit.

4 • Explain to students that the words in color are three more vocabulary categories. Ask students to work in pairs thinking of three more words for each category.

Suggested answers

Feelings: excited, worried, frightened, nervous, depressed, happy, sad
Animated movies: director, animator, stop motion technique, characters, camera, actors, rehearsal, shoot, designer, puppets
Animals: cow, dog, fox, pig, snake, spider, worm, crocodile

Optional activity

Confident students may like to write three words for each of the remaining categories in the box (rules, exhibits, jobs and occupations, digital cameras).

5 • Give students a few minutes to look through the questionnaire.

- Elicit from students the questions they will need to ask, e.g. *Do you like doing the dishes?*
- Students do the questionnaire individually, interviewing each person until they give a positive answer to one of the questions and then moving on to find another student.
- Students compare their results with other students, telling them anything interesting or surprising that they found out.
- Point out the "Believe it or not!" fact at the bottom of the page.

Questionnaire results project

Students interview eight other students and note down all their answers next to each question, so they have a tally, e.g. of how many people are scared of spiders and how many aren't.
Students write a short report about their findings, highlighting any interesting or surprising results. They can illustrate their report with drawings or pictures from magazines or from the Internet.
Display the projects in class so that students can look at each other's work.

Follow-up activities

- ♦ In groups of four, students brainstorm vocabulary for three other categories from the box on page 86: *exhibits, jobs and occupations,* and *digital cameras.* Give students an example from each category before they start, and tell them they have two minutes for each category to write as many words as they can think of on slips of paper. After the time is up for each of the three categories, students shuffle their slips of paper so they are jumbled out of order. They then swap their slips with another group, and the students then have another two minutes to sort another group's slips into the correct categories.
- ♦ **Game** *Memory chain* This is best played in groups of six to ten. Student 1 says *I went camping last week and I took some plates …* Student 2 repeats this and adds another household item. This continues around the group. A student who repeats or forgets is out.

Homework

Ask students to look at photo F on page 87 and to imagine what the characters are talking about. They write a short dialogue for the photo, including the line Steve says (*You don't have to come to with us.*).

1 They must eat insects and worms

Communicative Aims	**Language**	**Pronunciation**	**Vocabulary**
Expressing obligation and prohibition	*must* and *mustn't*	/m/ mistake	Household items Compound words

WARM-UP 1

Game *Password* Divide the class into two groups. One student from each group comes to the front of the class and sits down with their back to the board. Select a word from the box in the Opener or from previous lessons and write it on the board. The groups call out definitions of that word to their team member at the front. The first student to guess the word wins a point for their group.

WARM-UP 2

If students wrote questionnaires for the homework activity in the Review, they try them out on each other in pairs, to see how good their partner's knowledge of their town/city is.

1 Opener

- The aim is to pre-teach and recycle vocabulary, and to set the scene for the Reading text. Ask students to look at the photos on page 88 and explain that they are from a reality TV show. Ask *Can you guess where the place is?* (Australia). Then ask *What can you see in the photos?* and elicit *jungle, water, logs*.
- Ask students to read the words in the box and decide which are likely to be in the text. Help them with new words, e.g. *insects*.
- Ask students to scan the text to confirm their answers. Point out the irregular plural of *knife* = *knives*.

Answers

cell phones crocodiles insects jungle knives log snakes

Useful information

I'm A Celebrity—Get Me Out Of Here! is filmed in Queensland, near the east coast of Australia. The climate is very warm and there is plenty of rain.

2 Reading

- Students read the article and discuss the questions. Take a class vote to see how many students would like to take part in the show and how many would not.

Optional activities

- ♦ 2.25 Play the recording of the text for students to read and listen. Stop at any words you predict may cause pronunciation problems, e.g. *celebrities, luxuries, poisonous, emergency, viewers,* and ask students to repeat.
- ♦ Draw simple pictures on the board of the "basic supplies" listed in paragraph 2. Elicit the name of each item but don't write the words on the board. Then ask students to close their books and to write the names of all the items from memory.
- ♦ Students imagine they are taking part in the show. Which luxury item will they take to the jungle?

3 After Reading

- Students read the text again and decide if sentences 1–8 are true or false.
- Check the answers before students write corrections for the false sentences. Monitor and help where necessary.
- Ask students to read their corrections to the class.

Answers

1 *True.*
2 *False. Hidden cameras film everything they do and say.*
3 *False. They mustn't take things like cell phones.*
4 *True.*
5 *False. The TV viewers choose who does the task each day.*
6 *False. For one of the tasks, a celebrity must carry live snakes.*
7 *False. The King or Queen of the Jungle wins a lot of money for charity.*
8 *True.*

Optional activities

- ♦ Early finishers look back through the text and find sentences with *must/mustn't* in preparation for the next exercise.
- ♦ Students write more true/false sentences to check detailed comprehension of the text.

Your Response

- Introduce the topic of "reality" TV shows, where typically a group of strangers volunteer to spend time together and TV cameras film everything they do and say. Popular reality TV shows include *Survivor* (on an island) and *Big Brother* (in a house). Ask students if they watch any reality TV shows, and if they enjoy watching them.

- Have a class brainstorming session, and ask students to think of all the reasons why celebrities and other people want to appear on reality TV shows. Write all the reasons on the board.

LANGUAGE WORKOUT OPTION

If you want to pre-teach the language students will be using in the following activities, you may like to go to the Language Workout box now.

4 Speaking

- Ask students to read the notes for visitors to a TV show. Check vocabulary, e.g. *clap, smoke, trash, autograph, flash photographs.*
- Ask two students to read the example sentences aloud.
- In pairs, students take turns to tell each other what visitors must and mustn't do in the studio.

Answers

You must …
do what the director tells you.
stay with your group.
arrive and leave on time.
be quiet during filming.
clap when the "Clap!" sign is on.
You mustn't …
use cell phones.
smoke.
leave trash in the studio.
ask the actors for autographs.
take flash photographs.

Optional activity

Students work in pairs. One student closes the book and tries to remember as much about the notes as possible. His/Her partner listens and helps. Then students change roles.

5 Speaking

- Ask students to look at the signs from a TV studio. Ask two students to read the speech bubbles aloud.
- In pairs, students take turns to ask and answer questions about the signs. Monitor and correct if necessary.
- In pairs, students write sentences about the signs in their notebooks using *must/mustn't.*

Answers

You mustn't take photographs.
You mustn't use a video camera.
You must be quiet. You mustn't talk.
You mustn't go in here/there.
You mustn't eat in the studio.
You/Visitors mustn't go in this area.
You mustn't touch the equipment.

Optional activities

- Ask students where else they may see the signs in this exercise.
- In pairs, Student A closes the book. Student B checks whether Student A can remember the studio rules from exercise 5, e.g. *You mustn't use a video camera/take photographs.*

Extension In small groups, students think about their own school rules. They write signs like the ones in exercise 5 saying what to do or not to do at school. Then they write sentences. Display the lists of school rules in the classroom.

6 Pronunciation

- Demonstrate the /m/ sound. Play the recording and ask students to repeat the tongue-twister. Then students practice the tongue-twister in pairs, and say it as fast as possible!

2.26 **Recording**

/m/ *You must remember my number—you mustn't make a mistake.*

Optional activity

Students make up and practice more tongue-twisters using the /m/ sound.

7 Vocabulary

- Ask students to look at the example. Point out that it is a compound word, i.e. a combination of two words.
- Students work in pairs and make compound words by combining a word in box A with a word in box B and write them in their notebooks.
- Students look back through the lesson and find all the compound words from this exercise that appear in the lesson.

Answers

cell phone cutting board ice cream film crew
make-up notebook snakebites toilet paper
video camera
(notepaper (= writing paper) and film camera are also possible compounds)
ice cream is the only compound word which doesn't appear in this lesson

Optional activity

You could set a time limit and do this as a contest.

Extension Students have five minutes to think of more compound words they know. Ask a few students to read out their lists, then find the student who has the longest list and write it on the board.

8 Writing

- Ask students to read the list of places in the box. Ask a student to read out the example sentences.
- In pairs, students write at least one rule for each place in the box, referring to exercises 4 and 5 for ideas. Point out that they can add places of their own.
- Pairs join together to form groups of four. They compare their lists and add new ideas to their notes.
- Elicit feedback and write the rules on the board.

Optional activity

Students read out their rules and other students guess which place they are talking about.

LANGUAGE WORKOUT

- Ask students to complete the Language Workout box. Confident students can complete first and then check, while others can look back at exercise 2 and then complete.
- Students turn to page 120 of the Language File to check their answers.

Answers
must must must mustn't mustn't mustn't

- Highlight that:
  - *must* and *mustn't* are used to express obligation and prohibition, often when talking about rules. So *must/mustn't* is stronger than *should/shouldn't*.
  - *must/mustn't* always has the same form: it doesn't add *-s* in the third person singular.
  - *must/mustn't* is followed by the infinitive without *to*.
  - *must* has no past form, so we use *had to* for past obligation (see lesson 2).
- Explain that *must* is often pronounced /məst/ in affirmative sentences and questions (unless it is given particular emphasis); *mustn't* is pronounced /'mʌsnt/.
- Drill the examples chorally and individually for pronunciation and stress.

Practice

- Students do Practice exercise 22 on page 120 of the Language File. They complete the exercise on their own. Do the first one together as an example.
- Check the answers.

Answers
1 must 2 mustn't 3 must 4 must 5 mustn't

Optional activity

Students answer Practice exercise 22 question 4 and write one more question with *must.*

Follow-up activities

♦ Ask students to imagine that they are going camping in the jungle. They must protect themselves from danger and they must also protect the environment. Write word prompts on the board, e.g. *trash, animals, insects, water, clothes, swimming*, and students brainstorm things they must and mustn't do. Then they write a list of jungle rules using *You must/mustn't …*

♦ **Game** *Stand up, sit down* The students stand up. Each student is given two lives. One student is told the first half of a compound word and must supply a correct second half. If they are incorrect they lose a life, and another student is asked. If they are correct, they have control of the game and they nominate the next student to be asked. They continue nominating until another student is correct and wins control of the game. When students lose both lives they must sit down. The last student standing is the winner.

Homework

Students write the rules for a game they know well, e.g. a card game, dominoes, soccer.

NOTEBOOK SECTION

Complete the sentences using *must* or *mustn't* and one of these verbs: *eat, clean, wear, drive, be.*

1 Everybody ____ a uniform in this job.
2 If you want to go out, you ____ your room first.
3 You ____ be rude to the guests.
4 She ____ too much before her soccer game.
5 You ____ more slowly in the rain.

Answers
1 must wear
2 must clean
3 mustn't be
4 mustn't eat
5 must drive

Consolidation and Extension p97

Language File p120

Workbook Unit 7 Lesson 1 pp76–77

Photocopiable notes p159, worksheet p180

2 Do we have to go?

Communicative Aims	**Language**	**Pronunciation**	**Vocabulary**	**Optional aids**
Expressing obligation and lack of obligation	*have/has to* and *don't/doesn't have to*	/h/ hungry	Routines and rules	Exercise 8 Extension: small cards with different verbs written on them: *wear, do, make, open, close, send, win, take, remember, show, give, go*

WARM-UP 1

If students wrote the rules for a game as homework for the last lesson, they read out their rules, without saying the name of the game. Other students try to identify the game from the rules.

WARM-UP 2

Ask *What is the difference between homework and housework? Which do you prefer?* Brainstorm vocabulary connected with housework and write it on the board, e.g. *doing the dishes, cleaning your room, shopping*. In pairs, students ask about each other's favorite and least favorite activity. Which is the least/most favorite housework activity in the class?

1 Opener

- The aim is to encourage students to predict before reading.
- Students cover the text and look at the photo on pages 90–91. Ask *Who can you see?* (Steve, Silvana, Ramón, Lara, Alex, Jay, and Emma) *Where are they?* (in front of the Lincoln Memorial, in Washington, D.C.). Then ask students to guess why Emma doesn't look happy.

2 Reading

- Students read the dialogue, and check their answer to the question in the Opener. (Emma doesn't look happy because she doesn't want to visit the Washington stadium.)
- Students answer the question about Emma.

Answer

Emma will miss meeting the Redskins football players. She's disappointed.

Optional activities

- ♦ 2.27 Play the recording of the dialogue, pausing for students to repeat. Focus on pronunciation and intonation.
- ♦ Students act out the dialogue in fours. Choose one group to perform it for the rest of the class.

3 After Reading

- Students read the questions and choose the best answers.
- Check the answers with the whole class.

Answers

1 A 2 B 3 C 4 B 5 A 6 C

Optional activity

Early finishers look back through the text and note down examples of *have to* and *don't have to* in preparation for the next exercise.

Your Response

Have students discuss the questions in groups. Then as a class, see if everyone agrees.

LANGUAGE WORKOUT OPTION

If you want to pre-teach the language students will be using in the following activities, you may like to go to the Language Workout box now.

4 Writing

- Ask students to read the beginnings and endings and answer any vocabulary queries.
- Students work alone to match the sentences.
- Check the answers by asking individual students to read a sentence beginning and another to supply the correct ending.

Answers

1 b 2 d 3 a 4 f 5 c 6 e

Optional activities

- ♦ Students invent new beginnings and endings to test their partners.
- ♦ In pairs, Student A closes the book and Student B reads out a beginning. Student A must try to remember the ending.

5 Listening

- Before students listen, ask them to read the list of phrases 1–9 and try to guess which things you have to do to enter the contest.
- Play the recording. Students listen and put a check or a cross for each item.
- Check the answers with the class.

2.28 **Recording**

Here's some exciting news about the next World2day contest. Our last contest was about the United States, and the next one is about New York. All you have to do is answer three questions about New York and write a sentence saying why you think World2day is the greatest website in the world. The rules are very simple. The contest is free, so you don't have to pay to enter it. The winners will be on the Web, but you don't have to send a photograph yet—wait until you've won! Remember, you have to send us your answers by September 1st. Anyone can enter—you don't have to be an expert—this is a contest for everyone. You don't even have to know New York very well—you can always guess the answers! One thing is important: you have to give your e-mail address and phone number, so make sure your details are correct. And finally, this is a contest for all teenagers—anyone over twelve can enter. Enter now and win! Good luck!

Answers

1 ✓ *2* ✓ *3* ✗ *4* ✗ *5* ✓
6 ✗ *7* ✗ *8* ✓ *9* ✗

- Students take turns to tell each other about the contest rules. Monitor and make sure they are using *have to/ don't have to* correctly.

Optional activities

- 2.28 Play the recording again for students to check the correct rules.
- Students enter the contest: they write a sentence about World2day and make up three questions about New York or another capital city to test another student. Students who write good sentences and correctly answer all three questions are contest winners.

6 Speaking

- Students look at the prompts under the four headings and write a questionnaire in their notebooks, using the model questions for guidance.
- Before they start, ask some of the students the two example questions and elicit the answers, e.g. *Yes, I do. No, I don't.* Monitor as students write and provide help.
- In groups of four, students ask and answer each other's questionnaires. Demonstrate first for the whole class with two confident students.
- Ask groups to feed back to the class. Who has to do the most/least?

Optional activity

Students write sentences about the results of their questionnaire.

7 Pronunciation

- Demonstrate the /h/ sound. Play the recording and ask students to repeat the tongue-twister. Then students practice the tongue-twister in pairs, and say it as fast as possible!

2.29 **Recording**

/h/ *How hard does a hungry horse have to work before he has some help?*

Optional activity

Students make up and practice more tongue-twisters using the /h/ sound.

8 Vocabulary

- Remind students that it's useful to recognize and learn common word combinations, and point out that verbs like *catch, do,* and *make* appear in many idiomatic phrases. They should be familiar with all the collocations in this exercise.

Answers

1 set 2 do 3 catch 4 pass 5 make 6 do
7 make 8 do

Optional activities

- In pairs, one student closes the book and his/her partner tests him/her on the phrases.
- Ask students to suggest other nouns which can follow *catch* (a bus, a plane), *do* (the laundry, the cleaning, the housework), *make* (a sandwich, a cake, dinner).

Extension Students could do this activity in pairs, or you could divide the class into two teams, A and B. One student from team A says the verb. Students in team B have 20 seconds to note down as many nouns as they can which go with it. They get one point for each correct noun. Then teams change roles.
You might like to continue the activity using verb cards (see Optional aids) which each team uses to prompt the other team to note down nouns.

9 Writing

- Students use the ideas from the lesson to write a paragraph. They write about their weekday obligations and what they don't have to do on the weekend.
- Students exchange texts and correct each other's grammar, spelling, and punctuation.

Optional activity

Students include two false pieces of information in their texts for their partners to identify.

Extension Students write a paragraph about last weekend using the past forms *had to/didn't have to.*

LANGUAGE WORKOUT

- Ask students to complete the Language Workout box. Confident students can complete first and then check, while others can look back at exercises 2 and 3 then complete.
- Students turn to page 120 of the Language File to check their answers.

Answers

have to has to don't have to have to had to

- Highlight that:
  - we use *have/has to* to express obligation; *have to* in the affirmative form means the same as *must.*
  - we use *don't/doesn't have to* to express lack of obligation (= *it's not necessary*); it doesn't mean the same as *mustn't* (= *it's not allowed*).
  - the past form of *have/don't have to* is *had/didn't have to.* Remind students that the past of *must* is also *had to.* You may like to explain that for past prohibition we have to use alternative expressions, e.g. *They mustn't speak.—They weren't allowed/permitted to speak.*
- Drill the example sentences chorally and individually to practice the weak form of *have/has/had to* /tə/.

Practice

- Students do Practice exercise 23 on page 120 of the Language File. The aim is to highlight the meaning of different forms of *have to*. You may like to do the exercise orally with the whole class before students write sentences.

Answers

1 You have to 2 You don't have to 3 You have to 4 I had to 5 You have to 6 They didn't have to

Follow-up activities

- ♦ **Game** *Auction* Write ten sentences with different forms of *have to* on the board. Some of the sentences should be grammatically incorrect. Divide the class into small teams. Give each team "$1,000" to bet on the sentences. Give them a few minutes to decide which sentences are incorrect and note their answers on a sheet of paper. Start the bidding on the first sentence, acting as a fast-moving auctioneer, trying to create tension and enthusiasm. When you have the highest bid, ask the students who placed that bid to tell you if the sentence is correct or to correct the mistake. If the team is correct, they win back their bet. If they are wrong or they can't correct it, their bet is divided equally between the other teams. The winning team is the one with the most money.
- ♦ Review classroom rules. Write *do our homework, chew gum, arrive late,* etc. on the board. In small groups, students write out a classroom contract using *have to/mustn't/don't have to*. Compare classroom contracts.

Homework

Students imagine they are going on vacation together and they must live in the same house for a week. They write ten sentences about what they have/don't have to do during the vacation.

NOTEBOOK SECTION

Complete the sentences using one of these forms:
have to, has to, had to, don't have to, doesn't have to.

1 I can't go. I ____ take care of my sister.
2 I can go by myself. You ____ come.
3 The students ____ take a test yesterday.
4 He ____ get up at six every morning.
5 She's the boss. She ____ give a reason.

Answers
1 *have to*
2 *don't have to*
3 *had to*
4 *has to*
5 *doesn't have to*

Consolidation and Extension p97

Language File p120

Workbook Unit 7 Lesson 2 pp78–79

Photocopiable notes p159, worksheet p181

3 Don't be frightened!

Communicative Aims	Language	Pronunciation	Vocabulary	Optional aids
Making suggestions and expressing preferences	Participial adjectives ending in *-ed/-ing* Relative pronouns: *which/that* *want to/would like to* *I'd rather …*	/θ/ ear<u>th</u> /ð/ ra<u>th</u>er	Exhibits Animals	Exercise 4 Optional activity: cards for the Vocabulary box

WARM-UP 1

Write anagrams of animal words, e.g. *NAKES* (snake), *STINEC* (insect), *PRIDSE* (spider) on the board for students to solve.

WARM-UP 2

Explain that the text in this lesson is about Washington, D.C.'s National Museum of Natural History. Ask students *Have you ever been to a Natural History museum? What kind of things can you see there?* Elicit appropriate words and phrases, e.g. *different animals, dinosaurs, how our body works, plants and trees.*

1 Opener

- The aim is to pre-teach and recycle vocabulary and to introduce the context of the Reading text. Explain that the photos are from different exhibits in the National Museum of Natural History and ask students what the photos show, e.g. *a fish, a dinosaur, precious stones, a volcano, a desert/the frozen north.*

2 Reading

- Ask students to look at the five exhibit headings in the text, and elicit the meaning of new vocabulary, e.g. *amphibians* (e.g. frogs), *reptiles* (e.g. snakes), *gemstones* (e.g. diamonds), *habitat* (a place where something lives).
- Students read the text and answer the question.
- Check comprehension of vocabulary. The text includes several participial adjectives, some of which students will already know, e.g. *exciting*; highlight new adjectives *shocking, frightened, fascinating.*

Answer

The Dinosaurs exhibit is about the past. The Dynamic Earth exhibit is about people .

Optional activities

- ♦ 2.30 Play the recording of the text for students to read and listen. Focus on pronunciation and stress in multi-syllable words.
- ♦ Students choose one paragraph and practice reading it aloud to a partner to "advertise" the exhibit like a radio commercial. Encourage them to exaggerate stress and intonation.

3 After Reading

- Students read the text again and match the exhibits with questions 1–5.
- Check the answers with the class.

Answers

1 Dynamic Earth 2 Precious stones 3 Dinosaurs 4 Fish, amphibians, and reptiles 5 Volcanoes and earthquakes

Your Response

- In pairs, students tell each other which exhibit they would like to go to, and why. Write useful phrases for giving reasons on the board:
  … because it sounds interesting/exciting/fascinating.
  … because I'm interested in/fascinated by …
  … because I'd like/I want to know more about …
- Elicit feedback. Which exhibit is the most popular in the class?

LANGUAGE WORKOUT OPTION

If you want to pre-teach the language students will be using in the following activities, you may like to go to the Language Workout box now.

4 Vocabulary

- Students match the definitions with the correct kind of animal. Check students understand *lay eggs, wings, feathers.*
- Students check the answers in pairs and then as a whole class.

Answers

1 fish 2 amphibians 3 reptiles 4 birds 5 mammals

- Ask students for examples of each type of animal.

Useful information

Some common examples of the different animal groups:
Amphibians: frog, toad, salamander, newt
Birds: canary, chicken, dove, eagle, ostrich, parrot
Fish: cod, eel, salmon, shark, swordfish, trout, tuna
Mammals: ape, bear, donkey, leopard, elephant, whale
Reptiles: alligator, iguana, lizard, tortoise, snake

Optional activities

- With a confident class, write the words from the Word Bank on the board. Students write their own definitions and test each other.
- Students copy the animal words onto cards, putting the definition and some examples of each type of animal on the back. These can be added to the Vocabulary box.

5 Pronunciation

- Ask students to look at the words.
- Play the first part of the recording, pausing after each word for students to repeat. Point out that /θ/ is unvoiced—the sound is produced without using the voice-box in the throat. Ask students to say /ð/ and feel their throat vibrate. When they say /θ/ the throat doesn't vibrate.

2.31 Recording

both clothes feather fourth other south
then think thrill through together weather

- Ask students to copy the chart into their notebooks and write the words in the correct column.
- Play the second half of the recording for students to check their answers.

2.31 Recording and answers

/θ/ *earth*
both fourth south think thrill through
/ð/ *rather*
clothes feather other then together weather

6 Listening

- Ask students to read the sentences. Explain that *I'd rather* (*I would rather*) means *I'd prefer to* and *I'd rather not* means *I'd prefer not to*. Check that they understand the idiomatic phrases *That sounds ... -ing* and *I'm tired of ...* (= *I've had enough of ...*).
- In pairs, students guess who says each sentence.
- Play the recording. Students listen and check.

2.32 Recording

EMMA *Jay, what are we doing in this museum?*
JAY *Look at that giant octopus! There's some really interesting stuff in here.*
EMMA *But I want to go shopping!*
JAY *Later. Hey, I'd like to see the earthquake exhibit—it sounds exciting! Do you want to do that?*
EMMA *No way! I think earthquakes are very frightening!*
JAY *OK, how about the Dynamic Earth exhibit?*
EMMA *What's that about?*
JAY *It says it's fascinating. "See how human beings adapt to different habitats from the hot desert to the frozen north."*
EMMA *I'd rather look at snakes.*
JAY *Really? Ah.*
EMMA *Come on, then!*
JAY *Actually, I'd rather not ...*
EMMA *Are you frightened of snakes?!*
JAY *No, of course not! But I'd rather see the dinosaur exhibit.*
EMMA *Oh, I'm tired of dinosaurs.*
JAY *What about the gemstones? You can see the most valuable diamonds in the world!*
EMMA *That sounds really boring ...*
JAY *They're not at all boring! Well, would you like to go to the museum coffee shop?*
EMMA *No, I'd like to go to the museum store!*
JAY *OK, let's go shopping!*

Answers

EMMA—*Sentences 2, 3, 6, 8*
JAY—*Sentences 1, 4, 5, 7, 9, 10*

- Play the recording again, pausing where necessary to ask comprehension questions, e.g. *Why does Emma say "What are we doing in this museum?"* (She doesn't want to be there/She wants to go shopping.) *What does "No way!" mean?* (Of course not!)

Optional activity

2.32 Play the recording again, pausing for the students to repeat, and focus on stress and intonation.

Extension In pairs, students use sentences 1–10 to make short three-line dialogues about the exhibit. Model an example for students, e.g. *I'd like to try the earthquake simulator—it sounds exciting! No way! I think earthquakes are very frightening! What about the precious stones?* Confident pairs come to the front of the class and role-play one of their dialogues.

7 Role-Play

- Explain to students that they are going to act out a conversation between two friends who are trying to decide what to do/where to go, e.g. after school, in the evening, on the weekend.
- Ask students to read the phrases in the box for making suggestions and expressing preferences. Explain that *What/How about ...?* are commonly used to make suggestions, e.g. *What/How about a movie/game of tennis?* Remind students that when we use a verb form after *What/How about ...*, we use the gerund, e.g. *What/How about going to a movie/playing tennis?*
- Elicit example sentences for all the stems in the box to check that students have grasped the various structures. You may wish to play the recording from exercise 6 again for students to identify the phrases in the box.
- Write an example of a complete dialogue on the board and drill the pronunciation and intonation.
- Demonstrate the role-play a couple of times with confident students. Vary the activities/places.
- Students then act out their own dialogues in pairs.

Optional activity

While modeling the example dialogue, randomly erase parts from the board. The students continue practicing the dialogue, completing the gaps from memory. Eventually remove all the dialogue.

Extension In pairs, students write a six-line dialogue between two people who are trying to decide what to do or where to go. They use the role-play framework from exercise 7 and the phrases in the box to help them. Pairs read out their dialogues to the rest of the class.

8 Writing

- Ask a student to read out the e-mail. Ask students which phrases are used to make the suggestions (*How about …, Would you like to …, What about …*).
- Ask another student to read the instructions under the e-mail. Tell students to use their imagination for their Saturday afternoon plans—they don't have to be sensible!
- Monitor and provide help where necessary.
- Ask individual students to read their replies to the class.

LANGUAGE WORKOUT

- Ask students to look at the top half of the Language Workout box and complete the sentences. Confident students can complete first and then check, while others can look back at exercise 2 and then complete.
- Students turn to page 120 of the Language File to check their answers.

  Answers

  surprising surprised shocking frightened
- Read the explanations below the sentences with the class, and explain that there are lots of common adjectives like *surprised/surprising* which can end in both *-ed* and *-ing*, e.g. *interested/interesting, bored/boring.* Point out that all these adjectives are connected with feelings or emotions.
- Explain that the *-ed* ending is the past participle form, and the *-ing* ending is the present participle form (as in the present progressive).
- Drill the examples chorally and individually for pronunciation and stress.
- Ask students to look at the bottom half of the Language Workout box. They read the examples and then complete the sentence below.
- Students turn to page 121 of the Language File to check their answer.

  that

Practice

- Students do Practice exercise 24 on page 120 of the Language File. They choose the correct adjectives in sentences 1–6 on their own, referring to the Language Workout box explanations to help them make their choices.
- Check the answers by asking individual students to read out the completed sentences.

  Answers

  1 fascinating 2 interesting 3 amazed 4 frightened 5 exciting 6 tired
- Ask students to look at the example. In pairs, they write six more sentences using the remaining adjectives: *fascinated, interested, amazing, frightening, excited, tiring.* Write the useful collocations *fascinated by, interested in, excited by* on the board.

Optional activity

One student describes a feeling and the other identifies the *-ed* adjective, e.g.:

A It's how you feel when you've worked very hard.
B Tired.

Follow-up activities

- **Game** *Word Association* See Unit 3, Lesson 3, Exercise 7, Extension for further details.
- Students add words from this lesson to their word map for *Animals* (see Unit 6, Lesson 1, Follow-up activities).

Homework

Students write a dialogue between two friends who are trying to decide where to go on vacation. They use the role-play framework and phrases in the box in exercise 7 to help them.

NOTEBOOK SECTION

Complete the sentences using one of these adjective endings: *-ed* or *-ing*.

1 I like museums, but sometimes they're tir____.
2 That was a surpris____ thing to say.
3 I'm amaz____ that he's so relax____ about this.
4 Let's have a coffee here ... it looks so relax____.
5 I'm surpris____, I usually think museums are bor____.

Answers

1 tiring 2 surprising 3 amazed, relaxed 4 relaxing 5 surprised, boring

Consolidation and Extension p97

Language File pp120–121

Workbook Unit 7 Lesson 3 pp80–81

Photocopiable notes p159, worksheet p182

4 *Integrated Skills* Describing a journey

Skills

Reading Connecting ideas: *Ice Paradise* description
Listening Specific information: description of an Arctic trip
Speaking Exchanging information
Writing Description of a journey

Learner Independence

Learning words
Discussing learning strategies

Vocabulary

The Arctic
Useful expressions

Optional aids

Exercise 7: atlas or map of the world

WARM-UP 1

Review animal vocabulary from the previous lesson. Give definitions of different types of animal for students to guess and write down. Check their answers and their spelling.

WARM-UP 2

Ask students to brainstorm vocabulary connected with the winter, e.g. *cold, snow, ice*. Ask *What kind of clothes do you wear in the winter?* e.g. *hats, scarves, gloves, warm coats, boots*. Ask *What kind of sports do people play in the winter?* e.g. *skiing, ice-skating, tobogganing/sledding*. Do the students like the winter? Why/Why not?

1 Opener

- The aim is to pre-teach vocabulary and set the scene for the Reading text. Ask students to look at the photos on pages 94–95. Ask *Where are the places in the pictures?* and establish that they're in the Arctic.
- Use the pictures to explain the meaning of new vocabulary, e.g. *huskies, reindeer, sled.*
- Students make sentences describing the photos. Ask them to try to use all the words in the box.

Suggested answers

There is someone standing in the snow with a reindeer. He is wearing traditional costume. There's a woman on a sled with huskies in the snow. There is an actor on the stage in an ice theater.

2 Reading

- Ask students to read the first paragraph of *Ice Paradise*, and to find the names of four countries in the Arctic Circle. Point out that Lapland is a region, not a country.
- The aim of this exercise is to read and connect ideas. Ask students to decide which phrase (a–e) completes the first paragraph (c).
- Students read the rest of the text and complete it with the correct phrases.
- Play the recording. Students listen and check their answers.

2.33 Recording and answers

Ice Paradise

Lapland is a region north of the Arctic Circle, stretching across four countries from Russia in the east, through Finland and Sweden, to Norway in the west. Lapland is the home of the Sami people, (1) ***the original inhabitants of the region.***

Thousands of people now visit Lapland every year. A major attraction is the world-famous Ice Hotel, which is two hundred kilometers inside the Arctic Circle in a small Swedish town called Jukkasjärvi.

The hotel has an ice bar, ice bedrooms, and an ice church, which is very popular for weddings. They have to rebuild the hotel in November every year (2) ***because it melts every spring!*** *Most guests stay only one night in the Ice Hotel because it's freezing!*

And now there is also the Ice Globe, a replica of the Globe Theater in London! The theater is absolutely stunning. You sit on ice seats covered with reindeer skins, and above the ice stage, the Northern Lights flash across the night sky. All the performances are in the Sami language. The first was Shakespeare's Hamlet, *a seventy-minute version because the audience and actors couldn't stand the cold—*(3) ***on the first night the temperature was minus thirty-one degrees Celsius.***

The Ice Hotel has brought new life to the region and the increased tourism in Lapland is helping to keep the Sami culture alive. Jukkasjärvi has become a tourist center; popular activities include traveling on sleds pulled by husky dogs, (4) ***cross-country skiing, and "snowmobile safaris."***

The snowmobile is not only for pleasure and fun, (5) ***it's also an important means of transportation for the Sami people.*** *Traditionally, the Sami lived by herding reindeer, and they traveled across the ice and snow on sleds pulled by huskies or reindeer. Today, they also use snowmobiles to follow the reindeer herds and to travel across the tundra.*

1 c 2 e 3 a 4 d 5 b

- Ask questions about the text to check general comprehension, e.g. *Why do most people only stay one night in the Ice Hotel? Why was the performance of* Hamlet *so short?*

- Ask students which information in the text is most surprising. Ask *Would you like to go to Lapland/stay in the Ice Hotel? Why? Has anyone seen the Northern Lights?*

Useful information

The Sami people (formerly called Lapps) have inhabited the northern regions of Scandinavia and Russia since prehistoric times. It's estimated that 50,000 to 65,000 Sami live in Lapland, of whom about 10% still earn their living by reindeer herding.

3

- Students find the highlighted words and match them with the definitions. Then they compare answers in pairs.

Answers

1 audience 2 region 3 culture 4 replica 5 traditionally 6 freezing 7 herds 8 major

- Point out that *herd* can be both a noun and a verb (like many English words) and *herding reindeer = moving herds of reindeer from one place to another*.

Optional activity

Give students five minutes to memorize all they can from the text. Students close their books. Read out the text including some false information. Students shout *Stop!* when they hear incorrect information and correct it.

4 Listening

- The aim of this exercise is to listen for specific information and choose the best answers. Ask students to look at the photo of Gill and explain that she went to the Arctic for charity—to raise money to help people. Ask students to read the introduction to her story and the questions. Check comprehension.
- Play the recording. Students listen and choose the correct answers. Play the recording again, pausing to check the answers to each question.

Useful information

rucksack = backpack
£5,000 = approx. $8,000

2.34 Recording

I like the cold, I don't like hot places, and I'm interested in dogs, I love dogs, so when I saw an advertisement for an eight-day trip to the Arctic running a team of husky dogs, I thought—this is just too good to miss! I have to do it! But, um, I was worried because I'm very frightened of flying, and I had to fly for the first time in fifteen years!

But I was doing the trip for a reason—for charity. In the end, I raised five thousand pounds for charity, and paid for the trip myself. It costs a lot, and, uh, also you have to buy special clothes and equipment. So I worked very hard to raise five thousand pounds, and that helped me to not think about flying! And when I went to Sweden on the thirtieth of March, I knew I had to get on the plane because so many people gave me money!

We flew from London to the Arctic Circle in Sweden. The flight was really frightening because it was very windy—it was horrible! The next day we met the guide and then we all got a bit worried because we had to travel four hundred kilometers and it was freezing cold! You have to wear very warm clothes, of course, and when you pack your rucksack, you have to put all your things in plastic bags so they don't get wet.

We were a group of fourteen, including the guide and a doctor—because it's actually quite dangerous—and there were sixty dogs. That first day was terrifying! We got on our sleds with our rucksacks and we each had a team of four dogs pulling us. The huskies just want to run, and you may think the snow is nice and flat, but it isn't, and you go kerchoong, kerchoong, kerchoong, uphill, downhill, and round corners. Once, I hurt myself when I fell off, but other times it was just embarrassing—I was really embarrassed when I fell off. The hardest thing is when you're going uphill, you, you have to get off the sled, hold on to it, and run after the dogs, and then you have to jump back onto the sled. And it was absolutely exhausting, I was completely exhausted at the end of each day.

Answers

1 B 2 B 3 A 4 B 5 A 6 B 7 A 8 A

Optional activity

2.34 Play the recording again, pausing every so often to ask further comprehension questions, e.g. *When Gill packed her rucksack, what did she put all her things in?*

5

- This is a jigsaw listening activity, where Student A and Student B listen for the answers to different questions. Divide students into As and Bs and ask them to read their respective questions carefully.
- Students listen to the recording and note down the answers to their questions.
- Check the answers with the class.

2.35 Recording

Every night, we stayed in different places on the route, and we all had different tasks. Someone had to start the fire, um, someone had to go down to the lake and break the ice to get water, um, other people had to help with the dogs and feed them. I decided to do all the cooking every evening. And, um, we had to make sandwiches for lunch the next day. Usually we got up at about four or five a.m., had breakfast—hot milk, bread, and cheese—and we had to fill our water bottles, they're special bottles so the water doesn't freeze. You have to drink a lot of water when it's very very cold, just like you have to drink a lot when it's very very hot. Then we left at five thirty or six when it was light, and we traveled for six to eight hours.

On the last night we had to stay at the Ice Hotel. That was the worst part of the trip. I hated it, I didn't want to stay there at all. I was very tired after an exhausting week, and it was so cold in the bedroom I couldn't sleep. But I did see a wonderful Sami performance at the Ice Globe Theater—it was absolutely extraordinary. And one of the best things about the trip was seeing the Northern Lights—they were amazing.

I'm very glad I went on the trip—it was extraordinary, really surprising, and I surprised myself. And I want to go back to the Arctic—maybe next year!

Answers for Student A

1 Yes. 2 4 or 5 a.m. 3 6-8 hours
4 Staying at the Ice Hotel. 5 Seeing the Northern Lights.

Answers for Student B

1 The cooking. 2 5:30 or 6 3 On the last night.
4 At the Ice Globe theater. 5 Yes.

- Play the recording again, pausing every so often to ask further comprehension questions, e.g. *What tasks did they have to do when they stopped for the night?*

6 Speaking

- Student A and Student B use their answers to the questions to exchange information about Gill's trip:
  A *They stayed in different places every night.*
  B *Gill did the cooking every evening.*
- Encourage students to add any other information they can remember.

7 Writing

- Students write a description of a journey, using the questions in their books as a framework to help them. Less confident students will find it easier to write a paragraph about the trip to the Arctic. They can use all the information they have gathered from the Listening texts. More adventurous students can describe a different trip, and may find an atlas or map of the world useful. Encourage them to use their imagination.

8 Learner Independence

- The aim is to identify students' preferred way of learning new words and to encourage them to experiment with other ways. Ask students how they remember words.
- Individually, students order the list from 1–7 (1 = best) and then compare with another student.
- Elicit feedback on the most popular methods.

Optional activity

Write new vocabulary from the unit on the board. In small groups, students design an activity to help them learn some of the new words. They explain their activity to other groups.

9

- The aim is to encourage students to think about different strategies for improving their English, and to compare and discuss preferred strategies. Ask students to read through the list and choose the three that they think are most useful.
- Students discuss their choices with a partner. Then have a class discussion, and ask students how these strategies can help them.
- Ask students to try out their chosen strategies for a month. In later lessons, ask them for feedback.

10 Phrasebook

- Play the recording for students to listen and repeat the idiomatic expressions from the unit.

2.36 Recording

I'm not really into … (Emma, Lesson 2, ex 2)
I don't care. (Emma, Lesson 2, ex 2)
It sounds exciting. (Jay, Lesson 3, ex 5)
I'd rather not. (Jay, Lesson 3, ex 5)
That sounds really boring. (Emma, Lesson 3, ex 5)
Would you like to …? (Jay, Lesson 3, ex 5)
It's freezing. (Narrator, Lesson 4, ex 2)
I like the cold. (Speaker A, Lesson 4, ex 5)
It's too good to miss! (Lesson 4, ex 5, not recorded)

- Students work in pairs and ask each other *Would you like to go to the Arctic? Why/Why not?* Encourage them to use expressions from the box in their discussion.
- Ask students to write a short dialogue based on their conversation and including the expressions from the box where possible. Invite some pairs to act out their dialogues in front of the class.

Follow-up activity

Game *Definitions* Students work in pairs. Student A sits with her/his back to the board. Write a word from this unit on the board. Student B defines the word and Student A guesses it.

Homework

Students try out the methods from the Learner Independence section to learn new vocabulary from this lesson.

NOTEBOOK SECTION

Circle the correct option in each sentence.

1 I would like *go/to go* to the beach.
2 I want *to play/playing* tennis tomorrow.
3 How about *go/going* to the movies?
4 Let's *go/going* to the beach next weekend.
5 What *if/about* this weekend?.

Answers
1 to go 2 to play 3 going 4 go 5 about

Consolidation and Extension p97

Workbook Unit 7 Lesson 4 pp82–83

Inspired EXTRA!

LANGUAGE LINKS

- With books closed, ask students the question *In what countries of the world do people speak English?* Students may guess Britain and the U.S., and other English-speaking countries, but remind them that many people speak English as a second language in places like India and some countries in Africa, and that people all around the world speak English as a foreign language. Now ask students *How many people speak English?* and encourage them to guess. Write the highest and lowest guesses on the board.
- Students read the text and find the answer to the question. Help them with any difficult vocabulary, e.g. *accent, administration, estimated.*
- Check the answers, and see how close students were with their guesses. Remind them that the question asked how many people speak English, and the total number therefore includes speakers of English as a first, second, and foreign language.

Answer

Two billion people

Optional activity

Ask students more comprehension questions about the text, e.g. *How many people speak English as a first language? How many people speak English as a second language? In which countries do people speak English as a second language? How many people speak English as a foreign language? How many speakers of English as a second or foreign language are there for every speaker of English as a first language?*

Useful information

In the fifth century AD, three tribes from Denmark and Northern Germany—the Angles, Saxons, and Jutes—invaded Britain. They all spoke similar languages, from which Old English developed. When the Normans invaded England from France in 1066, many French words were added to the language, and it continued to change and develop over the years into Modern English, which we speak today. The English language is still changing all the time, and every year new entries are added to the Macmillan English Dictionary.

Game Desert Island

- Read through the instructions in the Student's Book with the class. Emphasize that each group must choose only five things to take to the desert island, apart from food and clothing.
- Divide the class into groups and give them five minutes to choose what they are going to take. Point out that they should have reasons for their choices. Be ready to help with necessary vocabulary.
- Ask a representative from each group to read out their list of items and explain the reasons. Write the lists on the board. Do groups have items in common?
- Ask students to vote on the best list.

Skit Rooms

- The aim is for students to enjoy using their English while also getting valuable stress and intonation practice. Ask students to look at the cartoon and establish that the skit is about two people who are looking for a hotel room.
- With a more confident class, play the recording with books closed. Then play it again with books open. With a less confident class, play the recording once while the students follow in their books, and then once again with books closed.

2.37 **Recording**

See text on page 96 of the Student's Book.

- Divide the class into three equal groups and play the recording again, with one group repeating in chorus as the boy, one as the girl, and one as the man. Encourage students to laugh and exaggerate stress and intonation.
- Ask students to close their books and play the recording again. Then ask students to work in groups of three and read the skit aloud. Choose several groups to act out the skit in front of the class.

Optional activity

Make an audio or video recording of students performing the skit.

Limerick

- Play the recording for students to read and listen. Then play the recording again with books closed.

2.38 **Recording**

See text on page 96 of the Student's Book.

Optional activities

- Students learn the limerick by heart.
- Confident students can try to write their own limericks. Remind them of the typical limerick rhyme scheme: A A B B A, and that lines 1, 2, and 5 usually have three stresses or beats, while lines 3 and 4 only have two beats.

Consolidation

Lesson 1

Suggested answers

at a swimming pool: *You mustn't run. People with long hair must wear swimming caps. You mustn't splash people. You mustn't eat near the pool. You mustn't chew gum in the pool.*
in a theater: *You must arrive on time. You mustn't smoke. You must switch off cell phones. You mustn't take pictures. You mustn't use recording equipment.*
in a library: *You must talk quietly. You mustn't write in the books. You mustn't eat or drink. You mustn't bring dogs into the library.*

Lesson 2

Answers

You have to answer three questions about New York.
You have to say why World2day is the greatest website.
You don't have to pay $10 to enter the contest.
You don't have to send a photograph with your answers.
You have to send your answers by September 1st.
You don't have to be an expert.
You don't have to know New York very well.
You have to give your phone number.
You don't have to be over 16 to enter the contest.

Lesson 3
Students' own answers.

Lesson 4
Students' own answers.
See Useful information on page 129 for suggestions.

Extension

Lesson 1
Students' own answers.

Lesson 2

Suggested answers

I have to …
find my passport.
change some money.
iron my clothes.
wash my hair.
borrow a camera.
buy an English phrasebook.
remember my plane ticket.

Lesson 3
Students' own answers.

Lesson 4
Students' own answers.

YOUR CHOICE!

The aim is to give students more learner independence and help them to identify their preferred ways of learning. Encourage students to choose an activity that they feel less comfortable with if they want a challenge or are aware that they need practice in a particular area.
How Did You Feel? is a free speaking activity in which students tell the rest of the group about a personal experience.
Words Beginning with Ex- is a vocabulary activity in which students work on their own.

Language File pp120–121

Workbook Unit 7 Inspired EXTRA! pp84–85

Saying it without words

1 Opener

- The aim is to set the scene for the Reading text. Ask students to discuss the questions in groups.
- Ask confident students to demonstrate the correct gesture for each situation.

Optional activity

Ask students to think of other common gestures and to describe the situations in which they are used.

2 Reading

- Ask students to look at the photos on page 98 and to describe the people. Ask *How old are they? What are they wearing? What are they doing?*
- Ask students to read the text and match the headings with the paragraphs. Remind them that they may only need to read the first few sentences of each paragraph.

Answers

1 Greetings 2 Facial expression 3 Eye contact 4 Silence

Optional activity

Ask students to look at each paragraph again and in pairs make a list of comparisons with their country. Students exchange lists and read them out so you can create a master list on the board.

3 Vocabulary

- Students work in pairs to match the words and definitions.
- Check the answers with the class.

Answers

1 d 2 g 3 f 4 a 5 h 6 b 7 e 8 c

- Students work on their own to find the sentences which describe what is happening in the photos, and then compare their answers in pairs.
- Check the answers with the class.

Answers

In France, many people shake hands every time they see each other.
… men in the Arab world often hug and kiss each other on the cheek.
In Britain, women often kiss each other …
… in Japan, people bow when they meet each other.

Optional activity

Students make a word map for *Parts of the body*. They use words from this lesson and add other words they know.

4 After Reading

- Students work through the text again to find the answers. They compare their answers in pairs. Check the answers with the class.

Answers

1 France
2 Many Asian countries
3 China, Japan, and Korea
4 In parts of Northern Europe
5 The Arab world
6 India

5 Speaking

- In small groups, students look at the topics for each of the paragraphs in exercise 2, and discuss how people in their country behave for each one.

Optional activity

Students write a few sentences about how people from their country behave for each of the topics. Make four displays of their writing, one for each topic, and illustrate them with drawings or photos.

6 Reading

- Before students take the quiz, ask them to read the ten statements in the quiz and check they understand all the vocabulary.
- Students work in pairs to decide which statements are true.
- Have a class vote on which are the five true statements.

7 After Reading

- Students use the information from the quiz to match the beginnings and endings.

Answers
1 g 2 e 3 j 4 a 5 i 6 c 7 h 8 b 9 f 10 d

Optional activity

Students make up similar sentences about life in their country. One student says the beginning of the sentence and the others try to guess how it ends. This is good oral preparation for the next exercise.

8 Mini-Project Cultural Information

- Ask students to look back over the information on pages 98–99.
- Students work in pairs. Tell them to make notes about how things are done in their country for each of the topics in the box.
- Each pair agrees which topic each student will write about, and they then work individually, writing sentences about life in their country like the (complete) sentences in exercise 7. Monitor and provide help where necessary.
- Students check their finished work and then check their partner's work, too.
- Students illustrate their work with photos from magazines or the Internet, or with drawings.
- Make a classroom display of the students' projects, so they can read each other's work.

NOTEBOOK SECTION

Draw a line to match the items in the two columns.

1 You shouldn't	It's possible.
2 You must	It's not a good idea.
3 You can	It's not allowed.
4 You don't have to	It's the law.
5 You mustn't	It's not necessary.

Answers
1 It's not a good idea.
2 It's the law.
3 It's possible.
4 It's not necessary.
5 It's not allowed.

Workbook Culture pp86–87

1 The characters seem to speak

Communicative aims	Language	Pronunciation	Vocabulary	Optional aids
Describing a process Expressing purpose and consequence	Verb + infinitive Infinitive of purpose Simple present passive	Syllable stress	Animated movies Jobs and occupations	Warm-up 1: small cards with jobs written on them, e.g. *architect, mechanic, firefighter, novelist*

WARM-UP 1

Game *Twenty questions* Students think of a job, or alternatively are given a card (see Optional aids). See Unit 1, Lesson 3, Follow-up activity for further information.

WARM-UP 2

Ask students to work in pairs or groups, and to list as many words for leisure activities, e.g. *playing the guitar, going to the theater*, as possible in three minutes. The pair/group with the longest list wins.

1 Opener

- The aim is to introduce the context for the Reading text. Students may have read or seen the movies: *James and the Giant Peach*, *Charlie and the Chocolate Factory*, *Danny, the Champion of the World*, *The BFG*, *Fantastic Mr. Fox*, and *Matilda*. Popular animated movies that they may have seen include: *Shrek*, *Ratatouille*, *Alice in Wonderland*, *Toy Story*, *Up*, *Bolt*, *Ice Age*, and *Madagascar*.

2 Reading

- Students read the text and answer the question. Encourage them to guess the meaning of new vocabulary from the context before they refer to a dictionary.
- Point out the use of sequencing adverbs (*first, then, next, after that*) to highlight the stages in the process of making animated movies with puppets.

Answer

They are the voices of the characters.

Optional activity

2.39 Play the recording of the article for students to read and listen. Stop at any words you predict may cause pronunciation problems, e.g. *technique, individual, 1,440,* and ask students to repeat.

3 After Reading

- Students find the answers in the text on their own, and then compare answers in pairs.
- Check the answers orally with the whole class.

Answers

1 *Wes Anderson.*
2 *"Stop motion" technique.*
3 *A series of pictures of the movie.*
4 *To make sure that everyone knows what they are doing.*
5 *Because the animator moves the puppets' mouths.*
6 *Because there are 24 pictures for every second of film./ Because the filmmakers often only manage to shoot a few seconds of film a day.*

Optional activities

♦ 2.39 Play the fourth paragraph of the text again, pausing for students to repeat. Focus on pronunciation and intonation. Pay particular attention to the stress on *characters, thumbnail, director, rehearsal, everyone, animator, designer, background.*

♦ Students write true/false sentences based on the text and test each other in small groups.

♦ Early finishers look through the text and note down examples of the infinitive of purpose and verb + infinitive in preparation for exercises 5 and 7.

Your Response

Ask students to discuss the questions in groups. Ask a confident student from each group to take notes, and then report back to the rest of the class.

4 Pronunciation

- Check students know the meaning of the words in the box. Ask them to give definitions, in English if possible.
- Ask students to work in pairs, read the words to each other, and mark the stress in pencil.
- Play the recording once, pausing for students to check their answers. Ask them to tell you the number of syllables in each word.
- Play the recording again for students to repeat in chorus.

2.40 Recording and answers

■animated ■animator ■background ■character
de■signer ■detail ■manage ■puppet ■storyboard

LANGUAGE WORKOUT OPTION

If you want to pre-teach the language students will be using in the following activities, you may like to go to the Language Workout box now.

5 Listening

- Tell students that they are going to hear a recording from the World2day farewell party, and check students understand the sentence beginnings 1–6.
- Play the recording once. Then play it again for students to match the beginnings and endings.

2.41 Recording

JAY	*Emma, do you remember the Independence Day Parade? I really enjoyed dancing with you.*
EMMA	*Yeah, that was a lot of fun.*
JAY	*Would you like to dance now?*
EMMA	*No, I just don't feel like it. It's the end of the vacation …*
RAMÓN	*Let me get you a drink. That'll make you feel better. What would you like?*
EMMA	*Actually, Ramón, I think I'd rather have some ice cream.*
JAY	*I'll get it. Ice cream, coming right up.*
EMMA	*Oh, thanks, Jay!*
RAMÓN	*Emma, can I ask you something?*
EMMA	*What is it?*
RAMÓN	*Will you e-mail to me after the vacation?*
EMMA	*I don't know, Ramón.*
RAMÓN	*Oh, come on. Please?*
EMMA	*All right, But don't tell Jay. Promise?*
RAMÓN	*Promise.*
JAY	*Here we are! Ice cream!*
EMMA	*That's great, Jay—thank you.*
JAY	*And when are you coming to see me in Chicago?*
RAMÓN	*Chicago!*
EMMA	*I don't know, Jay, I'll have to ask my parents.*
RAMÓN	*Come on, Emma, Guadalajara is much better than Chicago.*
JAY	*But Chicago is the best city in the world!*
EMMA	*Stop it, you two! I like both of you very much, you know that.*
JAY	*Why not dance with both of us, then? That'll make you feel better!*
EMMA	*OK. Why not? Come on!*

Answers

1 e 2 c 3 a 4 f 5 b 6 d

- Students work in pairs. Ask a pair to read the example question and answer.
- Students continue taking turns to ask and answer questions. Monitor and provide help where necessary.
- Check the answers by asking pairs to ask and answer around the class.

Answers

What did Jay want to do? He wanted to dance with Emma.
What did Emma refuse to do? She refused to dance with Jay.
What did Ramón offer to do? He offered to get Emma a drink.
What did Emma agree to do? She agreed to e-mail Ramón.
What did Ramón promise to do? He promised not to tell Jay.
What did Emma tell Ramón and Jay to do? She told them to stop arguing.

Extension Students write down what each character said for sentences 1–6. Play the recording again, pausing after *Would you like to dance now?* Elicit the first answer. Then play the rest of the recording and check answers.

Answers

1 *Would you like to dance now?*
2 *No, I just don't feel like it.*
3 *Let me get you a drink.*
4 *All right.*
5 *Promise.*
6 *Stop it, you two!*

6 Role-Play

- Read the instructions to the class. Work through the instructions line by line asking for suggestions. If possible, elicit several suggestions for each line. With a less confident class, list the suggestions on the board.
- Students do the role-play in pairs. Then they change roles and repeat the activity. If there is time, ask students to change partners and do the role-play twice more.

Optional activity

Ask several pairs to perform the role-play for the rest of the class. Ask confident students to act it out without books.

LANGUAGE WORKOUT OPTION

If you want to pre-teach the language students will be using in the following activities, you may like to go to the Language Workout box now.

7 Game

- The aim is to practice giving and understanding definitions using the infinitive of purpose.
- Brainstorm everyday objects, e.g. *camera, computer, map, cell phone, backpack, keys, spoon, knife, fork, cup, pen*. Write a list on the board, then point at one of the objects and ask students *Why do you use it?* Elicit the answer *You use it to …* Continue with the other objects on the board.
- Go through the example in the Student's Book with the class, then demonstrate the game using the same prompt in the example, but eliciting a different answer: *A fork*.

- Students play the game in pairs, keeping a note of their scores. Encourage students to use the words from the board or any other everyday objects they can think of. Ask students to call out when they reach ten points.

8 Vocabulary

- Ask students to read the words in the Jobs and occupations Word Bank. Check comprehension and pronunciation of the words. Encourage students to define each one, in English if possible.
- Students read the personal information and match the people and jobs. They then work in pairs to make sentences about each person, as in the example.

Answers

Jay loves cars, so he'd like to be a mechanic.
Lara is good at languages, so she'd like to be a translator.
Ramón likes mathematics, so he'd like to be an IT consultant.
Silvana is good at science and likes helping people, so she'd like to be a surgeon.
Alex likes organizing people and events, so he'd like to be a manager.
Emma likes cooking, so she'd like to be a chef.

9 Writing

- Students look at the example. Elicit a similar sentence about someone in the class, e.g. *X is good at singing, so I think she'd like to be a rock star.* Then students work individually and write at least five sentences.
- Students exchange sentences and check each other's work for grammar and spelling.
- Ask the class about any interesting skills they have or future careers they would like.

LANGUAGE WORKOUT

- Ask students to look at the Language Workout box. Confident students can complete first and then check, while others can look back at exercise 2 then complete.
- Students turn to page 121 of the Language File to check their answers.

  Answers

  to perform to shoot to be to plan why
  is are are

  Refer students to the list of verbs and phrases which are followed by *to* + infinitive on page 121 of the Language File.
- Drill the example sentences chorally and individually for pronunciation and stress.
- Highlight that:
  – the passive is often used to describe a process.
  – we use the passive when the "doer" of the verb is unknown, unimportant, or obvious.
  – we form the present simple passive with the present tense of *be* + past participle.
- To review past participle forms, refer students to the list of Irregular Verbs at the back of their books on page 127.

Consolidation and Extension p109

Language File p121

Practice

- Students do Practice exercise 25 on page 121. They match the words and phrases on their own.
- Check that they have matched correctly before asking them to write sentences beginning *You use a … to …*

Answers

1 *You use a camera to take photographs.*
2 *You use a computer to send e-mails.*
3 *You use a map to find the way.*
4 *You use a microphone to make a recording.*
5 *You use an MP3 player to listen to music.*
6 *You use a backpack to carry things on your back.*
7 *You use shampoo to wash your hair.*

- Point out that there is no article before *shampoo* in sentence 7 because it is an uncountable noun.

Follow-up activities

♦ Students update the word map for Jobs and occupations which they started in Unit 3, Lesson 4, Exercise 9.

♦ **Game** *Word rose* Write key words from the second half of the Animated Movies text in a circle on the board e.g. *animator, storyboard, puppets, designer, background, director, rehearsal, voices.* In pairs, students reconstruct the text about how animated movies are made, orally or in their notebooks, using these words.

Homework

Students write about an animated movie they have seen, e.g. a cartoon like *Tom and Jerry*.

Students make a word map for Movie-making.

NOTEBOOK SECTION

Complete the sentences using the active or passive form of the verb *use*.

1 Architects ____ mathematics to design buildings.
2 Cell phones ____ to send text messages.
3 Cocoa ____ to make chocolate.
4 Search engines ____ to find information.
5 Some travelers ____ backpacks to carry things more easily.

Answers

1 *use*
2 *are used*
3 *is used*
4 *are used*
5 *use*

Workbook Unit 8 Lesson 1 pp88–89

Photocopiable notes p160, worksheet p183

2 What will happen if ...?

Communicative Aims
Talking about future possibility

Language
First conditional

Pronunciation
Syllable stress

Vocabulary
Personal details

Useful information

The *Harry Potter* books are a series of seven fantasy novels by the British author J.K. Rowling. The books tell the adventures of Harry Potter and his best friends, Ron Weasley and Hermione Granger, who are all students at the Hogwarts School of Witchcraft and Wizardry. J.K. Rowling first had the idea for Harry Potter when she was on a crowded train journey. The first book, *Harry Potter and the Sorcerer's Stone*, was released on June 30th, 1997, and since then the series has sold more than 400 million copies and has been translated into 67 different languages.

WARM-UP 1

Elicit the meaning of *performance*, and ask students to brainstorm all the different places or media where you can see a performance, e.g. TV shows, movies, music concerts, theater plays, dance shows. Do a class survey to find out what kind of performance students prefer to watch. In small groups, students interview each other. While they are working, write these expressions on the board: *All of us prefer to watch, Two of us prefer to watch, One of us prefers to watch, None of us prefer to watch.* Groups report back to the class using the expressions on the board.

WARM-UP 2

Game *Teacher* Play with a word from the Vocabulary box. See Unit 2, Lesson 1, Warm-up for details.

1 Opener

- The aim is to introduce the context for the Reading.
- Point to the photos on page 102 and ask the questions. Allow the class to discuss the last question (*Do you like the books which the movies come from?*), giving reasons.

Answers

Daniel Radcliffe Harry Potter and the Sorcerer's Stone, Harry Potter and the Chamber of Secrets, Harry Potter and the Prisoner of Azkaban, Harry Potter and the Goblet of Fire, Harry Potter and the Order of the Phoenix, Harry Potter and the Half-Blood Prince, Harry Potter and the Deathly Hallows

2 Reading

- Ask students to read and listen to the article, writing down the three facts that they find most interesting. Answer any vocabulary questions.
- Ask a confident student to read out the three interesting facts they wrote down. Encourage them to say why they found the facts interesting. Invite other students to talk about more interesting facts they found in the article.

2.42 Recording
See text on page 102 of the Student's Book.

3 After Reading

- Students read the text again and write answers.
- Check their answers by asking one student to read a question, and then choose another student to answer it.

Answers

1 11.
2 No, we don't.
3 To take him seriously as a stage actor.
4 No, he isn't.
5 Some of the other boys bullied him.
6 Because he suffers from dyspraxia.
7 Attractive, beautiful, and intelligent.

Your Response

Ask students what bullying is, and encourage them to give examples of bullying behavior. Discuss the questions as a whole class or in small groups.

Optional activities

- ♦ Ask students to look through the text and find examples of the first conditional.
- ♦ Students look back at the text and write three more comprehension questions about it.

LANGUAGE WORKOUT OPTION

If you want to pre-teach the language students will be using in the following activities, you may like to go to the Language Workout box now.

4 Pronunciation

- Play the recording, pausing after each word for the students to count the syllables and mark the stress.
- Check the answers with the class before playing the recording a second time, pausing for the students to repeat each word.

2.43 Recording and answers

attractive (3) beautiful (3) fantastically (4)
frightening (3) intelligent (4) sensitive (3)
seriously (4) successful (3)

5 Listening

- Ask the students to look at the beginnings and endings. Point out to students that they are looking for endings where things are "going wrong," as stated in Murphy's Law. Then they work individually, matching.
- Play the recording. Students check their answers.

2.44 Recording

If you are early, the school bus will be late.
If you are late, the school bus will be on time.
If you want a book from the library, it won't be on the shelves.
If you do homework on a computer, it will crash before you save your work.
If you forget your calculator, you will have a math test.
If you copy someone else's homework, the teacher will find out.
If you lend friends your notes, they will lose them.
If you have to decide between two answers, you will choose the wrong one.

Answers

1 e 2 h 3 a 4 d 5 g 6 f 7 b 8 c

6 Speaking

- Students read the questionnaire. Write the following chart on the board for the students to copy into their notebooks. Continue the question numbers to 8.

Question	*Me*	*Name*	*Name*
1			
2			
3			
4			

- Give the students a few minutes to think about their responses to the eight questions in the questionnaire and write them in the *Me* column.
- Students interview two other students and note their answers in the second and third columns. Make sure students don't show each other their charts. Encourage confident students to give more information.
- Nominate students to say how they were similar or different from the students they interviewed. Identify some of the most popular answers.

Optional activity

Confident students invent two more questions to include in the questionnaire.

7 Writing

- Ask one or two students to tell the class about the answers they got for the first question. Use this information to show the students how to form sentences if the responses were the same (If …, both X and Y will …) and if the responses were different (If …, X will …, and/but Y will …).
- Students write sentences comparing the two students they interviewed.
- Students exchange their writing and check each other's work for spelling, grammar, and punctuation.

Extension Students write sentences about their own answers to the questionnaire. Monitor and help where necessary.

LANGUAGE WORKOUT

- Ask students to look at the Language Workout box and to complete the sentences. Confident students can complete first and then check, while less confident ones can look back at exercise 2 and then complete.
- Students turn to page 121 of the Language File to check their answers.

Answers

If … will gets … won't … think
will … changes will … don't

- Highlight that:
  - we use the first conditional to talk about future possibility.
  - in first conditional sentences, use the simple present tense in the *if/when* clause.
  - the *if* clause can follow the main clause.
- If necessary, highlight common mistakes: students use *will* in the present tense clause.
- Drill the examples chorally and individually for pronunciation and stress.

Practice

- Students do Practice exercise 26 on page 121 of the Language File. They match the beginnings with the endings.

Answers

1 You will feel better if you exercise more.
2 He will have an accident if he drives so fast.
3 They will pass the exam if they work hard.
4 I won't spend any money if I stay at home.
5 You will get a prize if you win the contest.
6 We won't go to the gig if we don't get free tickets.
7 She will find her keys if she cleans her room.
8 I won't get lost if I take a map.

Optional activities

- *Murphy's Law at home* In groups, students write (and illustrate) eight points similar to those in exercise 5, but based on home life, e.g. *If you don't clean your room, your mom will go in to look for something and get angry.*
- *Captions for pictures* Give students a selection of pictures from magazines. In groups, students choose two or three and write captions using the first conditional. These could be displayed around the classroom.

Homework

Students write about their plans for the weekend if the weather is good, or if it's raining.

NOTEBOOK SECTION

Complete the sentence using a form of the word in parentheses.

1 If it's rainy, we ____ to the movies. (✓go)
2 She won't like it if we ____ late. (✓arrive)
3 What will you do if the printer____? (✗ work)
4 If he doesn't study, he ____ the test. (✗ pass)
5 If they win this game, they ____ to the finals. (✓get)

Answers

1 'll (will) go
2 arrive
3 doesn't work
4 won't pass
5 'll (will) get

Consolidation and Extension p109

Language File p121

Workbook Unit 8 Lesson 2 pp90–91

Photocopiable notes p160, worksheet p184

3 When were the first movies shown?

Communicative aims	Language	Pronunciation	Vocabulary	Optional aids
Talking about past events	Simple past passive	Rhyming words	Review	Exercise 2 Extension: slips of paper

WARM-UP 1

Game *Outburst* Write five words you want to review on a card, e.g. some places: *hotel, bank, restaurant, movie theater, bar*; ways of saying hello and goodbye: *hi, hello, bye bye, goodbye, see you*. Divide students into small groups and give them 60 seconds to guess the five words you have written on the card. They get one point for every word they guess.

WARM-UP 2

Game *Hidden sentence* Students guess words in sentences based on the photos on page 105, exercise 5. For example, for photo 1 write this on the board:

_____ _____ _____ _____ _____ _____
1 2 3 4 5 6

Ask students to look at the picture and guess what words are in the sentence (The thin man is taking the girl's wallet.). They get one point for a correct word and one point for a correct position, e.g. students say *the—number 1* which gets two points. This could be a team game.

1 Opener

- The aim is to prepare students for the quiz, not to do it, so it's important to work quickly. Students work in pairs telling each other what the photos show.

2 Reading

- The aim is for students to test themselves to see how much they know about movies and TV. Ask students to take the quiz on their own.
- Students compare answers in pairs, but do not check the answers as a class.
- Play the recording for students to listen and check their answers. Play the recording again, pausing after each question to check the answer.

Answers

1 B 2 A 3 B 4 B 5 C 6 A 7 B 8 B 9 C 10 A

2.45 Recording

1 *When were the first movies shown?*
B In 1895.
2 *Who played Romeo in the movie of* Romeo and Juliet?
A Leonardo DiCaprio.
3 *In which series of movies does Emma Watson play Hermione?*
B Harry Potter.
4 *In* Fantastic Mr. Fox, *who was chosen to be the voice of Mr. Fox?*
B George Clooney.
5 *When was the first animated movie with sound made?*
C In 1928.
6 *What is the name of Bart Simpson's father?*
A Homer.
7 *In which country was Kylie Minogue born?*
B Australia.
8 *Who is the star of the* Pirates of the Caribbean *movies?*
B Johnny Depp.
9 *Where was the first broadcast of* Ugly Betty?
C Colombia.
10 *One contestant on* I'm A Celebrity—Get Me Out Of Here! *was asked to walk through water. What was the water full of?*
A Crocodiles.

Optional activity

2.45 Students listen and note down examples of the simple past passive in preparation for exercise 4.

Extension Give each student one or two slips of paper. Students look at the format of the quiz in exercise 2, and then write a quiz question on one side of the paper and the correct answer (A, B, or C) on the back. Collect the slips and read out the questions for a class quiz. Then check answers and see which student got the most correct answers.

3 Pronunciation

- Students match the rhyming pairs and write them in their notebooks.
- Play the recording. Students listen and check.
- Play it again, pausing after each pair for students to repeat.

2.46 Recording and answers

first—worst
full—wool
here—year
made—played
quiz—his
shown—phone
snake—break
through—true

4 Listening

- Remind students of what Emma told Carrie in Unit 4—she must choose to see either Ramón or Jay after the vacation. Students discuss in pairs what they think Emma will say to the boys. Ask pairs to tell the whole class their opinions.
- Play the recording and see who is right. Then ask *Who are Jay, Emma, and Ramón with at the end of the party?* Play the recording again for students to check.

2.47 Recording

CARRIE *And now here's the last dance for tonight—and for the vacation. Thank you, all of you, and goodbye. Don't forget to keep in touch.*
RAMÓN *Emma. You heard what Carrie said about keeping in touch. Are you going to come and see me in Guadalajara?*
EMMA *Oh, Ramón, I can't. I've decided to go and see Jay in Chicago.*
RAMÓN *Oh, OK. Right. So it's goodbye, then.*
EMMA *Yeah, Ramón. Sorry. Now, where's Jay?*
RAMÓN *He's over there, dancing with Silvana. See you around.*
EMMA *Thanks, Ramón, bye. Hi, Jay, hi, Silvana. Jay, I just wanted to say yes—I'd love to come to Chicago to stay with you!*
JAY *Yes, well, um … but you see, Silvana … um, Silvana …*
SILVANA *What Jay means is that he's coming to Argentina to visit me! So you can't stay with him in Chicago, because he won't be there. He'll be in Buenos Aires with me.*
EMMA *Oh no! Jay, how could you? I think I've made a terrible mistake. Now, where's Ramón?*
SILVANA *He's over there, dancing with Lara. Don't they look happy together?*
EMMA *Boys! They're all the same! Oh, here's Alex. Hi, Alex. How are you?*
ALEX *Hi, Emma. Would you like to dance? I've wanted to dance with you all evening.*
EMMA *I'd love to dance with you. Now, tell me all about Australia. I've always wanted to go there …*

Answers

Emma tells Ramón she is going to go and see Jay in Chicago.
At the end of the party, Jay is with Silvana, Emma is with Alex, and Ramón is with Lara.

LANGUAGE WORKOUT OPTION

If you want to pre-teach the language students will be using in the following activities, you may like to go to the Language Workout box now.

5 Speaking

- Ask students to look at photo 1 and read the example sentences out loud. Point out that the second sentence is in the present because it states who is in the photo, and the other two are in the past.
- In pairs, students tell each other three things about each of the photos using the passive, where possible.
- Ask pairs to say their sentences to the class. The important thing is that students should get the simple past passive and the past progressive tags right; it doesn't really matter if, for example, they get people's names wrong. There are lots of possibilities and no "right" answers.

Possible answers

1
The photo was taken in San Francisco, by the carousel.
Alex and Silvana are in the photo.
Silvana was helping Alex with his camera.
2
The photo was taken in San Francisco, at the street fair.
Steve and some other members of the group are in the photo.
Steve was telling the group they should stay together.
3
The photo was taken in San Francisco, on Nob Hill.
Jay and Silvana are in the photo.
They were standing in front of a cable car.
4
The photo was taken in the movie studio.
Everyone is in the photo.
They were doing drama exercises.
5
The photo was taken in Washington, D.C., in Rock Creek Park.
Silvana, Ramón, and Emma are in the photo.
They were making a video about life in the U.S.
6
The photo was taken in Washington, D.C., in front of the Lincoln Memorial.
Steve and everyone in the group are in the photo.
Steve was telling the group about the schedule for the day.

Optional activity

With a less confident class, ask students to note down their descriptions of the photos. They then read them out to each other in pairs. Change pairs and ask students to describe the same photos without looking at their notes.

6 Writing

- Students work on their own, and then read out their descriptions for a partner to identify the photo.
- Invite some students to read out their descriptions. Other students in the class call out when they identify the photo.

LANGUAGE WORKOUT

- Ask students to complete the sentences in the Language Workout box. The answers are in the Reading on pages 104–105.
- Students turn to page 121 of the Language File to check their answers.

Answers
was
was
were

- Drill the example sentences chorally and individually.

Practice

- Students do Practice exercise 27 on page 121 of the Language File. They complete the sentences on their own and then check each other's work.

Answers
1 was built
2 was made
3 was printed
4 were invented
5 was taken
6 were broadcast

Follow-up activity

Game *Just a minute* Play the game (see Unit 6, Lesson 4, page 117) with topics from Units 7–8.

Homework

Students write predictions about what will happen to Jay, Emma, Lara, Alex, Silvana, and Ramón.
Students choose one of the characters and write about what he/she did during the vacation in the U.S.

NOTEBOOK SECTION

Complete the sentences using the simple past passive form of the verbs in parentheses.

1 You look so different. When ____ this photo ____? (take)
2 Machu Picchu ____ in the 15th century. (build)
3 Their parents ____ to come to the school. (call)
4 Press this button to see when the last call ____. (make)
5 I'm sorry you ____ to the party. (not invite)

Answers
1 was, taken
2 was built
3 were called
4 was made
5 weren't invited

Consolidation and Extension p109

Language File p121

Workbook Unit 8 Lesson 3 pp92–93

Photocopiable notes p160, worksheet p185

4 Integrated Skills Describing a process

Skills
Reading Order of stages in a process: *Walking with Dinosaurs* article
Listening Order of stages in a process: computer animation
Speaking Exchanging information
Writing Process description

Learner Independence
Definitions
Resources for Practice

Vocabulary
Dinosaurs
Computer animation
Useful expressions

Optional aids
Exercise 6: monolingual dictionaries

WARM-UP 1

Game *Connect four* Draw this grid on the board.

Simple present (?)	Simple past (+)	Any tense you like	Present perfect (-)
Simple past (-)	Present progressive	Simple present (+)	Present progressive
Past progressive (?)	Simple past (?)	Present perfect (+)	Past progressive
Present perfect (?)	Any tense you like	Past progressive (-)	Simple present (-)

Divide the class into two teams and decide which team is Xs and which is Os. Team 1 chooses a square and makes a sentence using that tense, e.g. Simple past (+) requires a positive sentence in the simple past tense. If they answer correctly, write their symbol in the appropriate square. If they say it incorrectly, Team 2 can correct the sentence and win the square. The first team to connect four squares in any direction wins.

WARM-UP 2

Write jumbled sentences with question tags from the previous lesson on the board. Students re-order the sentences.

1 Opener

- The aim is to prepare students for the reading text. Ask students to close their books and discuss the questions in groups. Then elicit information from the groups. Write the different dinosaur names on the board.

2 Reading

- With a confident class, students read the text and note down the order. They compare their answers and then read the text again. With a less confident class, students read the text. Then students re-read the text and underline the sequencing adverbs: *First, Next, Then, After that, Finally*. They then match the sentences after the sequencing adverbs with sentences A–E and compare their answers. Finally they read the text again.

Answers
1 C 2 B 3 E 4 A 5 D

Optional activity

♦ Students write true/false sentences to check detailed comprehension of the text.

3 Listening

- Ask students to read the sentences and look at the pictures in exercise 4 before they listen. Pre-teach *scan*.
- Students listen and number sentences A–E. They compare answers in pairs.
- Play the recording again. Check the answers.

2.48 Recording

INTERVIEWER *So how does computer animation work?*
PRODUCER *There are lots of different ways of doing it, but we think our way is the best. First, a white model of the animal is made—it's fairly small, but exactly like the animal in every way, except that it's white. Next, the model is put into the computer using a machine called a scanner, which tells the computer exactly what the model looks like. So, the model is scanned into the computer. Then, the animal's skin is colored. After that, the computer is used to animate the animal—in other words, to make the animal move. That's why it's called computer animation. So, the computer is used to make the animal move. Finally, a movie of an actor against a real background is used, and the actor is taken away by the computer … then the animal is put into the picture. And then we can see the animal moving around on the screen. It's fantastic!*

Answers
1 E 2 B 3 D 4 A 5 C

Optional activity

Students can try to guess the order of the sentences before they listen.

4 Speaking

- Students work in pairs, using the pictures and the sequencing adverbs *First, Next, Then, After that, Finally,* to describe how to make a computer animation of an animal. Refer less confident students to the sentences in exercise 3 as prompts.

5 Writing

- Ask students to copy the description into their notebooks, adding the missing information as they do so.
- For a less confident class, elicit the missing information before students write.

Optional activity

One student closes the book and tries to remember as much as possible about how computer animation works. His/Her partner asks questions.

6 Learner Independence

- The aim is to encourage students to define words. This is a useful strategy if they don't know the English word for something. Students write definitions for the people and things in the box. If possible, bring dictionaries into class to help them.
- Students read out the definitions for others to guess.

Optional activity

Drill the words in the box for pronunciation. Students mark the stress.

7

- The aim is to help students organize their learning outside class and during their vacations. In pairs, they brainstorm what they can do to practice English during their vacations and discuss how they can use the resources from the box.
- Students match the resources with the activities on their own and then compare their answers in pairs.

Answers
1 yourself 2 TV and radio 3 video camera 4 the Internet 5 MP3 player 6 video or DVD player 7 graded readers 8 your coursebook 9 friends

- Check answers with the whole class.

8 Phrasebook

- Play the recording for students to listen and repeat.

2.49 Recording
I just wanted to say … (Emma, Lesson 3, ex 4)
How could you? (Emma, Lesson 3, ex 4)
I've made a terrible mistake. (Emma, Lesson 3, ex 4)
I've always wanted to … (Emma, Lesson 3, ex 4)
It wasn't easy. (Narrator, Lesson 4, ex 2)

- Students complete the two sentences for themselves. They exchange sentences and write their response.

Optional activity

Ask students to work in pairs and write a four-line dialogue using at least two of the expressions in the box. Invite pairs to act out their dialogues.

Follow-up activity

Students see how many words they can make from DINOSAURS in small groups. Students may only use the letter "s" twice in a word and the minimum length of a word is three letters. The group with the most words wins. Other students can add to the winning list. Possible words include: *air, and, nod(s), our(s), rain(s), ran, round, run(s), Russia(n), sad, said, sand(s), sir(s), soda, son(s), sound(s), sun(s)*

Homework

Students write a paragraph about dinosaurs using information from the lesson and other facts they have researched.

Students review vocabulary from the three previous lessons.

NOTEBOOK SECTION

Complete the sentences using one of these relative pronouns/adverbs: *who, where, which,* or *when.*

1 The crew is all the people ____ work on a movie.
2 The studio is ____ the movies are made.
3 Rehearsals are times ____ you practice scenes.
4 A storyboard is the thing ____ shows the scenes from a movie.
5 The director is the one ____ yells "Cut!"

Answers
1 who
2 where
3 when
4 which
5 who

Consolidation and Extension p109

Workbook Unit 8 Lesson 4 pp94–95

Inspired EXTRA!

Project A Day to Remember

1

- Explain to students that the aim of this project is to interview people and write about important days in their lives. Tell students to read the example text about someone's "day to remember" on page 108.
- Divide students into groups and appoint an "editor" for each group.
- In their groups, students make a list of special days. Encourage them to think about special days they remember well in their own lives to give them ideas.

2

- Students think of people they could interview for their project—friends, family, teachers, or other students. They may want to choose people who they already know have had very special days in their lives. Each student chooses two people to interview.

3

- The students in each group make a list of questions that they can ask people about their special day.
- Point out the questions in the book, and encourage them to think of others that they can ask, too.

4

- Each person in the group interviews the two people they have chosen, using the questions they have prepared and the list of special days to give the people ideas. They then write a short description of the people's "special days." Remind students to look again at the example text on page 108, for style.
- Students put their work together and read the texts through carefully to correct any mistakes. They copy their texts out neatly. The editor selects the order of the texts while others illustrate their work with photos of the people or drawings.
- Students show their work to other groups. Display it in the classroom if possible.

Game Compliments

- The aim is to generate a warm and positive end-of-term atmosphere and to personalize the language of compliments. Students work individually, writing positive adjectives to describe someone they like a lot. They compare their lists in pairs. Students either write their lists on the board or call out for you or another student to write them up.
- Students use the list to write a complimentary sentence about another student without using their name.
- Collect the sentences and shuffle them. Then read them out to the class and ask students to try to identify who the sentences are about and who wrote them.

Consolidation

Lesson 1

See Unit 8, Lesson 1, Exercise 5 answers.

Lesson 2

1 drop, will have
2 will be, eat
3 start, will go
4 will be, point
5 is, will bring

Lesson 3

1 was opened
2 were destroyed
3 was discovered
4 was sold
5 was called

Lesson 4

Answers

D B E C A

First, decide which show to record. Next, find a new DVD. Then, put the DVD in the DVD recorder. After that, set the time and channel on the DVD recorder and press "Record." Finally, watch the show after you have recorded it.

Extension

Lessons 1–4
Students' own answers.

YOUR CHOICE!

The aim is to give students more learner independence and help them to identify their preferred ways of learning. Encourage students to choose an activity that they feel less comfortable with if they want a challenge or are aware that they need practice in a particular area.
Words in the Mind gives students the opportunity to mime or draw words for other students in the group to guess.
Looking Back and Looking Forward gives students the opportunity to take part in a free-speaking group activity and to practice letter-writing.

You may now like students to do the song *The Miracle*. See p161 for the notes and p189 for the worksheet.

Language File p121

Song—photocopiable notes p161, worksheet p189

Workbook Unit 8 Inspired EXTRA! pp96–97

Units 7-8

1 Students choose the appropriate word for each space. Do the first one together as an example. This can be done in pairs or individually.

Answers
1 C 2 C 3 A 4 B 5 B 6 C 7 B 8 A 9 C 10 B

Optional activity
Confident students can first try to complete the text without looking at the words.

2 Explain that the rules are for another World2day contest. Tell students to read the rules all the way through and then choose the most appropriate answer in each case.

Answers
1 must 2 must 3 mustn't 4 mustn't 5 must 6 must 7 mustn't 8 must

3 Students choose one element from each box to make eight true sentences. Point out that *when* and *if* are both correct in each case. With a less confident class, do the first three as a whole class activity.

Answers
You have to buy a ticket when/if you go to the movies.
You have to exercise when/if you want to stay in shape.
You have to call the restaurant when/if you want to book a table.
You have to have lights when/if you bike at night.
You have to look both ways when/if you cross the street.
You have to wear sneakers when/if you go to the gym.
You have to be polite when/if you talk to teachers.
You have to speak English when/if you visit the U.S.

Optional activity
Confident students can do the exercise orally.

4 Students take turns asking and answering questions in pairs.

Answers
1 Does she have to paint for four hours a day? Yes, she does.
2 Does she have to call home every day? No, she doesn't.
3 Does she have to read a lot of books? No, she doesn't.
4 Does she have to go to all the classes? Yes, she does.
5 Does she have to eat French food? Yes, she does.
6 Does she have to share a room? No, she doesn't.

5 When you check the answers, ask students to explain their choice of *-ed* or *-ing* adjective.

Answers
1 interested 2 frightening 3 terrifying 4 embarrassed 5 exhausting 6 amazing 7 surprised

6

Answers
1 I'd like 2 I'd rather 3 I'd rather 4 I'd like 5 I'd rather

7 Suggest that students match the words to make the phrases first. With a more confident class, you could do this part orally. Students then match the phrases with the places. Check the answers before students make their sentences.

Answers
book a flight—travel agency
buy some medicine—drugstore
change some money—bank
see a movie—movie theater
send some postcards—post office
get a haircut—hairdresser's
Alex went to the bank to change some money.
He went to the drugstore to buy some medicine.
He went to the movie theater to see a movie.
He went to the hairdresser's to get a haircut.
He went to the post office to send some postcards.
He went to the travel agency to book a flight.

8 With a less confident class, elicit the infinitives first.

Answers
1 to write 2 to have 3 to get 4 to wait 5 to go 6 to see

9

Answers
1 are taken 2 is used 3 is recorded 4 are called 5 are mixed 6 is made

10

Answers
1 will cook, like
2 don't hurry, will miss
3 will be, passes
4 won't get, look
5 rains, won't have
6 will sleep better, open

11

Answers
1 The first printed books were produced in China.
2 The electric light bulb was invented in 1879.
3 Cell phones were first used in 1978.
4 The Washington, D.C. subway opened in 1976.
5 Potatoes were taken to Europe in the 16th century

Vocabulary

12 Point out that there are three extra words in the box.

Answers

1 grass 2 surgeon 3 autograph 4 trash
5 earthquake 6 shampoo 7 clap 8 intelligent

Optional activity

Students can write three sentences using the extra words in the box.

13 Confident students can first cover the list of words and try to work out what the definitions refer to.

Answers

1 technique 2 sled 3 luxury 4 storyboard
5 celebrity 6 checkout 7 equipment
8 animated movies 9 second

Optional activity

Students write definitions of other words from Units 7 and 8. They exchange definitions with another student and guess each other's words.

14

Answers

1 arrive on time
2 bring something to life
3 catch a train
4 tie your shoes
5 enter a contest
6 learn a technique
7 make a calculation
8 set the table
9 spend time

Learner Independence Self Assessment

- Explain to students that the aim of the self assessment is to encourage them to check their own progress and take any necessary action to improve. Point out that the list 1–7 covers areas of functional language from Units 7 and 8. Students check the "Fine" box for functional language that they feel confident using, but put a question mark in the "Not sure" box for functional language that they have difficulty with or still cannot use confidently.
- Encourage students to look at the Language File and re-do exercises from the Workbook in areas where they have problems. They may also like to re-do exercises from the lessons and from the Consolidation and Extension sections in Units 7 and 8.
- Students write an example sentence for each language area in the list. You may like to elicit the grammar students need for each example before students write sentences, e.g. *Expressing obligation and prohibition: must and mustn't.* Students can refer back to the lessons and the Language File.
- Ask students to compare their sentences with a partner's, and to discuss and correct any mistakes.
- Check their sentences and note down language areas for future practice.

Follow-up activity

Game *Teacher* Play with words for occupations. See Unit 2, Lesson 1 for further details

Homework

Students bring their vocabulary notebooks up to date.

NOTEBOOK SECTION

There is one error in each sentence. Rewrite the sentences correctly.

1 What a day! I'm exhausting.
2 You mustn't wash the car. I washed it yesterday.
3 I'd rather to go tomorrow.
4 I wait for you if you want.
5 The money was took out of my bag.

Answers

1 I'm exhausted.
2 You don't have to wash ...
3 I'd rather go tomorrow.
4 I'll wait for you if you want.
5 The money was taken out ...

Language File pp120–121

Workbook Review Units 7–8 pp98–99

1.1 Do you eat French fries every day?

Activity Questionnaire

Language focus Simple present for regular activities; asking and answering questions; review of vocabulary

Preparation Photocopy the worksheet for every student in the class.

Procedure

1 Give out a copy of the worksheet to every student in the class. They should read it and ask if they have any problems with the vocabulary.

2 Explain how to do the activity. Tell the students the aim is to guess information about their partner. Write *dog, cat, rabbit, no pet* on the board and circle *cat*. Say *I think Rosa has a cat*. Then ask *Rosa, do you have a cat?* or *Rosa, I think you have a cat*. If she says *Yes, I do*, put a check and if not, put a cross in the appropriate boxes.

3 Divide the class into pairs. First, they should work individually, going through the questionnaire and circling the information they think is true for their partner. If they don't think any of it is true, e.g. if they think Rosa has a pet rat, they could add *rat* to their list.

4 They then take turns to ask questions or make statements. When answering, their partner might like to add something true about themselves, e.g. *No, I don't have a cat, but I have a mouse.*

5 The students put a check or a cross in the appropriate box, depending on whether they guessed correctly or not. The person with the most checks knows his/her partner very well!

6 As a follow-up, the students could report back orally, in groups or in open class, on anything interesting they have found out about their partner.

1.2 Party time!

Activity Information gap

Language focus Present progressive questions and answers; review of vocabulary

Preparation Photocopy one picture for each student. Each student must also have one cue card. These can be duplicated for classes with more than 15 students.

New vocabulary *skateboarding*

Procedure

1 Give each student a cue card and tell them to write the name of the person who is on their cue card in the appropriate place on the picture. It is important that they do not let other students see their cue card or picture. Collect the cue cards before starting the second phase of the activity.

2 Tell the students that they need to find out the names of everyone in the picture. They only know the person who is on their cue card. They should go around the room asking questions like *Who is playing the guitar?* and giving responses such as *It's …* or *I don't know …* This is an opportunity to encourage contracted forms, e.g. *Who's …?/It's …*

3 The students walk around the room finding the information. Make it clear that they can only ask each person in the class one question before moving on.

4 The game ends when someone has written down all 15 names.

5 Go over the answers together in class.

Key

1.3 Clothes Bingo!

Activity Bingo

Language focus Vocabulary of clothes and accessories

Preparation Photocopy the worksheet and cut up the Bingo cards.

New vocabulary *pin, bangle, scarf*

Procedure

1 Distribute the picture cards. They can be duplicated for classes with over ten students.

2 Shuffle the 25 word cards and read out the words. The students cross out the picture on their cards if a word from their cards is called. (If they do this using a pencil, this can be erased and the game can be played again.) After you've read out the word, put it in a separate pile, so that you know which ones you have called.

3 The first student to cross out all his/her pictures should shout *Bingo*. Ask him/her to read back the words, so that you can check that they are correct. This also gives you an opportunity to check his/her pronunciation.

2.1 What's the difference?

Activity	Card game
Language focus	Comparative and superlative forms; review of adjectives
Preparation	Cut out the worksheet for each group of three or four students. The cards must be cut out along the lines.
New vocabulary	*chess, knitting, R&B*
Procedure	**1** Divide the class into groups of three or four. Give each group a set of both adjective and noun cards. Explain the activity, or demonstrate with one group. **2** Put the noun cards (the larger cards) in a pile, face down. **3** Each student takes five adjective cards (the smaller cards) and puts them face up in front of him/her. The rest of the adjectives should be in a pile, face down. **4** The first student turns over a noun card and uses one of his/her adjective cards to make a comparative or superlative form, e.g. *A supermarket is cheaper than a small store./August is the hottest month.* **5** If the rest of the group accepts the language and the content as valid, the student puts his/her adjective card at the bottom of the pile of adjective cards. If the student cannot use one of his/her adjectives, he/she can take one from the top of the pile or miss a turn. **6** The second student has a turn and so on, until one of the students gets rid of all his/her cards.

2.2 Where is it?

Activity	Information gap
Language focus	Prepositions of place and the verb *to be*; review of vocabulary
Preparation	Photocopy the worksheet for every two students and cut into two.
Procedure	**1** Explain the context. Two girls, Molly and Carol, are sharing a room on vacation. On Monday, Molly can't find her possessions, but Carol is able to tell her where they are. On Tuesday, Carol can't find the items that belong to her, but Molly knows where they are. In Molly's picture, Carol's possessions are clearly visible and vice versa. The possessions they can't find are written under the pictures. The students will have to ask each other questions to find out where their possessions are. Then they have to draw or write them onto their own pictures. **2** Divide the class into two groups. Group A has Carol's picture, and Group B has Molly's picture. Encourage them to work with a partner from their own group to name the objects in the picture and make questions about the things that are missing, e.g. *Where's my …?/Where are my …?* **3** Tell the students that they should now divide up so that a student from Group A works with a student from Group B. The students should ask questions about the things they can't find and listen carefully to the answers. Then they should either write the name of the object or draw it in the appropriate place on their picture.

2.3 The same or different?

Activity	Questionnaire
Language focus	Verbs + *ing*; short answers (*Yes, I do*; *No, I don't*)
Preparation	Photocopy one worksheet for every student in the class.
Procedure	**1** Give out a copy of the worksheet to every student. They read it and ask if they have any problems with the vocabulary. **2** Ask the students to check the appropriate column according to whether they enjoy/can't stand doing something. **3** The students should now walk around the classroom finding people who feel the same as they do. For example, they could ask *Do you like reading books?* If the student checked *enjoy/love* and the other person says *Yes, I do*, the student writes his/her initials on the line underneath the check box and moves on to the next question. If the person says *No*, then he/she has to move on and ask another person. The students should be encouraged to write down the initials of as many different people as they can. They can also be encouraged to ask further details, e.g. *What kind of books do you like reading?/What kind of foreign food do you like?* **4** The students form pairs and tell their partner what information they found. They could also report back to the whole class on any interesting information. Is there something a lot of people enjoy or don't like?

3.1 Looking back

Activity Game

Language focus Simple past

Preparation Photocopy the worksheet for each group, and cut it up into 15 A cards, 15 B cards, and 15 C cards. If time is limited, reduce the number of sentences in the game by using fewer cards in each category.

New vocabulary *direct* (v), *marry* (v), *paint* (v), *sink* (v)

Procedure

1 Put three word groups on the board, mixed up, e.g.

In 1885 Karl Benz	*In 1961 Yuri Gagarin*	*In 1938 László Bíró*
invent	*be*	*build*
the first ballpoint pen	*the first car*	*the first person to travel in space*

Ask the students to match them as quickly as they can, changing the verb into the past tense. Then drill the pronunciation. Point out the different endings /d/ and /t/ and the weak form of *was* (/wəz/).

2 Explain that they are going to play a team game, in which each group has to match three categories of cards as quickly as possible and put the verbs into the past tense.

3 Divide the class into groups of three. Number each group.

4 Student A in each group has the set of A cards, in a pile and face down. Student B and Student C in each group has their set of cards, shuffled well and face up in front of him/her.

5 Student A turns over the first A card, and Student B finds a verb and Student C a noun to go with it as quickly as possible. The three of them decide on the past tense and if the sentence is correct. If they're all agreed, they put the sentence to one side.

6 Student A then turns over the next card and they continue the game until all the sentences are completed.

7 The team that finishes first reads out their sentence first. If it is correct, they win a point. If the verb is correct, they win another point. After each sentence has been read out, the teacher asks *Is that correct?* If another team thinks the first team's sentence is incorrect, they can challenge them. If the challengers are incorrect, this team misses a turn. If they are correct, this team scores the points and wins the opportunity to read out their sentence. Keep a record of the scores on the board.

8 The winning team is the team with the most correct sentences and the highest score.

Key

Vesuvius buried Pompeii.
Christopher Columbus crossed the Atlantic.
Leonardo da Vinci painted the *Mona Lisa*.
Captain Cook traveled to Australia.
Antonio Meucci invented the first telephone.
The Titanic sank off the coast of Canada.
Walt Disney made *Snow White*.
Hillary and Tenzing climbed Mount Everest.
Neil Armstrong walked on the moon.
Steven Spielberg directed *Jaws*.
Prince Charles married Lady Diana Spencer.
J.K. Rowling wrote the first *Harry Potter* book.
Apple designed the iPod®.
The Brazilian soccer team won the World Cup.

3.2 Who? What? Where? When?

Activity Board game

Language focus Past tense forms

Preparation A copy of the board game, blown up for each group of three or four students. Provide a dice and three or four counters for each group.

Procedure

1 Tell the students to write three or four general knowledge questions each, using the past tense. Give and elicit examples to put on the board, e.g. *When did … win …?/Who wrote …?/What did … invent?*

2 Put the students into groups of three or four. Give them a copy of the board, the dice, and counters.

3 The students should take turns to throw the dice and land on a square. If a student lands on a square with a topic, he/she has to say a sentence about it. If the group agree it is grammatically correct, the student can stay there. If not, he/she must go back to where he/she was before.

4 If the student lands on a square with a question mark, one of the other students can ask him/her one of the questions they prepared earlier. The same rules apply.

5 The game continues until someone reaches the end and wins.

3.3 What were you doing yesterday at 11 o'clock?

Activity Memory game, information gap

Language focus Past progressive; review of simple past

Preparation Photocopy one worksheet for each pair, and cut it into two.

Procedure

1 Tell the class the situation. Yesterday at 11 o'clock, there were two robberies: one from a jewelry store on the street, and one from a classroom at a language school. Each student was at one of these places, and their task is to remember as much as possible about what was going on at the time. As they are witnesses, they will be asked questions by the police.

2 Divide the class into two groups: Group A and Group B. Give Group A Picture A and Group B Picture B.

3 The students first work with another student from the same group. Their task is to write as many questions as they can about their own picture. The idea is that they are going to ask a witness to the robbery these questions later. They have to use the past progressive and simple past, e.g. *What were you doing?/Who were you talking to?/What were you wearing?/Who did you see?/What were they doing?*

4 The students now swap pictures, so that Group A has Picture B and Group B has Picture A. Each student decides who they are in the picture. They cannot be the robbers! They have five minutes to memorize what was happening when they were at the scene.

5 The students take back their original picture that goes with the questions they have prepared.

6 Tell the students that they should divide up so that a student from Group A works with a student from Group B. They ask each other the questions they have prepared and answer the questions. They are not allowed to look at the scene they had to memorize again.

7 Discuss who made a good witness.

4.1 How well do you know me?

Activity Sentence completion

Language focus Open conditional with *if* and *when*; review of vocabulary

Preparation Photocopy one questionnaire for every student.

Procedure

1 Tell the students that they are going to finish sentences about their partner with information they think is true, using the open conditional.

2 Tell the students to work with someone they know well.

3 The students should complete as many sentences as they can with information about their partner, e.g. *When you have a free evening, you prefer to stay in and play on the computer*. They also make two sentences using *if* and *when*.

4 They should then ask their partner questions, e.g. *When you have a free evening, do you prefer to stay in?*

5 When they are given the information, they should put a check in the appropriate column. If they guessed wrongly, they should ask their partner what they (like to) do instead and write it down.

6 The students should compare the scores in pairs, and then as a class. How well do they know each other?

4.2 A romantic story

Activity Predicting the end of a story

Language focus *I'm sure, I hope, I think; will/won't*

Preparation Copy one worksheet for each pair of students, and cut up the pictures.

Procedure

1 Lead into the topic by discussing any romantic stories the students read or any soap operas they watch. Elicit examples of the "cliffhangers" they end on.

2 Tell the students that they are going to predict the end of a story using language such as *I think they'll/I hope he'll/I'm sure he won't*.

3 Divide the class into pairs and give each pair a set of pictures, jumbled up.

4 The students have to order the story first and discuss what is happening.

5 Tell the students to work in groups of three or four to predict what happens next, e.g. *Will Alessandro go back to his girlfriend?/Will he forget about Stella?/Will he decide not to leave?* The students should think of a one-sentence or a one-paragraph ending, depending on ability.

6 The groups report back to the whole class and decide which ending is the best.

4.3 Adverbs puzzle

Activity Adverbs puzzle

Language focus Adjectives; adverbs

Preparation A photocopy of the crossword for each pair. A copy of clues A for half of the class and clues B for the other half.

Procedure

1. Tell the students that they are going to fill in a puzzle with the correct form of the adverb formed from the adjective.
2. Divide the class into pairs. Give each pair a copy of the puzzle and give Students A clues A and Students B clues B.
3. Tell the students to work individually to complete the spaces in their sentences with the correct adverbs.
4. When they have filled in the correct adverbs, the students should work in pairs and take turns to give each other the definitions on their Clues sheets to complete the puzzle.
5. Set a time limit and check orally with the class.

Key

1			Q	U	I	C	K	L	Y		
2					L	O	U	D	L	Y	
3			N	O	R	M	A	L	L	Y	
4		C	A	R	E	F	U	L	L	Y	
5				S	L	O	W	L	Y		
6	P	R	O	P	E	R	L	Y			
7		Q	U	I	E	T	L	Y			
8					H	A	P	P	I	L	Y
9						B	A	D	L	Y	
10			W	E	L	L					
11		S	A	D	L	Y					

5.1 What are we doing?

Activity Information gap

Language focus Present progressive for the future; question forms

Preparation Photocopy one worksheet for each pair and cut the sheet along the dotted lines.

Procedure

1. Explain the situation to the class. Two boys (Tim and William) are going on a school trip to Washington, D.C. Their teacher has given them some information, but their notes are not complete. Their mothers/fathers call each other to find the missing information. The words with question marks next to the information indicate what they want to find out.
2. Demonstrate the first part with one pair of students, e.g.:

   Tim's mom: *Where are they meeting?*
   William's mom: *In front of the school gates. But at what time are they meeting?*
   Tim's mom: *At 6:15.*
3. Divide the class into two groups, A and B. Each student should work with another student from the same group to prepare questions together. Allow them time to ask about any vocabulary they need to know.
4. Tell the students that they should now divide up so that a student from Group A works with a student from Group B. Give them a time limit to practice asking and answering questions and to complete the worksheet.

5.2 Shopping list

Activity Role-play, information gap

Language focus Expressions of quantity (*some/any*; *much/many*); countable/uncountable nouns

Preparation Photocopy the page for each pair of students and cut up the page along the dotted lines.

Procedure

1. Explain the situation. A daughter has promised to make dinner. She's at school and has just decided she wants to make pizza. She calls her mom at home to find out what's in the refrigerator and what she needs to buy. Later that afternoon, her mom decides she wants a dessert as well. She's at work now and calls her daughter to find out what she needs to buy. Mother and daughter both write shopping lists while they're on the phone.
2. Divide the class into two groups, A and B. Group A have the worksheet for the daughter (Student A) and Group B have the worksheet for the mother (Student B). The students should work together with someone else from their group and think about questions to ask. Emphasize that they are using *Do we have any/a … ?/How much/many …?*
3. Tell the students that they should now divide up so that a student from Group A works with a student from Group B. They act out the role-play and complete the shopping lists.

5.3 Vowel snap

Activity Card game

Language focus The vowel sounds /ɔ/, /ɑ/, and /oʊ/

Preparation Photocopy the worksheet and cut up a set of cards for each pair.

Procedure

1 Explain the game by demonstrating it with one pair.

2 Each pair will have a full set of cards (38). They must shuffle them, divide them up equally, and put them face down in front of them.

3 The students then take turns putting a card down. If both cards put down have the same sound, either player can shout *Snap* and take the cards.

4 If the player is not correct, he/she must give the cards to the other player.

5 The game continues until one of the players has no cards left. The winner is the person who has the most cards.

Key

walk /ɔ/	stop /ɑ/	go /oʊ/
walk, talk, call, bought, taught, ball, pour, born, fall, saw, four, fork, store, more	want, what, stop, shop, cross, long, lost, clock, rock, strong, copy, top	most, don't, phone, go, show, joke, hope, slow, home, road, boat, coat

6.1 What just happened?

Activity Miming actions

Language focus Question forms of present perfect (+ *just*) and short answers; review of general vocabulary

Preparation Photocopy and cut out the cue cards. You need one set for every 12 students. They can be duplicated for bigger classes.

Procedure

1 If the class is bigger than 12 students, divide them into groups.

2 Put the cue cards in a pile, face down. The first student should take a card and, without showing the other students, mime the activity. The other students guess what he/she is doing, e.g. *Have you just …* + past participle or *You've just …*

3 The person who guesses correctly keeps the card. If nobody guesses, the card goes back to the bottom of the pile.

4 The game is over when all the cards have been used up.

6.2 My favorite things

Activity Questionnaire

Language focus Present perfect with *ever*; review of comparative forms; general vocabulary review

Preparation Photocopy the worksheet for every student in the class.

Procedure

1 Explain that the aim of the activity is to find information about what people like to do. The students should complete the sentences on the worksheet. Encourage them to write short answers, e.g. *J.K. Rowling*.

2 The students now ask their partner, e.g. *Have you ever read a book by …?* and put a check if their partner says *yes*. They put a cross in the column if they say *no* and ask their partner what they like instead.

6.3 How healthy are you?

Activity Questionnaire

Language focus *too much/too many*; *not enough*; review of vocabulary; ways of giving advice and suggestions

Preparation Photocopy a worksheet for every person in the class.

Procedure

1 Tell students they are going to interview their partner about their lifestyle.

2 Give a worksheet to everyone in the class and give them time to read it and ask any questions. They should complete the gaps with *how much* or *how many* and complete the unfinished sentences at the end with anything else they can think of (they can use the pictures for inspiration).

3 The students interview their partners and put a check in the relevant column.

4 The students should look at what their partner has written and give suggestions and advice, e.g. *You should eat more fish and less meat./Why don't you go running?*

N.B. This should obviously be done as a "fun" activity and not be taken too seriously!

7.1 Jungle survival

Activity	Board game
Language focus	*must/mustn't; can*; review of vocabulary
Preparation	Photocopy the board and two sets of sentence cards for each group of four and cut them along the lines. Bring a dice for each group and coins or small objects to act as counters.
Procedure	**1** Explain that the students are going to play a board game in pairs which is based on the reality TV show *I'm a Celebrity—Get Me Out Of Here!* The sentence cards are definitions of the illustrated objects on the board. **2** Divide the students into groups of four and give each group a copy of the board game, a set of sentence cards for each pair, and a dice and counters. Monitor and act as referee if the students aren't sure if the answers given are correct. **3** Explain the rules of the game: – They move forward by throwing the dice and landing on a square. They then match the picture on the square with the correct sentence on one of the cards they have and name the object. They put the sentence card face down to one side if the other pair think they have matched the card and object correctly. Then it's the other pair's turn. – If they cannot match the sentence or name the object, they move backwards one square and wait for their next turn. – If the other pair lands on the same square, they must throw the dice again until they land on a different square (or, alternatively, they must say the name of the object and/or a sentence with *must/mustn't* about the use of the object). – If the students land on a square without a picture, they must follow the instructions written there. If the square is blank, they do nothing until their next turn. – The winners are the pair who reach the *Congratulations!* square first.

7.2 How many sentences can you make?

Activity	Making sentences
Language focus	Recognition of language of obligation; *have/has to/don't/doesn't have to*; vocabulary related to household jobs and routines
Preparation	Make one copy of the worksheet per pair of students and cut out the squares along the dotted lines.
Procedure	**1** Divide the class into pairs and give each pair a set of jumbled-up cards (six cards per pair). **2** Explain that the aim of the activity is to arrange all cards into a table consisting of three rows and two columns. (Draw the model on the board.) Tell the students to ignore the words/phrases at this stage. Give them an opportunity to do this, and go around monitoring that they understand what they are doing. **3** Explain that they now have to make seven sentences with the words and phrases along the sides of the cards. Explain that cards can be moved or turned on any side as long as this does not alter the table structure outlined in point 2 above. The sentences are all made by matching a word/phrase on one side of the card with one on a neighboring side, e.g. *Mike has to wear his school uniform every day.* Make it clear that some words/phrases will not be used, e.g. *Tim and Ted* and some of the phrases with *have/has to*. **4** Elicit the sentences from the class, or get the students to come to the front and write them on the board.
Key	The answer is the combination of squares on the worksheet prior to cutting up.

7.3 Planning a night out

Activity	Role-play
Language focus	Making suggestions; expressing preference (*I'd rather/I'd like to*); giving advice
Preparation	Photocopy the sheet for each group of four. Cut up the role cards so that each person in the group has one.
Procedure	**1** Explain the situation. Four friends are planning a night out, and they are deciding where to go. **2** Elicit the sort of places students might go for a night out, and put them on the board. Review the language of suggestions, advice, and preferences. **3** Divide the class into groups of four and give each group a *What's On* sheet and each person a role card. **4** Give them time to read their role cards and think about what they are going to say. **5** Each student should say what they would like to do, and then they must try to agree on where to go. **6** Each group should report back on where they are going and the reasons why.

8.1 Make a sentence

Activity	Making sentences
Language focus	Verbs + infinitive or *-ing*
Preparation	Make one copy of the worksheet for each group of three or four students. Cut up the cards along the dotted lines.
Procedure	**1** Divide the class into groups of three or four and give each group a set of A cards and a set of B cards. **2** Demonstrate the game with one group: – Lay the cards face down on the table, with the A cards on one side and the B cards (shaded cards) on the other. – The first student turns over an A card and a B card and makes a sentence with them, using the A card first. The verb can be in the present, past, or future, but the sentence must make sense, e.g. *I offered to make dinner*. – If the group decides the sentence is grammatically correct and makes sense, the player keeps the cards. If not, the player puts the cards back in the same place and the game continues. – The winner is the person with the most cards.

8.2 Memory test

Activity	Pelmanism card game
Language focus	First conditional
Preparation	Photocopy the worksheet for each pair, and cut up the ten Picture cards and the ten Verb cards.
Procedure	**1** Divide the class into pairs and give each pair a set of Verb cards and a set of Picture cards. They are different shapes, so that they know which ones to pick up. Tell them to spread the cards out in front of them, face down. **2** Explain to the class that they are going to play a game of Pelmanism and demonstrate how to play with a couple of students. The idea is that the students have to find two cards that match from the cards which are spread out in front of them. Throughout the game, the students have to remember where possible matching cards are from having seen them in previous turns. **3** Student A turns over two cards: one Picture card and one Verb card. If they go together, e.g. the picture of someone dressed in tennis clothes, and the card *win the game—be happy*, the student has to make a sentence e.g. *If I win the game, I'll be happy*. If they don't match, the cards have to be turned over again in exactly the same place. Point out that if there's a speech bubble on the Picture card, the students have to use the pronoun "I," as if the person is speaking. **4** If Student A makes a mistake, he/she also leaves the cards where they are and turns them over in the same place. If his/her partner thinks the sentence is correct, Student A keeps the cards. **5** When the cards are all used up, the person with the most cards is the winner.

8.3 Do you agree with me?

Activity	Board game
Language focus	Review of grammar and vocabulary
Preparation	Photocopy the board game for each group of three or four students. Bring a dice for each group and coins or small objects to act as counters.
Procedure	**1** Explain that the students are going to play a board game in groups, which will review grammar and vocabulary from throughout *Inspired 2*. **2** Divide the class into groups of three or four and give each group a copy of the board game, a dice, and counters. **3** Explain the rules of the game: – They move forward by throwing the dice and landing on a square. If a student lands on a square with a topic, they have to speak on the subject for 30 seconds. The other students should time them. – If the other students don't understand, or if the student is unable to say anything, they must return to the previous square. – If the student lands on a square which says "Go back," "Go forward," or "Miss a turn," they must follow the instructions. – The winner is the student who reaches the "Finish" square first.

Dancin' In The Street

Activity	Song
Language focus	Review of language and vocabulary from Units 1–2
Preparation	Photocopy one sheet for each student. Get the recording ready. 2.50
Procedure	**1** Ask students if they can name some famous cities in the U.S., and write their answers on the board. **2** Students listen to the recording and follow the words of the song on their sheet. Ask them to listen out to see if they hear any of the cities listed on the board. **3** With the whole class, discuss the answer to 2. Ask students to find words in the song that support their answer. **4** Students work individually to answer 3 and 4. They then check their answers in pairs. Before they start working, elicit examples of a gerund.
Key	2 b 3 a) It doesn't matter b) guy c) grab d) nation e) folks 4 swingin', dancin', playin', laughin', singin', swayin'

Footprints In The Frost

Activity	Song
Language focus	Review of language and vocabulary from Units 3–4
Preparation	Photocopy one sheet for each student. Get the recording ready. 2.51
Procedure	**1** Students listen to the recording and follow the words of the song on their sheet. **2** In pairs, students choose their answers to 2. Check answers and ask pairs to read out the lines or words that support their answers. **3** Students work individually to answer 3 and 4. They then check their answers in pairs. Students who finish early can write down any regular simple past verbs they find in the song.
Key	2 a) autumn b) has had c) didn't work d) bad 3 c 4 spent, had, got, fell, did, rang

Father And Son

Activity	Song
Language focus	Review of language and vocabulary from Units 5–6
Preparation	Photocopy one sheet for each student. Get the recording ready. 2.52
Procedure	**1** Students listen to the recording and follow the words of the song on their sheet. **2** Students do exercises 2 and 3 in pairs. For 3, ask students to find sentences in the song that support their answer. **3** In pairs, students discuss the question in 4. Ask individuals to tell the class about their partner's experiences.
Key	2 a) ignore b) fault c) calm d) relax 3 a) True b) False c) False d) True

The Miracle

Activity	Song
Language focus	Review of language and vocabulary from Units 7–8
Preparation	Photocopy one sheet for each student. Get the recording ready. 2.53
Procedure	**1** Ask students if they know the band Queen, and see if they can list other songs by Queen. **2** Students listen to the recording and follow the words of the song on their sheet. **3** Students work in groups to discuss their answers to 1. Encourage them to read out words or lines from the song that support their answers. **4** Students work individually to answer 2 and 3. They then check their answers in pairs. **5** For 4, ask students to tell you their suggestions so you can put a list of miracles on the board.
Key	2 b 3 a) The Golden Gate, the Taj Mahal, the Hanging Gardens of Babylon, the Tower of Babel b) Captain Cook, Cain and Abel, Jimi Hendrix c) peace on earth 4 a) Taj Mahal b) Sahara Desert c) Test tube babies d) *Mona Lisa* e) Golden Gate f) Jimi Hendrix g) The Hanging Gardens of Babylon h) Captain Cook

1 Do you eat French fries every day?

Circle the fact that you think is true about your partner. Think of another fact if you think none of them are true.

MY PARTNER …

RIGHT ☐ WRONG ☐

has a dog / cat / rabbit / no pet /

RIGHT ☐ WRONG ☐

plays the piano / guitar / saxophone / no instrument /

RIGHT ☐ WRONG ☐

often eats Italian / Chinese / Mexican food /

RIGHT ☐ WRONG ☐

sometimes goes swimming / goes running / plays soccer /

RIGHT ☐ WRONG ☐

eats French fries / chocolate / ice cream every day /

RIGHT ☐ WRONG ☐

usually gets up late / goes to bed late / gets up early on the weekend /

RIGHT ☐ WRONG ☐

usually goes to school by bus / on foot / by car /

RIGHT ☐ WRONG ☐

prefers the spring / summer / autumn / winter /

RIGHT ☐ WRONG ☐

often listens to pop / rock / R&B music /

RIGHT ☐ WRONG ☐

often / never / sometimes helps around the house /

Now check your answers. Check the boxes under Right (✓) if your guess was right. Put a cross under Wrong (✗) if you were wrong.

Party time!

Cue cards

Helen is wearing sunglasses.	James is playing soccer.	Robert is skateboarding.
Andy is eating a hamburger.	Shannon is putting flowers on the table.	Tony is cooking sausages on the grill.
Milo is holding a soccer ball.	Lucy is drinking her water.	Molly is holding hands with her boyfriend.
Mark is holding a camera.	Anna is playing the guitar.	Tom is wearing a hat.
Sophie is taking a picture.	Alex is watching his girlfriend play the guitar.	Emma is speaking on her cell phone.

Clothes Bingo!

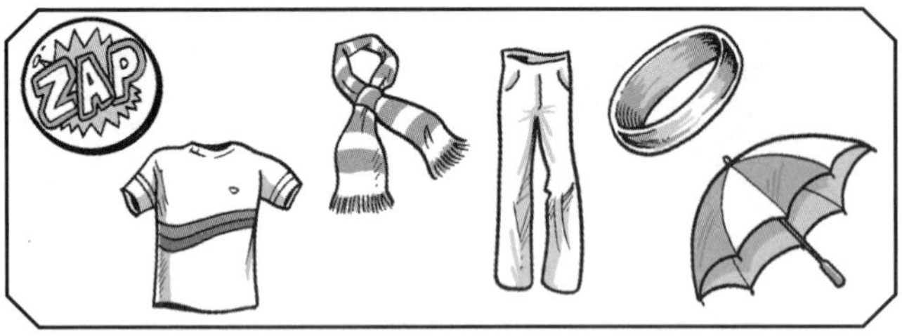

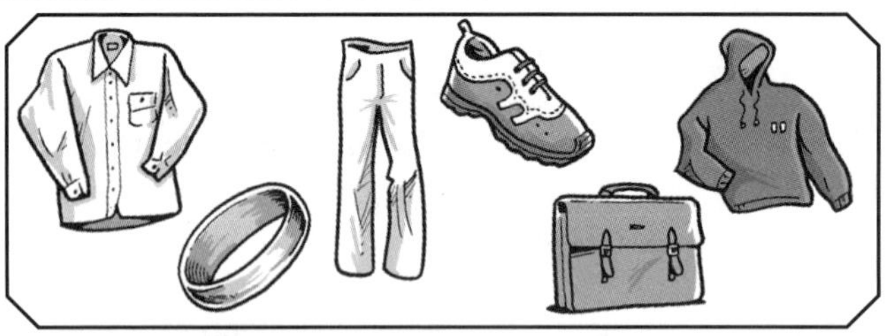

pin	bag	bangle	baseball cap	briefcase	camera	glasses
hat	jacket	jeans	coin purse	scarf	shirt	shoe
shorts	skirt	sunglasses	sweatshirt	T-shirt	top	sneaker
pants	umbrella	watch				

What's the difference?

Adjectives

bad	beautiful	boring	big	cheap	cold	colorful	dangerous	difficult
dry	expensive	exotic	easy	exciting	fast	fun	famous	friendly
good	high	hot	happy	healthy	large	important	long	loud
nice	noisy	new	old	ordinary	popular	pretty	quiet	relaxing
special	slow	safe	traditional	tall	unusual	wet	warm	young

Nouns

market small store supermarket	Australia Brazil Russia	train bus bicycle	coffee shop restaurant hotel
Chevrolet Nissan Volkswagen	sweater T-shirt	February April August	drums guitar piano
dog cat fish	chicken meat fish	swimming tennis soccer	chess knitting painting
a club a movie theater a theater	cheetah lion snake	rap R&B	geography history science
Italian food Chinese food Mexican food	Jennifer Lopez Kylie Minogue	men women children	Brad Pitt Sean Connery

2.2 Where is it?

You can't find: your sneakers, your cell phone, your watch, your guitar, a baseball cap, a magazine.

You can't find: your coin purse, your sunglasses, your keys, your shoes, your camera, a jacket.

The same or different?

	ENJOY/LOVE	DON'T LIKE/ CAN'T STAND
Reading books	☐	☐
Going for walks	☐	☐
Talking on the phone	☐	☐
Sending text messages	☐	☐
Watching sports on TV	☐	☐
Sightseeing	☐	☐
Watching *The Simpsons*	☐	☐
Buying clothes	☐	☐
Taking care of young children	☐	☐
Traveling by plane	☐	☐
Sunbathing	☐	☐
Eating food from other countries	☐	☐

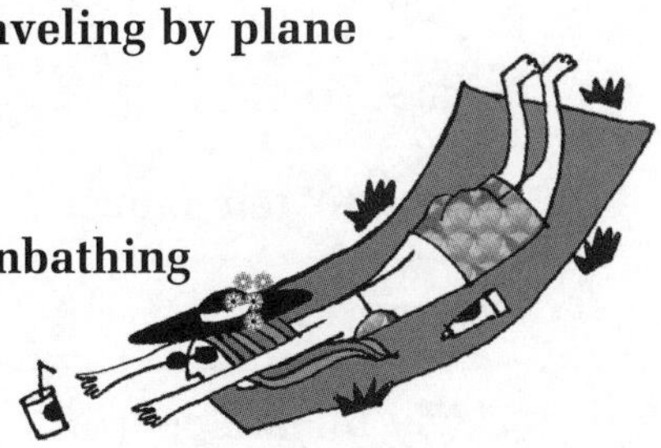

3.1 Looking back

A

(In AD 79) Vesuvius	(In 1953) Hillary and Tenzing
(In 1482) Christopher Columbus	(In 1969) Neil Armstrong
(In 1503) Leonardo da Vinci	(In 1975) Steven Spielberg
(In 1770) Captain Cook	(In 1981) Prince Charles
(In 1789) George Washington	(In 1998) J.K. Rowling
(In 1860) Antonio Meucci	(In 2001) Apple
(In 1912) the Titanic	(In 2002) the Brazilian soccer team
(In 1937) Walt Disney	

B

cross	travel to	bury
win	design	direct
sink	walk on	invent
become	paint	climb
make	write	marry

C

the Atlantic	Australia	Pompeii
the World Cup	the iPod®	*Jaws*
off the coast of Canada	the moon	the first telephone
the first President of the U.S.	the *Mona Lisa*	Mount Everest
Snow White	the first *Harry Potter* book	Lady Diana Spencer

Who? What? Where? When?

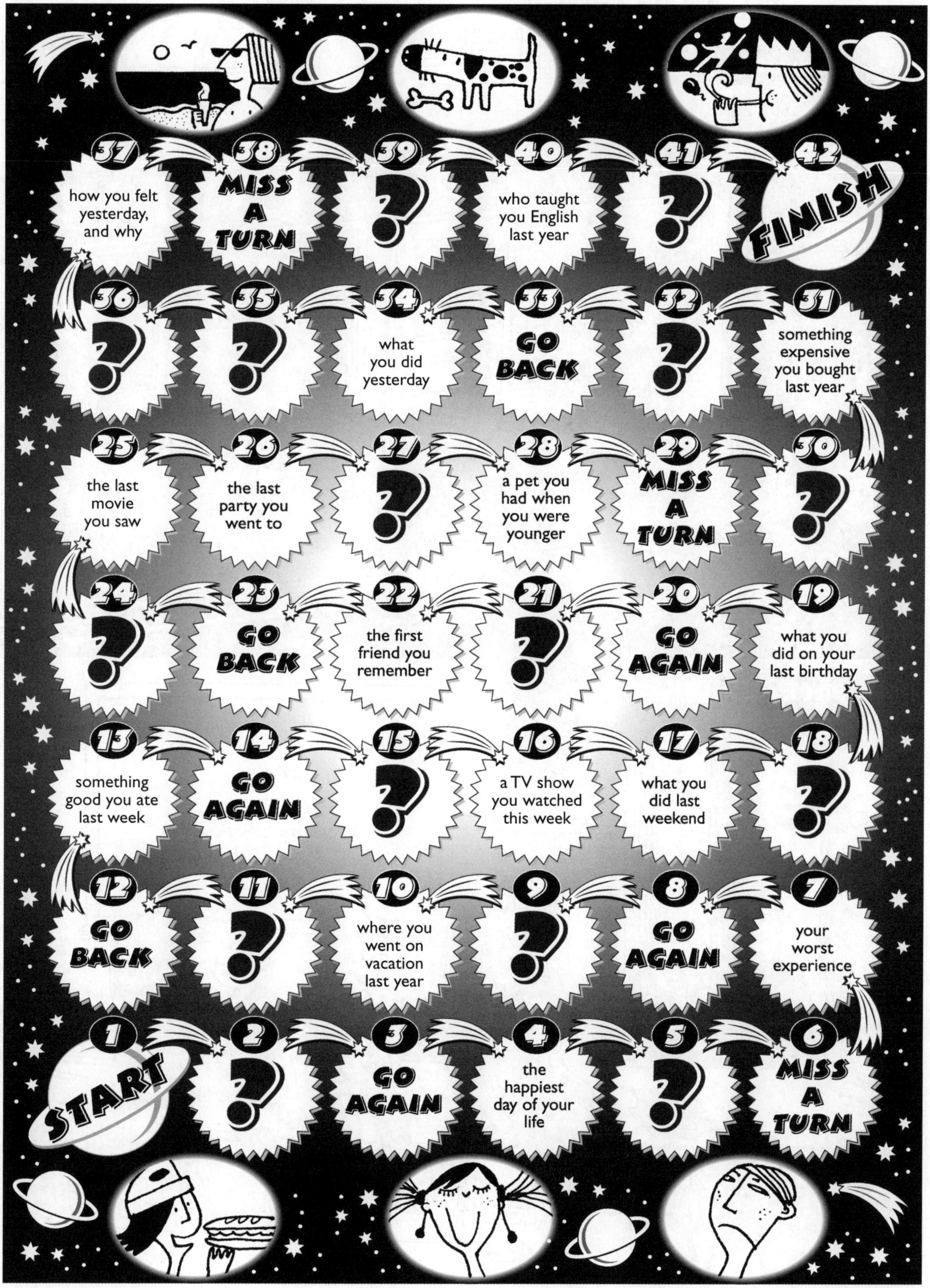

What were you doing yesterday at 11 o'clock?

Picture A

Picture B

4 1 How well do you know me?

Complete these sentences about your partner. Then ask questions. Put a check in the "Correct guess" column if you guessed right. If you guessed wrongly, ask your partner what he/she does instead. Write the answers down.

	Correct guess	Wrong guess
When you have a free evening, you ________________ ________________	☐	☐ ________________
If somebody tells you a secret, you ________________ ________________	☐	☐ ________________
You get angry when ________________ ________________	☐	☐ ________________
When you get some money, you ________________ ________________	☐	☐ ________________
If you walk into a room full of people you don't know, you ________________ ________________	☐	☐ ________________
If somebody says, "Do you like my new jeans?" (and you don't!), you say ________________ ________________	☐	☐ ________________
When you have homework to do, you ________________ ________________	☐	☐ ________________
If you are by yourself, you ________________ ________________	☐	☐ ________________
When you are buying clothes, you usually choose (the color) ________________ ________________	☐	☐ ________________
You get frightened if ________________ ________________	☐	☐ ________________
When ________________ ________________	☐	☐ ________________
If ________________ ________________	☐	☐ ________________

A romantic story

After finishing college, Alessandro decides to get a job in the U.S.

Two months later …
One day, he's walking along a beach and sees a beautiful girl looking for her earring.

Stella and Alessandro go for a coffee. His English is not very fluent so they have problems.

Alessandro decides to improve his English.

They fall in love.

A year later …
Alessandro is offered a job in Rome.

What will happen to Stella and Alessandro?

Adverbs puzzle

Fill in the right adverbs in the puzzle using the clues. Then work with a partner and tell each other the missing clues. Fill in the rest of the puzzle.

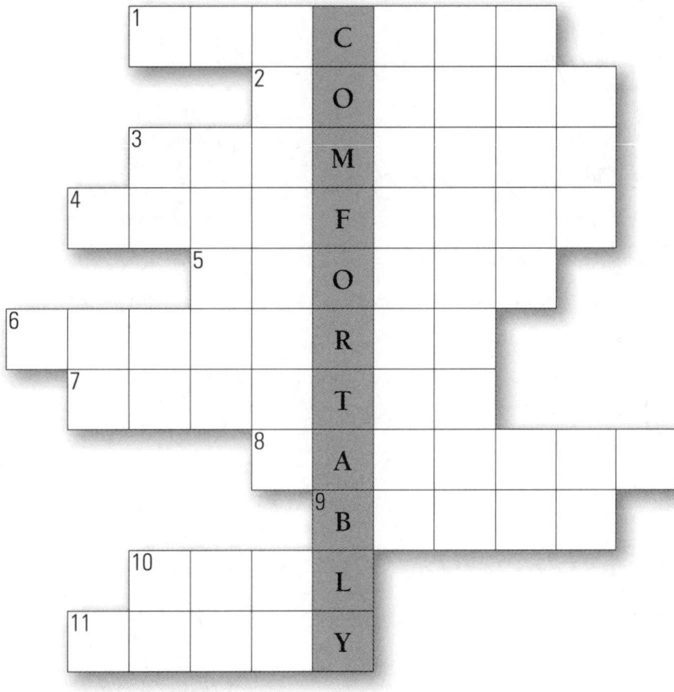

Clues A

1. This is a quick crossword. You can do it …
2. She has a loud voice. She speaks …
3. She is a normal student. She behaves …
4. Be careful on the stairs. Walk …
5. Bill is a slow runner. He runs …

Clues B

6. You should wear the proper uniform. Please dress …
7. She is very quiet in class. She works …
8. The children are happy. They're singing …
9. I am bad at drawing. I draw …
10. Julia is good at English. She speaks it …
11. You seem sad. You're smiling …

5.1 What are we doing?

A

Tim Clark Washington, D.C. trip
Saturday, 7th
Meet at 6:15 a.m. .... *Where?*
Go to airport (with Mr. Smith/Ms. Terry/Principal) .... *How?*
Flight leaves 11:15 a.m. .... *What airline?*
Arrive in Washington, D.C., take subway to hotel .... *Which hotel?*
Find rooms, unpack .... *How many per room?*
Afternoon: visit The White House
Evening: dinner .... *Where?*
Theater visit (The Lion King)

Sunday, 8th
Morning: Georgetown .... *Doing what?*
Afternoon: visit National Air and Space Museum
Evening: Flight home .... *What time?*
Arrive airport: 8:30 p.m.
Arrive school .... *When?*
Parents meet in front of school

B

William Bull Washington, D.C. trip
Saturday, 7th
Meet in front of school .... *What time?*
Bus to airport .... *With how many teachers?*
American Airlines flight .... *When?*
In Washington, D.C., go to Lincoln Hotel .... *How?*
Unpack (share room with Tim, Steve, and James)
Afternoon: visit .... *Where?*
Evening: dinner in hotel
Theater trip .... *To see what?*

Sunday, 8th
Morning: shopping .... *Where?*
Afternoon: visit .... *Where?*
Evening: Flight at 7 p.m.
Arrive airport evening .... *When?*
Bus to school, arrive 10:30 p.m.
Parents meet .... *Where?*

5 2 Shopping list

Daughter (Student A)

1 You are at school and have decided to make pizza this evening. This is what you need:
■ a big piece of cheese (about 500 grams) ■ a few slices of ham ■ six tomatoes (about 500 grams) ■ eight mushrooms ■ one egg ■ olives ■ a little flour ■ a little garlic

Call your mother and ask what there is in the refrigerator at home. Then write down what you need to buy. Ask: *Do we have any/a lot of … in the house? / I need a(n) … / some … / How much/many …?*

Shopping list

____

____

____

____

2 Your mother calls when you get home. Answer her questions using *We don't have … / some … / a lot of … / much … / many.*

Mother (Student B)

1 Your daughter calls you to ask you what food there is in the refrigerator at home. Answer her questions, using *There's … / We have … /some … /a lot … /not much … / not many … / There isn't …*

2 You are at work. You have decided to make dessert for six people and need to go to the store on your way home. Call your daughter and ask her what there is in the refrigerator. You need some:
■ fruit (to make a fruit salad, e.g. bananas, strawberries, apples) ■ ice cream ■ chocolate cookies ■ coffee ■ sugar ■ milk

Shopping list

____

____

____

____

5.3 Vowel snap

STOP	SHOP	CROSS	LONG
LOST	WANT	WHAT	CLOCK
ROCK	STRONG	COPY	TOP
WALK	TALK	STORE	FOUR
CALL	FORK	BOUGHT	TAUGHT
BALL	POUR	BORN	FALL
MOST	DON'T	PHONE	GO
SHOW	JOKE	HOPE	SLOW
HOME	ROAD	BOAT	
COAT	MORE	SAW	

What just happened?

You've just seen a ghost.	You've just run a long way.
You've just eaten something horrible.	You've just woken up.
You've just taken a shower.	You've just found something valuable.
You've just answered the phone.	You've just opened a gift.
You've just had an argument.	You've just hurt yourself.
Your soccer team has just won.	You've just fallen off a horse.

My favorite things

Complete the sentences with things that you like. Then ask your partner the questions you've written. Check (✔) the box if the answer is "yes." If his/her answer is "no," find out what he/she likes instead.

	Your partner	Instead
Have you ever read any books by ______________________?	☐	______________
Have you ever listened to a CD by ______________________?	☐	______________
Have you ever seen the movie ______________________?	☐	______________
Have you ever eaten ______________________?	☐	______________
Have you ever played/done ______________________?	☐	______________
Have you ever learned to ______________________?	☐	______________
Have you ever been to ______________________?	☐	______________
Have you ever watched ____________________ on TV?	☐	______________

6.3 How healthy are you?

Complete the gaps with *How much* or *How many*. Then interview your partner and check the right box. Give advice or suggestions after you've done the interview.

	a lot	too much/many	not enough	none
________ chocolate do you eat every day?	☐	☐	☐	☐
________ cookies do you eat in a week?	☐	☐	☐	☐
________ fruit do you eat in a day?	☐	☐	☐	☐
________ sugary drinks do you have in a day?	☐	☐	☐	☐
________ sports do you do in a week?	☐	☐	☐	☐
________ red meat do you eat in a week?	☐	☐	☐	☐
________ hours sleep do you get in a night?	☐	☐	☐	☐
________ glasses of water do you drink in a day?	☐	☐	☐	☐

How much ____?

How many ____?

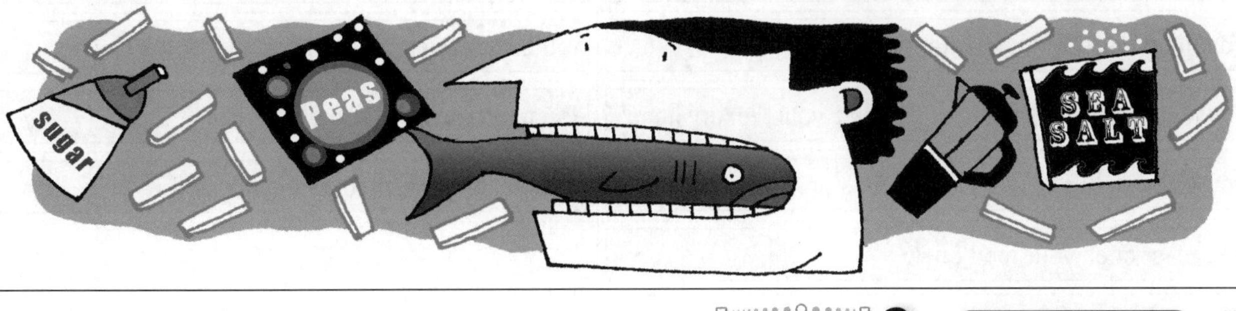

Jungle survival

Sentence cards

You must have a lot of them to light the fire.	You must learn what to do if they bite you.
You must be careful with them—they're sharp!	You can light these when it gets dark.
You must walk through water full of them.	You mustn't take this with you.
You must only choose one of these as your "luxury item."	You must eat this food every day.
You can use this to chop vegetables on.	You must eat them to win extra food.
You must cook your food on it.	

How many sentences can you make?

Tim and Ted

have to put our clothes away.

has to wear his school uniform every day.

Peter

Shirley

have to do my homework every night.

Ms. Smith

We

Mike

have to clean your room.

Does Bill

has to go shopping.

doesn't have to wash her own clothes.

has to catch a train.

I

You

have to help with meals?

have to make the bed?

Susan

don't have to set the table.

don't have to do the dishes.

She

I don't

Do you

Planning a night out

What's on

BLUE MOON NIGHT CLUB
Teens night
July 15
Open 8–midnight.
Over 16s only.
Tickets $7.50

BITZ & PIZZA RESTAURANT
Exciting new Mediterranean style menu
—pizzas, pasta, antipasti—
the best in town.
Special kids' menu available.
• Telephone 301-962-7117 •

WOO SANG CHINESE RESTAURANT
We serve a variety of Chinese dishes.
Space for private parties up to 40 people.
Please see our takeout menu.
9400 St. Paul Street
Telephone 301-495-7241

Jazz concert in Town Hall on July 15
Featuring: Woody Herman Big Band, Soul Survivors, and Sheena Davis Band
Starts at 8:00
Tickets $15
Concessions $12.50

FLAMES BURGER HOUSE
The best burgers in town!
3603 Dupont
Call us on 301-310-7241

HOLLYWOOD BOWL
28 lanes!
Kids' parties starting at $8.50 per person
Reserve your lane at 301-921-1145

MOVIE THEATER
showing 6&8
showing 7:30

A
You really don't want to go to the pizza restaurant—you had pizza last night. Suggest another restaurant because you're always starving. You would like to go dancing after the meal. You don't like bowling.

B
You are on a diet and want to eat healthily. Suggest you see a movie—you love romantic ones. Then you want to go to the jazz concert. You have to be home by midnight.

C
You don't have much money, so takeout and movie—you love science-fiction movies—would be good. You are only 15.

D
You like the idea of Italian food, followed by a concert or a movie. You've seen *Falling in Love* already, however, and would rather go bowling.

8.1 Make a sentence

A

decide	want	offer	agree
promise	like	enjoy	love
dislike	refuse	tell	manage

B

go	see	play	meet
have	eat	live	study
watch	help	make	be

What will happen if …?

Picture cards

Verb cards

win a game—be happy	get up late—miss the train	kiss—fall in love	have a party—be fun	go to the restaurant—have dinner
the weather is good—go jogging	it's rainy—watch TV	get up early—have a shower	eat French fries every day—get fat	friends visit—eat outside

8 3 Learn by heart

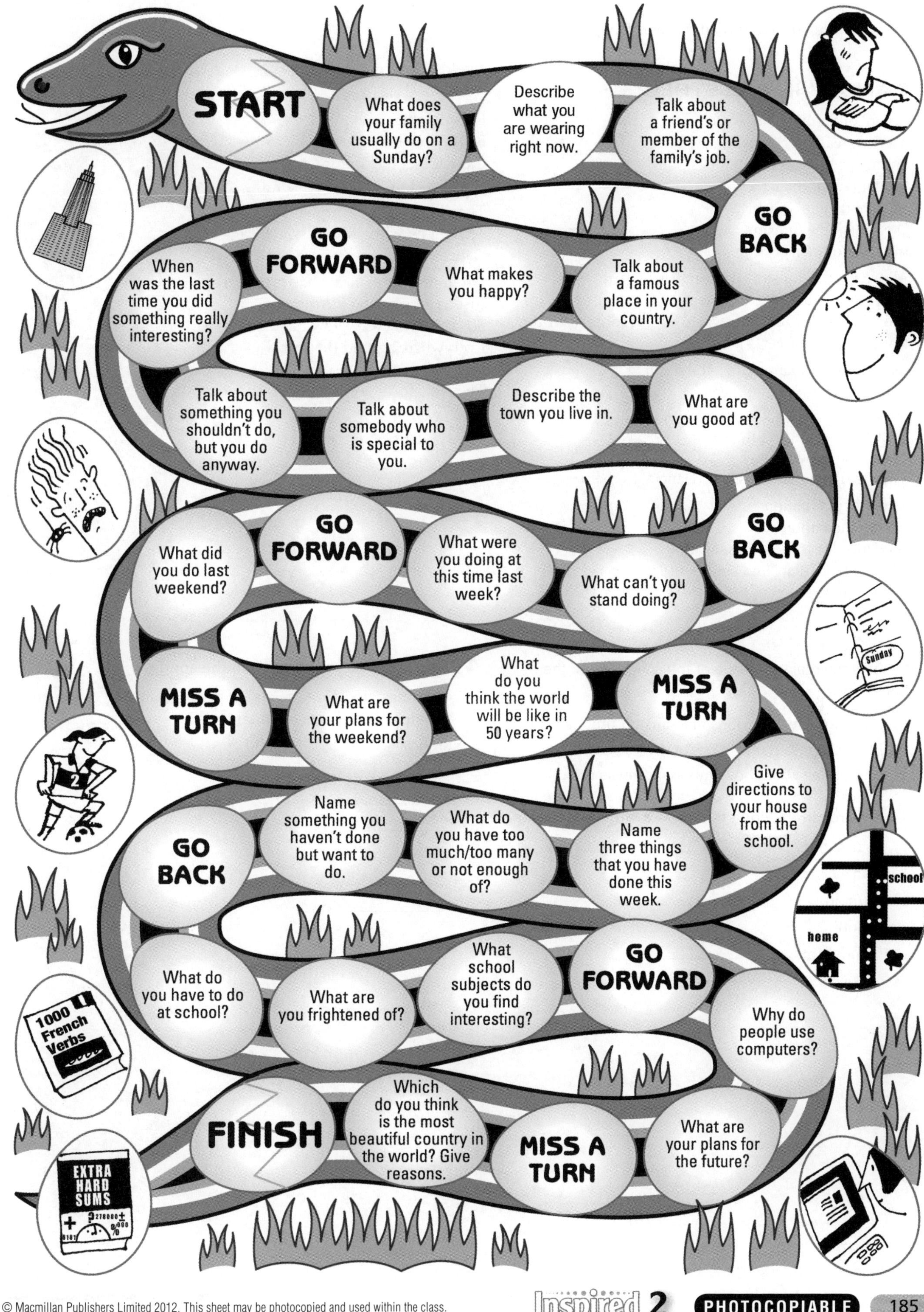

1–2 Song: Dancin' In The Street

1 Listen to the song and read the words.

DANCIN' IN THE STREET

Callin' out around the world
Are you ready for a brand new beat?
Summer's here and the time is right
for dancin' in the street
They're dancin' in Chicago
Down in New Orleans
In New York City

All we need is music—sweet music
There'll be music everywhere
There'll be swingin' and swayin' and records playin'
Dancin' in the street

Oh, it doesn't matter what you wear
Just as long as you are there
So come on, every guy grab a girl
Everywhere around the world
They'll be dancin'
They're dancin' in the street (Dancin' in the street)

This is an invitation
Across the nation
A chance for folks to meet
There'll be dancin' and singin' and music swingin'
Dancin' in the street

Philadelphia, PA
Baltimore and D.C. now
Can't forget the Motor City

All we need is music–sweet music
There'll be music everywhere
There'll be swingin' and swayin' and records playin'
Dancin' in the street

Oh, it doesn't matter what you wear
Just as long as you are there
So come on, every guy grab a girl
Everywhere around the world
They'll be dancin'
They're dancin' in the street (Dancin' in the street)

Way down in L.A. everyday
They're dancin' in the street.

2 What is the main message of the song? Check the correct box.

a) It is asking for help for some difficult times ahead. ☐
b) It is telling everyone to celebrate. ☐
c) It is talking about how important music is. ☐

3 Find words in the song that have a similar meaning.

a) it's not important ____________
b) man ____________
c) get/hold ____________
d) country ____________
e) friends/family ____________

4 Find six different gerunds in the song.

(In songs, the "*g*" at the end of gerunds or "*-ing*" words in progressive tenses is often omitted.)

swingin'
____
____
____
____
____
____

Song: Footprints In The Frost

1 Listen to the song and read the words.

FOOTPRINTS IN THE FROST

I spent too much money, I looked far too glad
Now I have so little of what I once had
I had too many parties I had too much time
I got so lazy and fell well behind

Now the summer is over I can count the cost
Footprints on the beaches are now footprints in the frost
The summer is over I can count the cost
Footprints on the beaches are now footprints in the frost

We did so much damage deep in our insides
The party's over it's going home time
The cathedral is empty, no one's at home
Winter's approaching paradise postponed

Now the summer is over I can count the cost
Footprints on the beaches are now footprints in the frost,
The rain won't stop falling and the people look lost
Footprints on the beaches are now footprints in the frost.

I rang lots of numbers and walked many miles
I watched the Flintstones and I turned my dial
To a brand new station where the beat comes in
Now it's all over the winter begins

The summer is over I can count the cost
Footprints on the beaches are now footprints in the frost
People with umbrellas disappear in the fog
Footprints on the beaches are now footprints in the frost

2 Read the song again and circle the correct answer.

a) It is **summer / autumn** now.
b) The songwriter **has had / is going to have** lots of parties.
c) The songwriter **worked / didn't work** hard in the summer.
d) The weather is **good / bad** now.

3 Check the sentence that best describes the way the songwriter is feeling.

a) He/She feels that he/she has no friends and nowhere to go. ☐
b) He/She feels that he/she has done some terrible things and must run away. ☐
c) He/She had too much fun in the summer, and now feels that everything is over. ☐

4 Find the irregular simple past forms of these verbs in the song:

spend ____________
have ____________
get ____________
fall ____________
do ____________
ring ____________

5–6 Song: Father And Son

1 Listen to the song and read the words.

FATHER AND SON

Father
It's not time to make a change,
Just relax, take it easy.
You're still young, that's your fault,
There's so much you have to know.
Find a girl, settle down,
If you want you can marry.
Look at me, I am old, but I'm happy.

I was once like you are now, and I know that it's not easy,
To be calm when you've found something going on.
But take your time, think a lot,
Why, think of everything you've got.
For you will still be here tomorrow, but your dreams may not.

Son
How can I try to explain, when I do he turns away again.
It's always been the same, same old story.
From the moment I could talk I was ordered to listen.
Now there's a way and I know that I have to go away.
I know I have to go.

Father
It's not time to make a change,
Just sit down, take it slowly.
You're still young, that's your fault,
There's so much you have to go through.
Find a girl, settle down,
if you want you can marry.
Look at me, I am old, but I'm happy.
(Son—Away Away Away, I know I have to
Make this decision alone—no)

Son
All the times that I cried, keeping all the things I knew inside,
It's hard, but it's harder to ignore it.
If they were right, I'd agree, but it's them they know not me.
Now there's a way and I know that I have to go away.
I know I have to go.
(Father—Stay Stay Stay, Why must you go and
make this decision alone?)

2 Find words in the song that have the following meanings:

a) take no notice of; pretend something's not there ____________

b) something you do wrong ____________

c) quiet; not excited ____________

d) have a rest; do nothing for a while ____________

3 Circle True or False.

a) The son wants to go away. **True / False**

b) The father wants the son to go away. **True / False**

c) The father always listens to his son. **True / False**

d) The father thinks his son is like he was when he was young. **True / False**

4 In pairs, talk about a time in your life when you tried to persuade someone not to do something.

7–8 Song: The Miracle

1 Listen to the song and read the words.

THE MIRACLE

Every drop of rain that falls in Sahara Desert says it all
It's a miracle
All God's creations great and small
The Golden Gate and the Taj Mahal
That's a miracle
Test tube babies being born
Mothers, fathers dead and gone
It's a miracle

We're having a miracle on earth
Mother nature does it all for us
The wonders of this world go on
The Hanging Gardens of Babylon
Captain Cook and Cain and Abel
Jimi Hendrix to the Tower of Babel
It's a miracle, it's a miracle, it's a miracle
It's a miracle

The one thing we're all waiting for is peace on earth—an end to war
It's a miracle we need—the miracle
The miracle we're all waiting for today

If every leaf on every tree could tell a story that would be a miracle
If every child on every street had clothes to wear and food to eat
That's a miracle
If all God's people could be free to live in perfect harmony
It's a miracle

We're having a miracle on earth
Mother nature does it all for us
Open hearts in surgery
(wonders of this world go on)
Sunday mornings with a cup of tea
Super powers always fighting
But Mona Lisa just keeps on smiling
It's a miracle, it's a miracle, it's a miracle

(wonders of this world go on)
It's a miracle, it's a miracle, it's a miracle
It's a miracle

The one thing (the one thing) we're all waiting for (we're all waiting for)
Is peace on earth (peace on earth) and an end to war (an end to war)
It's a miracle we need—the miracle
The miracle peace on earth and end to war today

That time will come one day you'll see when we can all be friends
(Repeat three times)

2 How would you describe the feeling of the song? Check the correct box.

a) Sad and thoughtful ☐
b) Positive and hopeful ☐
c) Fun and light-hearted ☐

3 Which of the following does the song describe as "miracles"?

a) Places	b) People
__________	__________
__________	______ and ______
__________	__________
__________	

c) What is the miracle the song says we are still waiting for?

____

4 Complete the sentences with the correct words from the song.

a) The __________ in India was built by the Shah Jahan for his wife when she died.
b) The __________ is almost as large as the U.S.
c) __________ are created when eggs are fertilized outside the mother's body.
d) The __________ is a famous painting by Leonardo da Vinci.
e) __________ is a famous bridge in San Francisco.
f) __________ was a famous rock musician.
g) __________ were built in Iraq in around 600 BC.
h) __________ was an explorer who discovered Australia and New Zealand.

5 What are four things in the world today that you would describe as miracles?

____
____
____
____

WORKBOOK Answers

WELCOME

1

1 T 2 F 3 T 4 T 5 F 6 F
2 Alex is Australian.
5 Emma is from Canada. (She's Canadian.)
6 Silvana is Argentine.

2

1 His name is Jay and he's American. He's from Chicago.
2 His name is Ramón and he's Mexican. He's from Guadalajara.
3 Her name is Lara and she's Brazilian. She's from Recife.
4 His name is Alex and he's Australian. He's from Sydney.
5 Her name is Silvana and she's Argentine. She's from Rosario.
6 Her name is Emma and she's Canadian. She's from Vancouver.

3

1 What's the name of the American boy? Jay.
2 What's the name of the Argentine girl? Silvana.
3 What's the name of the Australian boy? Alex.
4 What's the name of the Canadian girl? Emma.
5 What's the name of the Mexican boy? Ramón.
6 What's the name of the Brazilian girl? Lara.
7 Where's Emma from? She's from Vancouver.
8 Where's Silvana from? She's from Rosario.
9 Where's Alex from? He's from Australia.
10 Where's Ramón from? He's from Mexico.

4

1 e 2 f 3 a 4 c 5 d 6 b

5

1 Is Jay Mexican? No, he isn't. He's American.
2 Is Silvana Canadian? No, she isn't. She's Argentine.
3 Is Emma Australian? No, she isn't. She's Canadian.
4 Is Alex American? No, he isn't. He's Australian.
5 Is Lara from the U.S.? No, she isn't. She's from Brazil.
6 Is Ramón from Argentina? No, he isn't. He's from Mexico.
7 Is Silvana from Canada? No, she isn't. She's from Argentina.
8 Is Alex from the U.S.? No, he isn't. He's from Australia.

UNIT 1 LESSON 1

1

	Dogs	Basketball	Swimming	Music	Movies
Alex	✓	✓	✗	✓	✓
Lara	✗	✗	✓	✓	✓

2

1 goes 2 comes 3 like 4 plays 5 does 6 drink

3

1 Jay doesn't come from Australia. He comes from the U.S.
2 Emma speaks Italian. She doesn't speak Chinese.
3 Lara and Alex go to the movies on Saturdays. They don't go to the theater.
4 Alex plays basketball. He doesn't play soccer.
5 Jay and Alex like dogs. They don't like cats.
6 I don't come from San Francisco. I come from (students' own answers).

4

CARRIE **Do you speak** French?
A Yes, I **do.**
CARRIE **Do you come** from Vancouver?
A No, **I don't.**
CARRIE **Do you like** sea lions?
A Yes, **I do.**
CARRIE **Do you do** yoga?
A Yes, **I do.**
A is Silvana.

5

go: swimming, to bed, to the movies
do: yoga, karate, gymnastics
play: soccer, basketball, computer games
watch: DVDs, movies, TV

6

1 ✗ 2 ✓ 3 ✓ 4 ✗ 5 ✗ 6 ✓ 7 ✗ 8 ✓

7

Here are some facts ~~what~~ about our World2day contest winners. Emma from Vancouver ~~has~~ speaks English, Italian, and ~~fifty~~ French. Silvana chats with her ~~keys~~ friends online every evening in English and ~~but~~ Spanish! Ramón really likes music and he ~~never~~ loves hip-hop and rap! Lara does ~~opens~~ gymnastics every Friday afternoon and then she goes swimming in ~~a~~ the evening ~~door~~.
Q What has fifty keys but never opens a door?
A A piano!

UNIT 1 LESSON 2

1

a 6 b 5 c 4 d 1 e 7 f 3 g 2

2

1 is holding 2 is wearing 3 is telling
4 is standing 5 is helping 6 are listening
7 is taking 8 is watching

3

1 Alex is the boy who/that is holding a camera.
2 Steve is the man who/that is wearing a black jacket.
3 Steve is the man who/that is telling everyone about San Francisco.
4 Lara is the girl who/that is standing next to Steve.
5 Silvana is the girl who/that is helping Alex with his camera.
6 Jay and Lara are the students who/that are listening to Steve.
7 The thin man is the person who/that is taking the girl's wallet.
8 The girl is the person who/that is watching the juggler.

4

1 Jay isn't holding a bag. He's holding an umbrella.
2 Ramón isn't sitting next to Emma. He's standing next to Emma.
3 Lara isn't reading a magazine. She's looking at the map.
4 The girl isn't listening to Steve. She's watching the juggler.
5 Alex and Silvana aren't taking pictures. They're checking the camera.

5

1 Is Jay looking at the thin man? No, he isn't. He's listening to Steve.
2 Is Lara making a phone call? No, she isn't. She's looking at the map.
3 Is Steve wearing a hat? No, he isn't. He's wearing a jacket.
4 Is the girl taking pictures? No, she isn't. She's watching the juggler.
5 Are Alex and Silvana holding hands? No, they aren't. They're checking the camera.
6 Is Steve telling a joke? No, he isn't. He's talking about San Francisco.

6

T	P	A	N	T	S	H	S
O	T	K	I	R	K	A	H
P	J	E	A	N	S	T	I
S	W	E	A	T	E	R	R
H	M	J	A	C	K	E	T
O	D	I	L	Y	U	C	W
E	X	F	S	Q	O	E	N
S	N	E	A	K	E	R	S

1 sweater 4 jeans 7 hat
2 pants 5 sneakers 8 jacket
3 shoes 6 shirt 9 top

7

1 wide 3 hand 5 make 7 play
2 foot 4 feel 6 knows 8 dress

UNIT 1 LESSON 3

1

1 No, she isn't.
2 He's talking to his friend, Mike.
3 It's Teri's sister's birthday.
4 He's bringing a big birthday cake.
5 Mike is taking a picture.

2

1 Whose cell phone is this? It's Mike's cell phone.
2 Whose glasses are these? They're Jenny's glasses.
3 Whose jacket is this? It's Russell's jacket.
4 Whose sneakers are these? They're Al's sneakers.
5 Whose wallet is this? It's Kate's wallet.
6 Whose camera is this? It's Susie's camera.
7 Whose books are these? They're Tim's books.
8 Whose bag is this? It's Lola's bag.

3
1 Who's 3 Who's 5 Whose
2 Whose 4 Who's 6 Whose

4
1 is 2 possession 3 is 4 is 5 is
6 possession

5
1 It's her guitar. It's hers.
2 They're our flowers. They're ours.
3 It's your camera. It's yours.
4 They're her DVDs. They're hers.
5 It's my dog. It's mine.
6 They're their magazines. They're theirs.
7 They're his books. They're his.
8 It's their car. It's theirs.

6
1 make 2 day 3 hi 4 hour 5 week

7
1 B 2 A 3 A 4 B 5 B 6 A 7 A 8 B 9 A
10 B

8
1 reporter 2 pilot 3 firefighter 4 photographer
5 musician 6 receptionist 7 actor 8 teacher

UNIT 1 LESSON 4

1
1 j 2 f 3 c 4 a 5 h 6 b 7 e 8 i 9 d 10 g

2
Sample answer
Alex is our winner from Australia and he lives in Sydney. His favorite clothes are his blue T-shirt and black jeans. Alex's favorite colors are red and blue and his favorite English word is "peanut butter." When he plays chess with his sister and she wins, it makes him angry, and when his team wins at basketball, it makes him happy. He speaks English, of course. His grandmother is very important to him. He tries to write in his journal every day; and he is reading The Lord of the Rings *right now.*

3

1 J	O	2 U	R	N	A	L	I	3 S	T	
A		M						P		
C		B			4 T		5 T	E	A	
6 K	A	R	A	T	E			A		
E		E			X			K		
7 T	A	L	L		8 T	9 O	A	S	10 T	
		L		11 V		N			A	
12 P	L	A	C	E	13 S		14 A		K	
E				15 T	E	A	C	H	E	R
16 T	A	K	E		E		T		S	

Learner independence
1 miss 2 wallet 3 park 4 umbrella
5 musician

UNIT 1 Inspired EXTRA!

Consolidation

Welcome!
1 I 2 He 3 She 4 she 5 he 6 she
7 He 8 They 9 we

Lesson 1
1 teaches 3 plays 5 speak 7 comes
2 doesn't love 4 watch 6 goes 8 don't live

Lesson 2
1 Is Ramón wearing an orange shirt? No, he isn't.
2 Are Alex and Silvana listening to Steve? No, they aren't.
3 Is Emma wearing a green top? Yes, she is.
4 Is the girl in the orange top smiling? Yes, she is.
5 Is Ramón standing on Emma's foot? No, he isn't.

Lesson 3
1 Whose dog is this? It's Scott's.
2 Whose sneakers are these? They're Jay's.
3 Whose cell phone is this? It's Teresa's.
4 Whose magazines are these? They're Luke's.
5 Whose bag is this? It's Bill's.
6 Whose CDs are these? They're Anna's.

Lesson 4
1 What are your favorite clothes?
2 What makes you happy?
3 What languages do you speak?
4 Is there someone very important to you?
5 What are you reading right now?

Spelling
1 gymnastics 2 favorite 3 sweater 4 famous
5 musician 6 wallet 7 important 8 language

Brainteaser
A clock/watch

Extension

Welcome!
1 Australia, Canada, the U.S.
2 Canada
3 Argentina, Mexico
4 Brazil

Lesson 1
1 Alex **does** not live in the U.S.
2 He plays soccer every week.
3 What languages **do** you speak?
4 Jay **doesn't** believe Emma speaks Chinese.
5 Does she **drink** tea for breakfast?

Lesson 2
1 are having 3 Do … know 5 is playing
2 is giving 4 likes 6 do … get

Lesson 3
1 her map 3 his jacket 5 his sneakers
2 her bag 4 his camera

Lesson 4
Emma is from the ~~what~~ beautiful city of Vancouver in Canada. She lives ~~goes~~ with her parents and her brother, Ryan. Her favorite clothes are ~~to~~ party dresses. Her favorite word is "independence" and her favorite color is ~~bed~~ red. People who tell her what to do ~~with~~ make her angry, and shopping ~~its~~ makes her happy. Her two ~~shoes~~ cats, Fred and Ginger, are very important to her, and something she does ~~on~~ every morning is check her e-mail.
Q What goes to bed with its shoes on?
A A horse!

Spelling
1 phones 2 finishes 3 countries 4 does

Brainteaser
There's a door between them.

CULTURE

Welcome to San Francisco

1
1 Chinatown
2 Fisherman's Wharf
3 Golden Gate Bridge
4 Grace Cathedral
5 Golden Gate Park
6 A cable car

2
1–Fisherman's Wharf, 2–Chinatown,
3–Nob Hill, 4–Grace Cathedral,
5–Golden Gate Park, 6–Golden Gate Bridge

S	C	B	R	I	D	G	E	S	S	W	S
R	O	C	K	S	I	N	G	E	R	A	T
E	M	O	O	V	T	H	M	U	A	T	A
C	O	R	O	T	H	E	W	A	Q	E	S
A	V	E	E	V	E	T	A	R	U	R	T
Y	I	U	A	B	M	U	R	T	A	F	R
O	E	L	T	H	E	A	T	E	R	A	O
A	S	T	O	R	P	T	E	E	I	L	N
Y	T	S	R	T	A	E	R	S	U	L	A
R	A	T	O	U	R	I	S	T	M	E	U
T	R	P	I	C	K	P	O	C	K	E	T

People: astronaut, pickpocket, tourist, rock singer, movie star
Places: bridge, waterfall, aquarium, theater, park

4
1 cable car 5 circus show
2 movie star 6 suspension bridge
3 salt water 7 boat trip
4 theme park 8 tourist attraction

UNIT 2 LESSON 1

1
1 F 2 T 3 T 4 T 5 T 6 F

2
1 f 2 e 3 d 4 b 5 a 6 c

3
1 longer 2 better 3 more popular 4 colder
5 noisier 6 more exotic

4

Adjective	Comparative	Superlative
colorful	more colorful	the most colorful
dangerous	more dangerous	the most dangerous
dry	drier	the driest
expensive	more expensive	the most expensive
hungry	hungrier	the hungriest
nice	nicer	the nicest
old	older	the oldest
popular	more popular	the most popular
spectacular	more spectacular	the most spectacular
warm	warmer	the warmest
wet	wetter	the wettest

5
1 Brazil is larger than Australia.
2 Sydney is warmer than Vancouver.

3 Emma is noisier than Lara.
4 Taxis are more expensive than buses.
5 Driving is more dangerous than flying.
6 Steve is older than Jay.

6
1 less warm 2 the least modern
3 the least expensive 4 the least noisy
5 less usual 6 less tall 7 the least difficult
8 less safe

7
carnival famous giant million
parade region stadium

UNIT 2 LESSON 2

1
a 4 b 2, 6, 7, 8 c 3 d 1 e 5 f 1, 4

2
1 You should wear more comfortable shoes. You shouldn't walk so far.
2 You should leave it at the reception desk. You shouldn't take it out of the hotel.
3 You should get up for breakfast. You shouldn't stay in bed.
4 You should listen to him. You shouldn't go by yourself.
5 You should buy an umbrella. You shouldn't stay out in the rain.

3
1 near 2 next to 3 across from 4 in front of
5 behind 6 between 7 over 8 under 9 inside
10 outside

4
1 You can buy some aspirin at a drugstore.
2 You can buy some flowers at a flower shop.
3 You can buy a newspaper at a newsstand.
4 You can book a vacation at a travel agency.
5 You can buy fruit at a supermarket.
6 You can get a haircut at a hairdresser's.
7 You can ask for help at a police station.
8 You can get a cold drink at a coffee shop.

5
1 should, good 2 flower, hour 3 wear, hair
4 plate, great 5 crowd, loud 6 post, most
7 first, worst 8 break, shake

UNIT 2 LESSON 3

1
1 trash 2 rain and mud 3 getting up early
4 camping

2
1 Sue's very good at drawing.
2 Molly's good at playing the guitar.
3 David's bad at remembering things.
4 Jack's very good at choosing gifts.
5 Harry's good at taking pictures.
6 Emily's bad at telling jokes.
7 Maria's good at speaking English.
8 Beth's very good at making friends.

3
1 can't stand going 2 love going
3 can't stand camping 4 like camping
5 love being 6 can't stand being
7 can't stand waiting 8 don't mind waiting
9 love hearing 10 like sitting
11 can't stand sitting

4

C	A	J	H	G	E	M	U	R	C
H	E	A	V	Y	M	E	T	A	L
I	M	Z	O	L	E	L	E	P	T
P	U	Z	K	E	T	W	C	A	R
S	A	L	S	A	O	A	H	T	O
C	K	I	P	P	P	U	N	K	T
O	P	L	O	S	O	V	O	U	R
T	E	A	R	I	P	I	E	R	O
C	L	U	T	R	A	S	D	S	C
H	A	G	D	E	C	K	I	N	K

1 jazz 2 heavy metal 3 punk 4 Rap 5 salsa
6 pop 7 Rock 8 techno

5
1 making 2 using 3 watching 4 being
5 listening 6 writing 7 eating 8 going

6
1 better 2 hate 3 late 4 lost 5 forget 6 a lot
7 starting 8 front

7
1 ✗ 2 ✗ 3 ✓ 4 ✗ 5 ✓ 6 ✗ 7 ✓ 8 ✗ 9 ✓ 10 ✓

Extension
1 of 2 at 3 with 4 about 5 at 6 of 7 to
8 to 9 for 10 with

UNIT 2 LESSON 4

1
1 e 2 c 3 d 4 a 5 f 6 b

2
Students' own answers

3

1 C	A	2 N	D	L	E	3 S		4 B	E	5 D
E		O				E		A		A
6 L	O	W		7 H	O	L	I	D	A	Y
E				A		L		A		S
8 B	R	9 A	Z	I	L		10 I	T	11 S	
R		R		R		12 S			13 I	N
A		14 E	X	C	I	T	I	15 N	G	
T		U				A		16 E	N	17 D
18 E	A	T		19 T	H	R	O	W		O

UNIT 2 Inspired EXTRA!

Consolidation

Lesson 1
1 most romantic 2 largest 3 better 4 worse
5 most popular 6 more exciting 7 biggest
8 more famous

Lesson 2
1 between 2 behind 3 next to 4 near
5 in front of
1 under 2 shouldn't 3 in front of 4 inside
5 expensive 6 late

Lesson 3
1 meeting 2 doing 3 being 4 watching
5 playing 6 going 7 listening 8 sleeping
9 reading

Lesson 4
1 What; They eat lentils. 2 Where; In Brazil.
3 When; In January or February.
4 Who; People in Venezuela.
5 What; They throw water.

Spelling
1 celebrate 2 amazing 3 spectacular 4 exotic
5 noisiest 6 biggest 7 umbrella 8 medicine
9 interested 10 crowd 11 festival 12 visitors

Brainteaser
He isn't very tall and can't reach the button for the tenth floor.

Extension

Lesson 1
1 Holly thinks Glastonbury is the **best** festival in the world.
2 The weather in Chicago is **worse** that the weather in Recife.
3 Which is the **best** soccer team?
4 Lady Gaga is a **more** exciting singer than Madonna.
5 New York is **bigger** than Miami.

Lesson 2
1 You should leave home earlier.
2 You shouldn't buy so many CDs.
3 You should write it down.
4 You should keep it in your bag.
5 You shouldn't forget your homework.

Lesson 3
Students' own answers.

Lesson 4
Students' own answers.

Spelling

/k/	/s/
call	celebrate
computer	center
comparative	city
costume	circus
cup	once
carnival	dancer
excuse	December
cap	

The letter **c** is pronounced /k/ when it is followed by the letters **a**, **o**, or **u**, and /s/ when it is followed by **e** or **i**.

Brainteaser
Mary

REVIEW UNITS 1-2

1
1 D 2 C 3 A 4 B 5 B 6 C 7 D 8 B 9 C
10 B 11 A 12 C 13 C 14 A 15 A 16 B

2
1 tourists 2 dangerous 3 actors 4 winners
5 exciting 6 traditional 7 favorite 8 interested

3
1 This jacket isn't mine.

2 The man is standing behind the girl.
3 What does Steve do?
4 What are your favorite clothes?
5 The coffee shop is cheaper than the restaurant.
6 The flower shop is under the travel agency.
7 Alex isn't bad at dancing.
8 I can't stand feeling cold.

4
1 sister 2 pocket 3 stand 4 bag
5 costume 6 worry 7 bread 8 difficult

Learner independence

2
1 Of course not.
2 Let me see!
3 Now listen up!
4 I hope you like it.
5 What do you mean?
6 It isn't safe.
7 I'm coming with you.
8 The only problem is …

UNIT 3 LESSON 1

1
1 It started during the night.
2 The wind carried the flames to the rest of the city.
3 He was in Actium.
4 He helped look for people in the destroyed houses, he allowed people to stay in his palaces, and he bought food for them.
5 Because they don't burn easily.
6 Because they didn't like him.

2
1 was 2 wasn't 3 were, was 4 weren't
5 were, were

3
borrowed caused discovered helped liked missed designed invented practiced printed showed started buried carried married studied tried worried

4

Verb	Simple past	Verb	Simple past
begin	began	lose	lost
buy	bought	make	made
eat	ate	meet	met
find	found	put	put
give	gave	say	said
go	went	send	sent
hear	heard	sing	sang
hold	held	sit	sat
keep	kept	speak	spoke
know	knew	throw	threw

5
1 didn't happen 2 wasn't 3 didn't build
4 didn't have 5 didn't want 6 didn't last
7 weren't

6
1 1971 2 1989 3 1998 4 2002
5 sixteen sixty-six
6 eighteen twenty-six
7 nineteen ninety-four
8 two thousand and eleven / twenty eleven
9 two thousand and thirteen / twenty thirteen
10 two thousand and sixteen / twenty sixteen

7
1 cause 2 marry 3 spread 4 gold 5 smoke
6 damage 7 flames 8 helicopter
9 ballpoint pen 10 block

UNIT 3 LESSON 2

1
a 3 b 6 c 1 d 5 e 2 f 4

2
1 When 2 Who 3 When 4 What 5 What
6 When

3
1 Where did the group go?
2 What did they see at the academy?
3 Where did they go?
4 What did they visit after that?
5 What did Emma have outside?
6 Who did the group meet in the park?

4
1 Did they have fun? Yes, they did.
2 Did they see a play? No, they didn't.
3 Did they see an exhibit? Yes, they did.
4 Did they climb up Nob Hill? No, they didn't.
5 Did they all go inside the temple? No, they didn't.
6 Did they meet Alex in the park? Yes, they did.

5
1 on 2 in 3 at 4 in 5 in 6 at 7 on 8 on
9 on 10 in 11 in 12 at

6
Adjectives for people: asleep, awesome, exhausted, great, hungry, lazy, thirsty
Adjectives for things: awesome, great, steep, spectacular, long

7
ex~~h~~ibit clim~~b~~ s~~c~~ience desi~~g~~n ex~~h~~austed bou~~gh~~t

Extension
1 Did people go to the theater then? Yes, they did.
2 Did people go to the movies then? No, they didn't.
3 Did people make phone calls then? No, they didn't.
4 Did people visit cathedrals then? Yes, they did.
5 Did people drive cars then? No, they didn't.
6 Did people have MP3 players then? No, they didn't.

UNIT 3 LESSON 3

1
1 F 2 F 3 T 4 T 5 F

2
A was waiting for a bus
B was drinking a cup of coffee.
C was eating a sandwich.
D was reading a newspaper.
E was looking at a map.
F was using a cell phone.
G was taking a picture.
H was looking at the camera.

3
1 No, he wasn't. He was wearing a blue T-shirt.
2 No, he wasn't. He was standing in front of the temple.
3 No, he wasn't. He was standing next to Silvana.
4 No, she wasn't. She was wearing a blue top.
5 No, she wasn't. She was standing in front of the cathedral with Jay.
6 No, he wasn't. He was standing in front of the cathedral with Emma/in front of the cable car with Silvana.

4
1 Was Emma telling everyone about San Francisco?
2 Was Silvana standing next to Steve?
3 Was Ramón holding a map?
4 Was Alex holding an umbrella?
5 Was Emma helping Alex?
6 Was Steve stealing the wallet?

5
1 Why was Ryan feeling unhappy? Because he lost his cell phone.
2 Why were you running? Because I was late.
3 Why was Gerrit Blank smiling? Because he survived.
4 Why was Josh feeling happy? Because he got a real meteorite.
5 Why was Emma sitting outside? Because she was tired.
6 Why was Alex eating ice cream? Because he was hot.

6
1 d 2 c 3 f 4 e 5 b 6 h 7 a 8 g

7
bicycle e**mer**gency transpor**ta**tion **hel**icopter
dangerous **spa**ceship **speed**boat e**nor**mous

UNIT 3 LESSON 4

1
1 friends 2 believe 3 money 4 eyes
5 shouted 6 talking 7 disappeared 8 wearing
9 having 10 ghosts

2
1 F. Everyone was hard at work in Scrooge's office.
2 F. Bob Cratchit worked in Scrooge's office. His nephew's name was Fred.
3 T.
4 F. The ghost said "You should change your life."
5 T.
6 T.
7 T.

3

1 C	A	2 L	L		3 F	4 A	M	O	5 U	S
A		O		6 H		C			S	
T		7 S	E	A		8 T	A	K	E	9 S
10 H	O	T		P		O				E
E				11 P	A	R	T	Y		V
12 D	I	A	13 R	Y					14 B	E
R			O		15 R	I	C	16 H		R
A			D		A			I		A
17 L	A	T	E		18 N	E	X	T		L

Learner independence

Buildings	Occupations	Writing
cathedral	actor	bestseller
church	novelist	diary
factory	playwright	novel
theater	reporter	play
tower	teacher	poem
		story

UNIT 3
Inspired EXTRA!

Consolidation

Lesson 1
1 Walt Disney didn't study English. He studied art.
2 The San Francisco earthquake didn't happen during the day. It happened at night.
3 Silvana and Lara went out. They didn't stay in the hotel.
4 László Bíró didn't show the first movies. He invented the first ballpoint pen.
5 Gerrit Blank found a meteorite. He didn't find a ball.
6 Igor Sikorsky didn't invent the phone. He designed the first helicopter.

Lesson 2
1 Did San Francisco burn down in 1966? No, it didn't.
2 Did Emma visit the temple? No, she didn't.
3 Did Alex go to the Golden Gate Bridge? No, he didn't.
4 Did Silvana and Jay see an exhibit? Yes, they did.
5 Did the group meet Alex in the park? Yes, they did.
6 Did Alex sleep all morning? No, he didn't.

Lesson 3
1 Gerrit was walking when he saw a ball of light.
2 Josh was playing in his backyard when he found a shiny, black rock.
3 Emma's brother was sailing the boat when it hit a rock.
4 Ann Hodges was sleeping when the meteorite hit her house.
5 Lara was running in the park when it started to rain.
6 Jay was chatting online when the computer stopped working.

Lesson 4
1 c 2 e 3 h 4 a 5 f 6 d

Spelling
1 science 2 building 3 well-known 4 listen
5 playwright 6 school 7 walking 8 wrote

Brainteaser
A fire

Extension

Lesson 1
1 was 2 was 3 became 4 spoke 5 wanted
6 said 7 called 8 went 9 named 10 was
11 were 12 died

Lesson 2
1 Who **discovered** gold in California in 1848? James Marshall.
2 What **was** the date of the San Francisco earthquake? April 18, 1906.
3 How many blocks did the fire **destroy**? 500.
4 Who **made** the world's first phone call? Joseph Niepce.
5 Where did the group **see** an exhibit? At the museum.
6 What cathedral **did they** visit? Grace Cathedral.
7 **Did** Emma go into the temple? No, she didn't.
8 Where **did they** meet Alex? In the park.

Lesson 3
Students' own answers.

Lesson 4
Students' own answers.

Spelling
1 afternoon 2 asleep 3 bestseller 4 ballpoint
5 cartoon 6 collected 7 cell phone 8 happy
9 happen 10 hill 11 married 12 middle
13 occupation 14 suddenly 15 success
16 swimming 17 speedboat 18 million
19 feeling

Brainteaser
One person (the speaker)

CULTURE

1

Empire State Building—the facts

Opened	May 1931
Tallest building for	42 years
Height	443 meters
Number of floors	103
Number of windows	6,500
Number of elevators	73
Speed of elevators	366 meters a minute
Visitors a year	2.5 million

2

Sample answer

The Chrysler Building opened in May 1930 and for one year it was the tallest building in the world. It is 319 meters high and has 77 floors. There are 3,862 windows and 32 elevators. The elevators travel at up to 213 meters a minute.

3
1 F. Central Park is in the middle of New York City.
2 T.
3 F. The two ice-skating rinks become a swimming pool and a garden in July and August.
4 F. You can play sports in the park.
5 F. You can't drive a car through the park on weekends.
6 F. Many of the tickets are free.
7 F. You can sometimes see famous actors there.
8 T.

4
1 crimes 2 jogger 3 dangerous 4 mugger
5 fewer 6 injured 7 enormous 8 rink 9 free

UNIT 4 LESSON 1

1
1 b 2 f 3 a 4 e 5 c 6 d

2
1 get a good picture 2 ride a bike
3 go on vacation 4 blow the whistle

3
1 b 2 d 3 f 4 a 5 c 6 e

4
1 computer chip 2 ice cream 3 digital camera
4 camera phone 5 tour guide 6 primary color

5
1 black calculation picture science
2 answer brightness instant process
3 digital measure primary usually
4 language nervous computer trouble
5 light mathematics photo white

6
1 happy 2 terrible 3 angry 4 simple
5 nervous 6 rude

7
1 ✗ 2 ✗ 3 ✓ 4 ✓ 5 ✗ 6 ✓ 7 ✓ 8 ✗
9 ✗

UNIT 4 LESSON 2

1
1 T 2 T 3 F 4 T 5 F 6 F

2
1 Will the group go inside Alcatraz? No, they won't.
2 Will they take a boat ride? Yes, they will.
3 Will Emma have a surprise? Yes, she will.
4 Will Jay lose his phone? No, he won't.
5 Will Lara and Alex make a video? Yes, they will.
6 Will the weather be bad? No, it won't.

1 The group won't go inside Alcatraz.
2 They will take a boat ride.
3 Emma will have a surprise.
4 Jay won't lose his phone.
5 Lara and Alex will make a video.
6 The weather won't be bad.

3
1 will get some nice gifts 2 won't tell anyone
3 won't forget anything 4 will catch the last bus
5 will come to school 6 will win the game

4
1 popular 2 introduced 3 expensive
4 download 5 replaced 6 available

5

■▪	▪■
listen	invent
record (noun)	record (verb)
answer	cassette
money	replace
album	surprise
	prefer
	appear

6
1 cylinder 2 MP3 player 3 cassette tape
4 LP 5 CD

Extension
1 When will you be 21?
2 What time will you get up tomorrow?
3 What will you have for lunch tomorrow?

4 Where will you be on Sunday morning?

Students' own answers.

UNIT 4 LESSON 3

1
1 nervously 2 quickly 3 carefully 4 quietly 5 happily 6 Suddenly 7 immediately 8 sadly 9 fast 10 easily

2

Adjective	Adverb
bad	badly
correct	correctly
honest	honestly
loud	loudly
rude	rudely
slow	slowly
angry	angr**ily**
bossy	bossily
hungry	hungrily
comfortable	comfortab**ly**
terrible	terribly
beautiful	beautiful**ly**
special	specially
successful	successfully

3
1 terribly 2 rudely 3 hungrily 4 loudly 5 slowly 6 correctly 7 beautifully 8 badly

4
1 on 2 for 3 About 4 in 5 about 6 with 7 with 8 at 9 of 10 from 11 to 12 with

5
1 late 2 hard 3 well 4 high 5 long

6
1 drama 2 bodies 3 easy 4 ready 5 move 6 adverb 7 run 8 exercise 9 voices 10 talk 11 like 12 important

7

			↓					
1 C	H	A	R	A	C	T	E	R
2 D	I	R	E	C	T	O	R	
		3 T	H	E	A	T	E	R
	4 S	C	E	N	E			
			5 A	C	T	O	R	
		6 D	R	A	M	A		
			7 S	H	O	W		
		8 H	A	P	P	Y		
		9 P	L	A	Y	S		

UNIT 4 LESSON 4

1
1 popular 2 place 3 friends 4 parents 5 watches 6 questions 7 school 8 police 9 answer 10 wins

2
1 favorite 2 grow up 3 slum 4 correct 5 allow 6 explain

3
Students' own answers.

4

1 I	N	2 T	E	3 R	V	4 I	E	5 W		6 D
M		R		E		C		7 E	A	R
8 A	P	A	R	T	M	E	9 N	T		U
G		N		U			E			G
10 I	N	S	T	R	U	M	E	11 N	T	S
N		P		N			12 D	O		T
13 A	G	O			14 A	15 T		16 T	O	O
R		R		17 O		O				R
Y		18 T	A	K	E	P	L	A	C	E

Learner independence
make: a cake, a movie, friends, a list, a phone call, sure
take: a bus, a break, place, a shower, a picture

UNIT 4 Inspired EXTRA!

Consolidation

Lesson 1
1 c 2 a 3 d 4 e 5 b 6 h 7 f 8 g

Lesson 2
1 'll 2 will 3 'll 4 'll 5 won't 6 won't 7 won't 8 Will 9 won't

Lesson 3
1 loudly 2 late 3 politely 4 well 5 sadly 6 quickly

Lesson 4
1 Where (Springfield, U.S.)
2 How many (Over 70.)
3 What (A middle-class American family.)
4 What (Blue.)
5 When (1989.)

Spelling
1 character 2 documen**ta**ry 3 emer**ge**ncy 4 **e**pisode 5 ex**er**cise 6 nerv**ou**sly 7 perform**a**nce 8 rehe**ar**sal 9 calc**u**lation 10 thriller

Brainteaser
The future

Extension

Lesson 1
Student's own answers.

Lesson 2
Students' own answers.

Lesson 3
1 slept … well
2 works … hard
3 shouted angrily
4 rehearse properly
5 arrived … early

Lesson 4
Students' own answers.

Spelling

/k/	/tʃ/		
character	chair	China	lunch
Christmas	change	chip	teacher
schedule	charge	chocolate	which
school	chat	choose	
techno	cheese	church	
	child	each	

Brainteaser
The boy's mother

REVIEW UNITS 3–4

1
1 C 2 B 3 C 4 C 5 B 6 B 7 A 8 C 9 B

2
1 exhausted 2 buildings 3 rehearsal 4 playwrights 5 writer 6 invention 7 angrily 8 successful 9 imaginary 10 argument

3
1 When the earthquake started, the people of San Francisco were asleep.
2 Yuri Gagarin was the first person to travel in space.
3 If you mix blue and yellow paint, you get green.
4 Everyone was eating their lunch when Alex arrived.
5 When Ryan fell overboard, he was sailing with a friend.
6 Kafka is one of the most famous writers in the world.
7 We'll find out what happens in the next episode.
8 I really don't think that The Simpsons will end next year.

4
1 bridge 2 ship 3 expensive 4 politely 5 romance 6 hospital

Learner independence

2
1 Did you have fun?
2 I don't understand.
3 Oh, that's too bad.
4 It was awesome!
5 She wasn't feeling well.
6 It doesn't make sense.
7 I have some bad news.
8 What happend to you?

UNIT 5 LESSON 1

1
1 d 2 g 3 c 4 a 5 h 6 b 7 f 8 e

2
1 No, we aren't flying to Rome. We're flying to Venice.
2 No, we aren't flying to Florence. We're traveling by train.
3 No, we aren't spending three nights in Florence. We're spending two nights there.
4 No, we aren't flying to Naples. We're driving there.
5 No, we aren't returning to the U.S. on the 29th. We're returning on the 30th.

3

1 I'm seeing my bank manger.
2 I'm taking the group to the cathedral.
3 I'm having lunch with some travel agents.
4 I'm watching a rehearsal at the theater.
5 I'm giving an interview at Talk Radio.

4

1 When is he seeing his bank manager?
2 How long is he spending at the bank?
3 How long is he/are they spending in the cathedral?
4 When is he having lunch (with some travel agents)?
5 How long is he spending at the theater?
6 When is he giving an interview at Talk Radio?

5

First, he's seeing his bank manager. Next, he's taking the group to the cathedral. Then he's having lunch with some travel agents. After that, he's watching a rehearsal at the theater. Finally, he's giving an interview at Talk Radio.

6

1 trip 2 zoo 3 museums 4 tour 5 postcard
6 theater 7 shopping 8 hotel

7

1 Rome, home
2 friend, spend
3 who, zoo
4 daughter, water
5 street, seat
6 store, four
7 walk, talk
8 take, break

UNIT 5 LESSON 2

1

1 Two.
2 Jay doesn't want bananas.
3 A dessert without ice cream.
4 One tea and two coffees.
5 With sugar and no milk.

2

Countable nouns Singular	Countable nouns Plural	Uncountable nouns
egg	eggs	bread
mushroom	mushrooms	cheese
olive	olives	cola
onion	onions	fruit
pineapple	pineapples	garlic
strawberry	strawberries	ham
tomato	tomatoes	meat
vegetable	vegetables	spinach
		water

3

1 some 2 any 3 some 4 any 5 some 6 any
7 any 8 some 9 any 10 some 11 any 12 any

4

1 How much—C
2 How many—E
3 How much—A
4 How many—D
5 How many—B
6 How much
7 How much
8 How many
9 How much
10 How many
(6–10 Students' own answers)

5

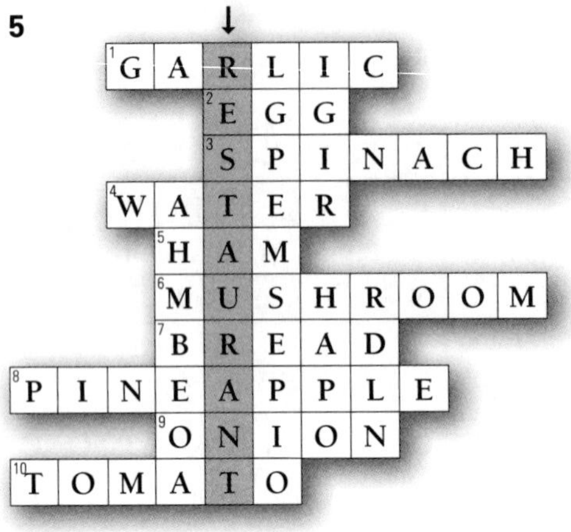

6

1 starving 2 waiter 3 glass 4 borrow
5 vegetarian 6 fried 7 menu

7

/e/ bread: any, egg, many, pepper, ready, says
/i/ cheese: cream, eat, meal, meat, need, pizza, please

UNIT 5 LESSON 3

1

1 F 2 T 3 T 4 F 5 F

2

1 us 2 me 3 them 4 it 5 her 6 you

3

1 They were looking for it.
2 She asked him the way.
3 They didn't want to miss it.
4 He ran after her.
5 He was waiting for them.
6 Can we sit next to you?

4

1 Please show me your photos.
2 Emma sent her parents a postcard.
3 We gave Ms. Fairfax some flowers.
4 Ramón sang us a song.
5 Did you write them a letter?
6 I'll get you a ticket.

5

1 through 2 across 3 along 4 past 5 up
6 down 7 around 8 into

6

1 through 2 across/over 3 through/across
4 into 5 out of

7

1 Excuse me, can you tell me the way to Market Road, please?
Turn left outside the museum and Market Road is the second street on the left.
2 Excuse me, can you tell me the way to Church Street, please?
Turn right outside the museum and Church Street is the second street on the right.
3 Excuse me, can you tell me the way to Wood Street, please?
Turn left outside the museum and Wood Street is the second street on the right.
4 Excuse me, can you tell me the way to Western Road, please?
Turn left outside the museum and turn left onto Market Road. Western Road is the first street on the right.

8

1 A 2 C 3 B 4 C 5 A 6 C 7 B 8 B

UNIT 5 LESSON 4

1

1 country 2 organization 3 farms
4 money 5 vacation 6 foreign 7 winter
8 fruit 9 people 10 tickets 11 food

2

Students' own answers.

3

UNIT 5 Inspired EXTRA!

Consolidation

Lesson 1

1 Silvana is returning to Argentina on September 1.
2 Carrie is getting married in November.
3 Jay and Ramón are visiting a museum today.
4 Ramón is flying to Mexico on August 31.
5 Steve is going on vacation in October.
6 Steve and Carrie are working on Sunday.

Lesson 2

1 some 2 many 3 any 4 some 5 much
6 any 7 some 8 any

Lesson 3

1 him 2 us 3 us 4 him 5 it 6 us 7 us
8 her 9 us 10 him
1 out 2 across 3 along 4 to 5 through
6 past 7 onto 8 on

Lesson 4

1 f 2 a 3 b 4 h 5 d

Spelling

1 hours 2 suitcase 3 right 4 building 5 suit
6 could 7 should 8 weight 9 straight
10 wrong

Brainteaser

Because it's the capital of England (The word England begins with the capital letter E.)

Extension

Lesson 1

1 *is taking*
2 *are … spending*
3 *are having*
4 *Are … coming*
5 *am going*
6 *Is … getting*

Lesson 2

1 A 2 D 3 C 4 B 5 D 6 C 7 A 8 B

Lesson 3

1 *Steve tells Emma how* **to** *get to the restaurant.*
2 *We asked a police officer to tell* **us** *the way.*
3 *Can you* **show me** *a map, please?*
4 *I'm looking for my friends, but I can't see* **them**.
5 *Could you lend* **me some money**?
6 *Turn left and you'll see the restaurant on* **the** *right.*

Lesson 4

Students' own answers.

Spelling

1 here 2 right 3 weigh 4 weight 5 meat 6 through 7 past 8 know 9 new

Brainteaser

She likes food/drink with double letters.

CULTURE

Teenage life

1

1 g 2 b 3 i 4 j 5 e 6 a 7 f 8 h 9 d 10 c

2

1 *big deal*
2 *stunt*
3 *hassle*
4 *internship*
5 *obsessed*
6 *complaint*
7 *hang out*
8 *hip-hop*

3

1 d 2 a 3 f 4 e 5 b 6 c

4

1 *skateboarding*
2 *high school*
3 *computer game*
4 *electrical store*
5 *designer clothes*
6 *night club*

5

1 do 2 spend 3 complain 4 get 5 treat 6 go

6

Students' own answers.

UNIT 6 LESSON 1

1

1 Lara 2 Jay 3 Jay 4 Lara 5 Jay 6 Jay

2

1 *Has Lara heard* Every Time I Miss You? *Yes, she has.*
2 *Has Jay heard* Every Time I Miss You? *No, he hasn't.*
3 *Have the City Boys been here long? No, they haven't.*
4 *Has Lara bought tickets for their concert? Yes, she has.*
5 *Has Lara invited Ramón to the concert? No, she hasn't.*
6 *Has Jay made plans for tomorrow night? No, he hasn't.*

3

1 *She hasn't filmed Jay and Lara. She's filmed Ramón and Silvana.*
2 *He hasn't bought a computer game. He's bought a DVD.*
3 *She hasn't sent an e-mail to her parents. She's sent an e-mail to her best friend.*
4 *He hasn't lost his watch. He's lost his map.*
5 *She hasn't called her parents once. She's called them three times.*
6 *They haven't recorded a song. They've recorded a video.*

4

1 *She's just gotten up.*
2 *They've just started the rehearsal.*
3 *They've just finished/had dinner.*
4 *She's just invited Jay to the concert.*
5 *He's just had a driving lesson.*
6 *He's just taken a picture.*
7 *The train has just left.*
8 *We've just seen the movie.*

5

1 *Emma is practicing with the camera.*
2 *Emma has been mean to Ramón.*
3 *Steve is wearing a jacket.*
4 *Jay is learning Spanish.*
5 *Emma has figured out how to use the camera.*
6 *She has recorded Ramón and Silvana's conversation.*
7 *Ramón has tried to talk to Emma.*
8 *Lara is friendly toward Jay.*

6

1 an e-mail 2 a shower 3 a picture 4 a song 5 a movie 6 a picture

7

1 squirrel 2 panda 3 cow 4 goat 5 deer 6 owl 7 duck

8

1 ✓ 2 ✓ 3 ✓ 4 ✓ 5 ✗ 6 ✓ 7 ✓ 8 ✗

UNIT 6 LESSON 2

1

1 *Alex and Silvana have both been on a high-speed train.*
2 *Yes, he has.*
3 *Silvana has been to Paris.*
4 *Alex has flown over Paris.*
5 *Silvana hasn't eaten Russian food.*

2

1 *Have you ever visited*
2 *I've never been*
3 *I've never visited*
4 *Have you ever seen*
5 *I've never had*
6 *anyone has ever seen*
7 *No one has ever painted*

3

1 *Have you ever been in the hospital? No, I've never been in the hospital. / Yes, I have.*
2 *Have you ever been on TV? No, I've never been on TV. / Yes, I have.*
3 *Have you ever ridden a motorcycle? No, I've never ridden a motorcycle. / Yes, I have.*
4 *Have you ever eaten Japanese food? No, I've never eaten Japanese food. / Yes, I have.*
5 *Have you ever forgotten your phone number? No, I've forgotten my phone number. / Yes, I have.*
6 *Have you ever used a video camera? No, I've never used a video camera. / Yes, I have.*
7 *Have you ever felt very angry with someone? No, I've never felt very angry with someone. / Yes, I have.*
8 *Have you ever had an argument with a friend? No, I've never had an argument with a friend. / Yes, I have.*

4

1 *important transportation modern*
2 *famous valuable route*
3 *crossing railroad station*
4 *somewhere magnet imagine*
5 *thought something schedule*

5↓

1 S	C	H	E	D	U	L	E	
2 T	I	C	K	E	T			
3 R	A	I	L	R	O	A	D	
4 E	V	E	R					
5 E	N	G	I	N	E			
6 T	R	A	V	E	L			
7 C	O	N	D	U	C	T	O	R
8 A	I	R	P	O	R	T		
9 R	O	U	T	E				

6

1 has ✓ *2 house* ✗ *3 seen* ✗ *4 let's* ✗ *5 museum* ✓ *6 stupid* ✗ *7 likes* ✗ *8 there's* ✓ *9 saw* ✗ *10 says* ✓ *11 was* ✓ *12 is* ✓

Extension

A … travels on metal rails on city streets.

UNIT 6 LESSON 3

1

1 crowded 2 shopping 3 low 4 expensive 5 free 6 fashionable

2

too much: coffee, homework, information, noise, rain, sun, sugar, cheese
too many: accidents, channels, pineapples, letters, mistakes, pickpockets, problems, stores

3

1 *There are too many passengers.*
2 *There is too much spaghetti.*
3 *There are too many police officers.*
4 *There is too much garbage/trash.*
5 *There are too many steps.*
6 *There is too much traffic.*

4

1 *The car isn't big enough.*
2 *The food isn't hot enough.*
3 *These pants aren't long enough.*
4 *The music isn't loud enough.*
5 *You aren't old enough to drive.*

5

1 b 2 h 3 e 4 d 5 c 6 j 7 i 8 g 9 f 10 a

6
1 expensive 2 small 3 win 4 popular 5 noisy 6 hard

7
channel de**scribe** de**scrip**tion ex**pen**sive **mu**sical **prob**lem **sat**ellite suc**cess**ful **suit**case **the**ater

UNIT 6 LESSON 4

1
Alex: *1 e 2 a 3 f 4 c 5 b 6 d*
Emma: *1 f 2 c 3 d 4 a 5 e 6 b*

2
Sample answers
Alex
My favorite place is a huge red rock called Uluru. It's the biggest rock in the world and it's in the middle of Australia, 450 kilometers south of Alice Springs. It's very old and it's 348 meters high. The quickest way to get there is to fly to Alice Springs and then go by car. But I prefer the train. There are always too many tourists. But the rock is so big you can still enjoy it.
Emma
… It's a wonderful park on top of a hill in Barcelona. The architect Gaudi worked on it from 1900 to 1914, but it didn't open until 1922. It's pretty high and there are wonderful views over the city. You can get there by bus or subway. Walking up is very hard work because the hill is really steep.

3

1 E		2 B		3 R	O	4 A	D	5 S		6 D
X		R		E		R		T		R
7 P	R	O	B	L	E	M		U		I
E		K		A		S		D		V
N		E		X			8 N	I	C	E
9 S	E	N	T			10 J		O		R
I				11 H	12 O	U	R		13 I	S
V		14 M	E	A	N	S			L	
E		Y		15 M	E	T		16 F	L	Y

Learner independence

Transportation	People	Seasons
airport	artist	fall
bus	musician	spring
harbor	poet	summer
plane	student	winter
ship	teacher	
station	tourist	
train	visitor	

The shortest list is Seasons because there are only four.

UNIT 6
Inspired EXTRA!

Consolidation

Lesson 1

Infinitive	*Past participle*
become	became
bring	brought
buy	bought
drink	drunk
eat	eaten
feel	felt
find	found
give	given
hear	heard
leave	left
pay	paid
say	said
speak	spoken
sing	sung
teach	taught
win	won

1 Silvana has just talked to Ramón.
2 Emma has been mean to Ramón today.
3 Alex and Lara have just gone to the museum.
4 I have done a lot of sightseeing this week.
5 Carrie hasn't had much free time this month.

Lesson 2
1 Has Emma ever visited Australia? No, she hasn't.
2 Has Ramón ever met anyone famous? No, he hasn't.
3 Has Carrie ever been in the hospital? Yes, she has.
4 Have Silvana and Alex ever eaten sushi? No, they haven't.
5 Has Steve ever ridden a horse? Yes, he has.

Lesson 3
1 much 2 enough 3 much 4 many 5 much, enough 6 many 7 enough 8 many, enough

Lesson 4
1 What's your favorite place?
2 Where is it?
3 How tall/high is it?
4 How old is it?
5 How do you get to the top?
6 Are there any problems?

Spelling
1 horrible 2 stunning 3 commercial 4 squirrel 5 sightseeing 6 really 7 questionnaire 8 ferry 9 speed 10 waterfall 11 giraffe 10 bullet

Brainteaser
In the dictionary

Extension

Lesson 1
Students' own answers.
1 has 2 is 3 has 4 has 5 is 6 has 7 is

Lesson 2
1 Have … visited 2 've been 3 've enjoyed 4 has … stopped 5 have watched 6 have … seen

Lesson 3
1 The hotel wasn't cheap enough.
2 It was too noisy.
3 The rooms were too small.
4 The place wasn't interesting enough.
5 The weather was too cold.

Lesson 4
Students' own answers.

Spelling
mosquito /ki/

Brainteaser
Bangkok (the opposite side of the world from Lima)

REVIEW UNITS 5-6

1
1 C 2 A 3 E 4 B

1 D 2 A 3 B 4 C 5 D 6 C 7 D 8 B 9 C 10 B 11 A 12 D

2
1 directions 2 visitors 3 shopping 4 argument 5 recording 6 suggestion 7 crowded 8 national

3
1 Why don't we go to the movies?
2 Can you tell us the way to Pizza Paradise?
3 Could I have a glass of water, please?
4 How much water do you want?
5 Could I borrow some money from you?
6 What time are we leaving for the theater?
7 I've just heard the news.
8 I've never won a prize.
9 We don't have enough money for the tickets.
10 The spaghetti was too cold.

4
1 sandwich 2 umbrella 3 backpack 4 nearly 5 statue 6 horrible 7 empty 8 harbor

Learner independence

2
1 Are you ready to order?
2 What would you like to drink?
3 Sure—coming right up.
4 Excuse me, can you help me?
5 But there's one problem …
6 Don't make too much noise.
7 The easiest way to get there is …
8 You can't miss it!

UNIT 7 LESSON 1

1
1 f 2 d 3 b 4 e 5 a 6 c

2
1 You mustn't have guests after 10 p.m.
2 You must leave by 10 a.m. on your last day.
3 You mustn't have/eat take-out food in the rooms.
4 You mustn't wash clothes in the rooms.
5 You must turn off the TV before you leave.
6 You mustn't make any noise after midnight.

3
1 must, mustn't
2 mustn't, must
3 mustn't
4 must
5 mustn't
6 must

4
1 hidden 2 jungle 3 insects 4 viewers 5 celebrity 6 trash 7 matches 8 clap 9 autograph 10 flash

5
1 ✗ 2 ✓ 3 ✗ 4 ✗ 5 ✓ 6 ✓ 7 ✓ 8 ✗ 9 ✓

UNIT 7 LESSON 2

1
1 ✓ 2 ✗ 3 ✗ 4 ✓ 5 ✓ 6 ✗ 7 ✓ 8 ✗

2

1	do … have to	6	don't have to
2	have to	7	have to
3	Do … have to	8	don't have to
4	has to	9	have to
5	Do … have to	10	have to

3
1 *Emma* **has to** *write some letters. How many* **does she have to write**?
2 *Ramón* **has to** *do some homework. How much* **does he have to do**?
3 *Silvana and Alex* **have** *to meet Lara in the park. When* **do** *they* **have to meet her**?
4 *You* **have to** *buy tickets for the concert. Where* **do we have to buy them**?
5 *You* **have to** *go to the airport tomorrow. What time* **do** *I* **have to go**?
6 *We* **have to** *clean up the room before we go to bed. Why* **do** *we* **have to clean up the room (before we go to bed)**?
7 **I have to** *get up at six o'clock. Why* **do** *you* **have to get up at six o'clock**?
8 *Carrie* **has to** *go to bed early. When* **does** *she* **have to go to bed**?

4
1 *They didn't have to spend a month in the camp, but they had to stay for up to two weeks.*
2 *They had to sleep in the open air, but they didn't have to go to bed early.*
3 *They didn't have to go shopping, but they had to win extra food.*
4 *They had to cook their meals, but they didn't have to set the table.*
5 *They had to wash their own clothes, but they didn't have to do any ironing.*
6 *They didn't have to make their beds, but they had to do other tasks.*
7 *They had to learn survival techniques, but they didn't have to learn another language.*
8 *They didn't have to give up food, but they had to give up luxuries.*

5
1 a postcard 2 a seat belt 3 an exam 4 a phone call 5 a bus

6
1 checkout 2 homework 3 school uniform 4 football 5 supermarket 6 takeoff

7
1 own, phone 2 pass, glass 3 care, wear 4 seat, feet 5 crash, flash 6 catch, match

UNIT 7 LESSON 3

1
a sun b cloud c tree d river e ocean
1 *The amount of the Earth which is covered by water—2/3*
2 *The amount of a tree which is water—50%*
3 *The number of liters of water that a big tree can lose in one day—200*
4 *The number of liters of water in the human body—30–40*
5 *The amount of the human body that is water—60%*

2

-ed adjective	-ing adjective
amazed	***amazing***
bored	*boring*
excited	***exciting***
fascinated	*fascinating*
frightened	***frightening***
interested	*interesting*
shocked	***shocking***
surprised	*surprising*
tired	***tiring***

3
1 *Why is Sandra shocked? Because the news is shocking.*
2 *Why is Peter frightened? Because the snakes are frightening.*
3 *Why is Laura bored? Because the show is boring.*
4 *Why is Pedro excited? Because the game is exciting.*

4
1 want 2 like 3 rather 4 like 5 rather 6 want 7 rather 8 want

5

O	B	C	A	T	F	L	U	J
C	R	O	C	O	D	I	L	E
T	P	W	O	R	M	O	S	V
O	R	D	H	T	X	N	H	S
P	H	U	G	O	A	T	A	H
U	I	C	P	I	G	D	R	E
S	N	K	E	S	N	A	K	E
H	O	R	S	E	Z	G	I	P

Mammals: *cat, goat, pig, horse, rhino, cow, lion, sheep*
Reptiles: *crocodile, snake, tortoise*
Ocean creatures: *octopus, shark*
Other creatures: *worm, duck*

6

■ ▪ ▪ ▪	▪ ▪ ■ ▪	▪ ■ ▪ ▪
fascinating	*conversation*	*amphibian*
fortunately	*information*	*celebrity*
supermarket	*obligation*	*emergency*
terrifying		*environment*
		experience
		intelligent
		reality

UNIT 7 LESSON 4

1
B c C e D a E d F b
A 5 B 3 C 1 D 6 E 7 F 2 G 4

2
Sample answer
Columbus left Spain on Friday, August 3, 1492 with 120 men in three ships. He sailed to the Canary Islands, the Bahamas, and the islands of Cuba and Haiti. The return voyage was difficult and frightening. Columbus finally reached Spain on March 15, 1493. The voyage was seven and a half months and he sailed over 15,000 kilometers.

3

1 R	E	2 I	N	3 D	E	4 E	R		5 T
E		N		O		X		6 S	O
7 P	A	S	S		8 I	T		P	
T		E		9 K	N	I	V	E	S
I		10 C	A	N		N		N	
11 L	E	T		I		C		D	
E			12 O	F		13 T	14 A	S	15 K
16 S	N	17 A	K	E	18 S		L		I
		C			E		O		N
19 I	N	T	E	R	E	S	T	E	D

Learner independence
1 rhino 2 snake 3 dog 4 worm 5 reindeer 6 crocodile 7 tortoise 8 horse

UNIT 7
Inspired EXTRA!

Consolidation

Lesson 1
1 must 2 mustn't 3 mustn't 4 must 5 must 6 mustn't 7 must 8 mustn't

Lesson 2
1 *Does she have to speak French? Yes, she does. She has to speak French.*
2 *Does she have to paint for four hours a day? Yes, she does. She has to paint for four hours a day.*
3 *Does she have to call home every day? No, she doesn't. She doesn't have to call home every day.*
4 *Does she have read a lot of books? No, she doesn't. She doesn't have to read a lot of books.*
5 *Does she have to eat French food? Yes, she does. She has to eat French food.*
6 *Does she have to share a room? No, she doesn't. She doesn't have to share a room.*

Lesson 3
1 *Would you like to go to the theater? I'd rather see a movie.*
2 *Would you like to play tennis? I'd rather go swimming.*
3 *Would you like to have a picnic? I'd rather go to a restaurant.*
4 *Would you like to walk home? I'd rather take a taxi.*

Lesson 4
1 d 2 f 3 a 4 g 5 c

Spelling
1 knives 2 lives 3 leaves 4 scarf 5 thief 6 wife

Brainteaser
Water/A river

Extension

Lesson 1
1 You mustn't park here.
2 You mustn't walk on the grass. / You must keep off the grass.
3 You mustn't smoke (in) here.
4 You must press here to open this.
5 You mustn't bring dogs (in) here.
6 You must stand in line here.

Lesson 2
Students' own answers.

Lesson 3
Students' own answers.

Lesson 4
Students' own answers.

Spelling
1 box 2 backpacks 3 snakes 4 cooks
5 Lakes 6 six books 7 extra 8 techniques
9 earthquakes 10 extinct 11 parks 12 extreme

Brainteaser
A pencil with an eraser on the end

CULTURE

Do the right thing

1
1 c 2 e 3 d 4 a 5 f 6 b

2
1 e 2 d 3 b 4 a 5 f 6 c

3
a 3 b 6 c 1 d 2 e 4 f 5

4
1 disagree 2 rude 3 unfriendly 4 boring
5 common 6 children

5
Students' own answers.

6
Students' own answers.

UNIT 8 LESSON 1

1
1 T 2 F 3 F 4 F 5 T 6 T

2
1 You go to a theater to see a play.
2 You go to the airport to catch a plane.
3 You go to a coffee shop to have a drink.
4 You go to the bank to take out some money.
5 You go to the stadium to watch a soccer game.
6 You go to a concert to listen to music.

3
1 Alex brought his digital camera to take a group picture.
2 Silvana went to the newsstand to buy some postcards.
3 Emma called Carrie to ask for help.
4 Jay borrowed some money from Emma to buy a gift.

4
1 offered 2 refused 3 agreed 4 warned
5 promised 6 managed

5
2 Lara knew the answers to the questions, so she won a vacation.
3 Emma had a wonderful time in the U.S., so she thanked Carrie.
4 Silvana and Emma were lost, so they asked a police officer for directions.

6
1 c 2 h 3 b 4 a 5 f 6 d 7 e 8 g

7↓

1 S	E	C	O	N	D	S			
2 T	E	C	H	N	I	Q	U	E	
3 O	N	E							
4 R	E	F	U	S	E	D			
5 Y	E	A	R	S					
6 B	O	O	K						
7 O	F	F	E	R	E	D			
8 A	C	T	O	R	S				
9 R	E	H	E	A	R	S	A	L	
10 D	I	R	E	C	T	O	R		

8
animator information journalist mathematics
translator surgeon rehearsal referee

Extension
This is used to plan an animated movie.

UNIT 8 LESSON 2

1
1 Jay is going to look for a job.
2 Because he is saving for driving lessons.
3 He will give her driving lessons.
4 She is nervous about some important exams at school.
5 She'll have to take them again.

2
1 f 2 h 3 e 4 g 5 b 6 a 7 d 8 c

3
1 What will you do if it rains? We'll have the picnic indoors.
2 What will you say if she asks what happened? I'll/will tell her the truth.
3 How will you get home if school finishes early? Anna will give me a ride.
4 Who will you tell if you pass your driving test? I'll/will tell everyone.
5 What will you buy if your parents give you some money? I'll/will get a new pair of shoes.
6 Who will you ask if you need help? I'll/will ask my brother.

4
1 will you win
2 if you answer
3 I win
4 'll/will go on a safari and see
5 will you do
6 you don't like
7 I'll sleep
8 will you do
9 gets
10 won't/will not
11 won't/will not win
12 will you invite
13 you win

5
1 frightening everyone novel seriously
2 intelligent sensitive bullied attractive
3 beautiful early because weather
4 actor listen height watch

6

■▪	▪■
always	affect
certain	agree
classmate	decide
finish	forget
homework	invite

UNIT 8 LESSON 3

1
1 F 2 T 3 F 4 F 5 T

2
1 The Golden Gate Bridge was designed by Irving Morrow.
2 Manhattan island was bought for $24.
3 The first 3-D movies were made in the 1950s.
4 Hundreds of buildings were destroyed in the San Francisco fire.
5 Shakespeare was born in 1564.
6 Grace Cathedral was completed in 1964.

3
1 Money was stolen from Emma's room when she was at the farewell party.
2 Her room was broken into.
3 One hundred dollars was taken from her wallet.
4 The wallet was hidden behind the curtains.
5 The theft wasn't discovered until after the party.
6 The police were called.
7 Emma's room was searched.
8 The empty wallet was found.
9 Everyone at the party was questioned.
10 The thief wasn't found.

4
1 does 2 are 3 Is 4 is 5 is 6 was 7 did
8 Has 9 Have 10 did
1 i 2 h 3 b 4 f 5 a 6 g 7 d 8 j 9 e 10 c

5
1 The 2 a 3 – 4 the 5 – 6 a 7 the 8 a
9 – 10 an 11 the 12 a 13 a 14 the

UNIT 8 LESSON 4

1
1 world 2 lessons 3 of 4 not 5 because 6 actors 7 faces 8 see 9 surprising 10 theaters

2
a 5 b 1 c 2 d 3 e 4

3
Sample answer
First, a team of artists had to draw all the animated characters and the backgrounds. Next, the actors went to Hawaii to see what a rainforest is like. Then they learned horseback riding and fighting and had lessons in Na'vi. After that, Cameron filmed the live action parts of the movie. Finally, they did the computer animated parts.

4

↓ ANIMATION

1 REHEARSAL
2 DOCUMENTARY
3 SPECIAL
4 FILM
5 DINOSAUR
6 ANIMATION
7 STUDIO
8 HISTORY
9 SCIENTISTS

Learner independence
1 producer 2 documentary 3 artist 4 animation 5 director 6 model 7 computer 8 effects 9 studio 10 camera

UNIT 8
Inspired EXTRA!

Consolidation

Lesson 1
1 *watch A watch is used to tell the time.*
2 *whistle A whistle is used to start and stop the game.*
3 *cell phone A cell phone is used to send text messages.*
4 *CD player A CD player is used to listen to music.*
5 *pen A pen is used to write a letter.*
6 *map A map is used to find the way.*

Lesson 2
1 d 2 b 3 e 4 c 5 a

Lesson 3
1 *were used*
2 *was heard*
3 *were published*
4 *was not eaten*
5 *were played*
6 *were invented*
7 *was made*
8 *were taken*

Lesson 4
1 *Who Tim Haines.*
2 *When 65 million years ago.*
3 *What They used computers.*
4 *Where At "Walking with Dinosaurs—The Arena Spectacular."*
5 *Which They went to Chile and New Zealand.*

Spelling
*1 anim**al** 2 penc**il** 3 success**ful** 4 met**al** 5 digit**al** 6 rehears**al** 7 festiv**al** 8 terri**ble** 9 beauti**ful** 10 tradition**al** 11 mod**el** 12 whist**le** 13 origin**al** 14 wonder**ful** 15 trav**el***

Brainteaser
The letter t

Extension

Lesson 1
1 *Ramón wanted to play soccer with Jay.*
2 *Jay agreed to play soccer with Ramón.*
3 *Silvana offered to get Lara a drink.*
4 *Jay promised to e-mail Emma.*
5 *Carrie decided to go to bed.*
6 *Emma refused to dance.*

Lesson 2
Student's own answers.

Lesson 3
1 *The electric washing machine **was** invented in 1907.*
2 *Paper cups were first **made** in 1908.*
3 *Correct*
4 *The first video recorders were **made** in 1956.*
5 *Correct.*
6 *Car seat belts **were** first used in 1959.*

Lesson 4
James Cameron, who directed Avatar, got the idea of the Na'vi from a dream ~~what~~ his mother had about a four-meter tall woman ~~was~~ with blue skin. Dr. Paul Frommer, a language expert at the University of ~~the~~ Southern California, invented the language that the Na'vi speak. It has a ~~name~~ vocabulary of about 1,000 words. Cameron added ~~of~~ 30 more after filming started.
Actor Sigourney Weaver plays a scientist who studies plants in the movie. A professor of plant biology helped ~~the~~ her, and the designers make the scenes with the plants look ~~planet~~ real.
Q What was the name of the planet?
A Pandora.

Spelling
give

Brainteaser
1 dad 2 dead 3 envelope 4 episode 5 engine 6 expensive 7 eye 8 high 9 remember 10 ticket

REVIEW UNITS 7–8

1
1 D 2 B 3 D 4 A 5 A 6 B 7 C 8 B 9 D 10 B 11 A 12 C

2
1 contestants 2 rebuild/build 3 scientists 4 unusual 5 reality 6 dramatic 7 calculator 8 animation

3
1 *You mustn't bring food or drinks into the studio.*
2 *We don't have to buy tickets.*
3 *She'd rather visit the rainforest.*
4 *He'd like to see the dinosaurs.*
5 *Ramón offered to buy everyone some ice cream.*
6 *An ice machine is used to make the snow.*
7 *The computer is used to make the model move.*
8 *If you go out in the snow without a coat, you'll freeze.*

4
1 glove 2 beans 3 computer 4 rice 5 walking 6 herds 7 animal 8 moon 9 actor 10 frightening

Learner independence

2
1 *How could you?*
2 *It wasn't easy.*
3 *I've always wanted to …*
4 *It's too good to miss!*
5 *I'd rather not.*
6 *I'm not really into …*
7 *It sounds exciting.*
8 *That sounds really boring.*

Stars

Stars encourages students to read for pleasure, while consolidating language covered in *Inspired* 2. Chapters 1–8 of the story correspond to Units 1–8 and Chapter 9 reviews language from the whole book. Each chapter begins with a question to focus students on the story and ends with a prediction question. The story is followed by a series of exercises practicing the language of each chapter. The story can be read in class, or teachers can set the reading as homework. Teachers may also find that some students read ahead because they're curious to know the end of the story!

It is a good idea to focus the students at the beginning of each chapter by asking them to retell the story so far or to describe the events of the previous chapter. This can be done in pairs or groups, with the students then sharing their ideas with the rest of the class, or as a whole-class activity. You can also use the illustrations to get the students to predict what will happen before they read the text. Ask questions about the pictures, such as *Who is this? Where are they? What is he/she doing?* to elicit ideas from the students. Sometimes get the students to read only part of a chapter and then stop and say what they think will happen next.

1 Late again!

1

1 Kristin's father 2 Kristin's father 3 Kristin's mother 4 Kristin 5 Kristin's mother 6 Kristin

2

1 the door 2 her watch 3 with a little smile 4 outside 26 Beach Road 5 up to the door 6 to cry

3

Students' own answers.

Optional activity

Books closed. The students retell the story so far.

2 Why not?

1

1 Kristin's father 2 Kristin's mother 3 Jo 4 Kristin 5 Kristin 6 Mary Mulloy

2

1 blond hair 2 angry 3 her eyes 4 jeans 5 in a band 6 her best friend 7 downstairs 8 with a smile

Optional activities

The students close their books. You read the chapter aloud to them.
Ask the students to discuss how they think the girls will get to New York.

3 Waiting for Mulloy

1

1 72nd Street 2 Mary Mulloy's building 3 a tall, dark-haired boy 4 all the people waiting for Mary Mulloy 5 Jo and Kristin 6 Kristin 7 the woman 8 Jo and Kristin

2

a 3 b 6 c 5 d 1 e 7 f 2 g 4

Optional activity

The students close their books and say what happened in this chapter.

4 Singers, singers, singers

1

1 b 2 c 3 d 4 a

2

1 e 2 c 3 b 4 a 5 d

3

1 hats dresses skirts jeans suits costumes shorts
2 chairs tables desk
3 long large big tall short

Optional activity

Books closed. The students retell the story around the class, getting the events in the correct order.

5 Stop!

1

1 Kristin 2 Kristin and Jo 3 Fred 4 Kristin and Jo 5 a boy with a hat

2

1 the room 2 into one of the microphones 3 up the bag 4 all morning 5 across the room

3

1 loudly 2 angrily 3 slowly 4 happily 5 nervously

Optional activity

Ask the students to make up a tune and sing Twelve at Night.

6 It's not right!

1

1 the boy with a hat 2 Kristin and Jo 3 the song 4 the audience 5 Kristin and Jo 6 the other singers

2

1 Fred 2 the boy with a hat 3 Mary Mulloy 4 Kristin 5 the audience 6 the boy with a hat

3

1 up on the stage 2 the same chance 3 in line 4 singing 5 the microphone 6 red

Optional activity

The students act out the conversation from this chapter. Parts: boy with a hat, Mary, Fred, Kristin, Jo, people in the audience.

7 We don't have to do what they say

1

a 7 b 1 c 4 d 2 e 5 f 3 g 6

2

1 our song 2 me 3 to finish it 4 the door 5 on the microphone 6 to be quick

3

1 up 2 on 3 up 4 over; out 5 off

Optional activity

The students make up words for the other songs mentioned in the chapter.

8 If you wait long enough ...

1

1 Mary Mulloy 2 the singers 3 the singers/450 people 4 the song 5 Kristin and Jo 6 Because You're Mine *7 the video 8 Kristin and Jo*

2

1 e 2 d 3 f 4 a 5 c 6 b

3

1 exhausting 2 the ones 3 don't believe it 4 is silly 5 found my stars 6 that

Optional activities

The students close their books and you read the chapter aloud to them.
Ask the students to predict how Mary will find Kristin and Jo.

9 I don't believe you!

1

1 To watch the ten o'clock news. 2 The number on the TV.
3 To call Mary Mulloy. 4 didn't you tell us where you were?
5 We were on TV last night! / We've won! / Mary Mulloy wants us to go to L.A.!

2

1 d 2 c 3 a 4 f 5 b 6 e

Optional activities

The students discuss these questions in groups: *What do you think will happen to Kristin and Jo in L.A.? Will they become famous?* Ask each group to share their ideas with the class.
The students make up a new chapter for the story about Kristin and Jo's adventures in L.A.

After reading activities

Write the ten activities below on the board. The students choose the ones they are most interested in. The written work can be displayed in the classroom. The first two activities could be recorded.

1. Choose a piece of dialogue from the story and act it out with another student.
2. Choose a chapter from the story. Work in a group. One student reads the chapter aloud. The others act out what happens.
3. Choose five pictures from the story and write a sentence about each one.
4. Choose three of the pictures and write as many questions as you can about them. Give your questions to a partner to answer.
5. Write one-sentence summaries of each chapter.
6. Which character in the story do you like best? Why?
7. Imagine you are Jo. Write your diary for the day you went to the studio.
8. Write another song for Kristin and Jo to sing in L.A.
9. Write a new ending for the story.
10. You are a movie director and are planning a movie of the story. What stars will you choose? You can only use two thirds of the story in your movie. What parts must you cut?

Unit 1–2 CLIL Teaching notes
Music

Music and festivals

Aims	To learn about different genres of music and the musical instruments used to create them.
Activities	Reading for gist and specific information; completing information in a table; matching and grouping vocabulary; multiple-choice quiz; project research and presentation.
Language	Simple present, present progressive, adverbs of frequency, possessive pronouns and adjectives, comparative and superlative adjectives, vocabulary relating to occupations, carnivals, festivals, and music.
To use	After Unit 2, either in class or as homework.

Procedure

- This CLIL spread can be given as homework or be done in pairs in class. For each activity, students can either check answers in pairs and then with the whole class, or use a monolingual dictionary to help with vocabulary if they are working at home.
- First, ask students to look at the pictures and describe what they see. Then ask them to quickly skim read the three texts for general understanding and match the pictures with the texts. You may wish to pre-teach the following vocabulary: *orchestra*—a large group of musicians using many different instruments to play mostly classical music; *composer*—someone who writes music, especially classical music; *invent*—to design or create something such as a machine or process that did not exist before; *rhythm*—a regular pattern of sounds in music.
- Ask the students to read the texts more carefully and complete the information about each festival in the table.
- Ask students to look at the pictures and complete the labels. Remind them that all the words can be found in the texts in exercise 1.
- Ask students to read the four short descriptions of keyboard, percussion, string, and wind instruments and then write the musical instruments in exercise 3 under the correct heading. You may wish to pre-teach the following vocabulary: *pedal*—a part on some musical instruments that you press with your foot to change or make a sound; *vibrate*—to shake very quickly with small movements; *bow*—a long thin object that you use for playing instruments such as the violin or cello; *blow*—to make a sound by pushing air through a musical instrument; *key*—one of the parts that you press on a musical instrument to make it produce sounds.
- Ask students to answer the music quiz questions individually. As an extension, students could write their own music quiz in small groups and then hold a class quiz.
- The project stage can be set as homework or, if possible, students can use school computers to research their projects. Students choose and research a particular type of music—it could be one of the genres covered in the lesson or something completely different. Remind them to find out about the origins of the music, why people like it, typical instruments, and famous artists or composers. Tell them to prepare a short talk with supporting pictures and audio to present to the class.

Key

Exercise 1
1 c 2 a 3 b

Exercise 2
1 classical 2 string 3 wind 4 cymbals 5 15 6 Jacksonville Jazz festival 7 4 days 8 clarinet 9 trombone 10 double 11 drums 12 50 13 rock 14 Summerfest 15 11 days 16 electronic 17 guitars 18 synthesizers 19 keyboards 20 700

Exercise 3
1 piano 2 violin 3 saxophone 4 clarinet 5 trumpet 6 double bass 7 drums 8 guitar 9 synthesizer 10 trombone 11 cymbals 12 flute

Exercise 4 *(Suggestions are in italics.)*

Keyboards	*Percussion*	*Strings*	*Winds*
piano synthesizer *organ*	drums cymbals *xylophone* *glockenspiel* *triangle*	double bass guitar violin *viola* *cello* *harp*	clarinet saxophone flute trombone trumpet *oboe*

Exercise 5

1 The orchestra is bigger—the Principality of Monaco has no army or air force. Its defense is provided by France. The Monaco Philharmonic Orchestra is a very successful and popular orchestra.
2 Frank Beard is the only member of ZZ Top who doesn't have a beard!
3 Yes. Some birds can sing when they are born, e.g. the chaffinch.
4 A sweet potato because of its shape and form.
5 Michael Jackson's *Thriller*, with 45 million copies sold worldwide.

Unit 3–4 CLIL Teaching notes
Science

Fire and fire prevention

Aims	To learn about how to create, prevent, and extinguish fire.
Activities	Matching vocabulary and definitions; reading for gist and specific information; labelling diagrams; project research and presentation about fire safety.
Language	Simple past, adverbial phrases of time, imperatives, *will/won't*, adverbs of manner, vocabulary relating to places, daily activities, natural world.
To use	After Unit 4, either in class or as homework.
Procedure	• This CLIL spread can be given as homework or be done in pairs in class. For each activity, students can either check answers in pairs and then with the whole class, or use a monolingual dictionary to help with vocabulary if they are working at home. • Ask students to match the vocabulary with the definitions. Tell them to scan the text in exercise 3 for the words and use the context to help them with meaning. • Next, ask the students to read the fire safety rules and choose *do/don't* as appropriate. You may wish to pre-teach the following vocabulary: *match*—a small stick that produces a flame when rubbed against a rough surface, used for lighting a fire; *damp*—something that is damp is slightly wet; *breathe in*—to take something into your lungs through your nose or mouth; *frying pan*—a flat metal pan with a long handle, used for cooking food in hot oil or fat. Students check answers first in pairs and then read the text to check their answers. • Ask students to read the text again carefully and then complete the diagram in exercise 4 with the appropriate words from the text. You may wish to pre-teach the following vocabulary: *break*—to separate into two or more pieces; *lighter*—a small container that produces a flame, used especially for lighting cigarettes; *lightning*—the bright flashes of light that you see in the sky during a storm; *explosion*—when something bursts with a lot of force and a loud noise, often causing damage; *spread*—to move from one place to another; *splash*—when a liquid moves or hits something; *conduct*—if something conducts heat or electricity, heat or electricity can move through it. • The project stage should be set as homework. Explain to students that they should first draw a plan of their homes, then identify and map the potential fire risks of each room on their plan. They should then identify solutions to each problem based on what they have learned about fire creation and prevention. Suggest they visit the websites listed to help them with their research. Finally, tell them to prepare a short talk to present to the class.

Key

Exercise 1

1 inflammable
2 liquid
3 smoke alarm
4 solid
5 smother
6 fire extinguisher
7 fuel
8 crawl

Exercises 2 & 3

1 Do 2 Do 3 Do 4 Don't 5 Do 6 Do 7 Do 8 Do 9 Don't 10 Do

Exercise 4

1 water
2 oxygen
3 Electrical
4 electricity
5 oven
6 lightning
7 wood
8 paper
9 gasoline
10 oil
11 Gas:

Unit 5–6 CLIL Teaching notes
History

History of transportation

Aims	To learn about the history of transportation through the ages.
Activities	Reading for gist and specific information; categorizing vocabulary; history of transportation quiz; writing own transportation quiz.
Language	Sequencing adverbs, expressions of quantity, countable and uncountable nouns, object pronouns, prepositions of direction, vocabulary relating to travel and transportation.
To use	After Unit 6, either in class or as homework.
Procedure	• This CLIL spread can be given as homework or be done in pairs in class. For each activity, students can either check answers in pairs and then with the whole class, or use a monolingual dictionary to help with vocabulary if they are working at home. • Ask students to look at the pictures of different modes of transportation and describe what they see. Then ask them to skim the text quickly for overall understanding and match a picture with each text. • Next, ask students to read the texts more carefully and categorize all the modes of transportation they find under the headings: land, sea, and air. When students have used all the words from the texts, ask them to write other modes of transportation in the three columns—provide dictionaries if necessary. You may wish to pre-teach the following vocabulary: *vehicle*—a machine that you travel in or on, especially one with an engine that travels on roads, for example a car, bus, van, truck, or motorcycle; *train*—to teach someone to do a particular job or activity; *sidewalk*—a path with a hard surface beside a road; *steer*—to control the direction in which a vehicle moves; *harness*—a set of strong leather bands used for fastening around an animal such as a horse so that it can pull a vehicle; *compass*— a piece of equipment used for finding your way, with a needle that always points north; *trader*—someone who buys and sells things; *steam*—power that is created when water is heated. • Ask students to take the quiz. Tell them to read the text again and look at the pictures. • The project stage can be set as homework or done in class if students have access to appropriate reference books, the Internet, etc. Ask them to prepare a short quiz about transportation. Suggest they visit the listed websites as part of their research. In the following lesson, students test their transportation knowledge by doing their classmates' quizzes.

Key

Exercise 1

1 d 2 a 3 g 4 c 5 f 6 e 7 b

Exercise 2

Land: *walking, sled, horse, steam railroad locomotive, subway, electric train, car, tram, bus, Maglev (bicycle, motorcycle, truck)*
Water: *boat, dugout, canoe, raft, ship, steamboat (ferry, hovercraft, submarine)*
Air: *airplane, space shuttle (helicopter, hot air balloon, glider)*

Exercise 3

1 b 2 d 3 b 4 c 5 d 6 d

a top speed of the Maglev train in kilometers per hour
b year when Christopher Columbus discovered the Americas
c year when Karl Benz made the first car in Germany
d number of years BC when the wheel was invented
e length in kilometers of the roads in the Roman Empire

Unit 7–8 CLIL Teaching notes
Geography

Tropical rainforests

Aims	To learn about the different layers that make up a tropical rainforest
Activities	Reading for gist and specific information; completing a table; tropical rainforest quiz; project research about rainforest animals.
Language	Relative pronouns, infinitive of purpose, open conditionals with *if/when*, vocabulary relating to animals, geography, and the natural world.
To use	After Unit 8, either in class or as homework.
Procedure	• This CLIL spread can be given as homework or be done in pairs in class. For each activity, students can either check answers in pairs and then with the whole class, or use a monolingual dictionary to help with vocabulary if they are working at home. • Ask students what they know about tropical rainforests and then read the sentences in exercise 1 individually and write *T* (true) or *F* (false). Students can check answers first in pairs and then skim read the text quickly to see if they were correct. • Next, ask students to read the text in exercise 3 carefully and complete the table with the correct information. You may wish to pre-teach the following vocabulary: *energy*— a supply of physical power that you have for doing things that need physical effort; *layer*—a part of something which lies between other parts; *smooth*—completely even with no rough areas or lumps; *root*—the part of a plant that usually grows under the ground, through which the plant gets water and food; *absorb*—to take in a substance; *soil*—the substance on the surface of the Earth in which plants grow. • Ask students to take the tropical rainforest quiz. Tell them to refer back to the texts and look at the pictures if they need any help. • The project stage can be set as homework or done in class if students have access to appropriate reference books, the Internet, etc. Ask them to prepare a short description of one of the animals in the rainforest layers text. Tell students that they should include information about where the animal lives in the rainforest, how it makes its home, what it eats and how its young are born. Remind students to write their descriptions in the form of a puzzle without mentioning the animal's name so that their classmates can guess the animal.

Key

Exercises 1 & 2

1 T 2 F 3 F 4 F 5 T 6 F

Exercise 3

Name of layer: *emergent layer*
Plants: *tall trees*
Conditions: *sunny, hot, and windy*
Animals: *macaws, bats, monkeys, butterflies*

Name of layer: *canopy*
Plants: *trees with pointed leaves, fruit, and flowers*
Conditions: *hot and sunny*
Animals: *snakes, spiders, toucans, tree frogs, monkeys*

Name of layer: *understory*
Plants: *short with large leaves*
Conditions: *cold and dark, not much sun or wind*
Animals: *insects, birds, and large mammals including jaguars, tapirs, and leopards*

Name of layer: *forest floor*
Plants: *not many plants, only leaves*
Conditions: *very dark and wet*
Animals: *elephants and gorillas, ants, scorpions, and earthworms*

Exercise 4

1 a 2 b 3 c 4 c 5 a

Audio Track List

CD 1

Track	Unit	Lesson	Exercise
1.02	**Welcome**		Exercise 1
1.03			Exercise 2
1.04	**Preview, Units 1 and 2**		Exercise 4
1.05	**Unit 1**	**Lesson 1**	Exercise 2
1.06		**Lesson 1**	Exercise 4
1.07		**Lesson 1**	Exercise 5
1.08		**Lesson 2**	Exercise 2
1.09		**Lesson 2**	Exercise 3
1.10		**Lesson 2**	Exercise 4
1.11		**Lesson 3**	Exercise 2
1.12		**Lesson 3**	Exercise 5
1.13		**Lesson 4**	Exercise 2
1.14		**Lesson 4**	Exercise 4
1.15		**Lesson 4**	Exercise 9
1.16		**Inspired *Extra!* Skit**	
1.17	**Unit 2**	**Lesson 1**	Exercise 2
1.18		**Lesson 1**	Exercise 5
1.19		**Lesson 2**	Exercise 2
1.20		**Lesson 2**	Exercise 5
1.21		**Lesson 3**	Exercise 2
1.22		**Lesson 3**	Exercise 4
1.23		**Lesson 3**	Exercise 6
1.24		**Lesson 4**	Exercise 3
1.25		**Lesson 4**	Exercise 8
1.26	**Preview, Units 3 and 4**		Exercise 4
1.27	**Unit 3**	**Lesson 1**	Exercise 2
1.28		**Lesson 1**	Exercise 5
1.29		**Lesson 1**	Exercise 6
1.30		**Lesson 1**	Exercise 7
1.31		**Lesson 2**	Exercise 2
1.32		**Lesson 2**	Exercise 4
1.33		**Lesson 2**	Exercise 5
1.34		**Lesson 3**	Exercise 2
1.35		**Lesson 3**	Exercise 5
1.36		**Lesson 3**	Exercise 6
1.37		**Lesson 4**	Exercise 3
1.38		**Lesson 4**	Exercise 5
1.39		**Lesson 4**	Exercise 10
1.40		**Inspired *Extra!* Skit**	
1.41	**Unit 4**	**Lesson 1**	Exercise 2
1.42		**Lesson 1**	Exercise 5
1.43		**Lesson 1**	Exercise 6
1.44		**Lesson 2**	Exercise 2
1.45		**Lesson 2**	Exercise 4
1.46		**Lesson 2**	Exercise 5
1.47		**Lesson 3**	Exercise 2
1.48		**Lesson 3**	Exercise 4
1.49		**Lesson 3**	Exercise 5
1.50		**Lesson 4**	Exercise 2
1.51		**Lesson 4**	Exercise 3
1.52		**Lesson 4**	Exercise 8
1.53	**Preview, Units 5 and 6**		Exercise 4
1.54	**Unit 5**	**Lesson 1**	Exercise 2
1.55		**Lesson 1**	Exercise 5
1.56		**Lesson 1**	Exercise 8
1.57		**Lesson 2**	Exercise 2
1.58		**Lesson 2**	Exercise 5
1.59		**Lesson 3**	Exercise 2

CD 2

Track	Unit	Lesson	Exercise
2.02		**Lesson 3**	Exercises 4 and 5
2.03		**Lesson 3**	Exercise 6
2.04		**Lesson 3**	Exercise 7
2.05		**Lesson 4**	Exercise 4
2.06		**Lesson 4**	Exercise 5
2.07		**Lesson 4**	Exercise 10
2.08		**Inspired *Extra!* Skit**	
2.09		**Inspired *Extra!* Limerick**	
2.10	**Unit 6**	**Lesson 1**	Exercise 2
2.11		**Lesson 1**	Exercise 3
2.12		**Lesson 1**	Exercise 4
2.13		**Lesson 1**	Exercise 6
2.14		**Lesson 1**	Exercise 8
2.15		**Lesson 2**	Exercise 2
2.16		**Lesson 2**	Exercise 5
2.17		**Lesson 2**	Exercise 7
2.18		**Lesson 3**	Exercise 2
2.19		**Lesson 3**	Exercise 4
2.20		**Lesson 3**	Exercise 6
2.21		**Lesson 4**	Exercise 4
2.22		**Lesson 4**	Exercise 9
2.23	**Review, Units 5 and 6**		Exercise 2
2.24	**Preview, Units 7 and 8**		Exercise 2
2.25	**Unit 7**	**Lesson 1**	Exercise 2
2.26		**Lesson 1**	Exercise 6
2.27		**Lesson 2**	Exercise 2
2.28		**Lesson 2**	Exercise 5
2.29		**Lesson 2**	Exercise 7
2.30		**Lesson 3**	Exercise 2
2.31		**Lesson 3**	Exercise 5
2.32		**Lesson 3**	Exercise 6
2.33		**Lesson 4**	Exercise 2
2.34		**Lesson 4**	Exercise 4
2.35		**Lesson 4**	Exercise 5
2.36		**Lesson 4**	Exercise 10
2.37		**Inspired *Extra!* Skit**	
2.38		**Inspired *Extra!* Limerick**	
2.39	**Unit 8**	**Lesson 1**	Exercise 2
2.40		**Lesson 1**	Exercise 4
2.41		**Lesson 1**	Exercise 5
2.42		**Lesson 2**	Exercise 2
2.43		**Lesson 2**	Exercise 4
2.44		**Lesson 2**	Exercise 5
2.45		**Lesson 3**	Exercise 2
2.46		**Lesson 3**	Exercise 3
2.47		**Lesson 3**	Exercise 4
2.48		**Lesson 4**	Exercise 3
2.49		**Lesson 4**	Exercise 8
2.50	**Song**	*Dancin' In The Street*	
2.51	**Song**	*Footprints In The Frost*	
2.52	**Song**	*Father And Son*	
2.53	**Song**	*The Miracle*	